This is number two hundred and five
in the second numbered series of the
Miegunyah Volumes
made possible by the
Miegunyah Fund
established by bequests
under the wills of
Sir Russell and Lady Grimwade.
'Miegunyah' was Russell Grimwade's home
from 1911 to 1955
and Mab Grimwade's home
from 1911 to 1973.

THE RED WITCH

A Biography of
Katharine Susannah Prichard

NATHAN HOBBY

THE
MIEGUNYAH
PRESS

THE MIEGUNYAH PRESS
An imprint of Melbourne University Publishing Limited
Level 1, 715 Swanston Street, Carlton, Victoria 3053, Australia
mup-contact@unimelb.edu.au
www.mup.com.au

First published 2022

Cover design by Pfisterer + Freeman
Cover image: Katharine in her sitting room, 1949 (D. Glass, NAA)
Text design and typesetting by Cannon Typesetting
Printed and bound in Malaysia for Imago

NATIONAL LIBRARY OF AUSTRALIA
A catalogue record for this book is available from the National Library of Australia

9780522877380 (hardback)
9780522877397 (ebook)

Contents

Preface

IN THE 1930S, a journalist's grandmother pointed out a wooden cottage near the top of a hill on the outskirts of Perth and said that a 'red witch' named Katharine Susannah Prichard lived there. Thirty years later, that journalist used the term in an article celebrating Katharine's eightieth birthday and 'red witch' began to catch on as a moniker for her.[1] It captures a notorious woman on the fringes, marked by her literary powers and her left-wing politics. She had other names too and the *Workers Star* ran many of them together when it used to call her 'Comrade Mrs Hugo Throssell: world famous revolutionary authoress'.[2] She was all of those things—founding member of the Communist Party of Australia, widow of a war hero who came from an establishment family, and an author whose distinctively Australian novels were published around the world.

My path to becoming Katharine's biographer began with a novel I had been working on. Writing about a fictional biographer for five years before abandoning the manuscript, I was intrigued by the pursuit of the past, the quest to tell the story of someone from their archival remains. It became clear to me that I needed to do that in real life, rather than only imagining it. I wanted to write about someone who had walked the same streets as me in Perth. The more I looked at Katharine Susannah Prichard's life, the more it seemed her many biographical mysteries and controversies hadn't been untangled and her story had not yet been fully told. What's more, I found her work as interesting as her life; I'd always liked *Coonardoo,* but I started reading through her other books from the beginning and found a breadth and vitality which surprised me.

Katharine's first story appeared in 1899 and her final novel in 1967. At the high point of that long career, she wrote two novels widely regarded as landmarks in Australian literature, *Working Bullocks* (1926) and *Coonardoo* (1929).[3] The *Bulletin* called *Working Bullocks* 'a work of genius' and 'probably the best novel ever written in Australia'.[4] In 1931, the critic HM Green wrote that she was 'the most representative novelist that Australia has yet produced … No set of novels by any one author gives a better idea of this country than those of Katharine Susannah Prichard'.[5] By then, she had written novels set in regional areas of four Australian states—nineteenth-century Gippsland, Victoria in *The Pioneers* (1915); the opal-mines around Lightning Ridge in outback New South Wales in *Black Opal* (1921); the karri forests of South-West Western Australia in *Working Bullocks*; Launceston, Tasmania in *The Wild Oats of Han* (1928); a cattle station in Western Australia's Pilbara in *Coonardoo*; and regional towns across several states in *Haxby's Circus* (1930). She would later add her saga of the development of the Western Australian goldfields, a trilogy beginning with *The Roaring Nineties* (1946). Given Australia was highly urbanised even then, it would be truer to say that Katharine largely gave Australia the idea of itself it wanted to read—an Australia of the 'bush' and the 'outback'. *Intimate Strangers* (1937), set in Perth, is her only significant novel with a metropolitan setting.[6]

Katharine lived long enough to feel neglected in the post–World War II literary landscape. She wrote in 1968 that it was a 'shock' to read in the introduction to *Modern Australian Writing* a reference to 'a "naissance", not a "renaissance", of Australian literature, implying that nothing worth mentioning had happened in the literature of Australia before the advent of Patrick White and Randolph Stow'.[7] Today, while White and Stow may continue to have a greater cachet, literary scholars view Katharine as a major twentieth-century Australian writer. *Coonardoo*, with its story of the thwarted love between a white man and an Aboriginal woman, had become part of the Australian 'canon' by the 1980s, taught in high schools and universities.[8] However, this century it has become a controversial novel, with scholars identifying problems in the way it depicts Aboriginal people, arguing it reflects racist assumptions of its time and fails to understand the white violence which formed the backdrop to Aboriginal lives.[9] At the same time as this ongoing reassessment of *Coonardoo*, other scholars have recently examined less well-known aspects of Katharine's work, including her drama and poetry, her reception in East Germany and the USA, and her first novel, *The Pioneers*.[10] As well as this continuing scholarly interest, Katharine has a popular following, with a number of her books remaining in print and her wooden cottage now a writers' centre named in her honour. In 2020, *Working Bullocks* and *Intimate Strangers* were selected for republication by Untapped: the Australian literary heritage project. All of this indicates Katharine's ongoing significance to Australian literature.

Katharine's life itself has also long been of interest to historians. She lived from the end of Australia's colonial period to the middle of the Vietnam War and her evolving worldview—from doubting Christian to progressive patriot to idealistic radical to stubborn communist—is an illustrative journey through responses to the upheavals of the first seven decades of the twentieth century. In *Exiles at Home* (1981), Drusilla Modjeska discusses Katharine as a key figure in a generation of women writers negotiating writing, politics, and sexism between 1925 and 1945. Other historians have a very negative take on Katharine's life. Desmond Ball and David Horner contend that she was at the centre of a Soviet spy ring during World War II; the claim, I argue in chapter 31, is unproven and dependent on an unreliable source. Just as *The Red Witch* is going to press, her granddaughter, Karen Throssell, has published a book telling of the effects of these allegations on the family and particularly her father, Ric. Conservative commentators such as Hal Colebatch believe Katharine's support for Soviet dictator Joseph Stalin make her legacy 'a strange and dishonourable one' to ever celebrate.[11] It's true that her loyalty to Stalin is a dark part of her legacy which needs to be reckoned with. In tracing her political journey in this biography, I found that she was guilty not of intentionally deceiving others nor of any evil intent but of deceiving herself; she had a fundamentalist faith in the Soviet Union and refused to accept anything which contradicted it.

Katharine had a troubled relationship to biography in her lifetime, and it carried over after her death as her son, Ric Throssell, became the guardian of her legacy. She found it harder to write her autobiography, *Child of the Hurricane* (1963), than any other book. She claimed she hadn't wanted to write about herself but needed to set the record straight after a postgraduate student 'wrote a very distorted version of my youth and childhood in a thesis'.[12] *Child of the Hurricane* is padded out with anecdotes about Katharine's family, celebrities she met, and passing crushes, while avoiding weightier matters. She hoped it would be the final word about her formative years. It is not that, but for a biographer it is a priceless record of her movements and memories, a road map for a fuller, historical account.

Just as Katharine wrote *Child of the Hurricane* as an act of self-defence, Ric Throssell's biography, *Wild Weeds and Windflowers: The Life and Letters of Katharine Susannah Prichard* (1975), was written to defend her posthumously. After her death in October 1969, *Overland* published an obituary by the writer Dorothy Hewett which was a brutal re-assessment of Katharine's life and work, reflecting Hewett's disenchantment with communism and with Katharine, who had been a friend.[13] Hewett wrote that it was 'as if, after the suicide of her husband, Hugo Throssell, she willed her own creative death' and in her unquestioning loyalty to the Soviet Union she closed off her 'artist's pagan and poetic sensibility'.[14] Ric responded angrily, resolving to write 'a factual biography' to again set the record straight.[15] Published in 1975, *Wild Weeds* is, in Ric's words, a 'personal picture', drawing heavily on his memories and the weekly letters Katharine sent him.[16] Ric's later work, *My Father's Son* (1989), is a hybrid work combining a biography of his father and an autobiography, as well as revisiting elements of Katharine's life. Ric's biographical writings about his mother leave room for a comprehensive, critical account of Katharine's life, one with some distance in time and relationship to the subject.

In 1969 at the end of Katharine's life, her pen-friend Catherine Duncan was thinking forward to our present: 'in fifty years, dearest Kattie, the KSP you are now will have become someone else—she will have escaped you'. Duncan wanted Katharine to preserve her remaining letters so that she would be more accurately understood today. Fifty years was also the distant horizon another friend, the writer Henrietta Drake-Brockman, imagined for Katharine's posthumous reckoning. 'Katharine Susannah Prichard, both personally and as a novelist, is still the most controversial figure in Australian literature. It is unlikely that her work and influence will be justly assessed for another fifty years.'[17] Drake-Brockman felt that the Cold War distorted opinions about

Katharine and that a fairer assessment would only be possible once it was in the past.

Katharine now exists on the edge of living memory. Midway through my research, I found five boxes of material left behind by a biographer from an abandoned attempt fifteen years earlier. She had interviewed half a dozen people who had known Katharine well; they had all died by the time I started. It is the archive that remains and Katharine left behind multiple sources for every year of her long life. The many letters held in other people's collections are as significant as the ones held in her own. *The Red Witch* is woven from her archival trail—letters, notebooks, clippings, ASIO files, government documents, and photographs—along with her published work and, importantly, the newly digitised newspaper articles on the National Library of Australia's Trove site which reveal so much about her life and world. While alert to thematic connections, this biography is a chronological account, narrating the intertwined personal, political and literary strands. It adds nuance and detail to the contours of Katharine's life, setting out to show what her life was like in its different phases and in the course of that, the biographical background to her literary works.

I hope this book will be of interest and use to scholars. However, I have written it for a general readership drawn to the peculiar pleasures of biography: the true drama of a life, the glimpses of a lost but familiar world, the recoverable details of the past. It is not a cultural history or a work of literary criticism but the story of one remarkable Australian life. The biographer Martin Edmond laments that the artists Rex Battarbee and Albert Namatjira—the subjects of his dual biography—had come to exist only as representatives of 'notions espoused by others', not as 'real people' acting in 'real situations'. His biography becomes a mission to restore them. He won't tell their story to prove a point—he will tell it to show a 'lived life'.[18] It's what I've sought to do also.

PART I

KATTIE, 1883–1907

1

Origins

Levuka, Fiji, 1883–1887

KATHARINE'S FATHER WAS Thomas Henry Prichard, usually known as Tom. He was the editor of the *Fiji Times* when Katharine was born. Late in 1882, on the eve of his departure to marry Edith Fraser in Melbourne and bring her back to Fiji, the Levuka community held a function to honour him. The German consul presented him with a purse of a hundred sovereigns collected from the other white colonists, saying, 'We recognise, sir, the services you have rendered the colony as a fearless, vigorous and able writer. We know that in you its interests have found a capable advocate'.[1]

Tom's response is a rare surviving instance of him talking about himself. 'When I came to Fiji I was a young man. As you now see, I am approaching middle age, yet I am one of the youngsters of my people. I am the waif, the stray, the wanderer of the lot; the rolling-stone that was expected to gather no moss.' He declared, 'I hold the journalist to be the great lay teacher of the age', and finished his speech by saying, 'My heart has ever been in my work, but when I return I shall resume it with redoubled energy, and if I fail to justify your estimate of me it will not be for want of trying, but because you have rated me altogether too highly'. He was a driven, sensitive man.

In his spare time, Tom wrote fiction and poetry with some success, appearing in a number of newspapers and magazines and even having one novel published in 1893. He regarded himself as a wit, writing satirical rhymes for his newspaper column which haven't aged well. A devout but theologically moderate Anglican, he was anything but moderate in his politics.[2] A hard-line conservative, he railed against a minimum wage, welfare and anything else progressive.[3]

Katharine spent long periods of her early life in the shadow cast by Tom's depression. She struggled against his desire for her to be a 'domestic angel', desperate for him to approve of her own ambitions. After he killed himself in 1907, she tried unsuccessfully to find publishers for his writing. He was on her mind the rest of her life. In 1950 she was planning to write a book about him. By 1969, she had conceded that it wasn't to happen, but in one sense it already had—the story of Tom's life as she knew it fills a good proportion of her autobiography, *Child of the Hurricane* (1963). Five days before she died, she wrote to the National Library enquiring about stories of her father's she had sent them years earlier, promising to send the rest when she'd finished submitting them to publishers.[4]

SOME OF THE family stories Katharine told in *Child of the Hurricane* aren't quite true, but it is true that all four of her grandparents were on the same boat, the *El Dorado*, sailing from Liverpool to booming Melbourne in 1852.[5] Over the decades that followed, three sets of Prichards and Frasers married, including Katharine's parents, 'so family relationships became somewhat complicated'.[6] Tom was seven years old on that voyage, having been born in 1845 in Monmouth, a town on the border of England and Wales.

Tom's father, Charles Allen Prichard, had 'set himself up as an importer of cheeses' in Australia; later he tried to make money in tallow but 'misfortune seems to have followed every attempt he made to be a businessman'.[7] The Melbourne directory for 1865 listed him as a grocer living on Gipps Street in the suburb of Collingwood. He and his wife, Agnes, died there within months of each other in 1867.[8]

In 1863, the year Tom turned eighteen, his older sister, Ada, married and moved to the goldmining town of Ararat; Tom and his younger brother, Frederick, seem to have moved with them while their parents remained in Collingwood.[9] He spent at least six years as a 'rolling stone' in different goldfields towns. He worked on a newspaper in Castlemaine, gaining his first experience as a journalist, and as a bailiff in the court at Beaufort.[10] By 1868 he was writing; that year, he took out second prize in a poetry competition for the Glassblowers' Exhibition in Ballarat.[11] He resigned as bailiff in May 1869 and migrated to Levuka, then Fiji's capital.[12]

Between 1868 and 1872 the 'Great Fiji Rush' brought many 'young, restless men' from Victoria and the other Australasian colonies to Fiji.[13] Alluvial gold was getting harder to find and wool prices were falling; newspaper reports led people to believe their fortunes were to be made in Fiji. Tom and the others who came hoped to turn Fiji into another of the white colonies of Australasia, prospering on the back of indigenous labour and resources. 'A rough-and-tumble time we had put in, as we helped to plan an outpost of the Empire in the very heart of barbarism', he wrote in a short story. 'It had been ten years of fry and frizzle, of sweat and swelter, of yams and bulamakau [beef], of sardines and square gin, of hard graft and unrealised hopes, of exile from civilisation and yearning to return.'[14] He worked for a time as the clerk of peace at the Levuka court before becoming the editor of the *Fiji Times* in about 1877.[15]

For years he courted Edith, nine years his junior, by mail. 'Father used to say that he fell in love with Mother when she was a schoolgirl, and made up his mind then that she was the girl he wanted to marry.'[16] One of his surviving poems is called 'To Edie, on her birthday', dated 25 April 1878, the day she turned twenty-three: 'Not with my hands but with my heart I wreathe / A natal garland for thy brows to-day.'[17] As sentimental and formal as it is, it would have impressed Edith as she waited to join her adventurer across the seas. 'My heart is sore for Somebody', she copied into her commonplace book in 1879.[18]

TOM AND EDITH married on 24 January 1883 at St Mary's Anglican in Caulfield.[19] He was thirty-seven; she was twenty-eight. By the time they set off on the SS *Hero* back to Fiji, Edith was pregnant. Though not Australian-born, Katharine was Australian-conceived.

Edith Isabel Fraser was born into a large middle-class family in 1854 in the Melbourne suburb of Williamstown. Her parents were from Scottish families, although her father had grown up in Ireland.[20]

She was the fourth of eight daughters from her father's two marriages, with just one brother surviving infancy. Katharine remembered 'the aunts' as a strong presence in her early life.

Edith was a gentle, conventional women who left few historical traces. She was adventurous enough to leave her family home and work as a governess for a time before she married.[21] Her commonplace book survives, filled with quotes and jokes by other people. There is a brief and formal letter she wrote to Alfred Deakin, a family friend, when he became prime minister in 1903. A couple of times, the facts of her presence and the colour of her dress at social events are recorded by newspapers. And then there is her sad testimony of her husband's final day preserved by the coronial inquest.

By 1883, the number of settler wives in Levuka had increased, but they were still far outnumbered by men. In that first year of marriage, a pregnant Edith was taken out of a close family network in Melbourne into a colonial outpost.

Child of the Hurricane begins with a hurricane destroying Levuka on the night Katharine was born. Their 'frail' huts smashed, homeless Fijians took shelter in the one house on the hill with its roof still on—her parents' house—just as she was being born. The Fijians 'gazed with awe at the baby the hurricane had left in its wake. "*Na Luve ni Cava*," they exclaimed. "She is a child of the hurricane."'[22] It was a messianic birth, foreshadowing the drama and tragedy of her life.

The problem is, there was no hurricane on 4 December 1883. There were some heavy rains on 29 November which caused the creek to flood, although the *Fiji Times* from the day after her birth doesn't mention the weather at all, let alone a hurricane which destroyed Levuka. Katharine's journalist father, Tom, chided the Australian press just a few months after her birth for exaggerating Fijian hurricanes, turning 'the most innocent gale' into a 'Frightful Hurricane in Fiji'. 'As a matter of fact,' he claimed, 'Fiji is no more subject to hurricanes than is Victoria'.[23]

Although Katharine had the reason for her nickname wrong, she *was* dubbed '*Na Luve ni Cava*' while still a baby. Tom wrote a poem of that title describing her—'a sprite of nature intense'—to send to her aunt.[24] In choosing the name, he may have been inspired by a novel about Fiji published the month Katharine was born, Henry Britton's *Loloma, or Two Years in Cannibal Land.* King Big-Wind declares that the narrator, who has arrived with a storm, is 'the Child of the Hurricane, a white God from unknown countries' and the tribe will adopt him.[25] It's one of the only other recorded uses of the phrase.

The earliest known version of Katharine's hurricane myth appeared in 1916 in an article by Mary Gilmore for the *Australian Worker.* 'Miss Prichard was born in Fiji during the worst hurricane known there for years. The roof of the house was blown off and the new-born infant wailed with the tempest. In Fiji she is called "Hurricane" by the populace.'[26] Katharine's mother, Edith, was still alive then but apparently never took the chance to correct the story Katharine had already begun telling.

KATHARINE WAS NAMED after her mother's late half-sister, Katherine Susan Davies. The original Katherine Susan died in Melbourne two weeks after giving birth to her second child in 1872.[27] In Katharine's autobiographical children's novel, *The Wild Oats of Han* (1928), the protagonist, Han, 'had been called Hannah Frances after a saintly great-aunt of whom a dark oil painting hung in the dining-room. She had excelled in good works, Great Aunt Hannah Frances ... Han was named after her in the hope she would imitate her virtues'.[28]

All her life, Katharine's names were regularly misspelt, even on the covers of some of her books, reporters and publishers blithely adding a 't' to Prichard, or turning 'Katharine' back into 'Katherine'. She 'detested' these misspellings, writes her son.[29] The problem began with her birth certificate, which she must never have looked at too closely. The loopy handwriting is a little ambiguous, but it recorded her name clearly enough as 'Katherine Susannah'.[30]

AFTER KATHARINE'S BIRTH, Edith had a nurse to help her, a man named N'gardo. It was customary, according to Katharine, for white women to have male nurses help them. When she was 'a few days old' N'gardo supposedly took her away for hours to see the chief without telling her parents. Over time, he taught her to speak the Fijian of the chiefly caste and told her stories from their mythology. 'Maybe N'gardo is responsible for the instinctive sympathy I've always had for people of the native races. It is, I think, a tribute to that dark, protective presence in my early life.'[31]

Tom tried to arrange for N'gardo to accompany Katharine and her mother back to Melbourne for the birth of Katharine's brother, Alan, in March 1885, but regulations prevented it. N'gardo died, she wrote, before she returned and 'it was nothing but grief for the child from whom he had been parted that caused him to will his own death'.[32]

It's a shocking story, but it might not be true. The shipping page of the *Sydney Morning Herald* recorded Mrs TH Pritchard [*sic*] with two children and a servant boarding the *Rockton* on 13 June 1885, bound for Fiji.[33] Katharine didn't mention any other servants, so this was possibly N'gardo, well and truly alive. Whatever actually happened, N'gardo became an antecedent for later tragedies. In her suicide-filled autobiography, he was the first man close to her to kill himself.

It wasn't long before Edith was pregnant again and Katharine's second brother, Nigel, was born in Levuka on 21 August 1886. Katharine's earliest memory was from this time. 'There's a picture in my mind of a balcony veranda with white rails, pink flowers below it, and blue sea beyond. Alan and I were playing on the veranda and a baby cried.'[34]

TOM WAS TO look back nostalgically on Levuka as a 'merry, bustling and busy' centre where 'adventurous spirits from the Australian colonies traded, paid their debts, drank, made merry and socially frizzled together under the torrid tropic sun'.[35] However, by the time Katharine was born the port was in decline and it had lost its status as Fiji's capital to Suva.[36]

Levuka's decline was hastened when a hurricane struck it on 4 March 1886, the event which probably formed the basis of Katharine's birth mythology. Katharine was two and a half years old; she may have had faint memories of it. 'The evil hap which Levuka, in common with the rest of the colony, has for so long experienced, culminated on Thursday morning in the heaviest hurricane which has visited the town since that of 1871.' The worst of it lasted from daybreak to 6 p.m., buildings 'going down in every direction', as debris flew through the streets.[37]

Katharine the toddler would have been huddled in the dark bungalow that day, her pregnant mother worried for her and baby Alan, who was eleven months old. Tom's scoffing at the dangers of hurricanes now seemed foolish. Writing for the *Argus*, he reported that 'the streets of a city under bombardment would not have been more dangerous'.[38]

Rather than rebuild, many white colonists left. The European population of Levuka fell from 2000 to less than 500. Levuka became, in Tom's words, a 'decayed, deserted fishing village'.[39]

At the end of the year, the *Fiji Times* moved to Suva and Tom moved with it. On 4 January 1887, the *Taupo* steamer arrived at Suva and he disembarked while Edith and the three children stayed on the ship, continuing on to Melbourne.[40] Their stay in Melbourne was only meant to be temporary—Tom still hoped that Fiji would prosper and the family could make a permanent home in Suva.

In September 1887, he led a deputation sent to Melbourne on behalf of the colonists to call for Fiji to be annexed by the colony of Victoria.[41] The settlers were unhappy with the British governors; they were looking for a government which would allow them to more easily exploit indigenous labour and land. When the premier finally met with Tom, he said the proposal had great difficulties and no advantages for Victoria.[42] Reported in newspapers across Australia, it was Tom's moment in the spotlight and it ended ingloriously.

With Tom's hopes for Fiji dashed, it seems he felt it was time to finally end his self-exile and settle the family in Australia permanently.

Fiji was to become a land of myth for Katharine, a place for her father to play out his exotic adventures in the stories he would tell her during her childhood. He was happy in these stories, carefree, a contrast to the anxious and depressed father she was to know for much of her childhood and youth.

2

'The Memory of a Storm'

Melbourne and Launceston, Tasmania, 1887–1895

The Wild Oats of Han (1928) is a memoir of Katharine's childhood in the form of a children's novel. In dreamy prose it captures the wonder of the world through a child's eyes. In the foreword, Katharine invited an autobiographical reading of the work: 'The first thing children ask about a story is usually: "But is it true?" And this one, it can be said, is a truly, really story. Katharine Susannah would stake her breath on it. Just here and there a few details stray from the strict path'. Even the name, Hannah Frances, is autobiographical, taken from Katharine's aunt, Hannah Frances Davies, who married the widower of her late sister, Katherine Susan, for whom Katharine was named.

Casting herself as a fictional character, Han, seems to have made it easier for Katharine to write about her life. As autobiography shaped into fiction, *Wild Oats* is an amalgam of childhood experiences, incidents from throughout her childhood added to Katharine's actual nineteen months in Launceston from 1893 to 1895. She depicts her childhood as a painful gaining of understanding and responsibility. Han begins with 'no conscience, any more than the birds or possums who lived in the great silver gum-trees' but as a 12-year-old, 'the weight of the world' descends on her shoulders and she must go 'down into the great mysterious world they had talked so much of, to take her part in the joy and the labour and the sorrow of it'.[1] This trajectory that Katharine compressed into the Launceston years for *Wild Oats* stretched in life from her early childhood in Melbourne to the sacrifice of her university ambitions at the age of nineteen in order to help her family.

KATHARINE HAD JUST turned three when she arrived in Melbourne with her mother and two brothers in January 1887. They lived for several years in Caulfield with her grandparents, Simon and Susan Fraser, in their Caulfield house, Clareville, along with two unmarried aunts.[2]

In *Wild Oats*, Han's parents are backgrounded characters, 'absorbed in each other'.[3] Her mother, Rosamund Mary in the novel, 'had never been required to consider domestic affairs' and it is Grandmother Sarahy, based on Susan, who keeps the household running. She 'dusted the mantelpieces, ordered the meals, mended, darned, made jam and the children's clothes, except when Rosamund Mary had what she called "twinges of conscience"'. Katharine called her grandmother 'the first person I became really interested in, perhaps because she was interested in me'.[4] The implication is that her parents were not interested enough in her.

The era of her grandmother and the Victorian era were one. Melbourne and the rest of the British empire was celebrating Queen Victoria's golden jubilee in 1887, with over 125,000 people converging on the Melbourne city-centre to witness its illumination on 21 June. 'As I remember her, Grandmother looked like the pictures of Queen Victoria. She wore her hair in silver wings over her forehead, and a little lisse cap on her head. Her dress was usually dull black silk, with a tight bodice and voluminous skirts.'[5] Her grandmother and the queen were to die within months of each other in 1901 when Katharine was seventeen, entwining them further. On the day of her grandmother's funeral she 'stood under the row of dark pines on the edge of the garden at Clareville, and watched the long train of vehicles file slowly away down the road, furious, yet grieving desperately about it all'.[6]

REJOINING THE FAMILY later in 1887, Tom was unable to find a job in Melbourne and in May 1888 he left the family at Clareville while he moved to Tasmania to take the position of editor at Launceston's *Daily Telegraph*.[7] He lasted less than six months before he resigned due to 'ill health', which, in view of what came later, could have been depression.[8]

In April 1889, Tom was appointed editor of a new Melbourne weekly, the *Sun*, and the family moved to the seaside suburb of Brighton.[9] He was in his element at the *Sun*, composing the satirical column 'Madcap Rhymes' each week. However, in late 1892, he lost his job just as Edith was pregnant with their fourth child.[10] In *Wild Oats* Han's mother tells her, 'We've no money … we don't know when father will get any more work to do. We haven't even a house to live in … and a little sister is coming to you soon … and there will be no home, no food—'[11] Beatrice was born on 2 November 1892, nine years younger than Katharine, the fourth and final of the Prichard children born after a gap of six years.

The economic woes of the 1890s were deepening and Victoria was at the epicentre; in 1893 its property bubble burst and the banks were in crisis. In July 1893, Tom was fortunate enough to find a new job as the associate editor back at the *Daily Telegraph* in Launceston.

'After a dark and troubled time that was like the memory of a storm, Peter Barry had climbed the hill which rose from the sleepy old township of Launceston and had chosen the house built right at the top of the hill.'[12] Peter's real-life counterpart, Tom, called that house 'Korovuna', even though he was only renting it. According to Katharine, the name means 'place of peace', but it actually combines the Fijian words for 'village' and 'for a reason'.[13] Tom would later give the same name to the family home in Melbourne. They lived next door to Tom's brother, Frederick, and his family; Frederick had taken up a role as editor of the town's rival newspaper, the *Launceston Examiner*.[14]

Tom and Edith were determined to establish themselves as pillars of the community, involving themselves in myriad committees and causes. Early impressions would have counted in the town, and they wanted to appear better-off than they were. They hired a 'general' to do the housework and they borrowed money to set their house up with quality furniture.[15]

Their house was in Trevallyn, backing onto the bush around the scenic Cataract Gorge. 'The hills which rose in misty, timbered brakes and ledges behind her home, were Han's happy hunting-ground.'[16] Katharine was enchanted by the trees and the flowers and the birds and the lizards, an enchantment which was to flow through her writing in the years that followed. 'She scarcely knew the world of the real from the world of the unreal; both were blended in the crystal of her mind.'[17]

ON 17 NOVEMBER 1893, Fillis's Mammoth Circus and Menagerie, a South African troupe, arrived in Launceston for five days of shows. 'Tier upon tier' of 'delighted spectators' watched a lion, a tiger, five elephants, 'Lilliputian marvels', a woman shot from a cannon, and acrobats.[18] In *Wild Oats,* Han 'was living in a world of enchantment, and could not think or talk of anything but the circus'; she hears the lions roaring in their cages and the music drifted up to her house on top of the hill.[19] She decides her great ambition in life is to be an acrobat, and she rehearses in her backyard, until she jumps from the tree before her watching family and falls hard to the ground. The visit of Fillis's Circus was the beginning of an ongoing fascination with the circus for Katharine, culminating in her 1930 novel *Haxby's Circus*.

In *Wild Oats*, the circus is paired with Han's brief attraction to another romantic vocation—the life of a missionary. She listens to a visiting missionary's stories of horror and martyrdom in 'darkest China' and decides she wants to 'convert the heathen from his blindness … I want to carry the light of the gospel to far Lao Tzu … I want to die by the sword of the Pig-Tailed Barbarian'.[20] In life, two missionaries visited Launceston three months before the circus in August 1893 and spoke of martyrdom. Perhaps Katharine was momentarily taken by their vision: 'To every land, the preacher urged, must the standard of Christianity be borne, every country invaded'.[21] For a 9-year-old girl working out her place in the world, the life of a missionary momentarily offered both adventure and a great cause.

In this period of trying on vocations in Launceston, she found her true calling. She remembered announcing to Tom that she wanted to be a writer:

> I can still see him as he used to stand on the verandah, in the evening, smoking his peace pipe as he called it, and looking out

over the shining river, or away to the mountains in the distance. Before that, the family had been disturbed by my ambitions to be a circus rider, or a missionary. So my father took my announcement about becoming a writer with an indulgent smile.

'Oh well,' he said, 'you'll need plenty of patience and plenty of postage stamps.'[22]

She wanted to follow in his footsteps. Tom's first and only novel, *Retaliation: A Tale of Early Melbourne*, appeared in May 1893 from the publishing arm of the *Sun*, just as the Prichards prepared to leave for Launceston.[23] *Retaliation* is a popular romance about an orphan girl's rescue by a wealthy widow and her revenge on a scoundrel. While competent and representative, it is not especially memorable. Many of Katharine's early works are also romances, bearing some resemblance to *Retaliation* in their coincidence-driven plots of beautiful damsels under threat from scoundrels.

KATHARINE WAS TO look back on her early teachers as benignly inept. Before the Prichards left Melbourne, she had started attending a school 'run by a gentle spinster' in Brighton, and then a private school run by her Aunt Lil.[24] By her own reckoning, she was the late age of eight when she started, but she had already learned to read and write and had been taking French lessons with her grandmother. She made her first known newspaper appearance on 23 December 1893 as 'Katty Prichard', the most awarded student at Miss Littler's private school in Trevallyn.[25] In contrast to the rebellious Han, Katharine was voted by her fellow students 'Best Conduct' for the entire school.

In August 1894, Katharine made her second newspaper appearance as one of the organisers of a children's bazaar, held at her family's house to raise funds for the poor. She and her friends made crafts and toys, selling them for a penny each. The event raised over a pound and the journalist—presumably Tom—held it up as an example to the rest of the community.[26] The charitable, community-spirited Prichard family living at Korovuna on top of the hill looked so assured of their place in Launceston society in 1894, seemingly unaware they were about to tumble.

IN KATHARINE'S ACCOUNT, the *Daily Telegraph* was 'on its last legs, and it was hoped Father would revive it', only for the paper to cease publication.[27] In reality, the newspaper kept going without Tom right up to 1928, but ructions did shake it in late 1894. The owner was in financial trouble and declared bankruptcy at Christmas. Two weeks later, the new owner sacked Tom.[28]

Six months after the bazaar at the Prichard house to raise money for the poor, almost everything they owned was auctioned onsite as they prepared to return to Melbourne. The advertisement placed on behalf of Tom in the *Launceston Examiner* for an auction of 'the whole of his household furniture' is a comprehensive and sad list: 'comprising walnut sideboard (mirror back), mahogany telescope table, dining room suite, new Brussells carpet, oil paintings (superior), mahogany wardrobe, cedar chest drawers, bedsteads and bedding, commode, dressing tables, washstands, fenders, curtains, poles and rings, kitchen utensils, dresser, garden tools, and sundries'.[29] They kept their piano and their books, but little else.

When Katharine gave a testimony of her conversion to communism sixty years later, the auction stood out as a landmark, her awakening to injustice in the world. She and her brothers had been sent out to play in the bush all day. On their return, they 'saw the family furniture piled on carts driving along the road, and a red auctioneer's flag over the gate'.[30] Her mother's grief stirred her to the realisation of 'some dark mysterious trouble' which she must prevent hurting her family.

Soon after the auction, on 7 March 1895, the Prichards returned to Melbourne. Despite their money troubles, they travelled not in steerage but saloon class.[31]

COMPARED TO THE plots fiction demands, lives are too repetitive. In writing about her life in the form of a children's novel, Katharine shaped the events of early 1895 into the decisive crisis of her childhood. In life, this crisis in the Prichard family was one of many, the circularity suggested by the 'memory of a storm' right at the start of *Wild Oats* as the family arrive in Launceston. Katharine lived her childhood with the memory of storms. Tom's difficulty finding work when he moved back to Australia from Fiji in 1887 was one; the loss of his job at the *Sun* in 1892 was another. This time, in 1895, Katharine understood some of what was happening to her family and the knowledge was bitter. In her memory, leaving Launceston became an exile from paradise, cast out from a carefree existence playing in the bush and forced back to suburban Melbourne with a new sense of responsibility.

3

'Enthusiasms and Ambitions'

Melbourne, 1895–1903

WHEN THE PRICHARDS returned to Melbourne in 1895, Tom couldn't find a job and Edith kept the family going. She 'was always sewing then ... smocking lovely little dresses for other children, or painting illuminated addresses which she sold to be presented to distinguished citizens'.[1] In this unhappy period they were staying in a 'dark, ugly' house in Caulfield lent to them by Katharine's wealthy uncle and aunt, Slingsby and Han Davies, who lived next door.[2]

Then, about a year after their return, Tom found a job as editor of Critchley Parker's *Australian Mining Standard*. 'Suddenly it was as if the dark and dreary days of winter had been chased away by the sunshine of spring. The house was filled with gladness. Father went off to catch an early morning train; Mother no longer sewed all day.'[3]

The Prichards moved two doors down to 401 North Road, 'a painted weatherboard house with a garden and lawn at the back, and open land covered with gorse, briars and bracken stretching before it'. It became the second 'Korovuna'. Katharine remembered it as 'a place of happiness and peace for a long time'.[4]

Despite interludes in Levuka and Launceston, North Road was the centre of Katharine's childhood and youth. At one end of the road was the Brighton General Cemetery where Katharine's parents were both to be buried; at the other end was the Ormond railway station. In between was 'Clareville', her maternal grandparents' house where she had lived from 1886 to 1888, 'Withersdane', home of Slingsby and Han, and, more humbly, her own family's 'Korovuna'. The 1896 Municipal Directory describes the Caulfield area as 'pleasant and healthy' and 'so increased in importance that it has become one of the leading suburbs' with a population of 8000.[5] In the depression of the 1890s, it was full of middle-class families like the Prichards struggling in genteel poverty.

THE ARTS WERE important in the Prichard house. 'During our bright times father's and mother's interests were chiefly literary and artistic. They talked to us about music, painting, and poetry. Mother played on the little Broadwood piano … She and Father sang together: he often read to us in the evening, usually Australian poetry.'[6] They took the four children to the National Gallery 'to see almost every new picture when it was bought'.[7]

Tom and Edith sent Alan and Nigel to state schools but Katharine was kept home for a time because 'the aunts were horrified at the idea of my going to a state school'.[8] Eventually, 'Father and Mother compromised with the aunts by letting me go to a state school in another district where Mother had heard there was a good teacher'.[9] It was Armadale State School and Katharine was there from 1895 to 1897. While she was there, the *Argus* reported that forty-five students were crowded into a classroom meant for ten.[10] In September 1896, two classrooms were destroyed in a fire and the fifth and sixth classes, Katharine among them, began attending classes at Toorak State School, still taught by Armadale teachers.[11]

With no public secondary schools, public school students wanting to continue their education competed for merit-based government scholarships to private schools. After the exam, Katharine was devastated to be disqualified because she had just turned fourteen. However, a few days later, 'a short fat man arrived on a bicycle who said he was JB O'Hara, headmaster of South Melbourne College … He had been so pleased by my papers that he had come to offer me a half-scholarship'.[12]

ACCORDING TO KATHARINE, she had her first story published in a Melbourne newspaper at age eleven; it awaits rediscovery.[13] At present, her earliest extant published story is from age fifteen, 'That Brown Boy'. Winning the *Sun's* quarterly children's prize for stories, 'That Brown Boy' is a lively, melodramatic tale which shows Katharine's early potential. It's the story of Nicholas Brown, a mischievous orphan who drowns defending some younger boys against a bully. She had to share the prize of ten shillings with another girl because of 'carelessness in writing, grammar, and orthography'.[14] Entering—and often winning—competitions would be an important part of Katharine's literary career in the decades which followed, the impetus for many new works.

This writing success meant much to Katharine. Despite her parents' appreciation of the arts, she felt they discouraged her literary ambition. 'Mother and Father were too absorbed in each other, and in their struggle to provide food and clothing for us all, to be interested in my scribbling.' She showed her grandmother a story called 'A Soldier's Love', only to later overhear her reading it out loud to her aunts in 'gales of laughter'. Then her family laughed again at her dramatic adaptation of William Tell, elaborately staged at home with her brothers and cousins.[15]

Although her parents were indifferent about her writing, South Melbourne College encouraged it; the principal, John Bernard O'Hara, was an established poet.

> He was very pleased with a contribution to the school magazine which the professor of English in a German university praised. One of our teachers had married this professor, and she wrote to say her husband thought the girl who wrote that sketch 'would become a famous writer some day'.
>
> How excited I was! To have my writing thought so well of was surprising. I decided forthwith to become 'a famous writer', and began consciously to study the work of great writers in order to learn something of how stories should be made, and why some were more powerful than others.[16]

Her French teacher, Irma Dreyfus, 'introduced her to French writers including De Maupassant, Anatole France and Victor Hugo'.[17]

Her mother encouraged her to read the great writers of the Victorian-era such as Alfred Tennyson and Charles Dickens as well as less enduring romances.[18]

Reading Miles Franklin's *My Brilliant Career* (1901) was another part of her literary formation. In Katharine's first letter to Miles in 1930 she remembered, 'It made a very vivid engraving on my mind, at about the time I had just left school, & I am sure it matured my mind in the direction of reality and truth at that moment as nothing else did'.[19]

THE FIRST DAY of 1901 marked both the federation of Australia and the beginning of the twentieth century. Melbourne was the temporary capital of the new nation. Federal attorney-general Alfred Deakin, a family friend of Edith's, sent a message to the Century Night held in the Melbourne Town Hall saying, 'May the new year of the new century usher in a new nation whose history shall be an illustrious record of progress'.[20] Katharine had arrived in Australia at the time of the centenary of colonisation; she was now on the cusp of adulthood at federation. This period of heightened awareness of Australian identity fed into an event significant to her personal mythology: the Prichard family reunion.

The reunion brought together fifty of the descendants of Tom's parents on 12 November 1902, the fiftieth anniversary of their arrival in Melbourne. While the other side of Katharine's family, the Frasers, had largely stayed in Melbourne, the Prichards had scattered across the Australasian colonies. All ten of the children were still alive, and they and their offspring came from around Victoria, New South Wales, Tasmania and New Zealand to gather at the house of Katharine's stern aunt, Agnes Church, in the Melbourne suburb of Canterbury.[21]

Katharine prefaced her account of the reunion by saying that her grandfather intentionally 'forgot the past' when he came to Australia, cutting off the 'myths and legends of family history which had captivated him as a young man' so that the next generations might truly start a 'new life' and 'make their own way in the colonies'. Katharine's grandparents were free settlers but her first novel, *The Pioneers* (1915) is marked by a concern with Australia as a fresh start for descendants of convicts, the past forgotten. In the epilogue, Dan, the grandson of the pioneers—the same generation as Katharine—is told by his mother,

'They may talk about your birthstain by and by, Dan … but that will not trouble you, because it was not this country that made the stain. This country has been the redeemer and blotted out all those old stains'.[22]

The intergenerational saga of *The Pioneers* owes something to the mood of this reunion when Katharine was eighteen. An original family of twelve had grown to eighty-three. The first generation brought up in Australia were now 'stout and grey-haired' elders 'disporting together'. Her own generation were bright and young with a new century ahead of them in a newly federated nation.

'I seem to be the only rebel among them', wrote Katharine, yet it was through her books that her grandfather's name would 'live on'. She wondered what that grandfather would say to her, having made his own 'bold venture into the unknown'. 'Would he understand that I am seeking to find as he did, a new and good life, though not only for the members of my own family, but for the families of mankind?'[23]

IN 1902, 16-YEAR-OLD Hilda Bull 'with glorious red hair' moved next door.

> Hilda and I had met at the Armadale State School, and were soon talking to each other over the garden fence. Before long we had broken a gap in the grey palings near a clump of lilac bushes, and could call to each other as soon as we got up in the morning. Living side by side, we shared our hopes and dreams in a friendship that grew stronger with the years.[24]

Such was their deep friendship that Hilda wrote years later of the 'telepathic sympathy' between them.[25] In the published version of *Child of the Hurricane*, Katharine wrote, 'there was never anyone with whom I could share my most intimate thoughts as I could with Hilda; and she, with me, I know, felt the same deep sense of security and understanding'.[26] The typescript contains a passage she deleted:

> Such intimate friendship between women is suspect these days. But there was never anything Lesbian in Hilda's and my association.

> We were both too much in love with men ~~always~~ later to need any other sexual interest. We could discuss the adventures of our minds in our love affairs as well as all the happenings of our lives, with complete freedom. That was what made our friendship the rare and lovely thing it was.[27]

It is an intriguing denial. 'Always' adjusted to 'later'. The love of men precluding same-sex attraction. What's more, it seems an unnecessary protestation—what prompted it in the first place?

Unlike Katharine, Hilda was her (wealthy) father's favourite, and he nurtured her aspirations. She was attending Presbyterian Ladies' College, Melbourne's most prestigious girls' school, and introduced Katharine to two of her PLC friends, Nettie Higgins and Christian Jollie Smith:

> We sat on the lawn between Hilda's room and mine, comparing notes about our enthusiasms and ambitions. We were each of us working for the matriculation examinations … I don't think we ever discussed the things that are supposed to interest girls—boys and dresses. We were interested mostly in ourselves, our future, and the first step towards it: those exams.[28]

The four of them were near-contemporaries, but the other three matriculated the year after Katharine in 1903 and went on to study for exhibitions in 1904. Nettie Higgins, later Palmer, was raised in a devout Baptist family. Christian was a boarder and only began at PLC in 1903; her father was a Presbyterian minister and she had been brought up in the South Australian town of Naracoorte.

All four young women were to go on to live remarkable lives—Katharine as a writer and Nettie as a critic, who both shaped the development of a distinctively Australian literature; Hilda as a patron of Australian drama and a medical doctor; and Christian as a lawyer. All four also came to hold left-wing political convictions, with Katharine and Christian both foundation members of the Communist Party of Australia in 1920.

Unlike any of Katharine's other close friends, Nettie kept many of her letters and diaries. The invaluable biographical insights into Katharine they provide also have the distorting effect of giving Nettie a bigger part in Katharine's known life than her closest friend, Hilda.

BAPTISED AS AN infant, it came time for Katharine to be confirmed into the Church of England. Despite Katharine narrating Han's brief desire to become a missionary in *Wild Oats*, her resistance to Christianity began early. She remembered attending a 'small, wooden Anglican church standing in the midst of bare paddocks' in Caulfield when she was eight and being outraged by the story from Genesis in which Jacob deceives his father Abraham to receive the birthright that was rightfully his brother's. She was with Uncle Arthur, her mother's only brother, and told him she didn't like God for allowing this injustice to happen. It is far from the most troubling story in the Old Testament, but with two younger brothers it touched a nerve. Katharine suspected Uncle Arthur shared her opinion.[29] 'The years of Bible reading, church-going, family prayers and religious instruction, which filled my youth, never removed my secret doubt as to the goodness of God, and the omnipotence that was claimed for Him.'[30]

According to Katharine, 'four clergymen in turn had undertaken to prepare me for confirmation; but I asked questions which they did not answer to my satisfaction'.[31] Tom tried his own arguments on her and she finally decided to not only be confirmed but to try harder to believe. It wasn't the arguments he used which changed her mind but rather his sadness at her apostasy. At her confirmation, the beauty of the ceremony in the cathedral impressed her.

> Very devout for a while, I prayed earnestly every night and went to church with Father and Mother on Sundays, giving God, as I thought, every chance to prove to me that He wasn't a myth like Santa Claus, Jack Frost, or the black dog on my back—those inventions which had beguiled my childhood.[32]

The surprise of Katharine's religious 'testimony' is that despite her retrospectively emphasising her many doubts, for a period of her youth she was a devout Christian.

> My imagination had been caught up by the inexplicable in religious ecstasy. I used to go out into the paddocks, gaze up into the sky and away in to the distance, enraptured by the gorse in bloom, its musky fragrance, the beauty of everything; and feel that I was communing with God.[33]

This sense of enchantment in nature stayed with her, even when she didn't believe in God any longer, and many of her novels have moments of it, notably *Working Bullocks* (1926) when Deb is among the trees and 'swung to them in a fury of worship and admiration. The invocation, passion and lamentation of the trees swayed her'.[34]

In 1907, Katharine watched Tom's depression worsen as he prayed fanatically each day, and she prayed too, promising herself she would believe in God if Tom got better. 'When Father died, I was finished with religious superstitions.'[35]

KATHARINE'S YEARS AT South Melbourne College from 1898 to 1902 were happy ones. She was stimulated intellectually and creatively and formed friendships she remembered fondly. She described the principal, John Bernard O'Hara, as 'a man of joyous and buoyant personality who taught by a sort of magnetism which brought the best out of his pupils'.[36] O'Hara was a highly regarded educator; under his leadership 'students prided themselves on being an educational elite. Girls and boys were encouraged in similar ambitions and competed on equal terms'.[37] However, his interest in bright girls was not all innocent; seven years after Katharine graduated, a student fell pregnant to him.[38]

In 1902, Katharine's last year of school, she worked hard, haunted by the fear she might fail her exams. 'I used to be out at dawn walking round the garden, with a book in my hands, and sit huddled up in a blanket on winter nights because there was no fire in my room.'[39]

A highlight of the year was the annual school ball at the South Melbourne Town Hall on Saturday 16 August. A local newspaper reported a long list of 'pretty and varied' dresses, including 'Miss K. Prichard—white silk and violets'.[40] She wrote about the dance for the school magazine: 'The quick hours are flying. A whirl of dainty frills, visions of light feet in pretty slippers, a subdued rustle and swish with the music, glimpses of flushed faces, waving hair, parted lips, graceful bows and curtseys, breathless laughter, and sighs. Clang! clang! and it is over'.[41]

Her friend, Maggie, was escorted by her father, the commissioner of police, Thomas O'Callaghan, 'a portly red-faced, old man, very pompous'. O'Callaghan asked Katharine to dance, and O'Hara 'chuckled hilariously afterwards, accusing me of having "captivated the commissioner of police"'.[42] This was just months after Katharine had charmed her grumpy Uncle Albert at the family reunion; in a rather naïve choice of phrases, that had been her 'first attempt at flirtation' as she 'coaxed him to dance' and 'made love' to him.[43] At times, Katharine's autobiography reads as a series of anecdotes about men she had, in one way or the other, beguiled.

The school's prize ceremony was held on 20 December, a couple of weeks after Katharine's nineteenth birthday. Katharine won the group prize for English, history and geography as well as individual subject prizes for German and physiology.[44] In algebra, she was equal bottom; O'Hara 'told Father that if I managed to pass in algebra in the matriculation examinations, I should return to school the following year and study for a university exhibition in the post-matriculation class. It was understood I was to do this'. It was one of the great disappointments of her life that she didn't return and was never to attain a degree.[45]

'Mother was suffering from sciatica when I should have returned to school. She lay in bed for six months, and I had to stay at home, do everything for her and look after the housework. There was no possibility of winning an exhibition after that.'[46] It wasn't simply a financial decision; the Prichards were in a better financial position than ever before. In September 1902, Edith's brother, Arthur Fraser—the same uncle Katharine had shared her doubts about God with—was thrown from his horse in a race and died; he had no heirs and left Tom his estate of £366, three years of a basic wage.[47]

As Katharine grew older, she became increasingly aware that her father's expectations of her were different because she was a girl. In *Wild Oats,* it is shown in Han's younger brother being given an axe to cut firewood. 'Being a boy, Han thought, must be more important than being a girl if it meant having an axe all to yourself to cut wood.'[48] When Katharine was in her early twenties and her brother Alan lay in hospital near death from acute appendicitis, she told Tom she wished it was her. Distractedly, he told her he wished that too. 'For the first time', she wrote, 'I realised that I was not the most important member of the family'.[49] Yet if it was the first time, then it was a realisation which had been growing for years.

Tom wanted her to be like Edith—a genteel housewife, a painter of watercolour copies, educated but not too educated. While her mother gave her books of poetry by Keats and Wordsworth as gifts for Christmas or birthdays, 'Father liked to give me pretty feminine things, a sunshade or a bottle of perfume, a pair of ear-rings, or a gauzy hand-painted fan'.[50]

As Katharine gave up her dreams of university to run the household, Tom 'was delighted to see me becoming more of a home-girl'. Edith's illness had played into his hands. Yet in misunderstanding his daughter, in trying to shape her to be something she didn't want to be, Tom provoked Katharine into proving him wrong and carving out a career—first as a governess then as a journalist and finally as a writer. 'Nothing', she wrote, 'was further from my thoughts than being the domestic angel into which he hoped I would be transformed'.[51]

4

Governess

Yarram, Victoria, 1904

THE HIGHLIGHT OF Katharine's desultory year of housekeeping was her first adult success as a writer, winning a love story competition run by *New Idea* journal with a tale called 'Bush Fires' despite 'knowing nothing about either love or bushfires'.[1] Katharine gave the main character her own name. She described Kath'rin' as 'an Australian woman, browned with the wind and sun, inured to the open-air life of freedom and danger. The countryside loved her for her fearlessness, the physical strength of her beautiful body, the sweet charity of her woman's eyes'.[2] Kath'rin' rides recklessly into a bushfire to save her estranged lover; she is reconciled to him, only for both of them to be killed by the fire. Like much of Katharine's early work, she sets romance against a quintessentially Australian backdrop.

In Katharine's memory, her decision to become a governess was connected to her literary ambitions. She decided, 'I must know more about bushfires, love, and the country beyond our ranges' and announced to her family her intention to work as a governess to a family in the country.[3] It was a chance to escape.

Governessing was one of the few respectable careers open to young women at the turn of the twentieth century. The status of governesses was ambiguous—not really one of the servants, if there were any, and not quite part of the family.[4] Although usually well educated, their need to work would have suggested their families were not wealthy.[5] Perhaps this implication of middle-class poverty was why Tom and Katharine's aunts objected to her plan. However, Edith had worked as a governess for a time before she was married; now recovered from sciatica, she 'quietly and practically sided' with Katharine against the objections.[6]

And so, at the beginning of 1904, at twenty years old, Katharine set out to live away from her family for the first time, as a governess in the isolated town of Yarram, 220 kilometres south-east of Melbourne in South Gippsland. With a population of about four hundred, it had recently become the largest of the cluster of towns settled in the 1840s and 1850s. She was to teach the two children of the local doctor William Muir and his wife, Lizzy—13-year-old Marjorie and 9-year-old Charles. 'It was an adventure into life, away from books.'[7]

Katharine was close to Dr Muir. On weekends she went with him 'on some of his long journeys to see patients in the mountains and along the coast'. It seems incredible that there was no scandal in the town about the 41-year-old doctor taking his 20-year-old governess with him on long trips, unchaperoned. He had 'intellectual interests beyond his surgery' and so they discussed literature and ideas; at home in the evenings he read Robert Burns to her 'in the broad Scottish tongue', giving her a new appreciation for the poet.[8]

There must have been some tension with Lizzy, even if Katharine couldn't remember it in retrospect. It comes through in Katharine's description of her as a 'pretty woman, in her thirties, plump and amiable. Her favourite occupation seemed to be sitting on a sofa, sucking her thumb and plucking fleas from her little dog's pelt. She played aristocratic roles in productions of the Yarram Dramatic Society as if to the manner born'. When Katharine arrived, Lizzy initially expected her to 'help with all manner of household tasks. I explained that I had been engaged to teach, and wasn't prepared to darn socks or do the ironing, after school hours. That being understood, we got on very well'. With typical ambivalence, Katharine added 'as a favour … I often did help with domestic doings'.[9] If Lizzy had felt threatened by her forthright, slim governess, she gave no hint in the reference she wrote her: 'We have great pleasure in recommending Miss Prichard as governess. She lived with me for one year in that capacity & gave every satisfaction. I consider her an excellent teacher, the progress my children made under her tuition was marvellous, & it is with great regret we parted with Miss Prichard'.[10]

Katharine was learning German that year and 'when a German doctor, temporarily living in the town, visited the Muirs ... he offered to help me with my studies'. Her encounter with him 'brought me closer to the dark realities of life, and left a psychological impression which was never obliterated'.[11] She called him 'Dr Paul' in *Child of the Hurricane* and described him as 'elderly'. His real name was far more unlikely—Otto Gmelin—and he was only 43 years old. Gmelin 'came twice a week and we read Goethe's *Faust* together'.

> Sometimes he talked brilliantly about famous places in Europe, or distinguished writers and artists with whom he was acquainted. Sometimes, strangely overcast and morose, he scarcely spoke at all ... These German lessons were a pleasant break in the quiet nights I usually spent in my room. Quite guileless, I looked forward to Dr Paul's visits.[12]

Lizzy heard rumours about Gmelin and warned Katharine about him—he was a married man and a cocaine addict; he was too fond of Katharine, and she must not 'encourage' him but put an end to his visits.

Gmelin lived a troubled life, a doctor always in desperate circumstances. After graduating in medicine from the German city of Leipzig, he came to Victoria in 1891, already a cocaine addict with 'completely shattered' nerves.[13] In 1893 he was sentenced to two months in prison for larceny. By 1899 he had recovered his fortunes enough to run a practice in Lilydale and marry, in an elaborate wedding, 18-year-old Edith Clarke, the niece of the minister for customs.[14] In their eventual divorce case, Edith testified that Gmelin became close to a Miss Blyth, who would come to their house until all hours. On 18 May 1904, heavily drunk, Gmelin announced he was leaving her, and departed at midnight with Miss Blyth and all his surgical instruments. The next month, Gmelin began advertising his practice in the local Yarram newspaper. By that time, he'd lost Miss Blyth.

After Lizzy's warning, Katharine initially tried avoiding him, allowing Lizzy to tell him she did not wish to continue the German lessons.

However, he was so persistent that eventually Dr Muir told Katharine to talk to Gmelin herself. 'It was an appalling interview. I was cruel and uncompromising in my youthful ignorance; astounded to hear this elderly man talk in such a distraught way about his love for me and beg me to go to Europe with him. "You're old, over sixty", I said. "How could I ever think of such a thing?"'[15] According to Katharine, Gmelin left town the next day; his final advertisement in the *Gippsland Standard* appeared on 26 October. In late November, Katharine was horrified to read in the newspaper that Gmelin was in hospital after collapsing at the Russell Street police station in Melbourne; in his pocket was 'a hypodermic syringe and a phial of atropine', a poison extracted from deadly nightshade and sometimes used with morphine to commit suicide.[16] Katharine blamed herself and spent anxious days wondering if he would live. He did, but for the first time—setting aside her nurse, N'gardo—the shadow of suicide had come over her life.

WITH LIZZY'S ENCOURAGEMENT, Katharine became involved in the Yarram Dramatic Society's production of Arthur Pinero's play *Sweet Lavender* (1888), a sentimental comedy which was one of the most popular plays of the period. Katharine played the eponymous Lavender, a young woman who must overcome obstacles to marry a law student. The locals started calling Katharine 'Lavender', a nickname which stuck for years afterwards as she cultivated an association with the plant. The one-off performance of the play was held on the night of the annual show, Wednesday 23 November, a public holiday in the shire.[17]

On the wet and muddy show day, Katharine came first in the ladies' trot to young men yelling, 'Ten to one on Sweet Lavender', but she was disqualified for galloping.[18] The Mechanics' Hall was 'filled to its utmost capacity' for the play by eight p.m. The newspaper recorded, 'The central figure of the play was Sweet Lavender, a fascinating young lady of undoubted charms, nicely acted by Miss Prichard'. The annual dance afterwards ran until 4 in the morning.[19]

The long show day was the climax of that year and a farewell to the town. The way she remembered it, she 'planned to stay only a year in one place' as she was determined 'to learn more about Australia, our country and people' but the character reference from Lizzy dated

December 1904 shows it was actually the Muirs who let her go: 'it is with great regret we parted with Miss Prichard, our reason for doing so was our approaching return to England'.[20]

THE YARRAM LOCALS found Katharine an interesting topic of conversation; Anne Home, then a child, remembered:

> I overheard the following conversation over the teacups one afternoon when the local gossip was being passed round, the new and only governess in the town being the highlight.
> Mrs A: 'Have you seen Dr M's new governess?'
> Mrs B: 'No, but I hear she is quite a blue stocking, one of those literary girls, the sort that has holes in her stockings and lives with her nose in a book. They say that she has come down here for copy.'[21]

Perhaps it was clear even at that point that Katharine was intent on turning her time in South Gippsland into 'copy', although it's also possible the knowledge of Katharine's later literary success influenced Anne Home's reminiscence in 1946.

In 1968, looking back on her career, Katharine wrote, 'In reaction to [Henry] Lawson's descriptions of the dreary and drought-stricken districts of New South Wales, I wanted to write of the beauty of forests and river meadows in South Gippsland'.[22] The area was to inspire two major works. The first was a 10,000-word short story, 'Diana of the Inlet' (1912). Drawing on her memories of the landscape from an Easter holiday with the Muirs at nearby Port Albert, Katharine evoked the power and beauty of nature in mythical and religious terms—'There is a mysterious spell in the lonely stillness and beauty of the forest hills. The air, with its mingled musky aroma of trees, its wild, heavy fragrance of flowers, is narcotic'.[23] The anonymous narrator visits the promontory and seeks out a hermit who lives in the bush, the survivor of a shipwreck whose ordeal caused him to embrace nature and decide that cities are 'plague spots—filthy and reeking of men's vices'.[24]

The second work inspired by South Gippsland was to be her breakthrough success—her first published novel, *The Pioneers* (1915). The novel begins with a Scottish couple, Donald and Mary Cameron, overcoming the hardships of the land to establish a farm in South Gippsland in the 1840s. Jumping forward to the next generation, it describes the development of the district and the rebellion of their only son, Davey, as he falls in love with Deirdre, an escaped convict's daughter, and strives to make his own way in the new country, free of the restraints of the old country.

Katharine obscured the geographical and historical setting of *The Pioneers* by renaming the places; the last page of a notebook for the novel reveals her key: 'Tarra = Wirrie; Tarraville = Wirrieford; Port Albert = Port Southern; Sale = Rane; Yarram = Ayrmuir'.[25] When the novel won a competition in 1915, her uncle's newspaper reported, 'Miss Prichard knows well the country of which she writes. Her material was gathered in talks with old people about the early days and the early settlers in the country. Some were survivors of the pioneering days. It is to a certain extent folk history'.[26] The pioneers of South Gippsland were dying off in 1904. In June, Katharine might have read in the local newspaper:

> One by one are the pioneers of the district entering the portal which is called Death ... They depart hence honoured in memory by those who, following in the pioneer's footsteps, have no regrets at having chosen South Gippsland as a field in which to labour, if not to ultimately reach the goal of mankind—wealth and comfort, and freedom from care.[27]

Like the editor of the *Gippsland Standard*, Katharine was to reflect on the meaning of pioneering and the legacy to the future generations. The major source of conflict between Donald Cameron and his son Davey is the wealthy father's meanness about money; if the next generation is not allowed to live comfortably, what is the point of all that striving? In the penultimate chapter, Davey's mother Mary declares, 'Oh God, we broke the earth, we sowed the seed. Let theirs be the harvest—the joy of life and the fullness thereof'.[28]

Katharine claimed to have met an escaped convict while in Yarram and she wove his tales into *The Pioneers.*[29] The colonial South Gippsland of *The Pioneers* is filled with escapees who have made their way by sea from Van Diemen's Land. One of the escapees, the Schoolmaster, reveals to Mary that he was an Irish political prisoner; he proves to be a sacrificial hero. Convicts, Katharine was arguing, were often the victims of a cruel system. Today, that seems an easy political point to make, even if it was more challenging a century ago. Katharine was, of course, less aware of aspects of colonial settlement which stand out today: the dispossession of Aboriginal people and the degradation of the environment. At this stage of her political awareness, she was oblivious to the first and only hinted at the second.

The Scottish explorer and pastoralist Angus McMillan was long honoured as someone who 'pioneered Gippsland and spent the rest of his life contributing to its welfare'; for decades his portrait hung in the Shire of Alberton chambers in Yarram and the adjacent federal parliamentary seat was named after him in 1948.[30] Yet in 2018, the seat was renamed; today he is notorious for his role in the 1843 Warrigal Creek massacre in which many Aboriginal people were murdered 30 kilometres north of the future site of Yarram.[31] Katharine may have had no knowledge of the massacre; 'a wall of silence fell across the incident'.[32] Aboriginal people only have a shadowy presence in *The Pioneers*, their existence mentioned in passing at several points, but without any awareness that the white settlement of the area involved their displacement and murder. The Aboriginal minor character, Teddy, is spoken to but never speaks; he often becomes 'the black boy'. Three decades later, when Katharine wrote another novel of pioneers—this time of the Western Australian goldfields—*The Roaring Nineties* (1946), she began with a short, violent story of the abduction of an Aboriginal woman by prospectors before gold has even been discovered; the novel is haunted by the presence of displaced and mistreated Aboriginal people.

With Katharine's rapturous appreciation of nature, and particularly trees, she may have experienced the denuded farmland around Yarram as a wound on the land. At the midpoint of the novel, Deirdre, the beautiful young heroine, contemplates a dead tree with its 'hacked zone that the axe of a settler had made when he ring-barked it years ago … It might have been an avenging spirit of the wilderness, it stood with an air of such tragic desolation by the wayside'.[33] The tree finally falls in a climactic chapter, killing Donald Cameron as he rides past it; Deirdre wonders 'if he had ring-barked the tree … and in turn it had killed him'.[34]

As she wrote *The Pioneers* in a cramped, cold London flat in the winter of 1914, she 'returned to the lovely countryside about the Tarwin River, with Wilson's Promontory outlined against the sky'.[35] The memory of South Gippsland was a quintessentially Australian space where she could play out her romance tale, interweaving it with her patriotic hope for a new, better nation as her generation, the grandchildren of the pioneers, took over. In the epilogue to the novel, Deirdre and Davey's son Dan remembers his grandmother Mary telling him, 'You will be a pioneer too, Dan … a pioneer of paths that will make the world a better, happier place for everybody to live in'.[36]

Katharine was only in Yarram for a year but it was a long year in her memory and, like Launceston, she revisited it in fiction and autobiography, in this case a time and place of adult freedom and sexual naïvety before tragedy struck.

5

Outback

Tarella Station, NSW, 1905

At the time she turned twenty-one, Katharine found herself back home for six months, without work and probably clashing with her family after a year of relative freedom. While she was away Tom had sent her a poem called 'Now that Kattie isn't Here', twelve stanzas of doggerel which give a picture of what it was like to live with Katharine. She is an 'audacious peace disturber' and without her 'my den is uninvaded'; in her absence, the family's 'grip on O'Mimosa' and other popular songs 'is relaxing very sadly'. She apparently not only moves all Tom's 'papers, books and pens' but now that she's gone even his 'hammer, planes & ruler / Can be found in half a jiffy'.[1]

Katharine's friend Hilda had been at Presbyterian Ladies' College with Hazel Quin, a boarder whose parents needed a governess for their younger children on their sheep station, Tarella, in north-western New South Wales.[2] Perhaps it was through this connection that Katharine was offered the job, starting in May 1905 when the Quin family returned to the station after spending the hotter half of the year at their house in Melbourne.

Tom sent Katharine on her way with another poem and a Bible. The poem, 'Magna Est Veritas' ('great is truth'), exhorts Katharine to 'do thou the right' and never lie, so that the truth's presence might 'guard thy life from stain' with its 'vestal purity'.[3] Even if the topic is ostensibly the matter of truth telling, it suggests a plea that Katharine retain her virginity.

Tarella is located so far west in New South Wales that the nearest capital city is Adelaide, and Katharine's journey with the Quin family began with a train ride there. After Adelaide 'came the slow train trundling to Broken Hill', the end of the line, and they then had a 500-kilometre, two-day Cobb and Co coach ride into the outback.[4]

While at Tarella Station, Katharine began writing a six-part serial called 'A City Girl in Central Australia', published in *New Idea* the next year. The serial is in the form of letters from 'Kit' to her mother from a station called 'Willara'. It's a strange work, having a deliberate basis in real events and people while consciously exaggerating many elements, culminating in high melodrama in the final instalment. 'While descriptions of the country and station life were vivid and realistic, I had strung them on a thread of fiction; silly, sentimental fiction at that.'[5]

In 'City Girl', the coach drive from Broken Hill to the station is perilous. Only the rough but honourable coach-driver, Billy Northwest, can save Kit from a drunk, 'evil-smelling Irish brute' travelling next to her. In *Child of the Hurricane,* Katharine confessed, 'As a matter of fact … the driver was a sober respectable middle-aged man, not in the least likely to tie himself in knots outside a female passenger's door. But my romantic imagination required a reckless and dashing cavalier'.[6] A letter writer to the *Barrier Miner* newspaper rebuked her for the exaggerations in her first instalment:

> She looks upon a trip into the heart of our back country as an adventure; she looks upon all who dwell here as specimens to be commented upon by her uncertain pen. She saw only in her travels the flippant side of life that appealed to her vanity—not the worth in those who in this land fight on bravely with the droughts and the duststorms and floods.[7]

The letter concluded, 'Let us hope that "Kit's" contribution to the next *New Idea* will smack of a little common-sense and be tainted with just a hint of truth'; the letter writer would have grown steadily angrier as they read on month by month and Kit's adventures became more and more outlandish. Yet ultimately, Katharine took the advice to heart.

Throughout her career she would often return to the people of the backblocks of Australia, but never again as a city girl encountering them as 'specimens'. Avoiding the first person and writing from the inside of communities, *The Pioneers* (1915) and *Black Opal* (1921) were the first of many novels in her oeuvre to valorise rural Australians.

EDWARD AND EDITH Quin had taken over the 685,000 acres of Tarella in 1872, expanding the flocks to 120,000 sheep and building a new homestead in 1879. The station 'was like a feudal domain ... with the homestead the centre of a village; the huts of stockmen and station-hands, a store, smithy, stockyards, and innumerable sheds'.[8] In between her duties as governess teaching her three students, Katharine witnessed horses broken in, cattle branded and the intense shearing season. In the past there had been industrial disputes between Edward Quin and the shearers. During the 1891 shearers' strike, Quin maintained control, paying the workers the rates set by the pastoralists.[9] Then, after another strike in 1902, he eventually conceded to the shearers' demand that he pay the union wage.[10] When the shearers strike in the fictionalised 'City Girl', the Boss sacks them all. Katharine's political awareness was low at this point and her alter ego, Kit, is just an observer, not taking a side.

On weekends, Katharine went on expeditions to the outlying parts of the property and beyond. She visited the White Cliffs opal field and described it in 'City Girl'; the experience planted the seed for her third novel *Black Opal* (1921). She spent much time absorbing the landscape and describing it in her 'big black exercise book'.[11] Those six months were the longest she would ever spend in the outback, and she stored up her experiences to draw on over the rest of her literary career, eventually revisiting station life directly in *Coonardoo* (1929).[12]

KATHARINE'S STUDENTS WERE 'sedate little girls of from twelve to sixteen, an elder sister for English and French, and the grown-up daughter of the house for drawing and painting' but she found the teaching hard, putting 'a great deal of nervous energy' into it and coming down with headaches at the end of each day.[13] She found the nightly dinners an ordeal; there was not only all the Quins to socialise with but usually guests passing through as well. Katharine was introverted. She could handle social interactions well enough, but needed solitude to recover.

The grown-up daughter Katharine mentioned was Tarella Quin, named after the station; she was a writer herself and published two adult novels about station life and several books of children's stories between 1907 and 1934. Nothing is known of the conversations Katharine and Tarella had, living for months under the same roof in 1905, two aspiring women writers in their twenties with an interest in depicting the outback.[14]

THERE WAS MUTUAL attraction between Katharine and Tarella's brother, Alfred Quin, the 29-year-old younger son of the family.

> He had a pointed red beard and eyes the colour of whisky. It was the beard which captured my imagination; but he also looked my ideal of an Australian stockman: tall, slender, reserved and sensitive; walking with the graceful slouch of a man more accustomed to riding than walking … When accidentally one day the red beard brushed my bare arm, it sent a quivering all through me. Such a thing had never happened before.[15]

She would befriend many poets and thinkers for their minds, but it was outdoorsmen like Alfred she was usually attracted to.

To celebrate the coming of the rains, 'folk from a hundred miles away were invited to a ball at the station'. Perhaps the ball would bring things to a head. In 'City Girl', it happens in mid-August: 'I resolved to depart the austere path of my youth … I swore to the moon and all the mute, gaunt mulga, to be young and merry. There is a ball coming, and a week of festivities, in which this interesting determination is to make its debut'.[16] The ball was held after a 'sumptuous dinner', Katharine wearing 'a frock of filmy cirrus and cumuli sewed with threads of starlight' as she danced with 'a tall gangling bloke with a walrus moustache before Red Beard came to me for a waltz. We sat in silence in the moonlight afterwards, beside an orange-tree in flower. It was the best part of the evening for me.'[17]

With the guests staying on for two nights, the next day was a tennis tournament, followed by a fancy-dress dance in the evening. Katharine stood out that night, dressed as a Spanish dancer with a tight bodice and an artificial rose in her hair. To the applause of the guests, she 'whirled into the Spanish dance of which Father had disapproved, long ago, when I was a schoolgirl'.[18] Afterwards, Alfred fought another man who 'boasted in the men's hut that "he had seen Miss Prichard's drawers"' as she twirled about. Yet even this was no proper declaration; she only heard about it from his sister.[19]

Katharine fictionalised this ball and the dance not just in 'City Girl' but also in *Black Opal.* In both of these works, the fickle young man chooses another woman only to realise his mistake, declare his love for the heroine and die.

Events were far less decisive in real life. Edward warned Katharine, 'No use your making eyes at my son, Miss Thinga-me-Bob. He's engaged to the daughter of an old friend'.[20] Denying she made eyes at anybody, Katharine 'would scarcely look at Red Beard after that'. The weather was heating up, the Quins were returning to Melbourne and Katharine was to go with them. Alfred's 'charm had diminished when he shaved off his beard. He looked like quite an ordinary young man then; but I was still aware of the mysterious attraction between us'. He came in to see her a few days before she was leaving, working up the courage to ask her if she had been told he was engaged to someone else. When she said she had, he told her it wasn't true. Katharine 'feigned indifference and went on correcting exercise books. No doubt if Red Beard had said something in the manner of a traditional lover, I would have responded. But he didn't. I thought he was afraid of displeasing his father. My pride was hurt'.[21]

6

Heavy Rocks, Icy Winds

Melbourne and New Zealand, 1906–1907

IN 1906, KATHARINE started teaching at Christ Church Grammar School. She struggled to control a class of thirty boys in three grades. The classes were all in one big hall, a 'babel of teachers and boys talking against each other'. She had to contend with sexual harassment from her students. When a hook in her 'flame-coloured blouse' came undone, one of the boys offered to help her; instead, he 'unfastened all the hooks'. Giving French lessons to the senior boys, one of them asked how to say, 'I'd like to kiss you'. 'Exhausted at the end of every day', she resigned and took up private tutoring, leaving her 'time to write in the afternoons, and to attend night lectures at the university'.[1]

These lectures 'were the fulfilment of a long frustrated desire'; they broadened her understanding of literature and gave her a taste of university.[2] Yet they were also a further frustration of her desire; unlike Hilda, Nettie and Christian, she wasn't working towards a degree. She remained defensive and a little bitter about some of those who did. 'I found that one of my cousins, who had got her degree, knew very little French, and less of international literature.'[3]

One of her lecturers was the academic and essayist Walter Murdoch; they talked when they caught the same tram, the beginning of a quiet friendship that would last the rest of their lives. He helped inspire in

Katharine a love of the English writer George Meredith. Later, they would both move to Western Australia and would be considered the two giants of Western Australian literature. A literary scholar, Murdoch reached a wide audience writing for newspapers, with his popular columns on a wide range of topics appearing from 1905 onwards. Although they only saw each other irregularly, he wrote to Katharine in 1954, 'What you mean to me, and have meant for nearly half a century, you will never guess'.[4]

IN MAY 1906, the first episode of 'A City Girl in Central Australia' appeared in *New Idea.* It was a major leap forward in her literary career, putting her name alongside established writers Miles Franklin and Mary Gilmore, whose serials had previously been published in the magazine. One newspaper called it 'a capital, racy sketch' while another wrote that the editor 'is to be congratulated on securing such an able writer as Miss Pritchard [*sic*] to follow Mrs Gilmore with descriptions of life in the inner parts of the continent'.[5] Katharine had forced her father to take her writing seriously. He composed a poem in response, one of his last, in which he wrote that 'our Kattie has taken wing'; it was 'a touch of Quin-sy'—a swelling of the throat, punning on the name of the Tarella Station owners—'ending in a case of swollen head'.[6]

IN JUNE 1906, Katharine attended a speech by a visiting Austrian academic named Rudolf Broda, a socialist in his mid-twenties. She described him as 'a little man, with "much of a balcony" (big tummy), as the French say, and a round angelic countenance. It positively beamed with the beauty of a high and noble character'.[7]

> He would discuss literature, art and music with eager joy in the manifestations of human genius, but always come back to the need for political and economic organization to release the potentialities of men and women from the poverty and injustices they suffered under a system by which the wealth and power of a few dominated the lives of a majority of the people.[8]

A journalist wrote that Rudolf's 'keen desire' on his visit to Australia 'was to meet the liberated, the enfranchised woman—advanced and intelligent men, he said, he could meet in Europe, but the Australian woman, who enjoyed a freedom social and political unknown elsewhere … he wished to … converse with'.[9] When Katharine met him, she told him she was saving up to visit Europe; he asked her why she would want to see Europe when she lived 'in the most progressive country in the world. You are making history here. You will write a new page in the story of the world. Helping to do that is more important than anything you can do, or write, in the old world'.[10]

Meeting Rudolf was Katharine's first exposure to left-wing politics, and even though she would later find his reformist approach inadequate, she was inspired. The third federal election was held six months later with Alfred Deakin's Protectionist Party retaining government in alliance with Labor. Katharine voted for the first time. Although women in Victoria did not have the right to vote at a state level until 1908, they had gained the right to vote in federal elections in 1902. There were three major parties contesting the election—the Labor Party representing the working class on the left, Deakin's Protectionist Party in the middle, and George Reid's Anti-Socialist Party on the right (formerly the Free Trade Party). Tom's vote was firmly with the Anti-Socialist Party. Defying the politics of her family and her class, Katharine voted for Labor without her father's knowledge. 'He was ill at the time and I could not tell him.'[11]

Tom had just been released from an asylum and she was right to think he would have taken it badly. She had difficulty coming to terms with his politics even long after he was dead. In 1950 she apparently told Cyril Cook that 'Tom Prichard was a liberal of the old school and a friend and admirer of Alfred Deakin'.[12] Perhaps Cook misconstrued her or perhaps she grew more aware of her father's politics in the years which followed as she read through his scrapbooks to research *Child of the Hurricane*; whichever was the case, she wrote in her autobiography that Tom's politics were conservative, 'anti one-man-one-vote, anti trade-unionism, anti even the liberalism of Deakin'.[13] She had written another line, which she crossed out for the published version: 'Strange it seems to me now, that so humane a man could have been so blind to the fundamental needs of humanity'.[14]

Tom had such strong conservative political convictions that he published a manifesto in 1902, *Australian Popular Delusions,* a collection of his columns from the *Australian Mining Standard.* He called for an expansion of cheap indentured labour from Asia, such as could be found in the plantations of the West Indies. He railed against the minimum wage in Australia, blaming it for the loss of investment in industry. Unions 'have striven to put workmen into artificial families in which all share alike, the able with the incompetent, the lazy with the industrious'.[15] He went on to condemn the welfare state, writing, 'That the government which be made to give most lavishly is the best for people and, therefore, worthiest of their support, is a delusion which the spineless section of the community hugs very closely to its heart'.[16]

If Tom had lived to witness it, the eventual conversion of his daughter to communism—far to the left of Labor—would have been the most outrageous thing he could have imagined.

IN OCTOBER 1906, Katharine's brother, Alan, nearly died from appendicitis. He was taken to hospital in an ambulance while the family waited at home. 'What an appalling night that was … [knowing] that Alan might not live until morning. Father walked up and down the hall all night, frantic with anxiety.' Alan lived but it 'was a shock Father never recovered from'.[17]

Tom couldn't sleep. He grew obsessively worried about Alan and about his job. Unable to work, he stopped going into the office, which only increased his worry. Edith and Alan had him committed to the Toorak House Asylum on 15 November. The doctors diagnosed him with delusions and melancholia. He was having trouble with dates and remembering anything from recent weeks. On 17 November, the doctor wrote, 'Saw patient today but he seemed suspicious of me & wouldn't converse'. A week later, he was discharged on probation, the doctor noting, 'I thought advisable recommend removal as he seemed well but greatly worried & vexed at detainment in an asylum'.[18]

The doctor advised a sea voyage and months of rest. Edith thought Tom should visit his brothers in New Zealand with Katharine accompanying him. Money was tight and Katharine paid for both their fares with her savings.[19] Katharine and Tom left on 12 December 1906, six days after the federal election, on the steamship *Monowai*.[20] They spent Christmas 1906 in Christchurch and a few weeks later Katharine returned home, leaving Tom at his brother Alfred's farm on the Canterbury plains.

> There were blue snow-capped mountains in the distance but the plains looked bare and dreary … Heavy rocks, scattered far and wide, seemed to hold down the soil which would otherwise have been blown away by icy winds.
>
> I hated to leave Father in such a place. He worked in old clothes, carting water and manure. It hurt to see him so humble and anxious to help out of doors. I felt that he should not be allowed to do such heavy work. But he insisted that this quiet, uneventful existence was what he needed for a while, and that physical toil would rest his mind.[21]

Writing her autobiography, the memory of leaving him in that bleak landscape—the heavy rocks and the icy winds—felt to her like a rehearsal for what came after.

THE DAILY LIFE of the Prichard household continued, anxiously, through the first half of 1907. Alan, twenty-two years old, was also working for the *Australian Mining Standard*. Nigel, now twenty, had left home to teach primary school students at Wangaratta Grammar, 230 kilometres north of Melbourne.[22] Beatrice was fourteen and—despite being Anglican—attending a Catholic convent school.[23] Edith's widowed sister, Lilly Williams, moved in with the family in March, the same month Tom returned from New Zealand. 'When Father came home from New Zealand he had lost weight and looked so much older. There were silver threads in the silky black hair he was so proud of.'[24] It distressed him that he felt unable to return to the office, but working from home he did start writing for the *Australian Mining Standard* again.

He may have pretended that the manual labour and fresh New Zealand air had cured him, but it hadn't. None of the family knew what to do for him. 'Often during those last months, when he couldn't sleep, he would ask me to sing to him. I sang for hours to soothe and comfort him.' He took to praying obsessively.

> We all knelt down round him in the little drawing-room, and long and earnestly he pleaded with God to restore him to health, give him another chance to provide for his dear wife and children. So humble and eloquent those outpourings were. Open-eyed I watched him, as he crouched over a chair, believing he was communing with God. It was torture to see the agony of mind he was suffering, and Mother's anguish as she wept quietly beside him.[25]

Katharine bargained with God, promising to believe in his existence if Tom recovered, but 'full of passionate resentment that Father and Mother should be suffering so cruelly; that their belief should require such humiliation. I felt that it was a farce, a tragic farce, to imagine there was a God who could hear their prayers and would avert the sorrow which threatened us'.[26]

IN *CHILD OF THE HURRICANE,* Katharine left the cause of Tom's death unsaid. 'In the end it seemed the struggle and frustration of many years had caught up with him.'[27]

On the morning of Thursday 27 June 1907, he was home with Edith, Katharine, Beatrice and Aunt Lilly. It had been a bad night and having been kept up by his restlessness, Edith returned to bed about 10.30 a.m. He came in to apologise and told her she should rest. Lilly saw him about 11.15 a.m. 'He was then on the lawn close to the door of his tool-house. I did not like to watch him too closely because he felt this keenly. I did not speak to him. He had some wood in his hand. He had been making a bookshelf.'[28]

Lilly must have been worried about him; about half an hour later she 'went to see how he was'. The door of the tool house was locked but she looked through the window and could see him hanging. 'I tried to open the door but failing that I ran to my sister [Edith] for help. We burst in the door. There is a beam cross to which he'd tied the rope … My sister cut the rope. He had not been dead long. He was quite warm.'[29]

Katharine and Beatrice must have come out by now. Between the four of them, they laid Tom's body out on a board in the shed. Someone was sent to fetch the family doctor as the others waited with the body. When the doctor arrived, he told them death would have been instantaneous. Someone placed a handkerchief over Tom's face.[30]

'Nothing was done', Edith testified, 'until the police came about 1.45 p.m.' It had been two hours since they'd found the body by then. Were the police slow to come, or were the family slow to fetch them? Constable Creed said, 'I went to the shed. I found the deceased lying on the board a handkerchief over his face. On removing the handkerchief I saw the marks of rope on his throat. He was quite dead. No marks of violence were visible … I was informed that the deceased was expert in making knots'.[31]

THE CORONIAL INQUEST was held the next day, Friday 28 June, by the district coroner. Edith, Lilly and Constable Creed gave their testimonies, leaving a fuller picture of this final, short day of Tom's life than any other—his insomnia, his final, inconsequential words, the bookshelf he never finished making. Edith testified Tom had never threatened suicide but he had said 'he would be better away than burdening us. He said this several times during the course of the illness'. After hearing the evidence, the coroner ruled that Tom had 'committed suicide while temporarily of an unsound mind'.[32]

The funeral was the day after this, Saturday 29 June. The mourners gathered at Korovuna at 3.15 p.m. and processed the short distance along North Road to the Brighton Cemetery. 'The very large number of mourners present testified to the high esteem in which he was held. These included journalists, representatives of the mining industry and commerce, and many friends.'[33] On his gravestone is a verse from Psalms: 'He sent from above, He took me, He drew me out of many waters'.

PART 2

FREEWOMAN, 1907–1919

7

The Preux Chevalier

Sydney, February 1907

'After father's death', Katharine wrote, 'for a long time I couldn't sing at all. There was no song in my heart and my voice would not lift'.[1] In a fictional echo, Sophie, the heroine of Katharine's novel, *Black Opal* (1921), loses her singing voice, too; for her it is tied up with her first sexual experience: 'I was so sick with the shock and shame of it all ... I couldn't sing any more. I wouldn't. My voice died'.[2] Earlier in *Black Opal*, mourning her mother transforms Sophie, causing Arthur Henty, the wealthy station-heir to notice her. 'And he seemed to be seeing Sophie for the first time, too ... He could not believe that this tall girl in the black dress was the queer, elfish-like girl he had seen running about the Ridge, bare-legged ... not much more than a year ago.'[3]

In life, it was a man Katharine called Preux Chevalier who noticed her; she said she was so naïve she had no idea what he wanted. 'He was married, of course, and had a daughter my own age, which I thought was why he was so courteous to me.'[4] His obsession with her escalated during Tom's sickness and he was waiting for her when she disembarked from the *Monowai* in Sydney on 12 February 1907 on the way home from New Zealand. 'He said he had heard from the family I was arriving from New Zealand that day, and thought he might be of some assistance, as he was on a business visit and knew Sydney quite well … "I'll be your *preux chevalier* and show you Sydney," he said.'[5]

The ostensible business the Preux Chevalier had in Sydney left him much time to spend with Katharine. 'Every night he took me to dinner and the theatre, or to a concert, or for a trip on the harbour. Every day we wandered about the city; or made excursions which revealed the dazzling beauty of its surroundings.' She was 'enchanted' by the city 'and flattered by the way this man discussed all manner of subjects with me'.

> We must have looked an odd pair, going about together. He, a man of the world, elegant and assured, accustomed to authority; and I in my home-made summer dress and floppy hat with a blue ribbon, or ingénue white chiffon evening dress at least three years old. I was not interested in clothes at that time, but conscious of being a little dowdy and gauche in the company of this Preux Chevalier.[6]

For someone who was uninterested in clothes, she had a vivid memory of what she wore. Rather than an 'odd' pair, they appeared all too familiar to a woman sitting beside them on a park bench who told Katharine not to trust him. The woman said, 'All men are gay deceivers'.[7] Later, as they walked along the harbour's edge near Mrs Macquarie's Chair, the Preux Chevalier asked Katharine if she thought he was a 'gay deceiver'. She told him she didn't; she wouldn't be deceived if he was. '"Don't wonder too much," he replied dryly. "There are all sorts of rapprochements between a man and woman beyond reason or argument."'

The Preux Chevalier was not only obsessive but patient. 'He did nothing to arouse my dormant senses. He never kissed me, or even pressed my hand suggestively. What he did was to capture my imagination by our companionship in the carefree atmosphere of Sydney, and create an intellectual bond between us.' When she arrived back in Melbourne, Katharine said nothing to her mother about him. 'People wouldn't understand', he warned her. 'There would be no end of malicious gossip.'[8]

They met often and in secret after their return to Melbourne.

> There were walks through the tea-tree at Black Rock, occasionally dinner at the seaside restaurant afterwards. But always our talk was of books, my studies and literary work. The intellectual companionship was stimulating with no hint of anything disturbing, except that these accidental, and not so accidental, meetings should not be mentioned. The Preux Chevalier was more interesting to talk to than any of the young men who were my friends. I was flattered, and thrilled too, at the thought of being his *chere amie*.[9]

Katharine's phrase 'anything disturbing' could mean 'anything sexual', yet sex didn't seem to particularly disturb her, as coyly as she presented her youthful self. Missing from the published account of the Sydney trip in *Child of the Hurricane* is a sentence in the draft suggesting she meant something else: 'Gradually the vines of a possessive passion began to twine about me, but I was not aware of that at the time'.[10] She was to be entangled with the Preux Chevalier for the next decade.

ONE CRITIC FINDS the name Preux Chevalier 'ludicrous'; another writes that 'her title for him itself tells much'.[11] Although Katharine claimed she 'never indulged in fairytale fantasies', the 'gallant knight' seems central to her ideal of romance at this time. In 'A City Girl in Central Australia' (1906) she refers to Bill Northwest as her 'cavalier' several times, a related term she also applies to the Preux Chevalier. 'Preux Chevalier' was a term borrowed from the romance serials appearing in Australian newspapers at this time. In 1905's 'Fair Lilias', as an example, a hero 'assisted her down the narrow, difficult path with the tenderness, devotion, and courage of a preux chevalier'.[12] Despite his stated intentions, Katharine's Preux Chevalier proved to bear more resemblance to the stock villains of the same serials. In ME Braddon's 'Dead Love Has Chains', serialised in 1906, the heroine is in love with a 'preux chevalier … radiant in the glory of enchanting youth', but is thrown into turmoil when she receives a letter from a villainous former lover. She 'remembered the tyranny of his love in the days when she had loved him. She was at the age when a girl adores a tyrant. His determined pursuit of her had been the charm that worked to such fatal issues. To be pursued, to be worshipped! It was the schoolgirl's dream of bliss'.[13]

IN 1962, AS Katharine was negotiating the publication of *Child of the Hurricane*, Beatrice Davis at Angus and Robertson asked if Katharine could reveal his name. 'It would hurt too many people', Katharine wrote back, 'so I could never do it'.[14]

He was probably Lieutenant-Colonel William Thomas Reay. Mentioned under his own name several times in *Child of the Hurricane*, Reay was a newspaper editor, politician and military officer with the Victorian Mounted Rifles who would become Katharine's boss at the *Herald* in 1909 and 1910 before moving to London at the same time as her. 'A chirpy, sparrow-like man is Reay—active, eager, energetic, and a regular tiger to work, he never has any leisure. As soon as his daily paper is … off his hands, he is hard at the work of some one or other of the numerous organisations to which he belongs.'[15] A man of a thousand causes and boundless energy, he was a progressive, successful version of Tom Prichard and he came into Katharine's life just as she was losing her father.

Reay was born in Balmain, Sydney on 10 November 1858. Katharine calls the Preux Chevalier a 'friend of the family'; like Katharine's mother, Edith, Reay spent part of his childhood in Williamstown in Melbourne. He was four years younger than Edith and twenty-five years older than Katharine. As a young bookkeeper, he saved enough money to buy the *Coleraine Albion* newspaper in country Victoria in 1883.[16] It was the year his first child was born, a daughter, to his wife, Lucinda; it was also the year Katharine was born. One hint that their marriage was troubled came in a 1911 trial of a burglar who had stolen jewels from the family; one of their daughters testified that 'she slept in the same room as her mother. Her father, who had met with an accident, slept in another room'.[17]

Reay had five daughters, his two sons dying in infancy.[18] Katharine was friends with at least one of them, Nan, a nurse. Another of the daughters, Beatrice, married Lionel Bull, the brother of Katharine's best friend, Hilda.[19] In 1962, when Katharine wrote that it would hurt too many people to name the Preux Chevalier, four of Reay's daughters were still alive.

Katharine's 'gaily irreligious and iconoclastic' Preux Chevalier influenced her to reject her father's political conservatism.

> He opened my mind to political questions, international problems of peace and war, the rights of women, with a broad humanitarian outlook on everything, and an ardent belief in Australia, its progress and future as a powerful, independent nation. Politics, history and poetry, he dipped into them all, with witty observations and amusing anecdotes of politicians and writers he had known.[20]

This description of the Preux Chevalier matches Reay. He was a member of the Victorian parliament from 1900 to 1902; 'describing himself as a radical, he often voted with Labor'.[21] He was active in the National Anti-Sweating League, a Victorian organisation of middle-class social reformers which had agitated for the passing of the Factory Act in 1896 and then continued as a watchdog and tribunal ensuring fair working hours and minimum wages in factories.[22] Matching Katharine's description of the Preux Chevalier's 'ardent belief in Australia', Reay was president of the Hawthorn branch of the Australian Natives' Association in Victoria before becoming one of the founders of the London branch in 1915.[23] With membership restricted to Australian-born whites, it had pushed for federation, and now in the 1900s 'supported the White Australia Policy, advocated a strong Australian defence force, promoted the celebration of Australia Day as a national holiday ... and defended wider powers for the Commonwealth Government'.[24]

Katharine carefully avoided mentioning the Preux Chevalier's occupation, but Ric Throssell reveals he was 'an influential figure in the Australian press'.[25] Reay was a newspaper editor for many decades; after editing the *Coleraine Albion* he later edited the *Hamilton Spectator* and then the *Herald*, Melbourne's major evening newspaper.[26]

Ric Throssell describes the Preux Chevalier's 'possessive jealousy'; in an earlier draft of *Wild Weeds and Windflowers,* he adds, 'that he imposed upon her, following her across the world'.[27] The deleted part explains the strange fact that the Preux Chevalier turned up wherever

Katharine was from 1907 to 1915. Reay's movements are the most telling circumstantial evidence he was the Preux Chevalier.

On 11 February 1907, the day before Katharine arrived in Sydney and was met by the Preux Chevalier, Reay travelled on the *Wyandra* from Melbourne to Sydney.[28]

In October 1908, the Preux Chevalier appeared in Paris to meet Katharine. That same month, Reay took a 'sojourn' to France, without his wife, 'for his health'.[29] When Katharine returned to Melbourne two months after Reay, he employed her at the *Herald.*

Several months after resigning from the *Herald,* Katharine unexpectedly travelled to New York in November 1910, where Reay was based for several months on another trip without his wife. The passenger list is difficult to decipher, but she appears to have been on the same ship as him leaving New York for Britain on 28 December 1910.[30] Katharine stayed on in London while Reay returned to Melbourne. He was expected to resume his post as editor of the *Herald,* but instead he created the post of manager of the newspaper's London office and moved there.[31] Reay stayed on in London all the time Katharine was there and beyond, eventually dying there in 1929.[32]

KATHARINE EMPHASISED THE Preux Chevalier's charm in *Child of the Hurricane*, only mentioning incidentally that he had threatened to kill himself if she ever married anyone else. Her son is less protective of him, revealing that Katharine privately 'warned my daughter, Karen, of the price she paid in years of possessive jealousy; of his demented threats to shoot himself when she attempted to leave him; of her regret for independence bartered to a man capable of the cowardice and deceit of playing upon her fear of suicide, knowing that she could not face the thought of becoming the cause of his self-destruction'.[33]

Reay's public persona is of a successful and relentless do-gooder. Beyond all that activity, hints of his weaknesses sometimes show through. In 1901, a gossip column described him as 'one of the most garrulous men in Victoria State Assembly'.

> He likes talking on all things, and one day, when he had held himself in, the *Argus* described him as 'suffering from suppression of speech'.

> This is one of the severest pains Reay can endure, but he very readily gets rid of it. Reay would be a real good man if he condensed more and did not drown his ideas in verbiage.[34]

Another gossip column in a Melbourne newspaper reported in January 1906 that Reay 'left for a holiday trip to Europe in the French mail steamer *Nera* on Thursday. That since his promotion to be chief [of the *Herald*] his duties have proved so arduous as to bring about nervous prostration, which renders a change of air and scene absolutely necessary'.[35] It was on his return he began pursuing Katharine, symptom of—or cure for—his middle-aged malaise.

THERE ARE SOME echoes of Katharine's relationship with Reay in her work. The most significant is in 'The New Pygmalion', one of her only surviving unpublished stories, written in the first year of her relationship with Reay. In late 1907, EJ Brady accepted it for publication in the *Native Companion,* but the journal folded before it appeared.[36] The Greek myth of Pygmalion tells of a sculptor who falls in love with his statue of a woman; the goddess Venus brings the statue to life. The myth was appropriated by many writers in the nineteenth and early twentieth centuries; Katharine's version predated the most famous one, George Bernard Shaw's play, *Pygmalion* (1913).[37]

In Katharine's story, Jean-Marie is a Frenchman who owns a beauty parlour by the sea. He is in love with his mannequin, Mimi. 'It was her beauty—her imperishable beauty—he adored, he told her … Madame his wife did not understand. She was not beautiful.' Jean-Marie treats his wife 'with formal chivalry, a ceremonious respect. Was she not his partner for life? But she was not an artist, Madame. She had not the soul of an artist'.

Madame also has a second rival for her husband's affection. 'The only ears besides Mimi's into which he could pour his trouble were the little ears, like tinted sea shells, of Lise, the orphan child.' Jean-Marie had promised Lise's father on his deathbed that he would take care of her. 'Perhaps he realised possibilities of beauty in the unformed grace of the slender little figure, despite its red, workworn hands and clumsy dirty clothes.'

After Madame destroys Mimi the mannequin in a fit of jealousy, Jean-Marie suffers 'exhaustion followed on nervous prostration'. Lise 'would do anything in the world to make him merry and garrulous again'. She tells Jean-Marie she has a secret; he assumes she has a lover and says he will rejoice if the man is worthy of her. Instead, Lise 'outlined her lips with scarlet, brushed her eyebrows with a tiny blackened brush, smoothed a delicate cream over her face and powdered it. She took the jewel from Mimi's hair and put it in her own. Then she bared her bosom and folded Mimi's scarf over it'. When she appears to Jean-Marie, he declares, 'It is Mimi … Mimi come to life, thou divine one'.[38]

In the story, Katharine showed a young woman naïvely enthralled by her Pygmalion, oblivious to his faults. Katharine seems to have had no sympathy for Madame, wife of the faithless Jean-Marie, not even giving her a name. Nor did she censure Jean-Marie for abusing his parental role in sexualising Lise. Lise herself shows no hesitation in embracing Jean-Marie; a poor, love-starved orphan, all she wants is to restore him to his 'garrulous' self.

8

'Astir with Great Things'

Melbourne, July 1907–May 1908

By the end of 1907, the Prichard family had moved out of the house where Tom had died to 94 Caroline Street, South Yarra, just a few kilometres from the Melbourne city centre. Alfred Deakin, then prime minister, lived nearby and not only knew Katharine's mother but also two of Katharine's admirers, Reay and Walter Murdoch. Katharine 'walked into town with him sometimes ... he, tall and stooping ... already worn and disillusioned; I, full of idealistic illusions, and my intention to become "a famous writer" as soon as possible'.[1] They talked of the writers they loved, especially George Meredith, whom Deakin had visited while in Britain earlier in 1907.[2] 'I did most of the talking', Katharine wrote, 'and Mr Deakin listened to my blithe chatter with a grave smile. So sensitive and sympathetic, that I knew when he was sharing my enthusiasm'.[3] Deakin wrote her a general letter of introduction to take to London in 1908 as well as one addressed to George Meredith.[4]

Many years later, Katharine wrote a didactic play about Deakin for the 1951 jubilee of federation competition. It was not shortlisted; nor was it ever performed. By that time, she was a rigid communist, but the play shows she still greatly admired the liberal politician for his role in achieving federation and shaping the new nation. Exaggerating her family connection to Deakin, the characters based on her parents, Tom and Edith Pollard, return from Fiji to witness key moments in Deakin's life and become his close friends and confidantes. Instead of dying in 1907, Tom outlives Deakin, saying in the epilogue after Deakin's death in 1919, 'You have gone beyond the Veil, Deakin. And we, old friends, grieve for you as we knew you—the soul of honour, poet, philosopher, and ardent lover of your country'.[5]

The influence of Deakin and Reay is apparent in 'Defence of Australia', a passionate opinion piece by Katharine published in the *Herald* in May 1908 marking the first known use of the initialism 'KSP'. Concern over Australia's defence had been growing since Japan's victory in its war with Russia in 1905. The influential Military Defence League brought together leaders from different sectors of society to agitate for compulsory military training for all young men. As a nationalist, Reay was a strong advocate for the policy and had written a series of articles on the Swiss military training system, published as a pamphlet in August 1907. Deakin had come around to the idea gradually, finally committing his government to it in December 1907. Conflict in the unstable parliaments over details of the legislation meant it was not passed for some time. The scheme eventually began in 1911 under the Labor government, with compulsory training for boys and men from ages twelve to twenty-six.[6]

As Deakin looked to grow popular support for the scheme in 1908, Katharine's article called on women to play their part by shunning any man who evaded training. 'Women will have nothing to do with him, for he is either a weakling who is unfit for, or a poor-spirited wretch who has evaded the discharge of a sacred and patriotic duty.' Katharine explicitly evoked the fear of an 'Asiatic invasion', writing with racism typical of the time but disturbing today, 'It is difficult for us to realise that the small yellow man, whose slant eyes squint at a woman in the street … hopes, in his secret brain, some day to be possessor and lord of our country. We must prepare against his hope …'. Among answers to common objections, Katharine wrote that although 'compulsory training sounds like a curtailing of public liberty … it is just the means whereby we may establish, emphasize and maintain our independence, safeguard our freedom, and snap our fingers at the suggestion of invasion'.[7]

Her strong support for the scheme might seem surprising, given her interest in the socialism of Rudolf Broda, whom she had met two years before. However, parts of the left were in favour of the idea. The federal conference of the Labor Party pledged its support in July 1908 while Reay's pamphlet noted that the Swiss socialists 'accept and uphold' the training system in their country.[8] Katharine's support for an Australian scheme in 1908 is the background to her dilemma over conscription during the first referendum on the issue in 1916.

IN DECEMBER 1907, Rudolf Broda published the first issue of an ambitious journal called *The International: A Review of the World's Progress.* Released simultaneously in French, German and English, he wrote that it 'will aim at being a mirror of the entire panorama of human evolution in all its many aspects'.[9]

In that first issue, alongside a piece on wage boards by Reay and 'The Women's Movement in Australia' by the suffragist Vida Goldstein, Katharine contributed a short manifesto on Australian literature. She wrote of how Australian literature was moving past the imitative stage of its infancy:

> It has reached the adolescent stage—it is astir with great things; growing daily in power and freedom. Bushrangers, drought, and dead sheep have too long been the entire tale of our existence. With our national feeling is growing a sane and vigorous treatment of the problems which affect our social and political life … The genesis of nationhood lies in its literature, and with the notion of elevating and glorifying the patriotic instincts Australian writers are dragging the minds of Australian people at the chariot wheels of their imaginations. Yet the muse of Australia is elusive—[Henry] Kendall caught 'A glimpse of her face and her glittering hair / And a hand with the harp of Australia'. But no-one has completely expressed the characteristic of our country, life and people. We await transfiguration at the hands of a great writer.[10]

Katharine's aspirations and opinions were not unique. They reflected the hope of the Australian Literature Society she was a part of with Nettie Palmer, the ideas of Walter Murdoch and writers like Bernard O'Dowd, as well as the vigorous nationalism espoused by Reay and the Australian Natives' Association. Yet her statement is remarkably prescient. Eight years before the publication of her first novel, she anticipated the goal she was to pursue throughout her long literary career: the attempt to express the 'characteristic of our country, life and people'. It is the thread which runs through her diverse oeuvre. In a poignant echo of this opening statement, she was to write in a kind of last testament in 1968, one year before she died: 'My work has been unpretentious: of the soil ... telling of the way men and women live and work in the forests, back country and cities of Australia'.[11]

In the 1907 statement, the development of an Australian literature was coinciding with Katharine's own literary development. She ascribed to the nation the very things she was striving for—to throw off 'imitativeness'; to grow 'daily in power and freedom'. She was 'astir with great things'. She wrote the piece with confidence and verve. Perhaps she dared to hope she would be the 'great writer' the nation awaited.

IN 1908, KATHARINE wrote the first draft of *The Wild Oats of Han.*[12] Ric Throssell imagines it as a 'turn from the pain-filled present ... to the memories of childhood in Launceston with her beloved young brothers, Alan and Nigel'.[13] Yet *Wild Oats* evokes not just a carefree idyll but also its shattering as Han becomes aware of death and the struggles of life. Katharine left the manuscript in draft form for years; for some reason she wasn't ready to try to publish it yet. Perhaps, as Jack Beasley speculates, she realised that 'the hapless father character she had created might have been regarded as an insensitive portrait of her own father, so soon after his death'. Or perhaps the draft still fell short of her hopes for the work. Ric Throssell notes that the version eventually published in 1928 'bears none of the hallmarks of Katharine's earliest stories', but instead shows the lyricism, sensitivity and perception of her best novels written in the 1920s; he believes she rewrote it extensively in that period.[14]

Ric might be right, but Katharine's most accomplished story of this period, 'The Kid', shows what she was already capable of, as well as having some resemblances to *Wild Oats*. Published by the *Bulletin* in January 1907, 'The Kid' is a gothic bush story. When the Kid's beloved baby half-brother dies, she runs away with his body, determined to stop

God taking him away to sell for his skin like her father does with dead cattle. A few days later, her body is found with the baby's under a white gum 'like a column of stainless marble'.[15] The theme and setting come together convincingly and Katharine gives death an emotional impact lacking in the melodrama of her other stories of the period. The *Bulletin* was at the centre of Australian literary culture and being published in it built on her success in *New Idea*. The grimness of the story befitted the bleak period in the Prichard household, published as it was while Tom was still alive but gripped by depression.

TURNING TWENTY-FOUR AT the end of 1907, there was a great sense of possibility for Katharine even in the midst of grief. She hadn't narrowed her choices by marrying. Her writing career was budding, her beloved but restrictive father was dead, and her well-travelled 'friend', Reay, was encouraging her to see the world. When a cheap fare was advertised for London, she decided to go.[16]

For young Australian women at the beginning of the twentieth century 'just embarking for London', writes Angela Woollacott, 'was often construed as a sign of success and ambition'.[17] Returning 'home' to the centre of the British empire seeking fame and success was a 'recognised cultural ritual in Australia'.[18] Katharine saw the trip as a literary and ancestral pilgrimage: 'I had hoped for years that some day I would see the historic places, and haunts of the great English writers'. It was also a chance to prove herself: 'I thought an Australian writer would never be appreciated in her country until she proved that her writing could win some recognition in England'.[19]

Yet her focus was not on fiction as it had been until now but journalism. She had freelance work guaranteed with *New Idea* on the strength of the popularity of the 'City Girl' serial and with the *Herald* thanks to her relationship with Reay. 'A Franco-British Exhibition was to be held in London that year. The *Herald* agreed to accept some articles about it, and the *New Idea* editor, my good friend William Somerset Shum, suggested interviews I might do for him. In a whirl of excitement I booked a passage.'[20] Katharine had turned her back on teaching and remade herself into a journalist. She was confident enough to list it as her occupation on the passenger list.[21]

9

Abroad

London and Paris, 1908–1909

KATHARINE LEFT MELBOURNE for London at noon on Wednesday 20 May 1908. 'The *Runic* to my enthusiastic imagination was a splendid ship. Crammed with passengers though she was, there were long decks to parade on in the mornings and evenings.'[1]

She shared a cabin with red-haired Robbie—real name Ethel Robson—from Sydney.[2] She was to be a close friend during Katharine's two stints in London. During the long journey to London, Robbie educated Katharine, telling her 'more about'—and here the manuscript shows Katharine had trouble choosing the right phrase—'the wicked ways of men than I had any idea of', or on the second attempt, the 'mysterious dangers of sex relationships', or thirdly, 'sexual intercourse about which I had never heard'.[3] In the manuscript, Katharine eventually settled on the more anodyne 'affairs', but then deleted the sentence altogether from the published version of *Child of the Hurricane*. In fact, Robbie confided in Katharine that she had gonorrhoea, having been infected at the age of sixteen by a friend of her father's.[4]

Katharine's other new friend on the six-week voyage was Harry Newton, 'a typically good-looking, athletic, young Australian, straight and reliable'. With 'a voice of remarkable range and bell-like purity … he was going to London, hoping to make a career as a concert singer'. Sitting together on the deck at night, he took her hand. She withdrew it.

'We decided', Katharine wrote, though she surely meant that *she* decided, 'there was to be no flirting or falling in love. We both had our careers to think of'.[5]

The voyage was good for Katharine; she was soothed by 'the dazzling blue of sea and sky' and 'the warm starry nights, free from strain and worry. The tragedy of Father's death lifted from me'.[6]

THE *RUNIC* REACHED London on 2 July 1908. The city was even busier than normal, with over a million visitors for the Franco-British Exhibition and the Olympics. In an article for the *Herald* and *Weekly Times,* Katharine gave the contrasting impressions of London from two newly arrived Australians. Agusta 'raves' about London's 'tragedy and poetry'. Bobbie complains about the city: 'to me it is just a great commercial centre—the world's core; and yet not half as fine a place to spend one's life in as any of the wide-streeted, open-air cities camped beneath the blue of Australian skies'.[7]

The poverty struck Katharine. 'The starved moan of the great degraded, hopeless, wretched poor of London is borne on the wind.'[8] She spent a night among the poor on the Embankment, visiting a soup kitchen and a homeless shelter in the slums with a stench of 'unwashed bodies, damp clothing, and physical decay'.[9] 'The problem of how such poverty and suffering could be prevented, haunted my mind.'[10] With hindsight, this experience became a moment of clarity about what was wrong with the world. She would come to understand the next decade of her life as a quest to find a solution.

A MAN TRIED to rape Katharine in her first weeks in London. 'I took a room in a street behind the Russell Hotel. It was a rather shabby house, and my room up three flights of stairs.' On a Saturday, she returned from the theatre with Harry. 'A clock had just struck twelve when we said goodnight on the door-step and Harry went off to his own lodgings. I tried to open the door before me, but the key wouldn't fit.' A young man offered to help her; he put the key in his pocket and told her he was coming in with her. 'Horrified by the look on his face and his pale shark's eyes' she appealed to him, but 'he laughed, and made his intentions quite clear'. If she called out for the police, he would accuse her of soliciting. She told him her husband was waiting upstairs. He handed her the key back on the condition she meet him at the corner on Monday night.

'I rushed upstairs and threw myself on the bed ... But before I undressed, a door on the other side of the room slowly opened.' The man had managed to get into the house and follow her up the stairs; he called out that he was coming in. There was a chair against the door and she pushed her trunk against it as well. She told him that if he came in, she'd jump from the window. Even after he seemed to have gone, she stayed sitting by the window all night. When she saw daylight, she ran downstairs and out of the house to find Harry. 'He came tumbling downstairs in his pyjamas.' His landlady told Katharine she could rent a room at her house, and even though it was more than Katharine could afford, she agreed.[11]

The threat of rape hangs over many of the women in Katharine's novels. In the finale of *Pioneers* (1915), Deidre accidently kills her villainous newlywed husband when he comes at her demanding his 'rights'; she is set to kill herself when an acquaintance, Mrs Cameron, reveals to her that 'something like what has happened to you happened to me, long ago'.[12] In *Black Opal* (1921, 1946), Sophie's great shame has different causes in the two editions, shifting from seduction to rape. In the first edition, she 'loses her head' with Adler at a 'drunken orgy'; in the second edition, she is 'sick with the shock and shame of being mauled by Adler'.[13] The pattern of sexual violence continues in Katharine's later novels, too, a trope which can't simply be traced to this incident in London, but which can be read in light of it.

ON 2 AUGUST 1908, four weeks after arriving in England, Katharine made a pilgrimage to visit 80-year-old George Meredith. Meredith was then ranked by many as one of the great Victorian novelists; in the decades that followed, he suffered a 'rapid and sustained decline of his posthumous reputation' such that he is now a forgotten novelist.[14]

Katharine had caught Walter Murdoch's enthusiasm for Meredith; she 'loved' his novels and poems for 'their exuberant vitality, intellectual brilliance, the exquisite quality of irony that informed them'.[15]

Widowed and ailing in the last year of his life, he lived in Flint Cottage at Box Hill, 40 kilometres south of London. He claimed to be unloved and unread, yet in the last years of his life, 'stricken down with paralysis, an unwilling Grand Old Man, [he] was haunted by journalists and admirers who hoped to write an essay on a Day with the Great'.[16] He refused many but thanks to the letter of introduction from Alfred Deakin, he agreed to meet Katharine.

> What happened in that moment, as I stood in the doorway, I've never been able to understand. A curious communication passed between us as Meredith's eyes reached me. I was aware of a magnetic personality, desolation and tragedy. The realization was so swift and devastating that I forgot to be shy and self-conscious. We seemed not to be strangers.[17]

Over afternoon tea, Katharine and Meredith talked about his writing and then about hers. He talked with the 'same brilliant, ironical exuberance' with which he wrote, yet he was also full of bitterness and despair. He had a writing chalet among the trees behind his house; it's possible this planted the idea for Katharine's own writing chalet, built twenty years later at her home in Western Australia.[18]

After she left, she sat down under a hawthorn bush and wept. 'I felt that I should not be young and Meredith old: that I should not have gone from the sunshine into that darkened room and stood in the doorway in my light summer dress ... He was waiting for death and I somehow had broken in on him, like his Daughter of Hades.'[19] She felt a painful contrast between her own youth and the dying generation who had formed the world she knew. She had felt it at the Prichard family reunion and when meeting the last of the pioneers in Yarram. She had felt it walking with a 'worn and disillusioned' Deakin 'when English trees along the road were yellow and shedding their leaves'.[20] She would feel it again in November in Paris interviewing the famous singing teacher, Mathilde Marchesi.[21] But she felt it most intensely now at the end of her afternoon with George Meredith.

Even if Meredith had been forgotten by many, Katharine would still talk of her 'passionate admiration' for him in an interview late in her life.[22] However, the influence on her work is not obvious. The ornate, convoluted prose of Katharine's 'Diana of the Inlet' (1912), written around this time, may owe something to him, but she moved away from it, adopting a more straightforward style by the time her novels began to be published.

KATHARINE TOOK A trip to Paris in October or November 1908, a plan she'd worked out with Reay, who'd told her he'd show her the city one day. 'There he was, at my hotel, one morning soon after I arrived. He … came from Italy to have those few days in Paris with me.'[23] What Reay was doing in Italy is unknown; he'd landed in Marseilles on the *Dumbea* in early October and was reported to be 'sojourning in the south of France for his health'.[24] Perhaps the trip and the tryst were timed to celebrate his fiftieth birthday on 10 November.

Katharine described her time with Reay in Paris with the ambivalence of all her depictions of him. They walked along the banks of the Seine, visited the Louvre, and dined at 'out-of-the-way restaurants'; at night, they visited the opera and the Moulin Rouge. She insisted he 'made my first visit to Paris a fabulous experience', but his obsessive streak shows through and she recounted two incidents where she 'incurred his displeasure'. He was unhappy when she didn't properly appreciate the 'famous soup' of the Café Royal. Then, on an afternoon when he was busy, she visited the cemetery of Père Lachaise to see the tombs of French writers. She wandered the cemetery alone on the foggy afternoon and found herself completely lost. 'The Preux Chevalier was furious that I had made this excursion without telling him where I was going'.[25]

She wrote that Reay 'was a fascinating companion, though I could not be in love with him' but she does not say their relationship was still chaste.[26] She wrote in the draft of *Child of the Hurricane* that she wouldn't let boys kiss her in her high school years, 'taking mother's advice about keeping everything for the man I would someday love and want to marry'.[27] She crossed it out; perhaps because it was not the way things had worked out by the time she married at the age of thirty-five. 'I was "late" in maturity!' Katharine wrote to a friend in 1964. 'Ideas really interested me more than sex—though later I "worshipped with the Egyptians".'[28] Katharine seems to have invented that Old Testament-sounding phrase in a 1928 story, 'The Cow', in which the female protagonist says, 'I worship with the Egyptians … adore life, the life-giver, fecundity, creation'.[29]

Reading between the lines of her autobiography, Reay was probably her first lover. In a foreign city without anyone to notice them, they had more opportunity for sex than they'd had back in Melbourne. In 1914, still involved with Reay, she published a sensual poem called 'Lips of My Love'.

Adventurous lips
That o'er me rove,
So swelling soft
And smelling like the rose
Lips of my love! My love!

Lips of the bee
That cling
And fall from clinging, Yearning,
Drunk with bliss!

Dear lips
That to me prove
My body
But a chalice, white,
For thy delight,
My love, my love

Oh, I am faint
When thy lips hang on mine
And there is ecstasy
In their mute questing,
Easting, westing.

So,
They are gentle
As the brooding dove,
Fierce as twin birds of prey,
Lips of my love! My love!

If the poem had a basis in her life, by this time she was 'worshipping with the Egyptians'. It depicts a woman positive about sex and pleasure but in the context of the uneven power balance between Katharine and Reay, there's something disturbing about the narrator offering up her body as 'But a chalice, white / For thy delight'.

IF ANYONE DESERVED to be known as Katharine's 'gallant knight' it was actually Harry. They spent much of their free time together in London, and Katharine ignored the signs he was in love with her. They danced together on Hampstead Heath; they went boating on the Thames; she took him with her when she went to stay with her mother's wealthy cousin in Huntingdonshire.

The romantic tension between them culminated at the notorious Covent Garden costume ball. They went with Robbie, the two women 'looking very demure in … pale mauve and pink evening dresses, wearing black masks', while Harry was 'handsome and impressive in his concert-platform dress suit'. The ball didn't start until after half-past eleven; 'we had never seen such love-making, kissing, and passionate episodes in public. Before long there were girls with torn skirts, and couples embracing in every alcove. But the floor and band were glorious. Harry and I danced happily together'. Somewhere near dawn, thirsty and adrenaline-filled, Harry kissed her 'for the first, and last, time' in a hansom cab on the way back to their boarding house. 'Harry was so staunch and reliable, so trustworthy as a friend and escort wherever I wished to go, that I did not want to complicate our camaraderie by sweethearting. He was quite pleased, too, to be free of any serious entanglement.'[30] Katharine may have been thinking of her career, but just as importantly, she was involved with Reay.

There's an echo of Katharine and Harry's 'platonic' partnership in her London novel, *Windlestraws* (1916). In it, Gene and Peter are two outsiders to the city who join forces to try to make it in London. They pretend to be a Russian noble couple to fool a theatre producer into staging their show. Despite their attraction for each other, they maintain—for most of the novel—a chaste distance, sleeping in separate beds of the same hotel room, just as Katharine had come to live in the same boarding house as Harry.

Windlestraws being a romance, it ends with Peter forsaking the rich woman he had loved for all his youth and marrying Gene. In real life, Harry eventually left London to work as a singer in Switzerland. He had minor success, but not enough, and he returned to Australia, abandoning his dream of being a professional singer. 'We did not meet again for years. Then we were both married and could laugh over the hopes and fears of those days in the "Old Smoke".'[31]

WHILE IN PARIS, Rudolf Broda, the socialist editor of *The International*, organised a reception for 'the esteemed young collaborator from Australia'. She met 'two medical students who were political exiles from Tsarist Russia'. Bloody Sunday, a massacre of petitioners in January 1905, had unleashed strikes and protests; in the government crackdown which followed, many radicals were exiled.

> [They] told me of the struggle going on in their country to overthrow the Tsarism … It seemed impossible that such a thing could ever happen. The power of the Russian autocracy stood in my mind like a massive wall … oppressive and impregnable, against which men and women had dashed themselves in futile protests …
>
> Quite ignorant of the people's growing resistance to such acts of ruthless cruelty, and the strength of the revolutionary movement, I pitied my first Russian friends, and wondered how they could attach themselves to such a vague, hopeless dream.

With hindsight, the encounter became more significant after the Russian revolutions of 1917. 'I never forgot them and, when their dream came true, began to study the ideas responsible for the success of the revolution in Russia.'[32]

RETURNING TO LONDON, her birthday came not at the beginning of summer but winter, 'cooped up … for dreary months of fog and cold weather'.[33] She shared the date with the essayist Thomas Carlyle, whose work she had loved at school, and so on 4 December 1908, she 'took a bus to Chelsea, put a bunch of violets on his statue, and sat communing with him for a while, remembering the struggles of his youth, and a spirit which refused to be defeated'.[34]

Her next step was undecided. The commission to write for the *Herald* was over, although she did continue to interview celebrities for *New Idea*. 'It was time to try an innings on the English press, but manuscripts were returned with discouraging regularity.' She was homesick and struggling financially when Reay sent an offer of a staff job with the *Herald* back in Melbourne. The prospect of a regular salary was 'heavenly'.[35]

She stayed in England long enough for spring, and spent time with her mother's cousin in Huntingdonshire. In the tranquil gardens surrounding the Georgian mansion, she wrote a poem which begins: 'My life will never be long enough to realise the beauty of the world'.[36] She was twenty-five and returning to Australia as a journalist who carried the allure of having interviewed a number of British and French celebrities. Her intense year away had confirmed her status as a single woman, focused on her career. She knew more about men and sex and she'd chosen a kind of freedom—an affair with a married man, Reay—over the limitations that marriage even to a man like Harry would have involved.

10

Pomona

Melbourne and New York, 1909–1910

ARRIVING BACK IN Melbourne on 16 April 1909, Katharine started work on 'Woman's World' at the *Herald* straightaway.[1] It wasn't simply a column—it was a whole section occupying two broadsheet pages, and printed each week in both the *Herald* and its rural counterpart, the *Weekly Times*. The headline promised 'Topics of the Week—Feminine Affairs Reviewed—The Fashions of the Moment'; Katharine delivered these and more. Each edition contained a lengthy, illustrated column on fashion; a report on a significant speech or meeting, often with a political or social angle to it; news relating to women; and sometimes an opinion piece. A couple of months into the role, Katharine adopted the pseudonym 'Pomona', the name of a lesser-known Roman goddess of fruit. The annual salary was reportedly a high one in the order of £320.[2] It was the only time Katharine would ever have a well-paying job, giving her more spending money and security than she would have again in her life.

If Katharine's appointment was an act of nepotism, Reay compensated by being a stern boss.

> Work on the *Herald* at first almost destroyed any confidence I might have had in myself as a writer ... Sometimes I was reduced almost

> to tears when paragraphs were blue-pencilled out of recognition. In despair I told the editor and general manager, Colonel W. T. Reay, that I was afraid I could never do the job satisfactorily. He was a drastic critic, and wielded that blue pencil mercilessly; but kind and helpful too, taught me to condense, and to avoid literary airs and graces in simple statements.[3]

Even here, Katharine's ambivalence about Reay comes through strongly. His 'drastic' criticism was destroying her confidence, yet he was 'kind and helpful too'. Apparently in thrall to Katharine sexually and emotionally, it's possible Reay revelled in the power he held over her at work.

After her initial contract expired, Reay sent a letter offering a new contract. He wrote, 'Allow me to take the present opportunity to express our high appreciation of your always fine work—marked, as it has ever been, by a high ability, strict care and punctuality, and a splendid enthusiasm'.[4] It is the only letter she kept from him.[5]

Back at the time he intercepted her in Sydney in 1907, she commented that she 'was not interested in clothes at that time' and felt 'a little dowdy' in his company; she remembered feeling it in Paris, too, prompting her to buy some glamorous clothes. He may have been encouraging her to become more interested in fashion with the 'Woman's World' job in mind. In a short time, she learnt how to write about fashion and at least sound like someone with a wide knowledge and deep interest in it. Week by week, she reported on the latest trends in dresses, coats, hats and accessories, sometimes reflecting feminist advances as women moved into new workplaces and dress became less Victorian. Her fashion news also reflected Edwardian technology and fads. She covered clothes for ice-skating one week—an important topic as the Glaciarium ice rink had opened in South Melbourne in 1906.[6] Another week she wrote of 'modes for motorists', opining, 'there is still a wide bridge between the motorist and beauty. Those dreadful goggles … and … those painful stiff leather coats, which no effort of tailor or designer can make otherwise than hideous'.[7]

Katharine usually maintained a mask of journalistic objectivity but in one column there is a striking glimpse of her disdain for men of her own age:

> At every dance one hears the same cry, 'Where are the men?' Certainly there is no lack of creatures masculine, but these are aggressively young, unbearded manlets, who consider they are conferring an honour by asking for one's programme, whilst the boredom that twenty minutes of their society entails is little worse than the ignominy of sitting out a dance by yourself, and pretending that you are frightfully tired, or that your shoe pinches.[8]

ON FRIDAY 28 May 1909, Katharine and Nettie Higgins were at the annual meeting of the Literature Society of Melbourne when the president, Bernard O'Dowd, delivered a lecture called 'The Poet Militant' that became legendary. In Katharine's account, 'that night, blazing away at his thesis, O'Dowd was a lean, wild figure, unconscious of anything but what he had to say, and saying it with all the passion there was in him'.[9] O'Dowd claimed that 'contemporary poetry is saying nothing' and the 'misdirected energies of too many modern verse-writers are being wasted in making crazy quilts out of pretty words; while a hungry and thirsty world, deprived of so many of its traditional nurses, is languishing for the help the poets can give it'.[10] The alternative was the poet as 'an Answerer' of the 'real questions' of the age, who wrote about 'politics, religion, science, sex and social reform'.[11]

In a tribute to him after his death in 1953 Katharine wrote, 'He made such an impression on those of us who were beginning to think seriously that, upon leaving the meeting, we were almost too exalted and exhilarated to speak. I felt that my eyes had been opened to what I could do, as a writer to help relieve the woes of the world'.[12] The didactic play Katharine wrote around this time, *The Burglar,* may have been influenced by O'Dowd's speech. Although it was followed by two romance novels, from *Black Opal* (1921) onwards her novels increasingly resembled what he called for—only in prose—such that her goldfields trilogy (1946–1950) is focused on politics and social reform; is frank in its treatment of sex; and also shows the 'simplicity of form' O'Dowd imagined.

AT THE *HERALD* Katharine became friends with William Moore, the art and drama critic. From 1909 to 1912 he organised four annual

Australian drama nights in which 'a group of enthusiastic amateurs would present a miscellany of one-acters in a hired hall'.[13] The nights had an egalitarian ethos, with no division between classes of seats and an injunction, 'Citizens in evening dress not admitted'. Although 'with the passing of years this little enterprise has taken on something of a rosy halo', these nights 'gave a fillip to Australian dramatic writing, much needed at a time when the silent cinema was beginning to gobble up available audiences for entertainment'.[14]

Katharine was travelling back from London at the time of the first drama night in March 1909, but for the second on Wednesday 5 October 1910, her play *The Burglar* was one of three produced. *The Burglar* was presented first, followed by *The Woman-Tamer*, written by a friend of Moore's, Louis Esson. The third play, *The Tea-Room Girl*, was by Moore. At the first rehearsal for *The Burglar*, Moore complained that the play wouldn't work and so Katharine took over production, organising everything from casting to set production.[15]

On 8 February 1910, a burglar broke into Reay's house in a wealthy suburb of Melbourne and stole £30 worth of jewellery.[16] Perhaps the incident inspired the scenario for Katharine's play. In *The Burglar*, Bill breaks into a bedroom only to be disturbed by the occupant, a young woman named Sally, who declares that she's a socialist and has always promised herself she would, on request, give her belongings to anyone who had less than her. Working as a governess, Sally is engaged to a diamond merchant. Bill the burglar is curious enough to stop and listen to Sally's opinions on the world. She gives a soliloquy reflecting Katharine's frustrations with the world she was reporting on as a journalist:

> Do you know there is nothing more unrespectable than so-called respectable society? It is a caucus of people who never think, and are stupid and cruel to those who do, who wear their beliefs like their skin, and cannot understand that what we believed yesterday we cannot today … Away with all stupid conventionalities, peradventures, and expediencies! I want to live in love with all the world, to kiss the children in the streets, to talk with whom I please, wander and play, sharing my purse with all who chance my way …

The play ends with a twist—Bill scrambles away, having sworn off burglary, and Sally reveals her fiancé entrusted her with diamonds for safekeeping which she has been hiding in her nightgown. 'She drops her head on the table over the diamonds, weeping passionately.' The diamonds she has protected represent a failure to live up to her own socialist ideals, the inevitable compromise a middle-class life involves.[17]

The brief reviews for *The Burglar* were mixed. The *Age* reported that 'the matter was cleverly constructed, and the sentiments uttered excellent in their way'.[18] The harshest review was published in the *Worker*, whose correspondent found Katharine's play the weakest of the three, 'too unnatural; the burglar horribly loquacious and given to excessive moralising. Fairly well acted'.[19]

Bernard O'Dowd probably liked Katharine's play better. He was there that night and would have at least approved of her attempt to depict issues which mattered.[20]

KATHARINE'S COLLABORATION WITH Louis Esson on that drama night was the beginning of a long friendship. Louis was born in 1878 and his biographer, Peter Fitzpatrick, writes that he was 'an attractive and most unusual man, who bore the marks of enough romantic suffering to leave him touchingly vulnerable. He was witty and erudite, a gifted and admired writer with a clear and confident sense of purpose in his life'.[21] On a visit to Europe in 1905, he had met the great Irish writer WB Yeats and been inspired to work towards the creation of a distinctly Australian theatre. He wrote a number of significant plays in the 1910s and 1920s before lapsing into literary silence, living the rest of his life in a cloud of depression. 'The ennui was persistent, and often there seemed to be no cause in particular.'[22] He was a foundation member of the Victorian Socialist Party in 1906, but in the years which followed he was to become less political as Katharine became more so.[23]

In the lead up to the drama night Louis had split for the final time from his first wife, Madeleine.[24] He met his second wife, Hilda Bull, during the planning of the drama night. Katharine had written to her, 'Bill Moore and Louis Esson are coming out to-night. Do come and help me with them darling!'[25] Katharine remembered Hilda was 'looking very beautiful' on that 'very wild, wet, wintry night'.[26]

Hilda and Louis were to marry in December 1913 while Katharine was back in London.

Katharine's friendship with Louis was independent of Hilda, and she kept up with him even when he had separated, amicably, from Hilda. She valued his opinion of her work, sometimes sending drafts to him, and dedicating her first book of short stories, *Kiss on the Lips and Other Stories* (1932) to him. Paying tribute to him in 1943, Katharine mentioned his 'gentle anonymity' and described him as 'generous in personal relationships: a man whose mind, vivid and intransigent where standards of art and literature were concerned, illumined every conversation'.[27]

KATHARINE SUDDENLY RESIGNED from the *Herald* in the middle of 1910. The writer Mary Gilmore, who Katharine came to know in this period, had warned her she was 'drawing on the Bank of Youth. Some day there'll be an overdraft'.[28] Katharine wrote of the job, 'I began to realize it was sapping my energy for creative writing. The experience had been invaluable as discipline and training for exact and condensed expression, but I became restless and dissatisfied because there was no time for the sort of writing I longed to do'.[29] A profile of Katharine closer to the time said that she 'resigned in consequence of ill health', which may have been the migraine headaches she suffered throughout her life during times of stress.[30]

After resigning, Katharine spent some months in 1910 trying to eke out a living as a freelancer in Melbourne, but wasn't making enough money. In October, just after *The Burglar* was performed at the Australian Drama Night, she took a 'brief holiday' in Sydney. She met an American journalist there, possibly Thomas Andrews, who was visiting from Milwaukee that month to cover a boxing match.[31] He told her 'of the wonderful opportunities and high prices paid for short-stories in the USA. With a swag of them, and some introductions from him, I sailed off across the Pacific, intending to make only a fleeting visit and return home in a few months'.[32]

If the American journalist was one reason for Katharine's impulsive trip to the United States, Reay was probably another one. Having been in Britain and Italy in the middle of 1910, he travelled on to New York, arriving there on 10 September.[33] Perhaps he invited or pressured her to join him there, talking up the prospect of another secret sojourn in a foreign city.

Katharine left Sydney on board the *Zealandia* on 24 October.[34] The ship stopped at Suva in Fiji for a day; Katharine had only ever lived in Levuka, on a different island, but 'a breath from the land was strangely familiar: the warm dry air, smells of seaweed, copra, native matting and guavas. In a dream, I walked down the long wharf and into the town as if my brain had retained some impression of them'.[35]

On 17 November, the *Zealandia* docked at Vancouver where Katharine spent just one night before beginning a long train journey across North America to New York on the east coast. She broke the train journey for a few days in Chicago, where she was inspired to hear a speech by Booker Washington, the African-American leader. Finally, she arrived in New York where Reay was presumably waiting for her.

Katharine's most evocative description of the city comes through the eyes of Sophie in the novel *Black Opal* (1921): 'A fairy city it had seemed to her with its sky-flung lights, thronged thoroughfares, and jangling bells. She saw a square of tall, flat-faced buildings before a park of leafless trees; shimmering streets on a wet night, near the New Theatre and the Little Opera House'.[36] But for Katharine, warned not to go walking alone as there was a murder every night, it was also a dangerous and unwelcoming place. It was freezing outside and overheated inside; the people were indifferent to her and she knew no-one. When her stories were rejected by an editor, she felt 'naïve and stupid' for embarking on her trip. She was running out of money and scared of being stranded in America. A fare to the United Kingdom was cheaper than to Australia, she wrote, so 'I looked up the shipping news, and almost ran to the Cunard offices to book a second-class passage on the first liner leaving for Liverpool'.[37]

Reay left New York on 28 December 1910 with a more positive impression of the United States, having 'learned to admire the wonderful organised power of the great Republic, which he describes as the greatest present force in the world'.[38] He was on board the *Lusitania*, a Cunard ship, sailing for Liverpool. Also on the passenger list is a woman journalist, single, travelling second class, with an indecipherable name that could be 'Kath Prichard'.[39] If it was her, after time together in

New York and—more furtively—on board the *Lusitania*, they had a month in Britain before Reay left for Melbourne on 3 February 1911.

IN *BLACK OPAL*, Sophie also flees mysteriously to Sydney and then the United States. The stationmaster reports that 'a girl in a black frock had taken a second-class ticket for Sydney' and she was crying; she told him she was going away to study singing.[40] She sails on the *Zealandia*—the same ship as Katharine. Sophie eventually writes back home saying 'when she had made a name for herself as a singer, she would come home to the Ridge to see them'.[41] Sophie's sojourn in America is much longer than Katharine's, becoming the fictional site of the sexual and political awakenings of Katharine's twenties. After finding success as a singer, Sophie is either seduced (1921 version) or raped (1946 version) by a playboy named Adler during a party on a yacht. Feeling ashamed, she decides that what happened was 'just the natural consequences of all the easy, luxurious living I'd seen'.[42] Following her 'awakening', she goes to live in a slum settlement in Chicago and works in a clothing factory as a kind of penance. Like Katharine, she hears Booker Washington speak there. Sophie's sojourn of several years in the United States is only told within the novel in a few retrospective descriptions. There are no biographical specifics that can be unpicked from them but they suggest the mythical significance Katharine ascribed to her own visit to the United States.

KATHARINE WAS IN London again. Having left Melbourne in September 1910 for what she had told her family and friends would be a 'brief holiday' in Sydney, she was not to return for five years. 'I was ready for a second assault on London, with more humility as to the chances of literary success than I had had on my first visit, but determined to earn my living somehow.'[43]

II

Freewoman

London, 1911–1913

WHEN KATHARINE RETURNED to London in 1911, the city 'was full of interest: the suffrage movement in full swing'.[1] In an interview for her eightieth birthday, she said that she had 'always resented the separation of women's interests from those of men'.[2] It was a conviction that developed during this second stint in London when she was most involved with feminist circles.

The first sighting of her is in a list of names of Australian suffragettes who marched in the Women's Coronation Procession in June 1911, five days ahead of George V's coronation. Forty-thousand women marched through the city that day demanding the right to vote, the largest of the British suffragette marches.[3] The marchers left from the Embankment at 5.30 p.m., five abreast, the column stretching 9 kilometres as they moved towards a mass meeting at Albert Hall. The banner carried by Katharine and the rest of the Australian contingent depicted Australia as a daughter saying to Britannia, 'Trust the women Mother as I have done'.

Katharine joined the Women's Social and Political Union (WSPU), led by Emmeline Pankhurst and her daughters, but she wasn't an active member. The organisation was riven by internal conflict. Even for men in Britain the vote was limited by a property qualification, requiring them to own or lease property of a certain value; the WSPU under the

Pankhursts had been pushing for the women's vote on the same terms. A wealthy donor couple, Emmeline and Frederick Petherick-Lawrence, wanted the group to campaign for the vote for all adults and opposed the use of violence.[4] 'Whether you were a Peth or a Pank became the burning question', Katharine wrote, declaring, 'I was a Peth'. It was a refusal to separate the interests of working-class men from those of women. In October 1912 the Pankhursts expelled the Petherick-Lawrences from the WSPU.[5]

At one point while staying with her mother's cousin in Huntingdonshire, Katharine debated the topic of the influence of women on history at the conservative Primrose League. Her opponent focused on the 'disastrous effect women had had on national affairs' as mistresses of kings and leaders. As the mistress of an influential man, Katharine may have taken the claim personally. She stood on the platform, 'quivering with nervousness' but 'so indignant at some of the things the first speaker had said that I forgot everything except the need to defend womanhood suffrage'.[6]

Katharine was passionate about women's suffrage, even if she didn't dedicate her life to it like her fellow Australians Muriel Matters and Vida Goldstein, both in London at this time. She was still searching for the cause she would commit everything to, something which could make sense of the world and its problems.

HOUSING WAS A problem, just as it had been her first time in London. She 'found a room in an old house at World's End … [but] I could not get accustomed to the noise, nor to the stench of a poverty-stricken area: damp, decaying houses, urinous walls, accumulated filth in drains and rubbish bins on the pavement'.[7] She couldn't sleep or eat. Despite her ideals, she was too sensitive to endure life in a slum. Her old friend Robbie rescued her and helped her find a basement flat in a complex called Chelsea Gardens, at the more genteel end of Chelsea. 'For several months, I lived and worked quite happily there beneath the pavement, with nothing but the feet of passers-by to see from my windows.' She was glad, though, to escape the 'dungeon' and be offered an upstairs flat. 'I soared to it, up six flights of stairs, with all my goods and chattels. How I loved that flat … It was a heavenly spot, within walking distance of Fleet Street, so quiet and restful, yet part of the great whirling life of London.'[8] Katharine was in the right place. Chelsea had a 'comfortable, Bohemian atmosphere'; a newspaper reported 'quite a little colony of Australians have congregated in this artistic centre'.[9]

It was even harder than she expected to make a living as a freelance journalist. 'Manuscripts kept on returning with "editor regrets" slips, day after day, week after week.'[10] The clippings she saved from her London journalism do not include any dated 1911. Her article 'Australia's Lesson: On Woman's Suffrage' appeared in the third ever issue of London's labour-movement newspaper, *Daily Herald,* on 17 April 1912.

Katharine was eventually desperate enough to apply for staff positions, a step backward. Freelancing gave her the flexibility to write creatively; a staff position like the one she'd held in Melbourne would leave her drained of time and energy. As it turned out, she wasn't able to get one anyway, meaning she was stuck with her original plan to try to make a living as a freelancer.

There were many other Australian journalists in a similar situation in London. A correspondent to Sydney's *Truth* wrote that year:

> Into this stinking pit of corruption Australian and New Zealand pressmen, journalists, writers (self-styled), and scribblers of all sorts drop under the astounding delusion that London 'wants' their sort, and that they can easily gather a fortune by their pens in a few years ... Instead of gathering a fortune ... it takes him all his time wandering round and round the pit snatching up a scanty living of tit-bits and scrag-ends, over which he and his fellow Australians quarrel as fiercely as any vagrant curs fighting over a bit of rotten meat.[11]

The correspondent mentioned that 'the latest arrival, whose descent caused quite a small stir in the Fleet Street pit, is Melbourne *Herald*'s own drapery "Major" [*sic*] Reay, who has opened an office in Fleet Street for that shocking example of Australian journalism, and may be able to throw out a few scraps on his own account for the battlers'. Reay doesn't seem to have thrown out scraps to Katharine; she had no attributed articles in the *Herald* and *Weekly Times* for this period. However, he may have opened doors for her at some London newspapers. All she recorded was that 'when the Preux Chevalier arrived from Australia, there was a round of theatres and dinners in luxurious hotels'.[12]

Reay had resigned as editor of the *Herald* and *Weekly Times* while in Melbourne in March 1911. He came straight back to establish a London office for the newspaper.[13] His career and his country meant much to him, but he was willing to take a demotion from the job he'd held since 1904 and leave Australia permanently in order to be with Katharine. A newspaper reported that his wife and five daughters were 'to join him in London, where affairs have decided he shall settle'.[14] By January 1912, they had arrived and the family had taken a house on Grosvenor Road, a kilometre or two from where Katharine was living.[15]

Was Katharine trying to escape, as Ric Throssell suggests, only for him to 'impose' on her his 'possessive jealousy … following her across the world'?[16] Perhaps, although her trip to the United States to see him in 1910 suggests reciprocity.

SOMETIMES KATHARINE DIDN'T have enough money to eat properly. During the winter, she would swallow a tablespoon of olive oil each day to prevent herself from getting too thin. 'At first it made me feel rather sick, but after a while I got quite to like it.'[17] Thomas Carlyle had lived on porridge when a struggling writer; she decided she would try it too. She became ill, and a doctor prescribed a proper diet and a stay in the country.

She went to live for two or three months with her mother's cousin, James Fraser, and his wife, Cissy, in their mansion, the Elms, in Houghton, Huntingdonshire. 'Although they disapproved of my independence, unconventional ways and radical views, they always treated me like a prodigal child and welcomed me with warm affection.'[18]

The Frasers had no children and James 'offered to make me his heir if I would regard writing more or less as a hobby, and give up my independent way of thinking and living. I wasn't even tempted.'[19] She seems to have been at least a little tempted, eating well, writing in a room set aside for her as 'Kattie's study', with cherry brandy served at eleven in the morning. 'I could have had a *dolce far niente* ["sweetly idle"] existence in this stately old mansion, and in the garden and woods surrounding, if only I had been content not to worry about my conflict with London.'[20] She came to see the tranquillity as an illusion. Agricultural workers were badly paid and couldn't afford meat: 'the contrasts between wealth and poverty were as disturbing here as in the slums of London'.[21]

KATHARINE WAS IN the midst of intellectual ferment in these years. She was drawn to politics, but in her account in *Why I am a Communist* (1956), she was also considering religious and supernatural systems of belief:

> I discovered the Fabian Society ... Guild Socialism, Syndicalism and the Anarchism of Kropotkin. My philosophical reading led me from Christianity to Rationalism, from Plato, Socrates and Epictetus to Buddhism, Theosophy and Christian Science. For ten years I studied these theories, taking each one in turn, discussing them with all manner of people, but committed to none, never a member of any organisation; still not satisfied that I had found the answer to the questions my mind was asking—still not convinced that any of them offered logical solutions to the problem of how the poverty and injustices suffered by so many innocent people could be prevented.[22]

It is apt that Katharine had a number of articles published in the *Daily Herald*, as its outlook on the world was similar to hers. It was radical and committed to reforms in the direction of socialism, as well as strongly pro-suffragette. But rather than become the mouthpiece of a particular party or organisation, it maintained political independence out of the conviction 'that contemporary unrest demanded a forum-style newspaper to debate the various issues raised'.[23] In this period before the shock of the Great War and the Russian Revolution, there was much 'cross-fertilisation of ideas and interconnection of personnel in debate and action' within radical circles.[24]

In November 1911, the first issue of the feminist journal *The Freewoman* appeared. The editor, Dora Marsden, had left the Women's Social and Political Union as she had become 'virulently opposed to a feminism which concentrated solely on the vote'. *The Freewoman* featured articles on various women's issues but frequently—and controversially—on sex.

Katharine had a letter published in the journal on 2 May 1912 while the world was still in shock about the *Titanic* disaster of a couple of weeks earlier. She felt, rather selflessly, that the push for women's equality called for a new chivalry from women: 'a man with responsibilities upon him, the responsibilities of providing for a wife and brood of little ones, has more right to a seat in a lifeboat, if seats are few, than any childless woman, be she maiden, widow, or wife'.[25]

On a Wednesday night a week later, the Freewoman Discussion Circle held its first meeting to continue the conversations begun in the journal.[26] Katharine joined the group and 'heard there that "marriage is a bargain in which a woman sells out all sexual rights in herself"'.[27] Yet if she felt comparatively free in her arrangement with Reay, she was shutting her eyes to how controlling he was. Late in life, she wrote to her granddaughter, 'A love affair that's restricting inhibits you when you're young [and] is worse than marriage, really. There's no end of unhappiness, quarrels and misunderstandings when jealousy not love is the motive of demands on your every action and thought'.[28]

In the journal and the discussion circle, Dora Marsden and those drawn to her were moving past the prevailing feminist concern with protecting women from unwanted sex and 'beginning to claim the right to *be sexual*'.[29] Katharine's poem 'Lips of My Love' goes some way to claiming this right, revelling in sexual desire and pleasure, even though it casts the man as active and the woman as passive. Published in 1914, it was possibly written in 1912 or 1913 while she was a part of the discussion circle and may owe some of its sexual frankness to her immersion in this milieu.

In September 1912, Katharine wrote to Dora Marsden, saying that her 'sympathies are very much with *The Freewoman*'. She would like to submit more writing to the journal, but a sketch accepted for publication months ago had still not appeared and she had come by the office several times only to find it closed.[30] The reason soon became apparent—due to lack of finances, Marsden published the final issue of *The Freewoman* a couple of weeks later.[31] The discussion circle continued meeting but Katharine stopped going.

KATHARINE'S MOST SIGNIFICANT friendship in this period was with a fellow Australian writer, Helena Sumner Locke, always known as Sumner. Sumner arrived in London in May 1912, but they'd already met in 1907 at the *Native Companion* office. Sumner had been sub-editor to EJ Brady, 'an elfish-looking little girl then, very slight and sprightly, with big, beautiful eyes'.[32]

Sumner was energetic and dedicated to writing. 'She usually wrote about 4000 words a day, and was ready for a jaunt, or party, or expedition of some sort in the late afternoon. She could write anyhow and anywhere.' They were 'comrades-in-arms', two talented women who were determined that they would be the ones to make the 'long-long climb' to the top of the literary ladder. At this point in their careers, Sumner was the more successful, with a best-selling humorous tale of the bush, *Mum Dawson, 'Boss'* published in 1911 and plays staged in Melbourne and Sydney.[33]

One conversation was to stand out in Katharine's memory. Sumner 'sat curled up on the sofa of my rooms in Chelsea, laughing—the sunshine on her hair, the green boughs of the elms in the garden below flapping behind her in the open window space'. When Sumner said she wouldn't want to write a book about herself, Katharine said she would write it and promised to give her a happy ending.

> The end was to be something like this: You and I—friends of struggling days, all that sort of thing—meet after a long time. You have become the brilliant and successful authoress, are married, have a handsome husband and a beautiful home. And you say to me, 'Come home and hear my masterpiece?' I go with you, but you will not tell me anything about the masterpiece—the plot, or characters, or where it is laid, or anything. 'It must speak for itself,' you say. Then in the garden of that beautiful home, overlooking the harbour, of course, we hear a baby yelling for his evening meal. And you stop and say to me, 'Hear him? *That's* my masterpiece!'[34]

As two single women turning thirty—Katharine involved with Reay; Sumner in a long and stalled engagement—they had put their writing ahead of marriage, children and beautiful houses by the harbour. Yet for Katharine to imagine this 'happy ending' for them suggests they still aspired to these things. In September 1930 when Katharine's son was eight and Sumner's son was twelve, Katharine wrote to Sumner's sister, saying, 'I suppose the two lads will meet some day and compare notes. But of the dreams and troubled way-faring of their mothers, that went to the making of the young men, how much will they ever know?'[35]

Perhaps taking a cue from Sumner's success with commercial fiction, Katharine wrote *Windlestraws* in 1912 or 1913, 'an attempt to please English publishers'.[36] A forgettable light romance, it only became her second published novel in 1916 because of the success of *The Pioneers. Windlestraws* presents a fantasy of artistic triumph in London. Gene is an orphan whose dreams of making it in the world of theatre have been dashed. She meets the mysterious Peter and like two pieces of whirling straw attaching to each other, they decide to band together. Peter has written a play and Gene is a performer. They will pretend to be Prince and Princess Varof of Russia and convince a theatre producer, on the strength of their name, to stage Peter's play with Gene in the lead role. The producers agree on the spot. Gene proves to be a brilliant singer and dancer and the show is a great success. The logic of *Windlestraws* is that it's only Britain's class prejudice which has been holding Gene—and, by extension, Katharine—back.

Katharine's earlier attempts at long narrative—'A City Girl in Central Australia' (1906) and *Wild Oats of Han* (written 1908)—both had stronger autobiographical elements than *Windlestraws*. After that, perhaps influenced by O'Dowd's 'poet militant' ideal, she created intentionally didactic, political works in her plays *The Burglar* (1910), *Her Place* (c. 1913), and *For Instance* (c. 1914), the latter two suffragette dramas. In *Windlestraws,* she struck out in an opposite direction, turning away from both politics and autobiography, only to find writing pure romance for the market was not enough to guarantee success. 'One can only wonder', comments the critic Jack Beasley, 'at the direction her writing may have taken had *Windlestraws* been a commercial success'.[37]

Then, in April 1913, Katharine's first book appeared, a modest, self-published twenty-page pamphlet of poems called *Clovelly Verses.* She wrote the poems on a visit to the village of Clovelly in Devonshire in the summer of 1912. Decades later, she described it as 'a first offering to my mother… I had not yet evolved from the "ye" and "thou" of poetical expression. So young and amusing they seem now; but maybe of interest to you as indicating the outlook of the young person before she encountered Marxism—as a key to KSP'.[38] They are the sort of poems her genteel, conventional mother appreciated—rhyming, descriptive, safely revelling in the charms of nature:

> I love the runes
> That the years write on the dunes
> And the tunes
> That the bee sings
> As it swings
> O'er the heather.[39]

Katharine's lack of creative achievement in this period reflects the priority she had to give to the grind of freelancing. By 1913 she was finally finding success as a journalist; she described the 'turning of the tide' after the editor of the *Globe* accepted a story about osier harvesting on the banks of the Ouse, written while she was staying with the Frasers. That article didn't actually appear for another year, but the editor asked for a couple more stories and her work was also being accepted by other London newspapers. Ironically, once she'd established herself as a freelancer she was offered a staff position at the *Star* and *Daily Chronicle*, but she didn't need it now.[40]

IN JUNE 1913, Katharine visited Rudolf Broda, the Austrian socialist, in Paris. He'd helped to inspire her political quest seven years earlier and she now had more things than ever to talk to him about. Broda relocated to Switzerland during the war, from where he published a pacifist supplement to his journal.[41] After the war, he and his wife divorced and he emigrated to the United States without her in 1923.[42] In 1932 he revived his journal after a ten-year hiatus and was teaching at a small college in Ohio when he died, aged just fifty-one.[43] Rudolf and his utopian vision of international progress have been forgotten; the Europe he thought was evolving towards justice and peace in 1913 was about to be torn apart. Yet if nothing else, Katharine was to remember his influence for the rest of her life.

ON 15 DECEMBER 1913, Katharine's best friend Hilda married Louis Esson in a quiet civil ceremony in Melbourne. Christian Jollie Smith was one of the witnesses. The fourth member of the circle of friends from high school days, Nettie Higgins, was now engaged to the writer Vance Palmer.

In London eleven days earlier, Katharine had turned thirty. Time was slipping by; there was a new urgency for a breakthrough, for the big literary success she had spent her twenties dreaming about.

12

Breaking Out

London, 1914–1915

IN FEBRUARY 1913 the London-based publisher Hodder & Stoughton announced with fanfare the opening of the £1000 Novel Competition 'for colonial and Indian authors'.[1] The competition was dominion-based, with prizes of £250 each for Canada, India, Australia and New Zealand, and South Africa. One columnist wrote, 'Whether the competition will produce the long expected Australasian masterpiece is a point upon which one may well remain dubious; still, it is a generous offer'.[2]

The deadline for the competition was over a year away—31 March 1914. Katharine was still working on *Windlestraws* in 1913, but she must have realised it was not the right novel for the competition, not only lacking in quality but also any Australian element. In that busy year as her thirtieth birthday approached, she saved up enough money to take off the first three months of 1914 from freelancing to 'write the book which I'd been waiting so long to do'.[3]

For *The Pioneers* Katharine returned to the regional Australian landscapes she had used as the settings for the story 'Bush Fires' (1903) and the serial 'A City Girl in Central Australia' (1906), still her most successful works to date. Her time as a governess to the Muir children in Yarram in 1904 was a whole decade ago but 'out came my notebooks of Gippsland; and, in a little while, the atmosphere of the great forests, cleared foothills of the ranges, the long plains, and the old township of Port Albert was filling my flat high up over London, despite the gloom and fogs of a northern winter'.[4] She wove her memories of the landscape and folklore of Gippsland around the narrative of Frederick McCubbin's triptych, *The Pioneer* (1904), which she had seen at the National Gallery of Victoria soon after it was acquired in 1906.[5] 'Casting about for a plot Mr McCubbin's picture came back to my memory. It was like a ground-plan ready to hand. I … built upon and around it.'[6] The novel follows the sequence of the three panels, the opening scene matching the left-hand panel as Mary and Donald Cameron set up camp in the uncleared bush at the end of a long journey. In chapter two, the narrative jumps ahead to the scenario of the middle panel—bush cleared, a baby born, a house built. Most of the novel's events occur in this time frame. The novel's epilogue, chapter forty-eight, evokes the third panel, as Dan, grandson of Donald Cameron, comes to a 'lichen-grown wooden cross', the grave of his grandfather, who had said that he wanted to be laid to rest where the wagon had come to a standstill.

Katharine had hired a charwoman at fourpence an hour, a Mrs Neal, who looked after her as she worked on the novel through the winter. 'On cold mornings, at about eight o'clock, she would bring me a cup of tea and run a hot bath in the infinitesimal kitchen. She would remind me to stir the porridge on the small gas stove while I took my bath, and then bring coffee and toast into the sitting-room.' Three months was an incredibly short time to write a novel. 'I wrote all day and far into the night, often falling into bed, too tired to get there without holding on to the wall between the sitting-room and my bedroom.'[7]

Despite the circumstances, *The Pioneers* was a leap forward in Katharine's writing. It has some of the exuberance of 'A City Girl in Central Australia' while being a far more disciplined work. Read alongside the politically strident suffragette plays she wrote at the same time, *The Pioneers* shows a pragmatic restraint for an idealist like Katharine, engaging with the less divisive issue of the injustices suffered by convicts and a safe vision of Australia as a new country of opportunity. It is also a far more substantial and interesting novel than *Windlestraws,* less tied up by the contrivances of the romance genre.

The judge of the Australasian prize, Charles Garvice, was the best-selling author of the time, having written over one hundred romances with sales of seven million.[8] Garvice's name was held in contempt by the literary community; the *Bulletin* called him 'Charles Garbage'.[9] One newspaper complained that 'to foist such a fifteenth-rate novelist as Mr Garvice upon Australasian writers as judge of their work was little short of an insult … Several … writers who had intended to compete simply laughed to scorn the idea of submitting their efforts to the critical judgement of a person such as Mr Garvice'.[10] Instead of scorning the judge, Katharine decided 'the story would have to be one of which he would approve'.[11]

The deadline was close by the time Katharine had finished her handwritten draft. 'The first typist she engaged worked too slowly and confessed it was because she had become so interested in the story.' A second typist finished it for her just in time, and Katharine hand-delivered it to the Hodder & Stoughton office on the day the competition closed.[12]

AFTER SUBMITTING *The Pioneers,* Katharine worked on two plays, *Her Place* and *For Instance. Her Place* is a twenty-minute 'curtain-raiser' in which a charwoman takes the blame for stealing a necklace actually lost by the landlady's vain daughter. The charwoman's 'true place'—the final lines declare—is 'on a pedestal or in a niche in a cathedral'.[13] The play's political message is the equality of *all* women, placing it on the side of the 'Peths' against the 'Panks' in the Women's Social and Political Union conflict.

Decades later, Katharine scrawled on the front page of the manuscript that *Her Place* had been staged by the Actresses' Franchise League, but she was probably confused with the other play, *For Instance,* the manuscript of which she lost. The production of *For Instance* was reported by a number of newspapers, while there are no known reports of the production of *Her Place.*

The Actresses' Franchise League staged one act 'playlets' for the cause of suffrage that were 'more propaganda than literature'.[14] Katharine wrote *For Instance* for the opening night of the inaugural conference of the British Dominions Woman Suffrage Union, held at the Westminster Palace Hotel on 9 July 1914. Women from dominions such as Australia which had won the vote encouraged women from dominions which hadn't.[15]

In the play, an English factory worker arrives in Australia and is amazed at the better conditions; one of her co-workers explains 'the civil, economic and social superiority enjoyed by women under the Southern Cross'. Reay sat in the audience that night and enthused about Katharine's play for the papers back home:

> The piece de resistance was a stirring dramatic sketch *For Instance*, written specially for the occasion by Miss K.S. Prichard (Melbourne), and the scene of which was a room in a white blouse factory, Australia.
>
> In this work, the writer showed a rare skill in compacting together romance, politics and social economics.

'The sketch won hearty applause', Reay concluded, 'which would not be stilled until the authoress appeared and bowed her acknowledgments'.[16] After many rejections and three years of literary obscurity in London, the staging of the playlet was a high point of public success for Katharine to that date.

ELEVEN DAYS BEFORE the staging of *For Instance,* Archduke Franz Ferdinand had been assassinated in Serbia. By the time Reay's report on *For Instance* appeared in Australia on 15 August, the Great War had begun. The momentum for women's suffrage was lost as many of the women's suffrage groups redirected their energy into supporting the war effort. In 1918, women over thirty with a property qualification—along with all men over twenty-one—were finally given the vote in Britain; only in 1928 were voting rights expanded to all women over twenty-one.

Britain declared war on Germany at 11 p.m. on 4 August 1914, with Australia and the other dominions following. It was the height of summer, and Katharine seems to have been on a trip out of the city that week. 'The countryside had never looked more tranquil and beautiful than during those first days of August. The stubble of cornfields lay golden with fringes of poppies ... It seemed incredible that war should break from the clear summer sky.'[17]

In response to the war, Katharine stepped back from the radicalism she had been flirting with. 'Neither I, nor anybody I knew, had much sympathy for pacifists and conscientious objectors in that period of patriotic illusions about the war, the justification for it, and the need to win.'[18] Reay and Sumner were both strong supporters of the war effort. Yet contradicting her memory of the mood, she also had friends who did not share the prevailing patriotism. Rudolf Broda began a pacifist supplement to his journal called *La Voix de l'Humanite*. And then there was her friend Nettie, not a pacifist but an early critic of the war.[19]

Reay immediately offered his services to the British War Office. He was appointed to help create and manage the special constabulary force, volunteers who would take the place of professional police sent to the front.[20]

Katharine wanted to help the war effort too, but not in a mundane role. She volunteered to train horses with the Women's Emergency Corps but she was knocked back. She proposed to a newspaper editor that he send her to Serbia as a war correspondent but was knocked back again because she was a woman.[21] She would have been disappointed to discover another Australian journalist, Louise Mack, had managed to persuade the *Daily Mail* editor to send her to report from Belgium just before the German invasion.[22]

AFTER A FIVE-YEAR courtship, Nettie Higgins had arrived in London and married Vance Palmer on 23 May 1914 at the Lower Sloane Baptist Church in Chelsea.[23] Katharine was living on the same road as the church, but there's no record of whether she was there.

Vance grew up in Queensland. Through his twenties, he'd travelled the world and was now making a living writing potboilers while also striving to create enduring literature. He and Nettie shared a dream of developing a distinctively Australian identity and culture.[24] Katharine saw him as 'one of those lamb-like men whom everybody loves. His kindliness and charm of manner are reflected in his writing; as also the tranquil depths of his austere mind and sensitive humour'.[25]

The newlyweds left soon after for a long honeymoon in France. After war broke out, they returned to London in September at the same time Sumner Locke left for Sydney. Nettie, Katharine's new best friend in London, was very different to Sumner—serious, intellectual, and at a different stage of life, being newly married. In October, Vance travelled to New York chasing writing work and Katharine went to stay with the pregnant Nettie for some weeks until he returned.[26] After the baby, Aileen, was born, Nettie brought her over to see Katharine in April 1915 for an afternoon tea with, of all people, Reay's wife and daughter, Lucinda and Nan.[27] Katharine would be a kind of secular godmother for the first five decades of Aileen's troubled life as the baby grew up to become a communist poet struggling with mental illness.[28]

IN EARLY DECEMBER, Katharine finally had a taste of war when she travelled to northern France to report on the Australian Voluntary Hospital. Lady Rachel Dudley had established the hospital, staffing it with Australian nurses and doctors who were in London when the war began. Dudley herself had lived in Australia while her husband served as governor-general of Australia from 1908 to 1911 and Katharine had stayed in touch with her after interviewing her for a newspaper. Nan, Reay's daughter, was one of the nurses.[29]

The hospital was in Wimmereux, near Boulogne, having taken over 'a great, rambling, muddily-white French hotel. When first you see it, you want to draw it as it stands against the sea, under a clear, shining sky'.[30] The First Battle of Ypres—fought only 30 kilometres away—had finished a week or two before she arrived and the hospital was quieter than it had been. Even before the war, Katharine's journalism had been patriotic; now it became more so. One of her articles proclaimed that the AVH was the 'best hospital at the front'; in another article, she wrote that 'in Boulogne I had seen all manner of hospital nurses, but none, I thought, looked as sweet as the Australian Sisters in their grey zephyr gowns, with little scarlet capes'.[31]

Visiting the wards, the misery and waste of war struck her forcibly. She found it hard to believe that the 'gaunt and weary-looking men … were the same strapping fellows whom I had seen leaving London blithely singing "Tipperary" a few months ago. There they lie, the wreckages of the war, so much splendid strength and virility maimed and thwarted'.[32]

SOON AFTER KATHARINE'S return to London, a journalist told her that he'd learned from someone at Hodder & Stoughton that Katharine was one of the winners of the £1000 Novel Competition. 'There was nothing to do but wait for official confirmation of the rumour; but, of course, my hopes soared.' It meant she was more devastated than she would otherwise have been when a form letter arrived one evening in February 1915, asking her to come and pick up her losing manuscript. It was winter and it was raining but 'I went out and wandered about London, walked for hours. Didn't know where: or why I was wandering'.[33]

The morning post brought another letter from Hodder & Stoughton, this one informing her that the previous letter had been sent to her by mistake and asking her to call by straightaway. At the office, the manager, Ernest Hodder Williams, told her she was the Australasian winner of the competition. When she left, she bought all the roses she could carry from a flower-girl and went along Fleet Street, finding friends to tell in the newspaper offices.[34]

Katharine's uncle, the editor Frederick Prichard, and her lover, Reay, reported her win in Australian newspapers straightaway, even though the results had not yet been publicly announced.[35] The official announcement came five weeks later in the April issue of Hodder & Stoughton's journal, *Bookman.* It was the month of the landing of the Anzac forces at Gallipoli. The other winners were AE Taylor (Canada); F Horace Rose (South Africa); and Samuel Foskett (India), none of them as well remembered as Katharine.[36]

Katharine had become a literary celebrity. Those who knew her understood her breakthrough was the culmination of years of determined struggle; she 'has been climbing into prominence by a kind of secret passage of sheer hard work for some time', wrote one journalist. The day after the official announcement, William Moore—the director of the Australian drama nights in Melbourne, now working in London—came to interview her at her flat. Other interviewers and a photographer had already been there; 'offers from publishers had come for serials and short stories' and 'some unknown financier had offered to advise her how to invest her money'.[37]

WITH PLENTY OF money for the passage home, Katharine planned a visit to Melbourne in the Australian spring, after the scheduled publication of her book in August.[38] 'Before I left London', she wrote, 'there were two or three things I wanted to do with my newly acquired wealth'. She took children from her street to the zoo and a restaurant, treats beyond their imagination. She sent her charwoman, Mrs Neal, and her sons on a month's holiday in the country. And she went on an 'orgy of shopping' for her sister's trousseau; Beatrice married a plantation owner in Melbourne in April.[39]

IN AUGUST, *The Pioneers* was published with the three other Hodder & Stoughton Novel Competition winners. It was a thick hardcover selling for six shillings and with a colour reproduction of Frederick McCubbin's *The Pioneer* as a frontispiece. The initial print run of 8000 copies had nearly sold out by 1920; Hodder & Stoughton went on to print 35,000 copies in cheap editions between 1917 and 1927 but Katharine only earned royalties on the original edition.[40]

The reviewer in the influential *Times Literary Supplement* wrote that Katharine 'has a sense of style, an intense love for more than the mere outer aspects of nature (and the book is drenched in Australian sunshine), an intimate acquaintance with the bush, and a faculty for conveying temperament'. The comment on Katharine's appreciation for nature beyond the external was prescient, anticipating the even stronger presence the landscape has in later works such as *Working Bullocks* and the goldfields trilogy. The reviewer went on to criticise *The Pioneers*, quite reasonably, for several improbabilities, including Deidre's unlikely marriage to the villainous McNab.[41]

The reviews in the Australian press were also very positive. Although her win in the competition had been reported around the country, it is a measure of parochialism that it was mostly newspapers in her home state of Victoria which reviewed the novel. The review in the *Argus* was typical:

> The atmosphere is genuinely Australian and Miss Prichard has succeeded in producing an intensely interesting and engrossing story without a hint of exaggeration or overcolouring. Her style is quiet and restrained, she has good descriptive power, her characters are well realised and the story is well constructed. A touch of humour would have illumined it, for Australian life can never be accurately described by anyone who lacks the capacity for revealing the humour of a situation; but the book clearly indicates that Miss Prichard will rank fairly high amongst Australian novelists.[42]

The review reflects concerns of the time: the question of how truly Australian works of literature were; the significance—in a less visual culture—of a novelist's descriptive powers; and the essential literary task of ranking writers. Perhaps Katharine took notice of the comment about the need for humour; from *Black Opal* onward her fiction often includes at least one comical character, from the layabout Paul in *Black Opal* to the larrikin Dinny Quinn in the goldfields trilogy.

Hodder & Stoughton's sister company, George H Doran, published an American edition of *The Pioneers* in January 1916. A publicity flyer collected praise from twenty-one reviews in newspapers around the United States, including the *New York Times*, with several reviewers finding it a fascinating reminder of the lawless days of the American West.[43] The nation which Katharine found unbearable in her brief stay gave her first novel an enthusiastic reception.

Overall, *The Pioneers* was seen as a fine debut of a potentially significant writer. If it was not generally thought to be a masterpiece, it was appreciated for its Australian setting and its homage to the pioneering generation who had now died out, as well as for its narrative skill. After years of disappointments and moderate successes, a novel written in haste but gestating for a decade had turned Katharine into a writer everyone was talking about.

13

Hugo

London, 1915

IN MAY 1915, German zeppelins began attacking London. Katharine saw one from her sixth-floor flat: 'looking out of the back window, I saw what I thought was a lighted cigar, high in the sky and presently a ball of fire seemed to fall from it … the inhabitants of the flats came rushing up and said, "Come down to the cellar at once"'.[1]

As Katharine waited for *The Pioneers* to be published, she was spending time with Australian soldiers. At an afternoon tea in June, she and Doris Carter—famous for her 'rippling, birdlike singing'—entertained thirty men evacuated from Gallipoli.[2] In September, the new London branch of the Australian Natives' Association established, at vice-president WT Reay's suggestion, the Anzac Club and Buffet.[3] Katharine was a frequent visitor in the six weeks before she left London—she could not 'extol too highly the value of its existence'. Offering free meals and the company of respectable Australian women, it aimed to give the soldiers 'a little bit of Australia in London', but just as much, it hoped to keep them away from prostitutes and alcohol.[4]

At one function, Katharine met Major Tom Todd of Western Australia's 10th Light Horse Regiment. Todd invited her to an afternoon tea at the opulent Royal Automobile Club, which had become something of an officers' club during the war. Here, on 14 September 1915,

Todd introduced her to one of his men, Lieutenant Hugo Throssell.[5] A gregarious 30-year-old, Hugo had been wounded at Gallipoli a couple of weeks earlier and only just evacuated to London.

Katharine and Hugo talked for a while and discovered their mutual love of horses. He proposed they go riding along Rotten Row, a track along the south edge of Hyde Park. When she said she didn't have a riding habit he suggested she sit astride the horse—something still widely considered improper for women—and show Londoners how Australians could ride. It made her think of Harry Newton showing off in a rowboat back in 1908. The proposed ride 'didn't happen, thank goodness'.[6]

Katharine wrote that 'there was an indefinable attraction to each other'. His 'irresistible manner' lifted her out of her 'usual aloofness'. He would later claim that he fell in love with her as he caught sight of her walking along the terrace towards him.[7] In a typically brief entry, all he recorded in his war diary was, 'Met Miss KSP'.[8]

HUGO VIVIAN HOPE THROSSELL was from Northam, a wheatbelt town a hundred kilometres inland from Perth. He was always known as 'Jim', a name Katharine said he gave himself.[9] His father, George Throssell, worked his way up from poverty to be a rich merchant, Northam's member of parliament, and even premier of WA for a few months. Born on 26 October 1884, Hugo was the thirteenth of fourteen children; his younger sister died as a baby and he grew up as the indulged youngest child. He 'had the best of everything. All the graces and pleasures of a country squire were his. There was always a horse of his own in the stables; his own dog; even … a pet monkey'.[10] Educated as a boarder at Prince Alfred College, a prestigious Methodist school in Adelaide, Hugo's great trouble in life, according to Katharine, was that he 'had not been trained for any definite job'.[11] After finishing school, he did office work for six years for his much older brother's business. He mucked around; he boxed; he sprinted; he acted in the local drama club; 'he was a popular escort, but as incapable of being serious about a young lady as he was about any of life's less significant pleasures'.[12] In 1910, the year his father died, Hugo worked as a stockman on Ashburton Downs Station, in the north of Western Australia.[13]

When he returned to the wheatbelt, he and his brother Eric tried to grow wheat on a family property in Cowcowing. After several years of failed crops, they owed a large debt and they decided to enlist, probably out of equal parts economic necessity, patriotism and the prospect of adventure. Enlisting together at Guildford in October 1914, they were original members of the newly formed 10th Light Horse Regiment.[14] During training at Rockingham, south of Perth, Hugo was made a 2nd Lieutenant; he left for the front in February 1915.[15]

Arriving in Egypt, Hugo was left behind in Cairo to look after the horses when most of the regiment sailed to Gallipoli in May to fight, dismounted, as infantry for the ill-fated campaign to capture the sea route through the Dardanelles and supply the eastern front.[16] In late July, Hugo led eighty-one soldiers sent to Gallipoli as reinforcements.[17] After several difficult weeks in the trenches, Hugo was sent with the remnant of the battalion to Hill 60, on the north-western end of the frontline. On 29 August came the battle that would see him awarded a Victoria Cross, the one costly success of his life. It was the same day as the first newspaper advertisement for Katharine's novel *The Pioneers*.[18] At 1 a.m., a group of soldiers led by Hugo ran, exposed, the 50 metres from their trench to a trench held by the Turks and took one end of it, putting up a sandbag barricade. Separated only by the sandbags and a 5-metre section of trench, the two sides exchanged bombs the size of cricket balls through the rest of the night. Turkish reinforcements arrived at 4.30 a.m. and the Australians were outnumbered. It was then, Hugo wrote, 'I got a bullet through the back of the neck and a piece of bomb through the left shoulder'.[19] Despite the wounds, he fought on and rallied the other soldiers. 'Men standing near me and next to me were blown to pieces or lost limbs, [or] were killed outright.'[20] At daylight, a machine gun arrived at the New Zealand line, and the Turkish soldiers who were not killed retreated. At about eight o'clock, Hugo agreed to have his wounds dressed; he was in such bad shape the doctor ordered that he be evacuated to the hospital ship.[21]

Arriving in London, Hugo was caught between making the most of the adventure of his first trip to Britain and getting better. A specialist blamed his hearing problems not on the noise of the trenches but adenoids. A week after meeting Katharine, Hugo was put under general anaesthetic and his adenoids removed. After the operation, he began developing a fever and was soon delirious and vomiting, fighting for his life for the next week.[22] He had bacterial meningitis; the surgeon's scalpel may have accidentally perforated the lining of his brain during the operation.[23] He was at his worst on 29 September and yet the next morning his temperature fell rapidly 'with general remission of symptoms'.[24]

Hugo remembered a doctor telling him as he recovered that 'he would never be normal again'.[25] On 14 October, the medical board at the Wandsworth Hospital ruled that he was unfit for duty for six months.[26]

The next day, while still in hospital, Hugo was announced as one of eight Anzac recipients of the Victoria Cross, the highest military honour awarded 'for valour in the face of the enemy'. Hugo wrote 'there was considerable excitement on my balcony where I was then domiciled that day. Many telegrams, letters and cables of congratulations were received, whilst a great number of visitors called, including seven people from Northam, press reporters after copy & camera fiends'.[27]

On 17 October, he recorded meeting two women—Miss Rene Sara and Miss Watson. At the time, he seems to have been at least as interested in them as he was in Katharine.

Rene Sara, turning twenty-six that year, was feted in Western Australia at the time of her early death from appendicitis in 1921 as 'perhaps the most brilliant of any of our singers'. She came to London to study at the Royal College of Music and stayed to work as a concert singer and to entertain troops.[28] In early 1916, Hugo took her with him to Ireland to stay at his father's birthplace, the town of Fermoy. Whatever there might have been between her and Hugo, she married another Western Australian soldier in March 1917.[29]

The other woman Hugo recorded meeting, Henrietta Watson, was a well-known British actress of forty-two. He had seen her perform in Adelaide when he was still at school and was entranced; after finding a photograph of her in a magazine in 1910 he wrote a fan letter. When Hugo reached London, he wrote again to let her know he was in town, which is how she came to visit him in hospital. They met up often over the following months. Hugo was to tell the story of his romance with Watson many times and at some stage he wrote it down, calling the story 'Intimate Strangers'. 'Of course, in a proper story, we should have got married and lived happily ever after, but this is a really truly story in every detail and so we just remained the very best of friends, or, as she aptly puts it—"Intimate Strangers".'[30]

It was a phrase which struck Katharine enough that she repurposed it as the title of a novel she wrote in the early 1930s in the years before Hugo's suicide. Her *Intimate Strangers* (1937) isn't the story of a coy romance between a war hero and an actress but a disintegrating marriage between a damaged war veteran and his wife.

READING IN THE newspaper that Hugo had been awarded the Victoria Cross, Katharine 'sent him a telegram of congratulations and forgot him, because without a word of warning my brother Nigel arrived on one of the hospital ships from the Dardanelles'. Katharine was overjoyed to see Nigel, the first family member she'd seen in five years. She made a bed up for him in her lounge 'and we spent a few happy days together'.[31] A blurry photo of the two of them survives, Nigel seated with Katharine perched on the arm of the chair and a tantalising glimpse of the inside of Katharine's flat, a framed photograph and a long, indistinct artwork on the wall, flowers on the side table. 'With Nige, during the war', Katharine wrote on the back, and with a different pen, 'Mostly feet'.[32]

Major Todd came to her flat to tell her Hugo had been suffering meningitis and wanted her to visit. When Katharine finally saw Hugo, 'we were chattering as if the undercurrent of that inexplicable attraction flowing between us needed no explanation'. Yet he sounds insensitive. He'd been reading *The Pioneers* and she wanted to know what he thought of it. His only comment was to correct her use of the term 'waggon' on the first page: it should have been 'covered-in dray'.[33] Katharine remembered the rebuke for decades, and made a special note in the preface to the revised edition in 1963 that she had taken the opportunity to finally correct it.[34]

At the hospital she met Hugo's brother Eric—known as Ric—for the first and only time. He was about to return to the front. 'The brothers were David and Jonathan in their devotion to each other. Ric, a splendid looking man, broader and taller than Hugo, had the same Australian-ness I admired in them both, a virility and the air of horsemen accustomed to deal with men and beasts.'[35]

Katharine was due to leave for Ceylon on the *Omrah* on 23 October. Hugo came to her flat to say goodbye 'in the midst of my luggage, packed cases of books and belongings. I couldn't believe there was more in his feeling for me than a sort of bushfire flare that would pass. So we parted, shaking hands, sadly, without any acknowledgement of an emotional stir between us'.[36]

She was only meant to be on a short visit to Ceylon and Australia; perhaps she didn't bother saying goodbye properly to all the friends she'd made, thinking she would be back within a year. There would have been a parting date with Reay—perhaps dinner at a fine restaurant. He was anxious for her to return soon. Yet 'now things were different', Katharine's son writes. 'Her success had given her more confidence.'[37]

A MONTH AFTER Katharine left, from 3 p.m. to 6 p.m. on Saturday 20 November 1915, the Australian Natives' Association held an 'At Home' at the Anzac Club and Buffet to honour the Australian Victoria Cross (VC) recipients. 'The floral decorations were wattle blossoms and grasses. At one end of the table stood a good-sized kangaroo in natural skin and colour.'[38] Four of the six VC recipients were there, including Hugo. It's not recorded whether Reay was present, but he was vice-president and it was the sort of thing he usually attended. If Hugo and Reay ever met, it was most likely this afternoon.

After songs by Hugo's love interest, Rene Sara, and others, Sir George Reid, the former Australian prime minister and now high commissioner, gave a rousing, patriotic speech. 'The King of Terrors meant a thousand deaths for each of you, but, in spite of all the thunderbolts which he launched, you stand before us not only alive but also braver, finer, and nobler for the experience.'[39] At that moment, at the height of his celebrity and before the death of his brother, Hugo may even have believed Reid. But the 'King of Terrors' with his 'thousand deaths' was not finished with Hugo yet.

Hugo, 'his head still in hospital bandages', was the only one of the VCs to give a substantial speech. He 'began by declaring that he was a farmer, and could not be expected to make a speech' but he went on to remember several brave soldiers he had seen die. He concluded by saying, 'My wounds are nearly well, and when they are I shall be off, too, although I have two maladies to cure—a heart affection and a swelled head. Folks here have made so much of us that we begin to imagine we are some kind of special pumpkin. Gallipoli will soon cure us of that'.[40]

14

Disquiet

Ceylon and Melbourne, 1915–1916

STAYING FOR SIX weeks on a rubber plantation in Ceylon, Katharine 'almost forgot the war'.[1] In April, her sister Beatrice had married the owner of the plantation, Patten ('Pack') Bridge, an old friend of the family. She was now four months pregnant. Beatrice had still been at school when Katharine last saw her and it must have been strange to find her little sister twenty-three years old, married and pregnant, already ahead of her in conventional life milestones. While she was there she wrote a poem to Beatrice with the lines, 'You went into the dark house of your love / I stayed in the twilight'.[2]

Beatrice was returning to Melbourne to give birth and the two sisters boarded the *Karmala* on 26 December 1915. Katharine wrote that they 'had an uneventful trip until the ship berthed at Melbourne'.[3] Yet it was on the voyage she met a wealthy student activist named Guido Baracchi who changed her life.

Katharine hid her tumultuous two-year romance with Guido. One of the few times she publicly acknowledged he had any role in her life was in a 1961 interview: 'I met Guido Baracchi on a boat, and he was getting interested in Marxism, too. He gave me a list of books to read, and when I got back to Australia my husband sent off and got them for me, all that were then available'.[4] The misleading reference to

Hugo was a deflection and she was conflating the events of three years. When she met Guido, neither of them were yet interested in Marx and she wasn't married.

In the version Guido told Katharine's son, Ric Throssell, in 1972, they met in the launch out to the *Karmala*. 'Katharine took one look at me &, as she told me, sighed hopelessly to her sister, "Another planter!"'[5] Guido was dressed like a planter because he had borrowed clothes from one. He wasn't meant to be in Ceylon at all. A friend of his was enlisting in London and Guido was only meant to be accompanying him from Melbourne to Fremantle, but during the six-hour stopover in Fremantle, Guido got drunk at a party onboard and woke up already out to sea. He disembarked at the first chance in Colombo and spent eleven days awaiting a ship which could take him back to Australia.[6]

In the words of one historian, Guido was 'the knight errant of Australian radicalism ... A man of considerable wealth and emotional spontaneity, utterly without guile or worldly ambition, of luminous innocence and limitless self-centredness—his marital and romantic arrangements ... in a constant muddle'.[7] He was the only child of a wealthy family, born in Melbourne in 1887 to an Italian father and a mother of Irish heritage. A perpetual student and playboy, he switched between studying science, medicine and law. His politics evolved over the next years 'from a hazy liberalism to something altogether more radical'—specifically, guild socialism at the time Katharine met him.[8]

In 1913 he'd written an article for a university magazine called 'Picking Up: The Finest Game on Earth', offering it as a modern alternative to the need for a formal introduction before a 'respectable' woman would allow a man to speak to her:

> A man sees a girl whose looks he likes, stares at her a moment friendly-wise, and if her eyes reciprocate, conversation is forthwith begun. The reverse process may also occur, the glance of invitation coming from the girl ...
>
> The uncertainty of picking up can only be described as gorgeous. She may be a blank or a treasure, married or single, slow or not. She may be much besides. You never can tell.

He goes on to claim the approach is about far more than romance or sex: 'Picking up is a very serviceable pestle with which to smash class consciousness in the mortar of socialism'.[9]

There was much which drew Katharine to Guido. He was on a political quest similar to her own and could talk confidently about political theory. He wrote poetry, as bad as it may have been. He was wealthy and charming and he had, according to his later lover, Betty Roland, a 'gift of being able to efface himself, to put aside his masculine aggressiveness and become the listener, the sympathetic, gentle, understanding recipient of confidences'.[10] In his obituary, Betty was quoted as saying, 'He wasn't exactly a handsome man—medium build, reddish hair, blue eyes. Yet he exuded such magnetism that all, friend and foe alike, were immediately attracted to him'.[11]

At the end of the voyage, Katharine gave him a copy of *Clovelly Verses,* 'a "Token of Amity"', Guido remembered, 'as she inscribed it for me on the fly-leaf'.[12] They arranged to stay in touch while they were both in Melbourne.

ON 12 JANUARY 1916, Katharine arrived back in Melbourne after five years abroad. Australia was unsettled. Her ship, the *Karmala*, was supposed to be carrying on to Sydney the next day but its departure was delayed by striking wharf labourers.[13] An ad in the day's *Argus* newspaper asked, 'HAVE YOU ENLISTED? The Call is to You Today! Australia needs at once 50,000 Men for the New Army and 16,000 Men each Month as Reinforcements of the New and Existing Armies'.[14] The day's editorial began, 'More deliberate and more wicked perversity was never displayed by an important body of workers than that which has culminated in the Broken Hill strike'.[15] The home-front battlelines were being drawn along class lines.

KATHARINE'S MOTHER, EDITH, had moved from South Yarra to the suburb of Armadale, an area of 'quiet respectability' where Katharine had previously attended primary school.[16] Katharine's brother Alan was still at home, about to turn thirty and feeling the burden of being the only one of the siblings left in the country with their widowed mother while working as the mining editor of the *Argus.* Katharine found herself suddenly re-immersed in family life as 'Mother and Bee chatted and sewed happily, making small garments' ahead of the baby's birth. 'I was no use to them either for sewing or pre-natal gossip, so tried out on them some of the recipes I had learnt in France.'[17]

After a month at home, she rented a house by the beach for five weeks at Black Rock, 20 kilometres south of the city.[18] She may have wanted her own space in order to write. She could only ever handle a certain amount of clamour and interaction; her need to retreat was a recurring one.

Her timing seems poor—just as she took the beach house she was honoured with a number of parties and receptions that required her to travel into the city, breaking the solitude. In mid-February, one columnist wrote that she 'is the woman of the moment in Melbourne this week, and we are just tumbling over one another to say "we are proud of you, and welcome home"'. Looking for signs fame had changed Katharine, the columnist reported, 'Outwardly and visibly it is the same bright, sweet face ... with a certain "spring" and vivacity of movement that betrays the alert mind and vividly "alive" temperament'.[19]

On Wednesday 16 February, Katharine's journalist friends organised a dinner to honour her at Café Francais on the corner of Swanston and Little Collins streets in the city. Years earlier, Edith had made a lace bertha for Katharine in the hope that she would one day wear it at her wedding; understanding the importance to Katharine of the dinner, she told her, 'If you don't want to be a wife and mother, dear, you might as well have the lace now'.[20]

She wore the lace to Café Francais with a white satin evening dress.[21] Her colleagues presented her with a souvenir menu painted with a scene from *The Pioneers*; on offer that night were devilled oysters, whiting, *cotelette d'Agneau à la Francais* (French lamb chop), and chicken casserole, with *bombe* and iced peaches for dessert and hock, claret, ale, lager and mineral waters to drink.[22] Among the guests in attendance was an aged Frederick McCubbin, whose painting had inspired *The Pioneers.* Despite all the adulation, decades later when she wrote her autobiography Katharine was still stung that Nettie and Vance and Hilda and Louis were missing. Oversensitive, she assumed it was because they didn't like *The Pioneers.*[23]

On 1 March, the Liberal premier of Victoria, Sir Alexander Peacock, held a luncheon in Katharine's honour at parliament and presented her with a six-month railway pass. The premier 'spoke at length on the value of Miss Prichard's novel to Australian literature and expressed his pride that an Australian woman had done so well in the English literary world'.[24] She seems to have got on well with Peacock and his wife; she also accompanied them on a visit to a flying school in July where she flew in an aeroplane for the first time.[25] The welcome the Peacocks gave her in 1916 suggests the life among the privileged Katharine might have enjoyed if she hadn't turned so forcefully against their world the next year.

That same week, Katharine watched a special screening of the silent film adaptation of *The Pioneers*, directed by Franklyn Barrett, at Hoyts Olympia.[26] Katharine was possibly the film's 'most dissatisfied critic' according to one columnist. 'One most annoying thing was the changing of the conclusion … and scenes that should properly have occurred in the wildest of backblock country are played in a setting of semi-civilised vegetation. Oh, the woes of an authoress!'[27] Only some stills and a few seconds of the film survive, a fragment showing Mary Cameron loading a rifle. A five-minute fragment is all that remains of a second adaptation by Raymond Longford in 1926.[28] Even if they were not good, the loss of these and so many other Australian silent films is a sad one, their 35mm prints worn as they did the rounds of the suburban cinemas and then sold on to itinerant exhibitors who toured the scratched copies around outback towns until they were discarded.[29]

FOUR NOTEBOOKS FROM 1916 to 1917 survived Katharine's purge of her papers before her death. They are the notebooks of a writer at work, sketches of scenes, dialogue, and other observations interspersed with candid moments of feeling and confession, interiority largely unmoored from known public events.

The first of these notebooks—'Australia I: Ti-Tree Studies 1916'—is from her stay at Black Rock in February and March. In this notebook, she is preoccupied with expressing a rapturous communion with the ti-trees which line the coast and with the ocean itself. Sometimes her connection to nature is a balm for the pain of love: 'Oh, it was good to go down to the sea this morning. To give myself to the sea's embrace, after the disquiet … the troubled thinking of the day & night'. At other times, her connection to nature is a substitute for romantic love: 'Oh it was the ti-tree. The wonder shuddering & whispering of it … My happiness had nothing to do with any person. It was for the world, of the world—that I, for a moment was contained within the world life …'

Early in her stay, she was thinking of Reay and their time in a 'little green parlour' in Black Rock. 'I walked & walked yesterday to find it … It was just as we left it. I sat down outside & thought of you & of the time when we used to come, plodding arm in arm through the sand together.' But now she was in love with Guido, the 'boy' or 'young man' as she referred to him in her notebook, a few years younger than her and decades younger than Reay. Taking on Reay's jealousy at her new love, 'the sea broke on the shore with a dull, heavy sound. I heard it early this morning, at dawn almost—& then its voice was that of a disturbed & jealous lover'.

Her seaside sojourn meant she and Guido had time alone together and he could stay overnight. Three days after her walk to the little-green parlour she asked, 'Does he feel as I do? Is he plagued like this? … Is he the *le jeune gars qui s'amuse bien* [the young man out for a good time]? … Is he angry, disappointed, practiced at bringing this phase into the … relationship … Is he simply agnostic, too?' On 1 March she recorded nothing of her visit to parliament, writing instead, 'Oh, there is something of the seas in our love—something restless, insatiable; something of its mute hunger, desolate passion, intensity & immortality!' On 3 March she wrote, 'The sick hungry suffering of these days! I cannot tell of them. I have offered three long days on the altar of my feeling for you, whatever it is'.

Katharine's longing turned to disappointment after another visit from Guido; on 14 March she wrote, 'For two nights & two days I thought that you were the wild adriatic lover I've dreamed of—but here you are now behaving like any other respectable, commonplace young man with no passion & dream in his soul to carry him out of his depth in the ocean of life'. On the next page of her notebook, she felt it was passion itself which was the problem, rather than the lack of it.

'The great love-passion is anti-social. There is a nice working comradeship & affection that is much better. It enables men & women to live peacefully together and breed. The other is simply destructive of mind, body, & soul.'

On the final day of her stay she recorded on the last page of the notebook, 'The ti-tree has bloomed for me! It is as if my love for it had brought the blossom, so unbelievably out of season'.[30]

IN KATHARINE'S NEXT notebook, 'Australia II 1916', she narrated at length a shorter retreat on Saturday 1 April 1916, visiting her old friend Hilda Esson in Emerald, 44 kilometres south-east of the city in the Dandenong Ranges. 'I thought that if I could see the hills, I would cease to think of you. The pain would lift from my heart and my mind would cease to plague me for a little while.' Between the train station and Hilda's cottage, she climbed up a hill beside the creek and spread her coat under a big blackbutt tree, feeling as small as the ants swarming 'over a gaping wound from which the red gum dripped & over me'. When the rain came, she stayed lying on her coat. 'The dampness … was stealing over my body, but I did not want to move. I wanted to lie there all night. I wanted to lie there in the darkness & see the stars come out …' Eventually, the 'thought of Hilda waiting for me … coming to look for me with lantern at night—& explanations—roused me'. At first, she went 'almost drunkenly down the track, intoxicated with the wild joy that had taken me'. Her clothes heavy with rain, the track slippery, she held her face up to the rain. 'It was one of those moments of ecstasy that even a lover's embrace cannot give—golden flooding, deepening of consciousness, wrapping from earth in an ether of exquisite joy.'

Yet her joy once more turned to misery as she lost her way, hurt her ankle on a sodden log and found herself wet and tired in the rain. 'I thought of you then—& went on sobbing.' She came out of the bush '& saw Hilda's house on the other hill side & the grey walls spoke of so much home comfort & the very drift of smoke from its chimneys told of the easy, domestic happiness from which I am forever divorced'. Louis was away and after 'talk & music all evening' with Hilda, Katharine slept before the fire until dawn came.[31]

Through the war, she would keep returning to that cottage which spoke of 'home comfort' and 'domestic happiness', first to visit the Essons and later the Palmers. Then, in 1918 her mother would buy it for her; and finally, two months after Armistice, she would honeymoon there.

IN 1916, KATHARINE spent much time reflecting on the 'domestic happiness' from which she felt forever divorced. Marriage had never been an expectation with Reay but it was more complicated now she was in love with Guido. Hilda was in the happiest phase of what would prove to be an unhappy marriage. Nettie was married with a baby; Sumner was to marry in December; and Beatrice was pregnant. After visiting another, unidentified friend, she wrote, 'B says she is happy. Her love for husband, his love for her, their quiet & harmonious life together for two years has been so serene'.[32]

If Katharine was sometimes attracted by the prospect of marriage and children, she was just as often repelled by it. In October, she glimpsed 'the flat, cheap suburb' of Gardenvale from the tram and imagined the father of one of the households coming home for the day and wondering whether his children 'have rooted up his broad beans growing in neat rows in the back yard. He probably does not think he is happy. Probably he does not think of enquiring whether he is happy or not. He has not time to think of such things, he would probably say'. She felt the residents of Gardenvale should take comfort from the 'prospect of the hills', but she suspected they took comfort from their red-tiled roofs instead.[33]

TRIPS ASIDE, KATHARINE herself was living a suburban existence in Armadale, even if temporarily, with Edith, Alan and Beatrice in the last month of her pregnancy. 'I always feel like a day when I've been home I want to go out and howl.'[34]

On 29 March, she recorded in her notebook a strange waking dream about a mother who has just given birth. The 'quiet of the valley of shadows' still hung in the room, the mother and baby having survived a dangerous passage. The father entered the room and knelt at the bed, full of 'reverence, tenderness, emotion'.[35] Ahead of her sister giving birth, Katharine was experiencing both awe and anxiety.

Beatrice gave birth to a daughter on 27 April and named her Katharine Beatrice, the first of several babies to be named after Katharine, although she was always known as Thea. In the first weeks, Beatrice was sick and Katharine took care of Thea. 'Her fingers curled round mine and she clung to me, wailing and refusing to suck from an ugly rubber-tipped bottle, instead of the rosy nipples of her mother.' Edith was worried the baby was growing too attached to Katharine and thought she should go away for a while once Beatrice was stronger.[36]

IN LONDON ON 1 March 1916, the medical board of the Wandsworth Hospital found that Hugo 'is still somewhat nervous and suffers from continuous headaches. In view of his meningitis the Board is of opinion that he should have extended leave'.[37] Ruled unfit for any service for three months, he was sent back to Australia.

On 20 June, he arrived in Melbourne on the train and sought Katharine out. 'There were a few days of whirlwind love-making', she wrote, 'from the moment Hugo arrived'.[38] Their time together was limited—Hugo had many functions to attend and toured regional Victoria. However, in the time they did have together in June and July, Katharine introduced him to her mother and brothers; Alan apparently told her she should marry him. 'More deeply stirred than I had ever been, I cursed myself for letting Hugo go back to the battlefields with no more than the memory of kisses and our last passionate embrace. Was it the end of this brief madness? Would Hugo survive the war? Would he ever return to overwhelm me again?'[39]

The posthumous revelation of Katharine's relationship with Guido—which was still smouldering until at least November 1917—complicates her account of Hugo's courtship in June and July 1916. Was she involved with them both at the same time or was her relationship with Guido on hold? Or could she be confusing aspects of this visit with Hugo's 1918 visit?

Whatever the case, with Reay waiting in London for her expected return in November and a complicated relationship with Guido, Katharine was now torn in three directions.

15

The Opal Fields

Lightning Ridge, NSW, 1916

Now Katharine was famous, there was interest in her unpublished novel, *Windlestraws*. In March 1916, Melbourne newspaper the *Age* began serialising it. A British press, Holden and Hardingham, published it as a book later in the year, misspelling her name as 'Pritchard' on the cover and spine. A reviewer noted that the plot contrivances 'show an ingenious indifference to probability, but they serve to stimulate the interest of those who only ask to be amused'.[1] The novel received several mixed reviews and was then forgotten forever, facilitated by Katharine herself mentioning it as little as possible. '*Windlestraws* proved to her that her heart could not be in a novel that was not about her own country.'[2]

Katharine felt that her success with *The Pioneers* had 'opened the door for more serious writing … Now I could devote myself to the literary work for which I had been paving the way for so long. I could write about Australia and the realities of life for the Australian people'.[3] It was more than two years since she'd written *The Pioneers*. After deciding to write about the opal fields, she spent the rest of the war working on *Black Opal* (1921).[4] She had visited the White Cliffs opal fields on a daytrip from Tarella Station in 1905, and included a description of the settlement and its miners in 'A City Girl in Central Australia' (1906).

Since then, opal mining had taken off at Lightning Ridge, in northern New South Wales near the Queensland border, and it was now producing the most opal in Australia. The first step for her opal novel was to be a research trip to Lightning Ridge.

Katharine's two assignments as a governess had been de facto research trips for her writing. This trip to Lightning Ridge was the first formal one as a published novelist. Research trips would become her signature method; among other adventures, she would stay at Turee Station in the Pilbara in 1926 for *Coonardoo* (1929) and tour with Wirth's Circus in 1927 for *Haxby's Circus* (1930). The approach reflected her background as a journalist, seeking a story outside her own world and building the setting and characters from observation. She explained her method in a letter to a scholar in 1938:

> I prefer always to live among the people and the places I write of: use notes taken at the time, and try to discover the thoughts and reactions of people under my microscope to situations they have been through, or may have to encounter. The law of libel necessitates variations from the original, of course. Otherwise I am concerned to draw as I see.[5]

Later she wrote: 'I do think those first, vivid impressions & the yarns one gathers on the spot are most valuable—the sense of gathering from the realities of a milieu, being a sponge for the absorption of speech & character'.[6]

Leaving for Lightning Ridge in early August, Katharine chose the isolated coastal route to reach Sydney. She travelled to the end of the eastern Victorian railway line at Orbost and then took a horse-drawn coach to Eden. The driver, Jack McAlister, was the son of South Gippsland pioneers; she was the only passenger. 'Driving from dawn until sunset through the southern forests, seeing again the thronging columns of mountain ash and messmate, the tangled fern gullies, breathing the fragrance of sassafras and dogwood ... made me feel as I were being newly baptized into Australia.'[7] Transferring to a motor coach for the trip to Sydney, she was 'unable to imagine anybody preferring to travel by motor-car when they could have had horses and a coachman like Mr McAlister'.[8]

From Sydney she took a train north-west to the end of the line at Walgett. 'So far this country lay from the chaos of war, no bombardment disturbed its remote horizons; yet, barren and desolate, it held its own tragedy. The bleached bones of drought-stricken bullocks glimmered beside the track.'[9] She set off from Walgett on 31 August on the all-night coach journey to Lightning Ridge, writing in her notebook: 'I thought Death must be like this—a journey out at sunset, on an unknown road with an unknown driver. But I loved it—the loneliness—the great unknown before me. The sky bright with stars—the dark trees. The keen air.'[10] As they came into town before dawn 'the white clayey soil gleamed in the starlight'.[11] Lightning Ridge was 'a lake of life in the country of wide plains'.[12] There were about two hundred miners in 1916; at the time of the initial rush in 1908, there had been two thousand.[13] Germans were major opal buyers and the loss of their market meant the value of opal had declined sharply.[14]

Katharine wrote that she was initially mistaken for a visiting prostitute and treated coldly by the pub owner, given a noisy room behind the bar. When she explained she was a writer, she was treated with much 'courtesy and kindness' by the miners on the Ridge. The main character of her novel, Michael Brady, was closely based on a miner who showed her 'every phase of work on the field'; an 'intellectual' and 'humane' man, he 'told me about the struggle of the opal gougers to maintain their independence' and their passion for 'the precious red fires in black matrix which made Lightning Ridge opal the rarest in the world'.[15] Katharine's notebook is filled with sketches of the characters of the town, the specifics of opal mining, and descriptions of the landscape. When she left Lightning Ridge later in September, some of the miners gave her pieces of opal as farewell gifts.[16]

AS SHE HAD done with *The Pioneers,* Katharine wove the folklore of the town—renamed Fallen Star Ridge—into *Black Opal.* The year before her visit, two miners had found an unusually colourful opal of 500 carats nicknamed the 'Empress of Australia'. Valued at £650, it was dropped and broken in three 'when being looked at by an inquisitive stranger'.[17] This incident, fresh in the minds of the miners, may have inspired the scene where Sophie drops Potch's precious stone.[18] In another story circulating the same month Katharine visited, 'An American buyer visited the Ridge some time back, and made purchases at considerably advanced prices for this inferior opal. The miners were delighted, and prophesied that they would never see him again. He came again quite recently and bought many thousands of pounds worth more'.[19] In *Black Opal,* an American buyer, Dawe Armitage, is inconsistently said to be offering the best prices to the miners for opal *and* depicted as ripping them off. His son, John, threatens the Ridge's way of life by proposing to buy up all the mining leases and turn the miners into employees, giving them a guaranteed income but depriving them of their independence and the possibility of making a fortune.

Katharine wrote about Lightning Ridge through the lens of her emerging political convictions, left wing but not yet communist. The miners in *Black Opal* represent an idyll of working conditions: 'Ridge miners find happiness in the sense of being free men. They are satisfied in their own minds that it is not good for a man to work all day at any mechanical toil; to use himself, or allow anyone else to use him, like a working bullock'.[20] Together they had resisted being bought out by large companies and becoming wage slaves. The novel opposes the greed of capitalists and extols collectivist action, but the miners are working for themselves rather than for the good of the state and this individualism does not reflect orthodox communism. By the time the novel was serialised in 1936 in the socialist magazine, *Women Today,* Katharine was a committed communist and felt the need to explain that although the miners' 'Utopian experiment' was bound to fail in a capitalist society, the 'same spirit will lead us to a Soviet Australia when there is nation-wide organisation to support the workers in their control of industry'.[21]

BLACK OPAL IS 'set in an imprecise time, not quite up to the minute, and decidedly not nineteenth century'.[22] It makes no mention of the war, suggesting Katharine's sense of distance from it during her stay at Lightning Ridge. After weeks in the back country of Australia hearing only snippets of news, when she returned to Melbourne she found that the war had come close to her again.

16

The Omen

Melbourne, 1916–1917

'EARLY IN SEPTEMBER', wrote a Sydney gossip editor after Katharine passed through the city, 'she returns to her home in Melbourne for a few weeks and will then proceed to London, where her work necessitates her presence'.[1] However, things worked out nothing like Katharine planned.

After Beatrice and baby Thea departed for Ceylon, Katharine 'was settling down to write *Black Opal* when the blow fell I had been fearing for some time. Alan told me he wanted to volunteer for active service'.[2] He had stayed home with widowed Edith for years while Katharine was overseas and now it was her turn. She still planned to return to London but Alan's enlistment meant she 'decided, under the circumstances to remain with her mother a few months longer'.[3]

ALAN WENT INTO training in the midst of an acrimonious public debate about conscription. On 30 August, while Katharine was travelling to Lightning Ridge, Labor prime minister Billy Hughes announced a referendum on the issue would be held on 26 October. He was pushing for conscription and yet leading a party in which many strongly opposed it. The previous December, the government had required all Australian men under forty-five years old to register whether they were willing to volunteer for military service and to explain any reluctance. Alan would have felt increasing pressure to enlist.

Katharine wrote that she 'was bewildered as to what was the right way to vote'.[4] A couple of days before the referendum, she attended an anti-conscription meeting in the inner-city suburb of Fitzroy, taking detailed notes, recording the speaker's words and the atmosphere:

> He talked in a husky voice with an earnestness that shook his meagre frame …
>
> 'It's the first time in the history of the world that a people have been asked to vote themselves into conscription. In every other country it has been forced on the workers. But this—the passing of the Referendum—will mean that the democracy will put the shackles on itself. It's like breaking into Hell & staying there.'
>
> And over all the clear night sky, thick with stars, the warm still night … These same stars gazing down on the battlefields of the Marne & Somme. What battles are waging there—& here?[5]

Guido, Nettie and Vance were all strongly opposed to conscription.[6] Yet Katharine also had influences pushing her in the other direction. Eight years earlier, in peace time, she'd written the opinion piece vehemently supporting compulsory military training. Hugo publicly supported the 'yes' campaign.[7] She had a brother training for the front; the influence of Reay; and a number of patriotic friends to balance out the 'antis'—including the journalist Masie Maxwell, her replacement at the *Herald* who later wrote in the second referendum campaign that every woman must ask:

> 'Shall I vote Yes and save my country, or vote No and play into the hands of Germany?'
>
> Maybe it will not be easy for her to arrive at a decision. The pacifists, shirkers, Sinn Feiners, socialists, and all the rest of that brigade will see to that. They will play upon the emotional side of her nature and bring forward fantastical arguments which they feel will appeal to her sentiment, and give her a distorted perspective.[8]

As much as anyone, Katharine was torn between the two sides. Eventually, she came to a decision. 'If recruits were needed, I thought, they would help to bring the war to an end, so with considerable misgivings I voted for them to be sent.'[9] There were many reasons for her to do so, but it is still a shock to find her voting for conscription less than three years before the Australian intelligence agency opened a file on her as a dangerous radical. In *Child of the Hurricane*, Katharine complained about government and press censorship of the 'no' campaign—yet she voted 'yes' with full, firsthand knowledge of the arguments put forward against conscription.

In voting 'yes' she was in the minority—the conscription referendum was narrowly defeated.

IN NOVEMBER 1916, the month *Windlestraws* was published, Hilda and Louis left for New York, where Louis hoped to have his plays produced. The day they departed 'several inky wayfarers wished the Esson literary couple bon voyage at Spencer-street station … Mr and Mrs Vance Palmer will take shelter in the Essons' shack at Emerald while the intellectual couple are facing the blizzards in New York'.[10]

It was a tumultuous time for Katharine. The week after Hilda left, Edith's sister, Christina, died; she had been one of the influential aunts shaping Katharine's life.[11] Then, on 16 December, her brother Alan embarked for France.[12] 'As the ship pulled out from the wharf I knew that I would never see that loved face again.'[13]

In the midst of this, there are signs Katharine had turned back to Guido only to learn he was involved with someone else. On 19 December, three days after Alan left, she wrote in her notebook:

> Some men are licensed to retail undiluted essences of hell—& they do it to the best of their ability. They are a danger to society, public nuisances. They ought to be locked up.
>
> *
>
> One drink's one's own tears—but tears are a poor drink. They increase thirst—and are bad for the digestion.
>
> *
>
> I want to swim in you—as one swims in a lake. Drown in you … It is only in the merging of souls that lovers become immortal—one flesh.[14]

In the aftermath of the referendum victory, Guido had fallen for a poet named Lesbia Keogh, better known by her later married name, Harford. Katharine may have already known her; Lesbia had been friends with Nettie since 1907.[15] Guido and Lesbia grew close in late 1916 working together on an organising committee for a proposed new journal, a review of politics, literature and arts. The journal never came about but 'what did eventuate from these meetings', wrote Guido, 'was our intimate friendship'.[16] Lesbia had a heart condition that was expected to kill her by thirty. Now twenty-five, she was living intensely. She completed a law degree in December 1916, but had joined the Industrial Workers of the World (IWW) and was working in a clothing factory out of solidarity with the working class. She introduced Guido to Percy Laidler, the Melbourne IWW leader and manager of Andrade's Bookshop, a meeting place for radicals.[17] Guido wrote that it was Lesbia 'above all who helped me to find my way right into the revolutionary working-class movement'.[18]

If Katharine's words on 19 December are in response to learning of Guido's unfaithfulness, she forgave him. Guido seems to have remained involved with both Katharine and Lesbia all through 1917, with probably neither Katharine nor Lesbia fully aware of the situation. Guido visited Emerald with each of them, writing of Lesbia, 'I well remember one Saturday in 1917, when this remarkable woman, despite her bad heart, insisted on our climbing a steep hill in the Dandenong Ranges, proceeding at the same time both to stir my mind deeply & to set my imagination on fire'.[19]

In May 1917, Nettie was dangerously sick with septicaemia after the birth of her second child.[20] While Nettie was in hospital, Katharine sublet the Emerald cottage from the Palmers for three weeks. She wrote to Nettie from Emerald while she was there. 'I am loving every minute of my time here ... I love going further into the wilderness with an axe in the morning and wheeling home a barrow-load.' She added as a 'by the way—although it is no by the way at all':

> Guido came to see me on Monday. We had all Tuesday together & he caught the train back on Wednesday ... The party was indiscrete, dear, but innocent to a degree—and I cannot tell you what it meant to us both. Mother would have hysterics if she heard of it—so this

> information is just for you dear. We had two perfect blue days wandering about the hills. I am better in mind and body than I have been for a very long time.[21]

It is Katharine's only known direct acknowledgement of her romance with Guido. What was the 'degree' of 'innocence' in their relationship? Guido is said to have suddenly married for the first time seven months later because the woman, Kathleen Tobin, 'refused to go to bed with me unless I did'; presumably, Katharine and Lesbia 'had been less resistant to his charm'.[22] And yet, for whatever reason, there was a degree of innocence between Guido and Katharine on those days in May 1917.

GUIDO'S BIG PROJECT in 1917 was to help establish the Victorian Labor College. The activist Bill Earsman was the initiator and he recruited Guido to join the organising committee and teach.[23] The constitution stated, 'the point of view of teachers shall be frankly working class, and the aim of the College shall be to enable working men and working women to serve their class'.[24]

Katharine's lack of a degree was a wound she still carried. Now, in 1917, it may have helped her to identify with the working classes cut off from tertiary education. In June, inspired by Guido, she wrote to the college committee asking if she could take classes even though she was not a member of a trade union. The committee accepted her application and the next meeting minuted her as the first student to be enrolled in the college.[25] Her enrolment was the most radical political step of her life so far. She was renouncing the middle class she had been born into and asking the working class to adopt her as an honorary member. It came only seven months after she had voted for conscription.

The Australian political landscape shifted dramatically after the first conscription referendum. In November 1916, prime minister Billy Hughes and thirty other pro-conscription government members split with the Labor Party over the issue. In May 1917, Hughes and these pro-conscription defectors won the federal election as part of a new centre-right party, the Nationalist Party of Australia. Presumably, Katharine's vote remained with the decimated Australian Labor Party, which now held a clear anti-conscription position.

There was an atmosphere of class division and turmoil in Melbourne. Cost of living pressures led to food riots. The Great Strike began in New South Wales in August and was affecting 20,000 workers in Melbourne by September, up to a half of them actually on strike while the other half were stood down as industry ground to a halt.[26]

At one point in 1917, Katharine experienced a political 'omen', with many of the markers of a religious experience:

> Walking into the city, across Prince's Bridge one evening, I saw the first posters proclaiming the revolution in Russia. It had happened. The dream of the exiles I had met in Paris, so long ago, had come true. There was a gash of gold in the cloudy sky. Everything was suffused in golden light. In a daze of excitement and rejoicing, it seemed this was an omen for the future ... I lost no time buying and studying all the books of these writers [Marx and Engels] available in Melbourne. Discussion with Christian [Jollie Smith], [Bill] Earsman and [Guido] Baracchi confirmed my impression that these theories provided the only logical basis that I had come across for the reorganization of our social system.[27]

In an earlier account of the experience, Katharine wrote that 'until then ... I had not heard of Karl Marx or Communism'.[28] This seems incredible from someone who had been mixing with socialists for years, but before 1917, Marxism was just one theory among many shaping the numerous movements opposed to capitalism.[29] Published in 1848, Karl Marx and Friedrich Engels' *Communist Manifesto* had finally found its moment. It spoke of history as a struggle between classes; in capitalism the workers who provided the labour were exploited by the minority class of capitalists who owned the means of production. It was time for the workers to throw off their chains and take power, forming a classless society in which production was decided according to human need rather than profit.

There were two revolutions in Russia in 1917. If the bridge experience is dated to the February Revolution—March 1917 in the modern calendar—it could have been one of the catalysts leading her to enrol at the Victorian Labor College in June. In the February Revolution, a series of strikes begun on International Women's Day shut down the Russian city of Petrograd and led to the abdication of the Tsar. A reformist Provisional Government came to power. When Katharine heard of these events, it would have brought to mind the Russians she met in 1908 whose dream was the overthrow of the Tsar.

As news reached Australia of the February Revolution, there was excitement in radical circles. The *Age* reported that on Sunday 25 March a group of Russians met on the banks of the Yarra under a red flag, rejoicing over the revolution.[30] Perhaps Katharine saw them there as she crossed Prince's Bridge, if not at the time of her omen then on another crossing. An Australian workers' newspaper declared: 'The Russian revolution, which has created such a wonderful sensation throughout the world, is literally a triumph for the countless number of noble men and women who for very many years have devoted every energy they possessed to the liberation of their glorious country'.[31]

Another influence on Katharine in this phase of her radicalism was the Industrial Workers of the World (IWW). Often known by the nickname the 'Wobblies', the IWW came out of the US labour movement and the first Australian group was formed in Sydney in 1907; a Melbourne group was formed in 1915.[32] The movement attracted those on the left disillusioned by the compromises the Australian Labor Party had made to win elections. The IWW opposed parliamentary politics and arbitration courts setting wages, and instead called for direct action, with all the workers uniting to seize control of their industry. Rather than dividing into unions according to different trades, the workers would unite across an entire industry and ultimately form One Big Union.[33] Opposed to militarism, the IWW was also protesting the war and twelve IWW leaders were arrested in Sydney in September 1916 and dubiously convicted of various offences, including arson and treason. Then, in December 1916, the federal government passed legislation banning the organisation. The prosecutions of IWW members stepped up in mid-1917, just as Katharine was radicalised.[34]

As Lesbia pulled Guido into the IWW circle, his theoretical interests seem to have turned to syndicalism, a theory which had shaped the movement.[35] 'Some of my friends', Katharine wrote, 'argued that syndicalism offered a more effective approach to the problems of industrial exploitation and poverty than guild socialism. I was myself more attracted to syndicalism'.[36] It was probably in the aftermath of the Bolshevik Revolution in November 1917 that she read the key syndicalist text, Georges Sorel's book *Reflections on Violence* (1908).[37] Sorel advocated workers staging a general strike to seize power in violent revolution.

The first term of the Victorian Labor College began at Unity Hall in the city on 9 July 1917. Guido Baracchi taught economics on Tuesday evenings from 8 p.m. to 9 p.m., giving a survey of different theories of how to emancipate the working class from 1750 to the present.[38] Later Guido was to remember that he had 'gone a fair way toward orthodox Marxism' in 1917, but he—and Katharine—may not have been as far along as they remembered.[39] The course did not culminate in Marxist theory, but instead offered several Marxist approaches as part of 'the dissenters'; this section was followed by more recent theories.[40] It is even likely that Guido didn't give his lecture on Marx and the dissenters at all that year. The last four weeks of the second term were cancelled so that everyone involved with the college could use their energy for the 'no' campaign in the second conscription referendum.[41] In December, Guido spoke not on Karl Marx but Georges Sorel's syndicalism at the Victorian Socialist Party's Sunday evening meeting.[42]

At the end of her life, remembering the architect of the revolution, Vladimir Lenin, Katharine wrote, 'Among my friends … there was excited and enthusiastic discussion about Lenin. Who is he? How had he won the soldiers, sailors, peasants and industrial workers to fight for the Russian revolution? Would socialism become practical politics with the establishment of the USSR?'[43] Katharine, Guido, and the other Australian radicals who would form the Communist Party of Australia in 1920 were inspired by the success of Russia's Bolsheviks in the second revolution of November 1917. However, the ideology of the Australian radicals wasn't settled yet. For several years they were still drawn to syndicalism and the IWW, which was re-created by Guido and others in 1918 as the International Industrial Workers to circumvent the IWW's illegality.[44] The IWW wanted power directly in the hands of the workers while the Bolsheviks believed temporary control by the revolutionaries was necessary 'to crush capitalist resistance' and 'confiscate capitalist property' before turning power over to the working class.[45] When historian Ian Turner interviewed Katharine in 1960, he commented that her 1919 pamphlet *The New Order* still showed the influence of syndicalism in its emphasis on industrial unionism and the strike. She agreed that she held a more syndicalist approach 'until the collapse of the Italian syndicates after the war', at which time she 'accepted the communist idea of the importance of political action'.[46] She seems to be referring to events in 1921, which dates her full conversion to communism later than her own official account.

Katharine's time at the college was a formal phase of her political education after years of eclectic personal reading. It put her in the midst of radical circles at a time of revolutionary urgency—the horrors of the war in Europe, the hope of a new order in Russia, and, at home, a government pushing for conscription and suppressing dissenters like the IWW.

SOMETIME IN 1917, Katharine and Edith had moved with a maid named Ethel to a 'dreary' two-storey house at 900 Malvern Road, still in Armadale. Katharine and her mother lived in shared anxiety for Alan at the front as they clashed over Katharine's bohemian and radical tendencies.[47] 'She was shocked to find that I had learnt to smoke while I was in England, and used to pull down blinds … for fear neighbours would see … Then, one day, when I had a frantic headache and no cigarettes, she trotted off and returned in triumph with a packet.'[48] They argued about sex education, conscription and communism. Though Edith sometimes asked, theatrically, how she came to have such a child, she began to accept that 'the old ways and ideas' did not work for Katharine.[49]

Katharine had spent all the money from the Hodder & Stoughton prize and she was now making a precarious living writing stories while also working on *Black Opal*. In a letter to Nettie in May she asked if she could delay paying rent for the Emerald cottage until the magazines had paid her the £12 they owed her.[50]

The effects of the war are felt in some of her stories of the time but rather sentimentally. Although the lightweight six-part serial, 'Granny Peace' (1917–1918), is set in the idyllic apple orchards of Sunny Creek, the romances and small intrigues of the Peace family and other locals are affected by anxiety for loved ones fighting at the front and the pressure on men to enlist. In December 1917's 'Danny Niel', the title character is a town drunk mistaken for Father Christmas by a little girl whose father has been killed in the war. Danny turns his life around in order to bring presents for the girl and her brother. It's a heart-warming story, probably written before October when the first of two deaths struck Katharine.

KATHARINE'S CLOSE FRIEND, Sumner Locke, was the first of the deaths. Sumner had married Corporal Henry Logan Elliott in Sydney at the end of 1916. It was a sudden marriage; the two had known each other when they were younger but had been close for just a few months. Less than two months after they married, Elliott—in Sumner's words her 'beautiful ten minutes husband'—left Sydney for the front.[51] In that time, Sumner had fallen pregnant. She went ahead with a trip she had already booked to the United States to gather experiences for a future novel and meet with her publisher.[52]

She came back to Australia in August and was admitted soon after to the Laurels Private Hospital, gravely ill with eclampsia. Her baby was ten days overdue when he was finally born on 17 October 1917. Late that night, Sumner's sister Lily sent a telegram to their other sisters in Victoria saying that 'Putty arrived this afternoon, splendid boy, eight pounds. Everything satisfactory'. Sumner was dead by the time the sisters received it the following morning.[53]

In a tribute to Sumner, Katharine quoted from Sumner's last letter to her. 'I'm a whole heap alone. And I don't like it… Since last week I've done a yarn and a war poem in bed, and that helps some … I've got big splendid hopes of my desert novel for next year.' Sumner counselled, 'Kathy, go slow! Run chickens and books but don't get downhearted dearest'. At the end of the letter was a note from Lily saying, 'We have laid her to rest among the gums and wildflowers of Illawarra, which she loved so much'.[54]

It was the first time a close friend of Katharine's had died. She wrote, 'The shock and grief of that announcement make it almost impossible to write. That sun-shiny personality not here any longer? Sumner not laughing and talking somewhere? It is unbelievable'.[55]

In November, Katharine wrote to newspapers as honorary secretary of the Sumner Locke Memorial, calling for donations from friends and admirers of Sumner's work to establish a permanent memorial.[56] Katharine's original idea 'was to plant an Australian tree on the bank of the Yarra, to form, perhaps, the opening of a memorial avenue to Australians who in their lifetime had contributed something of value to the art and literature of their country'.[57] However, it proved impossible and the eventual form the memorial took was the publication of a slim collection of Sumner's poetry in 1921. The proceeds from sales were used for the benefit of her son, Sumner Locke Elliott. He was being raised by his aunt and uncle and Katharine continued to send money from the fund until its closure in 1930.[58]

Katharine's 'ending' for Sumner in which Sumner introduced Katharine to her masterpiece, a son, had a strange fulfilment. Living much longer than his mother, Sumner Locke Elliott would go on to have the kind of career she dreamed of as the successful author of ten novels, acclaimed in both Australia and his adopted home of the United States. In a number of the characters he created he was to give 'fictional life to the mother he never knew, an act of creation based on his aunts' family memories and on a handful of letters, photographs, and memorabilia that survive'.[59]

ON 7 NOVEMBER 1917, just as the Bolshevik Revolution brought a communist government to power in Russia, prime minister Billy Hughes announced a second conscription referendum. Katharine remembered, 'I had no doubt by this time where I stood, and offered my services to the campaign directors'.[60]

Fifty years after the defeat of the conscription referenda, a committee set out to compile an honour roll of Victorian 'people and organisations active in the anti-conscription campaigns of 1916 and/or 1917'. An initial list was widely circulated in Victorian union and radical circles and additions, confirmations and corrections requested; it grew from 400 names to 700. Guido Baracchi was on it, as were Nettie and Vance Palmer. Louis Esson was raised as a 'possible' in one version. Yet Katharine Susannah Prichard was missing. She was not the only member of her circle notable by their absence—Christian Jollie Smith was nowhere to be found either. But given Katharine's high profile as a communist and a writer in the 1960s and her celebrity right back in

1917, it would be strange if she was heavily involved in the campaign and no-one consulted remembered it.[61]

Katharine was probably only involved in the last week or two of the campaign, spending the rest of the period in Pyramid Hill, a town in the goldfields, housekeeping for her brother Nigel at his request. Nigel's wife, Vera, had returned to her hometown of Geelong to give birth while, as one of the few doctors in the district, Nigel continued with his practice.[62] It seems an unlikely thing for Katharine to agree to do as a woman with egalitarian convictions, busy with writing and classes. Perhaps she felt a sense of family obligation; perhaps she wanted to escape her mother or Guido for a time.

Vera gave birth to a daughter on 23 November, Katharine's second niece, and it would have been some time after that before Vera returned to Pyramid Hill.[63] So it was probably from the isolation of Pyramid Hill that Katharine wrote a heartbroken unsent letter to Guido on 20 November, a double-sided page of which survives, sitting loosely in one of her notebooks.

> I've been reading some of your old letters today & I'm full to the brim with the spirit of them. A silly thing to do, but I longed so to read again some wonderful things you have said to me. I wonder do you still mean them … I say to myself—'he asked you to have faith' … Am I still to have faith? I mean that you are so indifferent, so careless of me.
>
> You say in some of these old letters—that there are only two things you ask of life—& one is that your life may not be 'devoid of me'—I wonder do you still mean that …
>
> I ask only those two things of life too. The first I have always been striving to—the second has grown with my love of you. And now I feel as if you were wanting to be 'devoid of' me. Why? … Is it just that with all the others to be seduced, I must be put to one side because I consent to be put there? I'm all middle-class female! If I went on a rampage & blacked your eyes for philandering with other women would you have more respect for me? I believe you would.[64]

Katharine returned to Melbourne and did what she could for the anti-conscription campaign. She wrote an article which a newspaper declined. Then she was asked to speak at an open-air meeting, and 'there was a dreadful scene with Mother', who felt like she was refusing to send help to Alan. As it turned out, she didn't speak that night; the meeting was 'broken up by a gang of hooligans and drunken soldiers'.[65] At a street meeting alongside Bill Earsman on 18 December 1917, she gave a speech titled, 'People of Australia, think for yourselves!' Her arguments against conscription were nationalistic and class-based. 'Members of the Government seem to think it a disgrace for people to declare themselves Australian above all things.' She called conscription, in this period of the war, 'anti-Australian', as the country was threatened by Japan and the goal of the conservative government was 'cheap labour and a spiritless working class; they are out after the bones of our industrial organizations, although they wear the sheep's-clothing of patriotism dyed the Imperial Purple'.[66]

It was only the second speech she had ever given, the first being the talk at the Primrose League in England. It wasn't reported by the newspapers or even remembered by the anti-conscription jubilee committee. And yet it was Katharine's most public act of radicalism so far and a harbinger of the role she was to adopt as an outspoken communist.

'As I was not an impressive speaker', she wrote, 'there were no more requests for me to address meetings'.[67] The referendum was just two days later, so the short amount of time is probably the real reason she wasn't asked to speak again. Yet her own sense of her lack of power as a speaker and her fear in the unsent letter that she was too middle class could have been felt in reaction to her rival, Lesbia. Guido wrote of Lesbia 'speaking against conscription night after night at street corners' until she was sent to hospital with heart problems, only for her to sneak out of the ward and 'break her silence the very next night from a soapbox'.[68] In activist circles there can be an implicit competitiveness over who is the most radical; Lesbia would have been difficult to beat.

On 13 December, a telegram came advising that Alan had been wounded in his left arm and back. He could still write, apparently, and the *Argus* reported that 'hope was entertained of his recovery'.[69] During that last week of conscription campaigning, Katharine prepared her speech full of worry for her brother.

The referendum was held on Thursday 20 December and to the surprise of many, conscription was defeated for a second time. That night,

Guido held a 'grand party'. Vance was there, and got so drunk that instead of returning to Emerald, he slept on Guido's bed with his boots still on.[70] It's unknown whether Katharine was at the party.

The day after the referendum, there was a knock on the door of Edith and Katharine's house.

> As [Mother] lay in bed, she heard me open the door and take the telegram from the small boy who brought it. There was no need to tell her what I read on that scrap of paper. Her broken cry told me she knew. I fell into her arms, pressed against the soft bosom that had been a place of comfort in many distresses. But there was no consolation for either of us now. Mother rolled about in the turbulence of her grief, distraught and moaning: 'Oh God, how can I bear it? My boy! My boy!'[71]

Alan had been wounded by a bomb on 2 December and transferred to No. 2 Casualty Clearing Station, Le Veau. Despite the initial hope of recovery, 'the injury to the spine had caused paralysis, followed by pneumonia' and he died on 12 December, nine days before Katharine and Edith received the second telegram.[72]

The breeze died down at sunset that day, the *Argus* reported on the same page as an article on Alan's death, and it was a humid, oppressive evening.[73] Just a few days before Christmas, Katharine and Edith were grieving in the summer heat, their scattered family hit by a second tragedy a decade after Tom's death.

'I liked Alan so much', wrote Hilda to Nettie when she heard the news. 'We grew up together, and had many experiences, good and bad, together, that his death was a terrible shock. It seemed one of those unnecessary catastrophes. For Kattie it will be terrible because she loves so intensely, and grieves so fiercely, that it is too much for her to bear.'[74]

Sometime later, Katharine or Edith wrote to Reay in London, seeking his help to arrange photographs of the grave. It was noted on Alan's military record, 'three photographs of grave sent … to Lieut. Col. W. T. Reay (for relatives)'.[75] Alan's effects were eventually put on board the *Barunga* to be sent back to Edith. However, the ship was torpedoed by a German submarine on 15 July 1918 and everything of his was lost at sea.[76]

17

Retreat

Emerald, Victoria, 1918

KATHARINE DIDN'T DEPICT the Great War directly in her fiction of the 1920s and 1930s. There are several returned soldiers—notably Greg, the shell-shocked husband in *Intimate Strangers* (1937), a significant psychological portrait of the lingering effects of the war—but that is all. She was not alone: 'It is as if a whole generation of writers by tacit agreement declined to incorporate the Great War into their imaginative fiction'.[1] Katharine and other Australian writers may not have had enough distance yet. The communities she wrote about in those years—the timber workers of *Working Bullocks* (1926), the cattle station in *Coonardoo* (1929), the touring troupe of *Haxby's Circus* (1930)—had a similar sense of timeless isolation from world events as the miners of Lightning Ridge in *Black Opal* (1921). She only came to write directly about the Great War late in her career in *Golden Miles* (1948), the second volume of the goldfields trilogy.

The protagonist of *Golden Miles*, Sally Gough, was born on 25 April like Katharine's mother, Edith. After Gallipoli, Sally's birthday is filled with 'sadness and mourning for her, and for hundreds of mothers throughout Australia'.[2] Sally has two sons in the war; one, Lal, is killed, and the other, Dick, is shattered by his experience. Sally's response to Lal's death echoes Katharine's response to Alan's death. 'But it was no earthly use to curse and wail: she must be calm, she told herself. She must think about this scourge which afflicted humanity: find out whether there was anything in what Charles O'Reilly, Dinny, and Tom were saying—that this war could be stopped, and the outbreak of future wars prevented.'[3] Sally moves from voting 'yes' in the first conscription referendum to 'no' in the second one; she also develops new sympathy for the convictions of her communist son, Tom.

Although set in the 1950s, Katharine's final novel, *Subtle Flame* (1967), also fictionalises aspects of Katharine's political conversion during the Great War. In a psychologically intriguing union, the protagonist, David Evans, has elements not only of Katharine but also of her father, Tom, and her lover, Reay. Unsubtly echoing Reay's position at the *Herald* and the *Weekly Times*, David is the editor and general manager of the *Daily Dispatch* and the *Weekly Budget*. Like Tom Prichard, David has two daughters and two sons—one of the daughters a committed political activist, the other quite conventional; one son a doctor and the other dying in a futile war. The novel begins with David learning of the death of that son, Rob, in the Korean War. It causes such a crisis of his worldview that he resigns from his job. On a retreat to read and think in a shack in the bush, he is converted to the cause of peace.

> He was simply a man who had become conscious of a colossal confidence trick worked on the people: a sane man, in his time, concerned to look squarely at his own life; and the lives of men and women who made the population of this country. They had become like a mob of sheep rounded up by the press, the churches and big business, which doped and betrayed them to the shambles of war.[4]

David embarks on a one-man crusade to stir the apathetic masses to action. His activist daughter, Myff, guides him into using his journalistic skills for good: 'He could use that "brilliant ironical style" of his more effectively. Not find himself limited and leg-ironed by the policy of a newspaper. He would make a name for himself as an independent writer of courage: turn out special articles exposing political skulduggery, religious hypocrisy, economic chicanery'.[5] In fiction Katharine found a chance to give her father another chapter, erasing his suicide and redeeming him politically.

In life, Katharine had already radicalised before Alan's death. Yet coming in the midst of that intense conversion, Alan's death became a crucial part of it. The Russian revolutions had given her hope for a better society; Alan's death made her feel just how appalling the present one was. In 1918 she retreated to the cottage in the bush of Emerald to finish writing *Black Opal,* to read Karl Marx, and to 'absorb some of the vigour and beauty of the earth as an anodyne to realization of the woes of the world'.[6]

VANCE PALMER'S UNEXPECTED reaction to the anti-conscription victory was to announce that he was enlisting. Later, Vance suggested that if he hadn't enlisted, he'd have been left feeling he'd missed out on something of great significance.[7] On 7 January 1918, Nettie recorded in her diary that Katharine visited them in Emerald.

> She had come up to persuade V not to enlist & she showed him some of her brother Alan's letters … Says 'no man can hope to get through it'. Also gravest belief that Australians have not only the most dangerous work but the heaviest. None of these sufficient reasons to keep a man from enlisting! Katharine very sweet & kind: also very broken down about her brother. She wouldn't stay.[8]

With Vance enlisting the Palmers would be moving out of the cottage—which the owner had also put up for sale—and were on the lookout for someone to take over the lease.

Guido was meant to visit the Palmers at midday on Thursday 17 January. Vance walked to the railway station to meet him, but he wasn't there. Instead, he'd sent a note dated Tuesday saying he would be delayed as he was 'committing a rash & extreme act' at 2 a.m. on Thursday morning in Upwey.[9] The Palmers knew what he meant; Upwey was where their mutual friend, Reverend Frederick Sinclaire, minister of the Free Religious Fellowship, lived. 'Passed a horrid afternoon', Nettie wrote in her diary, 'wondering precisely who was his wife'.[10] Was Nettie upset that Guido hadn't married Katharine, or was she worrying that he might have? The 2 a.m. ceremony adds to the bizarreness of the marriage.[11]

Guido walked 11 kilometres from Upwey and arrived at the Palmers' cottage at six o'clock in the evening without his new wife, who'd already returned to Melbourne. She was Kathleen Tobin—known as Katrina or Toby—and working as a pantomime chorister. The *Labor Call* newspaper reported, derisively: 'Guido Baracchi, the plutocratic socialist … has acquired a wife in the pleasing person of Katrina Tobin, a decorative feature of the *Aladdin* panto chorus'.[12]

Guido returned to Melbourne the next day, Friday, on an evening train; Katharine arrived soon after, narrowly missing him. She seemed frenzied to Nettie, full of thoughts about the Wobblies after talking to Percy Laidler at Andrade's Bookshop. On Saturday, Nettie and Katharine walked into town in the hot afternoon; when they returned, Katharine refused to rest. She was finally 'finished by an atrocious headache (back of head) & collapsed till evening. Sat outside & K said her illness had decided her that she needed a rest in the country & would take the house & perhaps buy it. Talked plans of her novels & stories'.[13]

Nettie didn't connect Guido's impulsive marriage to Katharine's collapse, but it would have been a shocking thing for Katharine to learn when she arrived. Marriage had seemed so far from Guido's intentions when she was with him. It was only two months earlier that she'd written the unsent letter asking if she should still have faith in him. She had her definitive answer now.

Katharine and Nettie—as well as everyone else—would have been wondering why Guido married Toby. Betty Roland, Guido's lover, wondered years later, and actually asked him; it was then she said he gave the candid answer that Toby would only go to bed with him if he did.[14]

On 25 January, Katharine moved in with a vanload of furniture and the Palmers moved out to live with Nettie's aunt.[15]

THE EMERALD COTTAGE—home to the Essons and then the Palmers—was now Katharine's.

It was a train ride of three hours from the city to Emerald, the 46-kilometre journey made slower by a transfer to a narrow-gauge line at Fern Tree Gully and the steep climb through dense ferns from there to Emerald.[16] The village had 'less than thirty houses, a few stores, a wine bar, a blacksmith, and a police station'.[17] Two kilometres down the road, the cottage stood at the end of a driveway of wattles on 8 hectares of bush. The land had been cleared by a pioneer family, the Charmans, forty years earlier, but the trees had regrown and the eucalypts were now more than 7 metres high. The cottage had been built in 1908 for Rose Charman and even though she had only lived in it less than a year before she married and moved out, it's still known by her name today. 'It had a sitting room, kitchen, two bedrooms and a makeshift laundry on the back verandah. A primitive wood stove cooked the food and boiled the water for bathing.'[18]

David's retreat to the bush in *Subtle Flame* after the death of his son in the war seems to reflect Katharine's quiet months in Emerald. 'At night, sprawled before a log fire', he read poems and political pamphlets and spent time thinking 'as he had never done before. The trouble and pain of the last few months brushed aside, still lurked at the back of his mind'.[19]

EDITH DIDN'T LIKE Katharine living in Emerald alone and sometimes came to stay with her for a week at a time.[20] Katharine remembered the two of them sitting by the fire one cold evening, Edith working on a lace cushion while Katharine read Karl Marx's *Capital.* Edith told her to put down that 'dry old book' and give her head a rest. It wasn't dry at all, Katharine replied and read her an excerpt about working conditions for women and children in English mines and factories. Her mother's sewing stopped and she said, 'I'd no idea there was ever such a terrible state of things'.[21]

In April, Edith inherited Alan's estate valued at £1354, half of it real estate and the other half a life-insurance payout.[22] With the money, Edith bought the Emerald cottage in July, perhaps as an inducement for Katharine to remain in Victoria with her rather than returning to London.[23]

Nettie came to stay with Katharine at Emerald in September. Katharine was 'sweating and groaning under the last chapters of her novel [*Black Opal*] which will have to be two volumes long. I do my whole duty by avoiding her all day long, though we talk by the fire at night'.[24]

In a 1961 letter to Nettie's younger daughter, Helen, Katharine related an incident which she dated to about 1918:

> It happened soon after I returned from England. I had written some stray verses, *The Earth Lover & Other Verses* & not knowing what to think of them sent them to Hilda & Louis. They passed them to Vance & Nettie. None of them were impressed by the verse—in fact rather damning. So I put them aside.
>
> When I went to see Nettie & Vance at Emerald, there was [Bernard] O'Dowd over by the mantelpiece & you & Aileen—lovely children—Aileen about three, & you just toddling—evidently brought up to regard O'Dowd & poets generally with veneration.
>
> Aileen exclaimed eagerly, 'Katharine poet? Katharine poet?'
>
> I said (under the disapproval of my critics), 'No, Katharine not poet'!
>
> Aileen burst into tears & c[oul]d not be consoled until she answered that 'Katharine might be a poet someday'.
>
> I remember that lovely little face, all tears, & the sunshiny smiles breaking through.[25]

Despite Katharine's success as a fiction writer, she craved acclaim for her poetry, something neither the Palmers nor Essons could honestly offer. When she said she wasn't a poet, the Palmers and their friend Bernard O'Dowd probably thought she was just being perceptive about where her literary gifts didn't lie.

The Earth Lover and Other Verses was eventually published in 1932 in a limited edition of seventy-five copies. She dedicated it to Hugo, obscuring the origins of the poems, many of which developed out of her notebooks of anguish over Guido, replete with references to the ti-trees of January 1916. The collection follows an arc, beginning with several poems professing joy in 'the beloved' only for it to turn to heartbreak. In 'Love Philtre' she described a love potion she would brew with 'all her wit and witchcraft' which would either win him over or demonstrate for sure that he was untrue. She addressed the 'whilom' (that is, former) lover in another poem. It was a farewell:

> I have washed your feet with my tears,
> my love;
> and dried them with my hair.
>
> But you are not Jesus, my love,
> you are only my love;
> and I wonder if ever a god above,
> or anywhere on the earth, my love,
> would have failed to notice these things
> and gone on his way whistling rag-time.[26]

The poem after this is 'For Alan', evoking her ongoing grief at her brother's death—'No fruits are sweet now / The flowers are done'. Yet the second stanza of the short poem tempers the present struggle with a sustaining hope:

> My way is like this way
>   Which goes through the hills—
> A rough path—it seems to ascend, ascend:
>   But I know it will come to the sea,
> And long day end.

The Earth Lover and Other Verses is more strongly felt than *Clovelly Verses* (1913) and has some striking imagery and moments of illumination. Katharine was developing as a poet, even if she had not come far enough to impress the Palmers or the Essons. It seems she was so sensitive about her poetry that their lack of enthusiasm was a major reason she stopped writing it.

KATHARINE HAD HER life worked out in 1918. Now her brother was dead, her mother needed her more and she gave up her plans to return to London. She probably expected things to continue as they were for years to come, her time split between her mother's house in suburban

Melbourne where she had a workroom with a piano, and the rustic Emerald cottage she loved. She had found time and space to write. She could stay connected to the literary and political bustle of Melbourne while maintaining a necessary distance from it in Emerald.

But just as things seemed to have settled into this pattern, Hugo was writing to her from Egypt. They now had a shared grief in the deaths of their brothers in the war. His letters were growing more passionate and urgent. He wasn't going to leave her alone. In September, he cabled to tell her he was coming to see her.[27]

18

Armistice

Emerald and Melbourne, 1918–1919

After being part of the Allied forces capturing Jerusalem in December 1917, Hugo's health was bad for months and eventually the AIF sent him back to Australia to recover and help recruitment.[1] He left Cairo on 4 September 1918 aboard the *Suffolk*, bound for Melbourne. 'Cable followed cable', wrote Katharine, 'from every port on his journey'.[2] He arrived in Melbourne on 17 October and came to see her at her mother's house in Armadale. 'I still felt afraid to commit myself where Hugo was concerned. But when … he stood at the foot of the stairs, a tall, masterful figure in uniform—returned from the maelstrom of war—my irresolution vanished. He held out his arms, and I walked down the stairs into them.'[3]

He had decided he wanted to marry Katharine and he came to her at just the moment she was willing to be wooed. A few ecstatic weeks of courtship followed. She would keep looking back on them for the rest of her life. 'He was really a deliriously exciting and romantic lover … Such a gallant, striking figure he made as he strode through the streets. If we dined in town, I could hear the whispers going round, "Throssell, VC", and the crowds collected to cheer as we passed.'[4] A mythology had grown up around him and other Victoria Cross recipients as exemplars of the Anzac hero. The *Age* reported that year that he was 'seven feet in height' and 'holds the distinction of being the tallest man in the Australian army' when he was actually 5 feet 10 inches or 178 centimetres.[5]

If Katharine's irresolution 'vanished' the instant she saw him, she still felt there were obstacles to their marriage—politics being one. 'I told Hugo my political beliefs and he accepted them with me.'[6] It was a stunning conversion for the son of a conservative politician but he was an impulsive man in love with Katharine and ready to be excited about whatever she was excited about. It was common enough to change religious denominations in order to marry; he could have seen a political conversion as an analogous compromise. Having lived through so much horror, Katharine's claims of war-profiteering and the lives lost in the interests of capitalists must have rung true for him.

Katharine's other obstacle was the promise she'd made to Reay that she would never marry. She took seriously his threat to shoot himself. When she told Hugo about it, he refused to accept it as a reason and told her he'd 'kidnap' her if he needed to.[7] He might have been the first person she'd told about Reay's manipulative threat. It was three years since she'd seen Reay and in that time she had distanced herself from him emotionally and sexually with Guido and now Hugo. Katharine and Hugo decided they would marry once the war had finished. She sent Reay a telegram to tell him. 'There was no disastrous repercussion … a promise was broken, but no fatal shot fired.'[8] She was finally free of 'the vines of a possessive passion' that had bound her for a decade.[9]

After many Allied victories over the Central Powers through October, in November there were rumours an armistice was about to be signed. In Victoria on Monday 11 November 'the feeling that the great news was near at hand pervaded all sections of the community and a strong desire to be ready to celebrate in a fitting manner was evident'. Shops were selling as many flags and as much ribbon as they could stock. Then, in the evening, 'the glad news that the German delegation had signed the armistice terms spread like wildfire. It reached the country almost as quickly as the more distant suburbs, and it kindled a blaze of feeling such as the State has never before known. Everywhere there was joy—deep unrestrained heartfelt joy'.[10]

Katharine and Hugo had spent the day at Emerald 'and were walking to the train at twilight, when flares lit up the distant hills'.

> Hugo gazed at them, a strange expression on his face. So moved and silent, he was, as flare after flare cast a yellow light across the sky ... His arms folded round me. 'The war's over', he said. 'Those are armistice rockets. We can be married now. I won't have to go away again.'[11]

They told Edith they were marrying. She was thrilled but also horrified by Katharine's insistence she didn't want a church wedding. 'I warned him and Mother that I could be married at the Registrar's office, or not at all.' When Edith protested, Katharine threatened to live with him without being married at all. 'Terrified' Katharine would follow through with that, Edith said she would be content with a registry wedding.[12]

SOON AFTER HER engagement, Katharine finished writing *Black Opal.*[13] The machinations of Sophie's complex love-life continue to the end of *Black Opal.* She is still in love with the station heir, Arthur Henty, even though he is now married. She decides to marry the devoted, reliable opal miner, Potch, saying to him that she was afraid of the power of her love for Arthur 'and there's no future that way. With you there is a future ... You know I do care for you too, Potch dear, and I want to have the sort of life that keeps a woman faithful ... to mend your clothes [and] cook your meals'.[14] Returning to the couple after their marriage, Katharine wrote, 'The days had been long and peaceful since they were living together ... She believed her life had found its haven; that if she kept in tune with the fundamentals of love and service, she could maintain a consciousness of peace and rightness with the world'.[15] Yet there is a further twist. Arthur comes to Sophie, desperate, and begs her to run away with him. When she refuses, he shoots himself. In a tribute to Arthur, Sophie rides his horse to his funeral. Leaving the cemetery, she starts singing for the first time since she lost her voice in America. 'The notes of Sophie's singing, with its undying tenderness triumphing over life and death, flowed.' The novel ends with Sophie and Potch riding through Lightning Ridge. 'In everybody's mind was the enthusiasm of a new endeavour.'[16] The nature of the 'new endeavour' is vague in the novel; it seems to be spilling over from Katharine's new-found sense of political purpose in her own life.

The original manuscript—now lost—was the length of two standard novels at about 160,000 words. She felt confident about it. When, in 1919, a friend compared her to Jack London and Walt Whitman, she didn't reject the comparison but wrote that it would only be true on the basis of the unpublished *Black Opal.*[17] She submitted the manuscript to Hodder & Stoughton in London, the publisher of *The Pioneers* (1915). They wrote back in mid-1919, wanting her to drastically cut the length by 50,000 words and alter two of the main characters. 'I told them to "go to hell"—or words to that effect.' Yet she then realised that the 'propaganda would go further' if she made the cut, even if the novel 'loses from a literary point of view'.[18] Despite partially following Hodder & Stoughton's advice, she still resolved to never send it or any other manuscript to them, the publisher who had made her famous. The novel would eventually find another British publisher, Heinemann, appearing at the end of 1921, five years after her second novel, *Windlestraws.*

ANOTHER REFRACTION OF Katharine and Hugo's marriage is found in her play, *Bid Me to Love,* written in 1927 but only produced and published posthumously in the 1970s. Ric Throssell notes that the setting 'was unmistakably the verandah at Greenmount' where Katharine and Hugo were living in the 1920s.[19] In the play, the husband, Greg, tells his wife, Louise, 'Of all the trophies I ever won for running, swimming or boxing, I'm proudest of you, darling. Did it in record time too, didn't I?'[20] In *Child of the Hurricane,* Katharine depicted only her wedding as unconventional, giving no hint the terms of the marriage itself were also unconventional. In *Bid Me to Love*, Louise discusses her marriage with an old flame who happens to be visiting, a writer named Woodbridge.

> LOUISE: When we were married, I said to Greg: 'If I don't like it, married life, don't expect me to stick it, will you? And if you don't like it, I won't expect you to stick it, either'.
>
> WOODBRIDGE: Not a point of view he was accustomed to, I should think.
>
> LOUISE: Greg has been a very well brought up young man. It was *rather* a shock to him, but—

WOODBRIDGE: He got used to it.

LOUISE: I believe really, the success of our marriage has been due to … a sense of its impermanence. *(Frowning slightly)* I've said: 'If ever there's anyone you care for more than me, Greg, I'll make way. We'll be good friends. Only tell me.'[21]

Louise goes on to tell Woodbridge that 'physical fidelity doesn't mean as much to me as psychological fidelity'.[22] Even though these are characters in a play, it's possible there's more insight into Katharine and Hugo's marriage in *Bid Me to Love*, written in the midst of it, than in the ostensibly autobiographical account in *Child of the Hurricane,* written when Hugo was long dead and the years of their marriage had become an idyll in Katharine's own mythology.

ON 4 DECEMBER 1918, Katharine's thirty-fifth birthday, she and Hugo publicly announced their engagement. One columnist commented:

> Despite his experience of the horrors of war on Gallipoli and in Jerusalem, Capt. Throssell does not take either life or himself too seriously, and if there is any truth in the theory that those marriages are happiest in which the parties are of opposite temperaments, this particular match should prove a conspicuous success, for Miss Prichard is earnest and rather serious-minded.[23]

Making a slightly different point about their compatibility, Guido's partner Betty Roland would ask years later how Katharine came to marry a 'swarthy' 'virile' war hero, when they had so little in common.[24] If Betty had known Katharine better—or her fiction—she might have understood that Hugo was the kind of macho, outdoorsman Katharine was attracted to; his antecedent was Alfred 'Redbeard' Quin, whom she had a crush on in 1906 at Tarella Station.

Katharine would always insist, though, that she and Hugo also had an intellectual connection. In 1950 she wrote to her son Ric:

> My Jimmy had a wonderful brain, that was never properly appreciated by his family, or even given a chance when he was young.

> Everybody seemed to live in the shadow of the old man [Hugo's father, George Throssell]. Jim could have been & done anything, as far as his mental ability was concerned, I'm convinced. But they all treated him as a good sport & a playboy. Damn them! Never understood his great qualities. He'd never have married your mother if he hadn't appreciated the intellectual things of life. He did: we had great times reading & discussing books, & always his points of view showed a clear & rigorous brain, capable of sound judgement.[25]

In Katharine's mind, she saw a side of Hugo no-one else recognised.

THE DAY AFTER the announcement, Hugo left on the train for Perth to spend a month with family. He and Katharine had been together for just six weeks. Asked about his future movements, he 'said that after his visit to his old home in Western Australia he would probably return and settle in Victoria'.[26]

In his first week in Perth, he was sent to the Army General Hospital in Fremantle for a medical assessment. The malarial symptoms had returned the previous month; he was suffering shivering fits and heavy sweats. The doctors declared him permanently unfit for general service and granted him a 50 per cent disability pension on the basis of his malaria, with the expectation that he would be fully recovered in a year. The part-pension was to begin after his discharge on 13 February.[27]

'Out of work', Hugo declared to a reporter, 'but never so pleased to lose a job in my life'. The question of employment—something at thirty-four he had yet to properly resolve—was weighing on his mind. While returning from the front in September, a repatriation form asked what occupation he desired to follow after discharge. He responded, 'Undecided'.[28] He was still on that voyage when he was encouraged to stand as an independent candidate for the federal by-election in the seat of Swan.[29] His nomination was handed in on the last morning, only to be apparently withdrawn ten minutes before the deadline.[30] He was a celebrity son of a politician, beloved by the merchant and pastoralist classes he had been born into and yet also, as a war hero, by the working class. Despite his lack of interest in politics, he might have won the by-election.

While he was in Perth, he was offered a job as the soldier's representative on the board of the land settlement scheme for soldiers, a full-time position paying a reasonable salary of £300 per year. The scheme granted land and loans to returned soldiers to set themselves up in farming. Hugo's job would involve assessing soldiers' applications and recommending how much the state-owned Agricultural Bank should loan successful applicants.[31] He had accepted the job by the time he left Perth on 16 January 1919.[32] There's no record of the long-distance negotiations with Katharine, if there were any. According to Nettie, he had only taken the job for a year, which may have made Katharine feel able to leave her mother without any sons or daughters in Melbourne. Katharine 'approves of this job a good deal', Nettie wrote, 'because Jimmy does know land & he'll do his best for the soldiers'.[33]

Hugo and Katharine would have seemed to be setting themselves up for a sound financial position, the new job supplemented by the £80 part-pension, earnings from his family's estate, and Katharine's income as a writer. However, Hugo was still carrying a debt of at least £1000 from his unsuccessful years of farming. 'After the war', Katharine wrote to the Repatriation Commission years later, 'he was left with obligations on his own and his brother's farm to meet, and tried desperately, in many ways, to fulfil them'.[34]

HUGO ARRIVED BACK in Melbourne on 22 January 1919. He had less than a week to prepare for the wedding and he only bought Katharine's ring on the day itself from a jeweller on Collins Street, the same street as the registry office.[35]

Katharine and Hugo were married on 28 January 1919, the day Victoria and New South Wales were declared infected with Spanish influenza. The pandemic had been spreading around the world since the middle of 1918, but until now Australians had been living normally. The day before had been the Foundation Day public holiday—as Australia Day was then known—and in Melbourne, many spent the day 'at the Australian Natives' Association fete, in the fern gullies or hills, at the races or by the sea ... In all the parks and gardens round the city and suburbs youngsters and their guardians frolicked to their hearts' content'.[36] At 4.30 p.m. on the day of Hugo and Katharine's wedding, after autopsy results showed the disease had reached Melbourne, Victoria was declared infected and traffic into South Australia, a state not yet infected, was stopped. All theatres and schools in Melbourne were closed.[37] The epidemic killed about fifteen thousand Australians over the next six months—half of them aged in their twenties and thirties.[38]

A newspaper article from the period reported that registry marriages cost £2 4s 6d and 'the ceremony can be performed in twenty minutes, provided everything is in order, without fuss or ostentation. These unceremonious weddings are becoming increasingly popular'.[39] The witnesses were Katharine's brother, Nigel, her mother, Edith, and Hugo's sister and brother-in-law, Ada and Frederick Constable. Katharine still gave her occupation as 'journalist', three years since she had worked as one. It was probably Hugo who gave her age as thirty-four, matching his. Katharine wrote decades later, 'My husband objected to me being born a few months before he was, & always insisted that we were the same age. Because I was born in December, he declared I had no right to claim a year more than he had. So the mistake in my date arose, I suppose'.[40] There are still sources which give the year of her birth as 1884 rather than 1883.

They held a small reception at Edith's house in Armadale. 'Aunt Lil decked the house with branches of magnolia from her garden … The perfume of the big moon-white blooms was everywhere.' Katharine's friend, composer Henry Tate, 'played the suite he had composed in honour of my marriage'.[41] It's not recorded who made speeches. Possibly Nigel, the conservative doctor, made one; he and Katharine never understood each other but he would have approved of her marriage. He might have joked, seriously, about Hugo being a good influence on Katharine, straightening out the strange ideas which had filled her head during the war.

Edith gave Katharine the deeds to the Emerald cottage as a wedding gift. The transfer officially occurred on 28 February, during the couple's honeymoon.[42] Nigel and Beatrice do not seem to have received anything from Alan's estate. Both of them were financially stable; perhaps Edith had heard that Hugo was carrying debt from his farm and wanted to provide Katharine with some security.

On the day of the wedding, Nettie was writing to Vance, who was still serving with the AIF in Britain. 'Katharine's marriage is taking place just about this minute … I think she & Jimmy Throssell are going to be happy … Katharine's married life shows signs of being more orderly & better "found" than she thought.'[43] Nettie had a cold and, fearing the influenza outbreak, was staying home that Tuesday rather than heading into the city, as planned, for something unspecified—possibly Katharine's wedding.

After the reception, Katharine and Hugo 'drove away into the hills'.[44]

KATHARINE AND HUGO's honeymoon in Emerald lasted most of February. The single surviving memento is a grocery receipt from the Emerald Corner Store, dated 1 February 1919. Their honeymoon fare was simple: bread, butter, rice, curry powder, apples, and Beefine ('the original fluid beef', an advertisement from the time proclaimed, is 'more economical than meat' and 'makes delightful sandwiches in a moment'). Hugo kept it in his scrapbook, perhaps by chance or perhaps because it was one of the first documents to bear the name of the new 'Mrs Throssell'.[45]

'She is never Mrs Hugo Throssell', wrote Betty Roland, 'always Katharine Susannah Prichard, poet, playwright, novelist … never a mere wife. It must be very difficult for him'.[46] Yet Betty was wrong; after her marriage, Katharine went by the name 'Mrs Hugo Throssell' socially and even had a calling card with the name on it.[47] She maintained her maiden name only as her literary identity. Even though the Freewoman Discussion Circle would have encouraged her to keep her own name in every sphere of life, gender issues had long been secondary for Katharine. As if to compensate for the radical political position Hugo took to marry her, she embraced a degree of conventional domesticity in her marriage and would be 'as proud of her cupboards of jams and preserves as any good farmer's wife'.[48]

Katharine and Hugo would have been glad to be out of the influenza-ridden city, but after days of hot temperatures, bushfires broke out around Emerald and were at their worst on 2 February. 'Several dwellings had narrow escapes from destruction.'[49] For Katharine and Hugo, the fires were 'the only disturbing element of the honeymoon', a newspaper reported. The fires 'raged around with fierce and frightening intensity. Trees fell, and the wicked cracklings caused by the leaping flames were only too much in evidence'.[50]

Sixteen years earlier, Katharine had written 'Bush Fires', the winning entry in the *New Idea* love story competition. In that story, a stockman named Angus was lying drunk in a hut in the bush in the midst of fires when his estranged lover, Kath'rin', came riding in to rescue him. Reunited, they embrace and, even though the fires will soon kill them, 'life seemed all fair now—a flower-strewn meadow, sunlit, winding tranquilly into Eternity'.[51] The deaths aside, elements of Katharine and Hugo's honeymoon—idyllic love in a hut in the bush in the midst of fire—were a neatly literal fulfilment of the naïve love story she'd written as a teenager. The success of that story had encouraged her at a critical point and made her resolve that 'I must know more about bushfires, love, and the country beyond our ranges'.[52] As it turned out, she learnt of the three elements in reverse order, finally completing them with her experience of a bushfire on her honeymoon.

ON 28 FEBRUARY 1919, Nettie and Christian came to say goodbye to Katharine at her mother's house. Quarantine permits had been granted and a berth had opened up on a ship and so Katharine and Hugo were leaving for Western Australia sooner than expected. 'We found Katharine in her study', wrote Nettie

> ... tearing up mounds of old letters & she made us stay while she tore & tore & chattered. She seems well & rested & also quite comfortably mistress of her fate—and charming & young too, of course. When she took me to her room & showed me half-packed trunks of trousseaux things—sets of things sent her by her Ceylon sister, prodigiously beautiful & others made by her relatives here—I was astounded to find myself suddenly envious to the point of passion![53]

The letters Katharine tore up probably included those from Reay and Guido; she was making a new start.

On 3 March, Katharine and Hugo left Melbourne on board the *Somali*.[54] Katharine probably still expected she would be coming back one day to live in her home city. She never did; she would only ever return to Melbourne as a visitor.

She is rarely remembered as a Melbourne writer, despite living there for much of her early life. One reason is that she only ever wrote about the city in her final, largely unread novel, *Subtle Flame* (1967). She described writing *Subtle Flame* as if it were a literal trip to Melbourne: 'For the setting of this story I left my spiritual home in the West, and went to Melbourne and the Dandenong Ranges, well known to me as a girl'.[55] Despite calling Western Australia her 'spiritual home', the fond way Katharine evoked the Melbourne of her youth in the novel suggests it also had some claim to that title. Critic Jack Beasley notes that even though the novel is ostensibly set in the 1950s, the Melbourne it depicts is that of a much earlier period.[56] As the main character, David, forsakes his comfortable existence to embark on an idealistic campaign for peace, 'A stirring of pride and love for the city, and all that it held of human energy, swept him'.

> Thought of the city's history surged. He could see it as a ramshackle settlement of canvas and wattle and daub huts during the early days of pioneering and the gold rush, when bullock waggons and horse-drawn drays ploughed the streets: chase its growth though boisterous prosperity of the land boom, the chaos of economic collapse: follow its gradual resurrection and the renaissance of civic pride, until now Melbourne was being advertised to tourists as 'The Queen City of the South': a modern city vaunting its order, cleanliness and culture, its university, National Gallery, public libraries, hospitals and theatres, tree-planted streets and gardens.[57]

Katharine's Melbourne years took her from Queen Victoria's jubilee in 1887 to Armistice in 1918. Her life would have been very different if she had grown up in Launceston or Levuka. As significant as stints in the outback and London were to Katharine's development, it was Melbourne and its people that shaped her more than any other place. There were her parents, old Melburnians, pioneers who brought her up with some of the optimism of the Marvellous Melbourne boom days they had known in their childhood and youth. With the new century, Katharine came of age in a city with a sense of its place in history, the capital of a new nation at work defining what it meant to be Australian. Conversely, the depression which clung to Tom through the 1890s and beyond reflected the long economic gloom of the city itself. Then there was her ambitious circle of school friends, Hilda, Nettie and Christian, all of them breaking through gender barriers; she was to keep up friendships with them for the rest of their lives. As disappointed as Katharine was by her lack of a degree, the educational opportunities she did have were crucial: the influence of the poet principal, JB O'Hara, at South Melbourne College, the evening classes with Walter Murdoch at Melbourne University, and the things she learned as the first student of the Victorian Labor College. She also furthered her literary formation informally at the Victorian Public Library, Cole's Book Arcade, the Australian Literature Society, and the Melbourne Literary Society. Significantly, Melbourne gave her Colonel WT Reay and then Guido Baracchi, the older man and the younger man who helped her shift, respectively, from the conservatism of her parents to nationalistic reformism and then to the radical ideology of syndicalism and the foundations for communism.

Katharine was formed in Melbourne, and while she was there she was the student or mentee. When she arrived in Western Australia, she shook that off and right from the beginning assumed the role of political and literary sage. She was thirty-five years old, the author of a new novel she knew would cement her literary reputation, the wife of a war hero, and a syndicalist-communist with all the zeal of a new convert, preparing to publicly declare herself. She was ready to begin a new season of her life.

IT SEEMED, UNBELIEVABLY, after so many tragedies, that Katharine had found peace. In September 1919, she wrote to Nettie from her new home in Greenmount in Perth's Darling Ranges:

> I never thought life could be as good as it is. Jim is so unbelievably thoughtful, devout & adorable in all the little everyday ways.
>
> I'm surer every day of the rightness of having married him. He is the best thing that could have possibly happened to a lone literary female. I really think I've been happy lately for the first time in my life ...

> I didn't think it could ever happen to me. The Furies had chased me so far & so hard. And now this tranquil back water where I just live & am afraid something may happen!
>
> The only way with happiness, it seems to me, is not to seek to hold it, not to peer at it too closely—& to be very humble about it and try to be working on it—by being willing to sacrifice even it to the great objective values.[58]

Katharine was aware of living temporarily in a happy ending like she had given Deidre and Davey in *The Pioneers* and Sophie and Potch in *Black Opal.* But she also knew that happy endings could only be found in books, where the author could stop the story at just the right point.

PART 3

MRS THROSSELL, 1919–1933

19

The New Order

Greenmount, 1919–1921

When Katharine and Hugo arrived in the port of Fremantle on 11 March 1919 aboard the *Somali*, they'd been married six weeks. Perth's *Daily News* noted their arrival; Hugo was a Western Australian celebrity and needed no introduction while Mrs Throssell was described as 'a well-known writer and daughter of the late TH Prichard, editor of the *Mining Standard*'.[1]

There were 320,000 people living in Western Australia in 1919, half of them in the metropolitan area.[2] A tourist book from 1914 claimed that 'small and youthful' Perth was 'fast becoming a well-built city', up to date with its electric light, and electric tram cars.[3] Yet two years later a soldier from New South Wales on his way to the front wrote, 'Perth is a place curiously behind the times. It is not very large, poor in public buildings [and] peopled with extremely nice citizens …'[4] Katharine had only briefly visited Perth before for stopovers on voyages home from London to Melbourne. Having lived in London and Melbourne, it seemed a 'backwater' to her.

Hugo and Katharine rented a house called 'Wandu' in Greenmount, 25 kilometres east of the city in the Darling Ranges. In a letter to Nettie Palmer, Katharine gave her address as 'House of the White Gums, On the Green Mountain'.[5] Wandu was a 'ramshackle' eight-bedroom bungalow built in 1902, and described in 1919 as having 'bath room, tanks, stables, and tennis court, 22 acres ground, including 8 acres orchard and vineyard'.[6] Katharine wrote that there was 'a wild garden screening us off from the road. We lived in only two or three rooms, and on hot summer evenings disported ourselves like Adam and Eve in the garden'.[7]

Katharine's new life in 1919 was happy and busy. Hugo wanted her to hire a maid, but she was reluctant, 'not wanting to be an employer of labour', while also aware that there were people looking for jobs. 'So far I've done all the housework, cooking etc', she wrote to Nettie, as well as milking the cows. She hadn't milked before and she found it 'a most exacting business'; she sung arias in an attempt to 'beguile' the cows.[8]

The artist Tom Roberts visited their house on 5 December 1919 during a stopover; he was on a ship from London for his first trip back to Melbourne for years. Roberts had volunteered as an orderly at the London hospital where Hugo recovered from meningitis in 1915; he had been assigned to Hugo as a 'batman' and the two became good friends. Roberts' account of his visit gives a glimpse of the Throssells' life at Wandu:

> [A] white gate & brushed against the shrubs & silver wattle of the wild garden Mrs Throssell got the key & opened up the house & I watched the VC feed the ducks & fowls, milk the cow …
>
> We all helped the supper out the verandah from the kitchen through a passage from the hall. Kerosene lamps—one a hurricane. Cold roast duck salad with a dressing, thick butter & cream & fruits. Jasmine climbing up the verandah & pomegranate red flowers learning over to us, leaving a gap looking through towards the valley & distant hills. To go outside was to be in a strange stillness, only now & again a cricket or cicada & the pony moving in the yellow grass of the garden. But we had to set back to the ship at midnight …
>
> Throssell looks first rate, & his wife is the same.[9]

After Hugo and Katharine moved out of Wandu the next year, the new owner, Mrs Blanche Hunter, turned it into a guesthouse and added the attractions of a golf course and the state's first electrically lit tennis court. At the bottom of the block, right on York Road, she built a shop and let it out as the Wandu Weekend Tea-Rooms. For the next three decades until the original house was dismantled in the early 1950s Wandu was to be 'a landmark and almost a symbol of hospitality and good cheer' in the Greenmount area, including for Hugo and Katharine, who became friends with Mrs Hunter and her family. A remnant of Wandu still stands today—the old tearooms, most recently operating as a liquor store.[10]

IN THEIR WHIRLWIND courtship at the end of 1918, Hugo had told Katharine he agreed with her new-found political beliefs before he proposed to her. They didn't have time to work out just what that meant and Katharine's convictions were evolving anyway. Now over in Western Australia, she wrote to Nettie that 'Jim has grown so to my point of view that he usually describes himself as a Bolshevik & certainly has done more explanations of what Bolshevism is than any man I know in this state. Can you hear him explaining what the word means to the State Attorney General?'[11] In this initial phase, Katharine and Hugo saw themselves as partners in revolution. 'I owe a great deal', Hugo wrote, 'of my new faith and understanding of the trouble and sorrow in the world to my wife, and that we hope to work together in ways which will make our lives of real service to our fellow men and women'.[12] They were settling in Perth at a time of ferment; a long-running industrial dispute at Fremantle wharf culminated in a day of violence on 4 May dubbed 'Bloody Sunday' in which a unionist was killed by a police officer.[13] Rather than seeking out the writers of Perth, Katharine launched herself into the city's radical political circle. She and Hugo came into the city on Sunday afternoons for the Social Democratic League meetings on the Esplanade, 'the green flats beside the shining river where the people of Perth gather for such occasions'.[14]

In the winter of 1919, Katharine and Hugo both made speeches revealing they were socialists. Hugo went first in July. Peace Day was celebrated around the world to mark the long-awaited signing of the Treaty of Versailles after months of negotiation over the terms of peace. It came just as the influenza pandemic had finally started to take hold in Western Australia and one author speculates that the spike in cases in August was due to the celebrations.[15] Hugo was invited to speak at his hometown, Northam, on 19 July 1919. He wasn't meant to be a controversial choice of speaker. 'A scion of the Tory Throssell family', one newspaper wrote of him, 'a mighty warrior, a returned hero who sooled during the first conscription campaign—he possessed every qualification to keep up the Tory reputation of sleepy Northam, his native heath'.[16]

That Saturday started out overcast but the sun had come out by the time the long procession left the Northam Town Hall at two o'clock. The Salvation Army band marched first followed by Hugo leading the mounted light horsemen. The town's war hero was dressed in full-uniform, 'looking very splendid', Katharine wrote, 'on a great bay charger'.[17] After the light horsemen was a car with Hugo's sister-in-law, Nurse Isabella Throssell, and 'three maimed soldiers', followed by thirty returned soldiers, one hundred cadets, a motor ambulance, a fire truck, a tradesman performing a burlesque, decorated motor cars, and, at the end of the procession, a tin-can band. The procession followed a circuitous path along the streets of Northam, finishing at the showgrounds. The streets were lined with people waving flags of the Allies and making noise with whistles, kazoos, drums and conches.[18]

After a football match at the showgrounds, twelve hundred people gathered on Avon Street in the evening in front of a platform for a 'demonstration' beginning at eight o'clock. Gerry Throssell, Hugo's 17-year-old nephew, remembers it was strange that Katharine came up to him and the other nephews and nieces beforehand telling them to give 'uncle a loud clap & a big cheer when he made his speech'.[19] There were five speeches interspersed with a choir of one hundred singing patriotic songs from the victorious Allies, including 'The Star Spangled Banner', 'The Marseillaise', and 'Australia Will Be There'. Hugo was the fourth speaker. The first speaker, a Catholic priest, declared it was 'now the duty of the people to preserve Peace'. An Anglican priest spoke second and 'appealed to all creeds and all classes to work together'. James Mitchell, the state premier and local conservative member, spoke third; he was an old family friend of the Throssells. His message was far more hawkish, looking to the future and declaring 'it would be absolutely necessary for Australians to prepare to defend their Country, and if that became necessary, to endeavour to emulate the deeds of the Australians in the great war'.[20]

With this lead-in, Hugo took to the stage and began his speech innocuously enough, saying how good it was to be back in old Northam again. He mentioned his football-playing days and boxing matches; at the time he left for war, the district would have known him as a somewhat irresponsible 'lad' but the war had made him a 'man'.[21]

> 'The war has made me a Socialist. It has made me think and inquire what are the causes of wars. And my thinking and reading have led me to the conclusion that we never shall be free of wars under a system of production for profit, with its consequent over production, periodic crises, unemployment and the struggle for markets …'[22]

As he spoke, Katharine wrote, his face was 'all torn with emotion. It was terrible—but magnificent'. One newspaper reported applause at the end of his remarks, but his nephew claims decades later that 'he was greeted with silence—except we nephews & nieces who clapped & cheered'.[23]

A bugler sounded the last post after Hugo's speech and then the final speaker stood, 83-year-old Saul Solomon, a retired businessman and politician. Solomon wasn't going to remain silent about Hugo's incendiary words. Departing from his prepared speech, he claimed there 'was no country in the world that gave so much in return for labour' as Australia. He concluded by declaring that socialism had already failed in Australia. He sat back down next to Hugo, and the band played the national anthem, 'God Save the King'.[24]

NOT MUCH OF the reaction to Hugo's speech was recorded. The *West Australian* noted the 'impressive speeches' without any detail about what was said. It took the *Northam Advertiser,* to break the story on Wednesday with a neutral summary of the five speeches. On Friday the *Westralian Worker* called the speech a 'veritable "bombshell"' and published a lengthy verbatim transcript. It's probable Katharine herself wrote the article—she knew the editor, the future Labor prime minister John Curtin, and was contributing some unsigned articles to the newspaper at this time.[25]

According to his nephew, Hugo would tell people he lost all but five of his friends over the speech and it's this interpretation taken by

Hugo's biographer, John Hamilton.[26] Yet the reality was more complex than that, other factors over the next fourteen years contributing more to the long unravelling of Hugo than just the announcement of his political radicalisation. After the speech he kept his job with the land board; one of the few public mentions of disfavour was in a gossip column in November saying that he 'seems to have suffered a "slump" in those circles that were wont to honor' his conservative father, George.[27] Although there's no record of him being asked to give further speeches at commemorative events, he continued to make appearances at ceremonies as an honoured veteran.

HUGO HAD BEEN Katharine's first convert, won over so easily and completely that it had filled Katharine with hope and the expectation that many more would follow. The next month the 'Perth Prattle' column in the *Sunday Times* reported: 'Mrs. Hugo Throssell's address on "Socialism" at the Karrakatta Club last Thursday left the members thinking. Seems that it was Mrs Hugo who converted Hugo to Socialism. Socialism and novel-writing are her hobbies'.[28]

The speech was not publicly advertised as it was only open to the club's members, the wealthy and high-status women of the state. Entitled 'The New Order', it was a much longer speech than Hugo's, a carefully developed argument against capitalism and for socialism. Her tone was strident and her message uncompromising. 'We are standing on one of those periods of history when the old order is changing and yielding to a new one', declared Katharine. 'Socialism stands for justice, light, reason, love, and honesty; Capitalism for greed, for war, for oppression of the weak, over-working and under-paying of men, women, and children.' Only two things kept people from embracing socialism. The first was ignorance, because no-one who studied socialism 'with an open mind' could fail to be convinced. The second was greed, because some people were convinced but still said, '"Nevertheless, I want my profits, and I don't care how I get them"'.[29]

Her speech shows extensive reading and thinking, outlining centuries of economic history and peppered with stories and statistics from around the world. At the end she gave a list of twelve books for 'preliminary reading'. The speech was the culmination of her own period of intense reading, initially as the first student of the Victorian Labor College in 1917 and then in the isolation of her cottage in Emerald throughout 1918. She wasn't yet a communist in a narrow sense, still placing hope in several movements, including both the Bolsheviks in Russia and the syndicalists in Spain. 'Guild Socialism, Syndicalism, and Industrial Unionism all outline paths along which the workers may achieve … emancipation.'[30]

It was an unlikely audience to bring her message to and it's not recorded that she made any converts. The invitation to speak shows an openness to Katharine from the elite women of Perth, but the contents of her speech marked her out from them. She was to exist on the fringes of the city's cultural elite for the rest of her life, admired for her writing but separated by her politics.

IN NOVEMBER 1919, the government opened a surveillance file on Hugo. It came after he gave a speech one Sunday that month on the Esplanade denouncing Allied support against the Bolsheviks in the Russian Civil War and Katharine gave a speech explaining socialism to the Anglican Social Committee.[31] Surveillance of left-wing radicals had begun during the war when the IWW were active and the conscription referendums caused such disquiet. At the end of the war, the government had decided to continue surveillance and secretly opened an Investigations Branch of the Attorney-General's office, its staff drawn from military intelligence.[32] A war veteran named Robert Weddell was one of the officers in Perth. His brief report stated:

> The latest recruit in the ranks of the Social Democrats is Captain Hugo Throssell, VC … Many attribute his leaning towards Socialism to his wife's influence, but he states that he saw the need of such principles whilst on service and on his return to Australia. However, he was struck on the head at Gallipoli and further he was a victim to Cerebro-spinal Meningitis, his mind perhaps having been affected.[33]

Weddell didn't add anything to the file until March 1921, reporting that he had met Hugo and intended to 'draw him out' about communism. 'A medical authority informed a friend of mine that he would not be surprised if Throssell went "off his head" at any time, so it is evidently his wife who must be regarded as the more dangerous.' Hugo's fragile mental state wasn't observed on his medical record until much later, but the second-hand account from one of his doctors in 1921 was prescient.

Weddell or one of his colleagues compiled a two-page report on the couple in March 1922. The report writer was almost certain by then that Katharine was one of the 'leading members and advocates' of the Communist Party. The writer details Katharine's 'inflammatory' speeches and her 'mischievous propensities', concluding that she 'is regarded as a visionary but at the same time she is responsible for much harmful propaganda'.[34] Before too long, Hugo's file was relabelled with Katharine's name as Weddell and his successors observed that only she remained politically active.

'THE GALLAVANTINGS HAVE been interesting', Katharine wrote to Nettie. 'Trips with Jimmy on land settlement business into the country districts, down to the S[outh]-W[est] pastoral, grazing & orange growing, into the timber country, & out to the big wheat grazing lands. I'm simply gorged with stuff to write.' Although so full of subject matter, she didn't have the time she needed to write.

Under the influence of his brother-in-law, Percy Armstrong—a keen motorist and car dealer—Hugo bought a motorbike, a red 7.8 horsepower Indian Powerplus with a basket sidecar for Katharine to travel in.[35] He took her out to his farm at Cowcowing, a journey of 200 kilometres. Travelling the bumpy roads in the sidecar of a noisy motorbike reduced Katharine 'to the mental condition of a scrambled egg in the shortest time on record. But the journey was gorgeous! Every stockman and drover on the road knew Jim—and of course it was a case of pull up and yarn with everyone!'[36] Hugo employed a farm manager, but he and Katharine made the trip out sometimes to help.[37]

Out of Katharine's observations of Cowcowing came the only short story she published in her first five years in Western Australia, 'Christmas Tree', appearing in December 1919 in the *Australasian.* In it, Jinny Gillard and her husband are packing up their meagre possessions and leaving their wheat farm after fifteen years of struggle. They had come to the farm as newlyweds and the toil had taken their youth, only to leave them with nothing. The Western Australian Christmas Trees on the horizon 'had thrown their blossoming crests', but Jinny had read in the newspaper that the tree was actually a parasite, 'Its roots throw suckers round the roots of other trees, and draw the sap from them', she tells her husband. 'That's why the trees around it are so poor and dreary lookin', and it's so big and strong—and has all those yellow flowers'. On their way to their new place, they stop by the Christmas party at the town hall and encounter the banker who wouldn't show mercy to the Gillards and other farmers forced off their land. They leave the party in disgust, the story ending with Jinny drawing a parallel between the banker and the parasitic Christmas Trees.[38] It is her first mature literary work, restrained and lacking the melodrama of her earlier stories.

Katharine lapsed into a literary silence after writing 'Christmas Tree'. 'During this period of strenuous and exacting organisational activity', she remembered later, 'I did no literary work at all'.[39] The silence was disguised by the delayed publication of *Black Opal* in November 1921, but the novel had long been completed. She cut the 50,000 words from it that Hodder & Stoughton requested and sent it to the London publisher, Heinemann, who accepted it in April 1920.[40]

Despite Katharine gaining notoriety for her political views, both the *West Australian* and the *Sunday Times* carried positive reviews of *Black Opal*. The reviewer for the *West* called it 'a remarkably well-written and interesting novel, which may unhesitatingly be recommended to every reader of fiction. It is hardly necessary to say that the whole atmosphere of the book is essentially Australian'.[41] The most enthusiastic review came from *Triad* in Sydney, which wrote that it was 'the best Australian novel we have read for a long time', praising the authenticity of its characters and plot.[42] Overall, however, the reviews were more in line with the modest praise in London's *Daily News* which called it a 'wholesome, pleasant, virile story'.[43] Its sales were hampered, according the *Bulletin,* by the fact 'very few copies had come to Australia', even months after its publication in London.[44]

KATHARINE'S MOTHER, EDITH, was in bad health and Katharine had been meaning to visit Melbourne for Christmas 1919. She was too busy and had to delay the trip, but finally set off on 12 June 1920.

Once Katharine was in Melbourne, she became sick too and Hugo took the train over in July to be with her. In August, they were staying with the Palmers in Emerald for a couple of weeks while Katharine built up her strength for 'a severe operation', its nature unknown.[45] The operation took place on the morning of Thursday 19 August; Hugo wrote to Nettie, 'my woman came safely through … everything was very different from the last performance & [Dr] Lloyd told me he was perfectly satisfied … every minute now will see her making strength for which Glory be'.[46]

While Katharine was in hospital, Hugo was staying with Edith at her house in the Melbourne suburb of Armadale. Katharine hadn't been discharged on Sunday 22 August when Edith unexpectedly died in her sleep from heart failure caused by an infection. She was sixty-six years old. 'Mrs Prichard has never been really well since her son Alan was killed at the war,' a newspaper reported, 'and the added grief of the deaths of her two sisters following shortly one upon the other, further weakened her resisting power'.[47]

Edith probably knew nothing of Hugo and Katharine's speeches in 1919; she didn't live long enough to see Katharine become truly infamous for her politics. She died thinking life was turning out well for her eldest child, that married to Hugo Katharine had achieved middle-class respectability and normality. With Edith dead, Katharine had only her brother Nigel left in Victoria and her ties to her home state had been loosened.

KATHARINE AND HUGO returned to Greenmount in October 1920, the same month a group of radicals met in Sydney to form the Communist Party of Australia (CPA). There had been socialist and revolutionary parties in Australia before, but what set the CPA apart was its alignment with the Communist International (Comintern) in Moscow. The Bolsheviks had formed the Comintern to spread communism around the world; the newly formed CPA were to do their part in Australia. Bill Earsman telegrammed Katharine with the news and she wrote back to say her health was improving and 'she was prepared to work very hard to form a branch of the party' in Perth.[48] For the next year, Katharine worked desperately hard trying to fan the flames of revolutionary zeal in her adopted city.

At a meeting in the Perth Trades Hall in late 1920, six comrades signed a letter to the general secretary of the CPA, agreeing to accept its principles and policies and submit to its discipline. Katharine's name was second on the list after the inaugural secretary, George Whitbread.[49]

Whitbread expressed doubts to Earsman about Katharine's ability to contribute because of her ill health. Earsman responded, 'I have worked with Mrs Throssell for a number of years and I strongly recommend that the branch secures her active co-operation in all work. I know her as a good teacher and a good tactician and her knowledge of the revolutionary movement is based on a good experience and a very wide reading'.[50]

From December, the fledgling Western Australian Communists held fortnightly Saturday night public lectures—explicitly called 'propaganda meetings'—and a weekly study circle on Sunday mornings. The propaganda meetings soon faltered: there were usually about ten people who came to the public meetings in the Trades Hall 'but even these dwindled', Katharine reported, 'until there were only four of us one evening the lecturer, the Secretary (then GW Whitbread), myself and my husband'.[51]

The study circle was more successful. Starting at eleven o'clock straight after the morning church services, it met with the seriousness of a new religion. Advertising the circle, the *Westralian Worker* wrote, 'We are in the period of the collapse of capitalism. Crisis will follow upon crisis. The revolution is developing rapidly in Italy, France, and in England. It must hit Australia. But with sufficient understanding and an intelligent lead the problem of carrying on production for use here should not be difficult. Study groups should be formed everywhere.'[52] Katharine later explained that it was called the Labor Study Circle 'to get a foothold in the orthodox trade union movement'; the name also echoed the Victorian Labor College she had been a part of.[53] While the relationship between communists and the wider labour movement was strained from the start, John Curtin promoted the study circle in the *Westralian Worker*. Katharine and her co-organiser, George Ryce, alternated leading the group week by week as they worked their way through the writings of Marx.

In September 1921, Katharine fell pregnant, worsening her poor health. She struggled on for a couple more months until the group went into recess in November. The *Westralian Worker* proclaimed, 'Socialism is the nearer for what has been done. A great deal of self-sacrifice went to its achievement, and in this connection, Mrs Throssell's health has suffered greatly as the consequence of the strain the Circle work added to her literary and other activities.'[54] The study circle was the most successful communist activity in the state in the early 1920s and it continued for several more years under George Ryce's leadership. 'The influence of our study circle', Katharine claimed, 'was carried into the trade unions, unemployment camps, and ALP branches'.[55]

Hugo, despite his conversion and attendance at some meetings, soon became politically disengaged. After the Northam speech, he wrote an account of why he became a socialist at the request of Sydney's *Sun* newspaper but they decided not to publish it.[56] He made just one more political speech in November 1919. He never joined the Communist Party and instead became obsessed with making money from real estate. He'd once taken Katharine down the hill to Perth for the public meetings on the Esplanade on Sundays but by 1923 Katharine was reporting there are 'no Sunday trains from our district which makes it almost impossible for me to attend Esplanade meetings on Sunday'.[57]

There was still much hope of a radical turn in Australian politics. In October 1921, the Australian Labor Party adopted the socialisation of industry as part of its platform. John Curtin was there at the conference and on his return to Perth came out to Greenmount, bursting 'with the excitement of a schoolboy' to tell Katharine the good news.[58] Yet the CPA itself was struggling. A dispute rocked the state branch in late 1922 and early 1923 when one member publicly attacked George Ryce. The Central Committee tried to resolve the conflict from Sydney, the secretary, HL Denford, trusting Katharine enough to seek her opinion on the matter.[59] Things did not improve over the years that followed and the party had only a weak presence in Western Australia over the rest of the 1920s.

Katharine's health had broken down from overexertion worsened by tensions in the fledgling party and she didn't attend party meetings in 1922. She gave birth in May and explained to the Central Committee, 'my health is very uncertain and we live a long way from Perth'.[60] Years later she wrote, 'the birth of my son, and ill health for some years prevented me from doing organisational work … But those years of contact with the workers and the everyday struggle for improvement of their living conditions, bound me forever to their interests'.[61]

20

York Road

Greenmount, 1920–1929

KATHARINE AND HUGO decided to settle permanently in Greenmount. Life there in the Darling Ranges suited them both. Their house was on York Road, gateway to the Wheatbelt where Hugo had grown up, close enough to the city to remain connected but semi-rural so they could keep horses, an important common interest. Describing Hugo to an old friend who'd never met him, Katharine focused on horses: 'My Jim is a wonderful horseman and beauteous & behaved with horses'.[1] On her return from a trip to Melbourne, she wrote of 'a stolen hour or two on my beloved red Wyburn among the deep hills—where not the signs or the sound of a soul but ourselves and the birds'.[2]

Katharine loved the Darling Ranges:

> Every spur of the range is heavily timbered with jarrah and red gum, through which white-bodied trunks of wandu stand, with their saplings about them, slender and graceful as nymphs in the dark forest. Townships are scattered among the hills, of course. There are isolated farms, orchards, and vineyards; but for the most part, the country still belongs to the trees and wild flowers. It becomes a wilderness of miraculous beauty during the spring time.[3]

The wildflowers meant much to her. 'When I came to live in Western Australia I was enchanted by the wild flowers. With the help of the government botanist Mr C. A. Gardner I learnt their names and was able to greet them like friends when we met in the bush which covers the hills of the Darling Range.' For several years she arranged to give lessons on wildflowers to the children from the Greenmount State School, taking 'a flock' each Wednesday afternoon during spring 'through nearby stretches of bush where over a hundred specimens of wild flowers could be found'.[4]

After living at Wandu for fifteen months, they bought a cottage a few hundred metres down York Road in June 1920. Built in 1896, the cottage was made of jarrah weatherboard and had four rooms coming off a central passageway, with an outside kitchen and verandahs on three sides. The Guildford Grammar headmaster, Rev. Percy Henn, had been using it as a weekender. Years later, first Hugo then Katharine were to die in that cottage. They bought an adjacent vacant lot as well, giving them a hectare of land with an orchard and enough of a paddock for horses, and then 140 acres of grazing land on the other side of York Road where Hugo kept cattle.[5]

It was a modest house and Hugo always talked of building something grander once he'd made money. 'It would be made from granite cut from the old quarry, with wide windows overlooking the plain and vine-covered verandahs.'[6] The aspiration stoked his financial recklessness.

IN JANUARY 1921, Katharine and Hugo had been married two years without children. Unlike many of her generation, Katharine knew about contraception and wasn't embarrassed to use it. She once wrote of a visitor with too many children, 'Evidently, she doesn't know all she ought to. I'll have to have a word with her, or her great big husband, which I'm quite capable of doing'. She went on to tell her adult son, newly married, 'there's plenty of time, and you've got so much to do together, before any infant need apply, I hope'.[7]

Katharine and Hugo were ambivalent about children. Katharine was sick and busy trying to establish the Communist Party. Ric, their only child, later imagined Hugo's reluctance: 'Still, a baby! A man might not be ready to be a father'.[8] In *The Roaring Nineties* (1946), Morris, husband to the novel's protagonist, 'had decided they must not have children until they had made their fortune'.[9]

They had a taste of parenthood that year. Katharine's five-year-old niece, Thea, nicknamed Biddy, arrived on a boat from Ceylon on 11 February 1921. Thea wasn't flourishing on her parents' plantation and was sent to Perth so she could eat better. She was to stay at boarding school but come to Greenmount with Katharine and Hugo on weekends and holidays. Ric writes that 'Katharine used to think of [her] as her daughter'.[10] 'Greenmount, with Katharine and Unc', writes Thea, 'was my real home and refuge. I remember the feeling of sanctuary and love that those two offered and I loved Greenmount'. After Ric was born and Thea's brother Alan also came to school in Perth, 'in many ways we formed a family group'.[11] Years later, Katharine wrote to Ric of Thea, 'So close to us, she is really. Seems to belong to me, as well as Bee … somehow, I feel, the affinity is with me & the point of view & interests in life, more my way, than towards golf & bridge wh chiefly interest my little sister'.[12]

It seems Hugo and Katharine were ready for parenthood in September 1921 and their child was conceived on 'a glorious spring morning':

> I returned from a trip to Albany [on the south coast] to welcome Hilda [Esson] who was coming home after some time in London & New York. It was an all night train journey, and Daddy met me at the station with horse & buggy. Then, it was coffee for two, and—— Such a joyous occasion for both of us, the reunion after a few days separation & a glorious morning of sunshine & wildflowers out along the road, hovea & scarlet bottle bush. I remember it so well and being intoxicated with happiness.[13]

Their baby was born at dawn on 10 May 1922, a fortnight early. Katharine gave birth at home—on the jarrah dining-room table, she later told guests, as uncomfortable as it sounds.[14] She wrote that 'the incidents' of the birth 'went into' her play, *The Great Man* (1923).[15] In it, the baby is born at home because the hospital is so full that there are 'patients sleeping on the verandah'.[16] A neighbour named Ethel Parker helped Katharine give birth.[17] 'Then I saw you', Katharine remembered to Ric years later, 'so fat and red and lovely, and they bathed you beside the fire and I said: "Put on his Bolshevik gown, please". That was the little gown I had embroidered with wheat ears and a hammer and sickle'.[18] Hugo was outside 'hanging onto the clothesline in an agony of mind' when Mrs Parker came out to tell him he had a son. 'How gloriously happy we were! Daddy's shouting with joy & telling everybody he weighed 8lbs, & me just holding him tight, as he snuggled beside me'.[19]

They called the boy Ric Prichard Throssell. His first name was in honour of his dead uncle, Hugo's brother Eric, who had always been known as Ric. In *The Great Man,* the baby's aunt complains, 'That's why they call the babe "the great man". Expect him to revolutionize the world, abolish poverty, misery, battle, murder and sudden death'. As a young man, Ric left Western Australia to serve overseas during World War II and he never returned to the state to live. His birthday became a lonely occasion for Katharine and each year she would write him a letter recounting again her 'great day' and then go to visit Ethel Parker in celebration.[20]

Years later, she told her daughter-in-law that having a baby was a 'glorious experience' but the fulfillment was mixed with a sense of 'having given "hostages to fortune"'.[21] She articulated those maternal anxieties in a letter to Ric in 1961. 'Oh darl, I used to be so afraid that you were too wonderful to last. The world seemed full of germs & wild beasts of all sorts wanting to devour you. How cd I ever protect you from them—and yet make you strong enough to fight them yourself?'[22]

Katharine was thirty-eight when Ric was born and sick in the years which followed, two possible reasons he turned out to be an only child. Hugo, she wrote, was 'jubilant when our son was born … though he never wanted more children'.[23] Perhaps he was reacting to growing up in such a big family. In a short story Katharine wrote in 1924, Rose, the main character's wife, 'did not want any more children; she dreaded having another baby. It seemed simple and natural enough for a man and woman to have children. But not for Rose, or for him'.[24]

IN 1923 LOUIS ESSON was setting up the Pioneer Players in Melbourne—dedicated to staging Australian drama—and he wanted a play from Katharine. She wrote *The Great Man* for him and it was performed as one of five short plays on 16 August without Katharine to witness it.

A reviewer dismissed it as 'a rather artificial trifle, showing the love-making and quarrelling of an emotional and a not very sensible young couple, who had been thrown out of their stride by the advent of the first baby'.[25]

The play was written out of the frustrations and anxieties of Katharine's first year of motherhood. She called it a comedy, but the tone is one of conflict and unhappiness. Isabel is trying to raise her infant son according to the principles of a pamphlet called *The Care and Feeding of Babies*—the title of an actual publication issued by the NSW Department of Public Instruction in 1914. The sterilised bottles and the timed feeds are met with disdain by Isabel's sister and sister-in-law, who give her conflicting advice. Meanwhile Isabel and her husband, Robert, argue terribly, too; Isabel only has time for the baby and her housekeeping is no good. She tells Robert, 'Ours wasn't an ordinary marriage. Don't you remember it was to last as long as we liked. Not a moment longer than either of us liked'.[26]

THE NIGHT KATHARINE went into labour, Hugo had read in the newspaper that DH Lawrence was staying in Darlington, just a few kilometres away. 'I explained to Jim that D. H. Lawrence was the most brilliant of modern English writers and that I would like very much to meet him. Jim promised to drive me over to Darlington the next day.' Hugo called and wrote after Ric was born, but when Lawrence eventually wrote back he was in New South Wales and said he'd already left Western Australia by the time the letter came. Katharine and Lawrence exchanged books and several letters with Katharine telling him she thought her baby had arrived early in order to try to meet him.[27]

The Australian novelist Henry Handel Richardson wrote to Nettie after reading *Working Bullocks* (1926), 'Katharine Prichard has great talent—but I fear for her, if she cannot shake herself free of the apeing of D. H. Lawrence … the undoing of more than one promising novelist'.[28] Critics often noted Lawrence's apparent influence on *Working Bullocks* and Katharine's story 'Grey Horse', both written soon after his visit. Katharine denied it, dating her period of interest in him much earlier to her London years when she wrote *The Pioneers* and *Windlestraws*, novels which bear no sign of his influence. She remembered she read

Sons and Lovers soon after it was published in 1913 and 'felt as if a comet had swung into my ken'.[29] She was so affected she paced around her Chelsea flat all night.[30] In the rest of his work she 'did not find quite the sensitive realism and power which had impressed me so much' and she became 'dissatisfied with the diffuseness, arrogance and morbid mysticism which had become associated with his work'.[31] The only debt she would acknowledge to him was a general 'liberating effect on the writers of his time, with regard to style, construction, the discussion of sex and thought processes'.[32]

KATHARINE'S ONLY LITERARY friend in the Darling Ranges was Mollie Skinner. Mollie, seven years older than Katharine, had written newspaper articles and a book about her experience as a nurse during the war. She ran the guesthouse in nearby Darlington where Lawrence stayed while he was in Perth. He was so intrigued by Mollie he collaborated with her on a novel, *The Boy in the Bush*, published in 1924.

In December 1924, a profile of Mollie written by Katharine appeared in the magazine *Woman's World*:

> That the writing and ideas of M. L. Skinner are naive and individual, we can believe. She herself is. She has strength of will and mind to go her own way; say her own say; courage, too, taking attacks of the Furies with energy and placidity, the precipitate of years of sensitive and tragic realisation.
>
> The impression you have of her is of a tree that has been blasted by lightning. A tree lithe and beautiful in its growing time.[33]

Katharine did not particularly like Mollie's writing. When Nettie was curating a collection of Australian stories and looking for a recommendation for a story of Mollie's in 1928, Katharine wrote that there was nothing of hers she was 'particularly shook on', though she liked her 'immensely' and found her as a person 'much more original & individual than anything she's written'.[34]

Mollie was more interested in spirituality than politics and she exasperated Katharine at times, but they maintained an uneasy friendship for thirty years until Mollie's death.

ANOTHER OF KATHARINE'S somewhat unlikely literary friendships in Western Australia was with the younger writer Henrietta Drake-Brockman, daughter of the prominent feminist doctor, Roberta Jull, and married into a Perth establishment family. 'It was an intimate friendship, despite political differences', Katharine wrote years later. 'She confided in me as I'm sure she didn't to anyone else.'[35] In 1926 Katharine wrote a profile of her for *Home* magazine, declaring, 'Witty and well informed, a lover of Australia, our life and people, by temperament and ability, Henry Drake is splendidly equipped for her career as a writer'.[36] The fact Katharine's friendship with the politically conservative Henrietta was to survive the Cold War and the most rigid phases of Katharine's politics shows her commitments never completely closed her off to other people.

IN 1924, KATHARINE re-immersed herself in writing, producing two major works that year, the novel *Working Bullocks* and the story 'The Grey Horse'. She had just turned forty and it was the beginning of the creative peak of her career. Over the next five years she would also write the novels *Coonardoo, Haxby's Circus,* the play *Brumby Innes,* and many of her best short stories. Her peak can't be explained simply. She largely gave up political activity over those five years but she was busy with parenting and housework, and she had a more active social life than ever before. Her health was often bad and financial problems were beginning to trouble the family. It wasn't the happiest time of her life; the joy of her first year or two of marriage had faded. She wrote out of the disappointments and frustrations of marriage and middle age. When Nettie saw Katharine in Melbourne at the end of these years, she wrote perceptively:

> In a way she's found herself. Even in those old days in London she knew the kind of books she wanted to write, but she was wavery in her approach to life and unsure of her powers. Now without having lost any of the sensitiveness … she's gained a sort of toughness. She can be deeply moved by the treatment of natives on the stations … yet can look at the whole question with clear unsentimental eyes.[37]

The first fruit of her creative peak, 'The Grey Horse', was written for a £50 short-story competition announced by *Art in Australia* in April and closing on 31 August 1924. It was open to its subscribers 'with the object of encouraging a perfection of style and treatment, which is so evidently lacking in the shorter fiction appearing in Australia at the present time'.[38] Katharine's entry was the judges' unanimous choice for the prize and appeared in the December issue.

In the story, a farmer will neither share his coveted grey stallion nor let it mate. One day it breaks through a fence to reach a mare and, tasting sex, can never be controlled again. The stallion is contrasted with the farmer's neighbour who is trying to make a success of an orchard so he can marry. He gets what he wants, at least at first, and marries his sweetheart but then their firstborn baby dies, the orchard fails, and his wife turns off sex.

Katharine was never to write a novel about Greenmount, but 'The Grey Horse' and a number of her other short stories are set in the area. She wrote to the American critic Hartley Grattan in 1938, 'The grey horse lived in the yard below our verandah. You know where you stood with me, and I told you a fire had burnt down all the wattles. I watched the grey horse at his gambols for a year or so—and was always afraid the old couple who lived there would sue me for libel!'[39]

The elegant *Art in Australia*, with its high aspirations for Australian art and literature and its tolerance of the avant-garde, was important to Katharine's literary career.[40] Winning the short-story prize boosted her confidence after a hiatus. She became a favourite of the literary editor, Leon Gellert, and in the December 1925 issue, he published 'Ti Tree' and 'The Wild Cherry-plum Tree', two poems Katharine had written during the war and put aside after the indifference of the Essons and the Palmers. It would have helped resolve Katharine to pursue the publication of her second book of poems—including these two—eventually released in 1932.

In 1926, Gellert asked for a story, written 'freely, in any way that I wished'.[41] She had been reading James Joyce's *Ulysses* (1922), and she wrote the most experimental story of her career, 'The Curse'.[42] The story describes a hut in the bush overgrown with Patterson's Curse, with a dialogue between two disembodied voices remembering

Alf who used to live there and preferred to read rather than subdue the bush:

> 'The curse!'
> 'Patterson's curse?'
> 'A noxious weed …'
> 'That's what it is, he says.'
> 'Salt and poisonous as the sea.'
> 'An enchanted sea.'
> 'Sea of dreams.'
> 'Dead sea.'[43]

In her youth she had emerged as a writer publishing fiction in newspapers and popular magazines; in her publications with *Art in Australia* she was consciously writing literature, not entertainment.

As well as being literary editor for *Art in Australia*, Leon Gellert was the editor of the company's lifestyle magazine, *Home*, and after persuading the other directors to make it a monthly from January 1926, he needed to find more material.[44] He probably asked Katharine what she could send him; she decided it was time to revisit *The Wild Oats of Han,* written nearly twenty years earlier but possibly revised at this time. It was serialised from July 1926 to May 1927.

Katharine asked Gellert to send the manuscript on to the publisher Angus and Robertson; after initially rejecting it because they feared it would not sell, they eventually published it under their Cornstalk imprint in October 1928.[45] It had proved harder for Katharine to publish books in Australia than in Britain and *The Wild Oats of Han* was only a temporary breakthrough; despite her growing reputation, she was not to have another book released by an Australian publisher until 1944 when Angus and Robertson brought out her collection of short stories, *Potch and Colour.*

The Wild Oats of Han was marketed as a children's book which may have caused critics to take it less seriously; the short, positive reviews described it with adjectives like 'delightful'. Some reviewers, however, noted that it was more suited to an adult readership. HM Green found room for it in his *Outline of Australian Literature* (1930), writing that it was 'removed by a whole world from the ordinary children's story'.[46]

It had a print run of 1500, and by the end of 1929 had sold nearly one thousand copies, earning Katharine a modest £28.[47]

AS KATHARINE WAS coming into her creative peak, her health was worse than ever. In late 1923, she had another unknown operation. Then, a few days before Christmas 1924, she came down with typhoid and was in hospital until 23 January 1925. Typhoid is a bacterial infection spread through contaminated water or food; it sets in with a worsening fever, abdominal pain, and severe weakness lasting weeks. Before antibiotics, it killed one in ten people who contracted it and a newspaper reported Katharine 'has had a hard struggle for life'.[48] After epidemics in the goldfields in the 1890s and 1900s, by the 1920s it had become a rare disease in Western Australia but a boy from Greenmount came down with it at the same time as Katharine.[49]

Writing the novel *Coonardoo* in 1928, Katharine gave typhoid to Hugh, the main character. He suddenly becomes sick and 'could not eat, rolled about with a pain in his stomach; his eyes and hands blazed feverishly'.[50] He is near death for a time. 'Each day Hugh became weaker, more exhausted … and, although the fever abated, his heart seemed to swim all over his body, his breath came in such faint windy gusts, that he lay without speaking more than he had to.'[51] Drawing on her experience again, Katharine has Sally suffer typhoid in *The Roaring Nineties* (1946) while prospecting in particularly harsh country; an Aboriginal woman, Kalgoorla, nurses her through the sickness, saving her life.[52]

KATHARINE WOULD TALK of her marriage to Hugo as the happiest years of her life. Ric writes that she 'remembered only the "halcyon days" in Greenmount before anxiety and stifling domestic triviality settled about her'.[53] Tensions in her marriage were already apparent when she wrote the play *The Great Man* in 1923; in 1927 she wrote a kind of sequel to it, a comedy called *Bid Me to Love or The Caught Bus.* In it, marital happiness has come to an end.

Set, according to the directions, 'on a sunshiny autumn morning in the late 1920s', *Bid Me to Love* is the story of Louise, married for six years to Greg with two children. He tells her, flippantly, that he doesn't need to bother romancing her any longer because 'a man doesn't run after a caught bus'. Later that day, she discovers he's secretly planning to meet a woman on his business trip to Sydney. Physical fidelity doesn't matter to her, she declares, but she hates deception. Until now, she's been faithful to him, saying, 'I've been so busy trying to be a good mother and model housewife. There hasn't been any time or energy for diversions of any sort'.[54] She decides to exact her revenge by having her own tryst with Don, 'a good looking young man of Italian extraction, but Australian in every word and gesture'. She says, in words Katharine would reuse in the novel *Intimate Strangers* (1937), 'Every woman of forty needs a lover to keep her self-respect … and her husband's'.[55]

Ric finds the play obviously inspired by the family's home life:

> To me the reality of the settings and characters of the play was transparent. The verandah of our home at Greenmount was described in the stage directions; my father spoke in Greg's every word; I saw my mother's romanticism and unconventionality in Louise; found my own childish sayings recalled; even Phoebus Apollo, the family cat, was included in the cast. As to the plot—fact, or fiction to tease her own Jim? That remains KSP's private joke.[56]

If the play was Katharine's private joke, Hugo didn't find it funny—she wrote that although she called it 'an honest-to-God attempt at comedy', 'Jim says it isn't!'.[57] Elsewhere, Ric remembers Katharine's flirtations with the Italian 'who used to plough the orchard, showing off by singing all the operas for her. She pretended that she had run off with him for the day and put it all in that blasted play, *Bid Me to Love* for him to see'; Hugo threatened to beat the man up.[58]

Despite the marital difficulties, *Bid Me to Love* is set in a middle-class idyll—the family are well-off and spend their time playing tennis on the nearby courts, riding horses in the bush and attending social nights. 'This contented, unawakened life as it existed in the twenties is most delicately portrayed by Katharine Prichard, with an accuracy which today we can place in perspective.'[59] There is no shadow of the Great Depression over the play, as there would be over the related novel, *Intimate Strangers*.

The family in *Bid Me to Love* do not have a maid, but the Throssells usually did have one in this period, an important factor in giving Katharine time to write. In 1924 Katharine wrote to Vance Palmer just before she came down with typhoid saying, 'the domestic affairs [are] overwhelming. I barely have a minute to think much less talk. And now the aged virgin who does my chores has sprained her wrist & the book has had to be set aside again'.[60] In July 1925, Katharine advertised in the local paper, 'WANTED: Capable Houseworker, fond of children, washing done, four in family; 30s per week'.[61]

Even with a young child, Katharine and Hugo had an active social life. In April 1924, Hugo officially opened the state's first electrically lit tennis courts at Wandu, playing in the first match. The court 'presented a brilliant appearance, and its glowing outline could be discerned at a distance of several miles. The house beside which it lies … stands in a picturesque old garden and the powerful lights, shining on trees and shrubberies, transformed the scene into a veritable fairyland …'[62]

In September 1926 they hosted a racially insensitive 'gipsy' party at their house for the engagement of Hugo's niece, Grace Throssell. There were one hundred guests. 'The gardens were prettily illuminated and made to resemble a gipsy camp'. When the couple arrived, they were led down a 'gaily' lit path to 'the wishing well, where, under the guidance and counsel of Mrs Hugo Throssell they were asked to drink of the delicious love potion'. A band played fiddles and sang as the guests danced the foxtrot on the verandah. Hugo sang 'The Bandolero' on horseback. 'Supper was then served on the verandah, in gipsy fashion, seated on bags of chaff and other rustic seats on the floor; after which Mr and Mrs Throssell arrived in their donkey cart, which was laden with every possible kitchen utensil, and presented them to the happy pair.'[63]

It was the foxtrot that year; in 1927 it was the Charleston. 'We have … parties on the verandah', Katharine wrote to Vance, 'where everybody practices the Charleston with various results. It's so thoroughly ridiculous, but splendid exercise really. When you see fat middle-aged men & women taking themselves quite seriously. Trying to do the absurd shuffle & genuflexion!'[64] This detail found its way into *Bid Me to Love,* with Miss Kenny, the local gossip, comically practising her Charleston moves.

In 1928, Katharine and Hugo visited the Green Room Club Cabaret most Thursday nights. Katharine's varied costumes were noted: once it was 'black taffeta silk'; another time a 'striking frock, with fitting bodice of oxidised silver lace and skirt of cloud grey georgette in pointed flares'.[65] Each New Year's Day they were at Perth's Ascot Racecourse for the Derby.

Katharine's political involvement thinned out as the 1920s went on. It wasn't that her political convictions had consciously changed, but she was no longer giving it priority, uninspired by the embers of activity in Perth and busy with other spheres of life.

One 'thoroughly depressing and disappointing experience' was attending her first conference of the Communist Party of Australia, held in Sydney from 26 to 28 December 1925. Katharine said of the conference later that she was delayed getting to Sydney on the train and two unemployed activists from Western Australia were 'accepted as credentialled delegates. I, the first communist in Western Australia, was allowed to attend only as an observer'. Afterwards, the delegates had no money and Katharine was asked to help. 'I gave them enough for food and paid their fares back to Western Australia, where they were instructed to build the party. They disappeared and weren't seen by us again.'[66]

After that conference, Katharine's main link to political activism was through her friendship with the radical unionist Cecilia Shelley, who had been part of the Labor Study Circle with her. Cecilia was ten years younger than Katharine and had grown up on the goldfields. She controlled the WA Organisation of Labor Women but in a tussle over the influence of communists in the Australian Labor Party, the party expelled her in 1925. The organisation continued without ALP endorsement and by 1927 Cecilia had persuaded Katharine to be one of its executive councillors. For years, Cecilia and the organisation—with Katharine's help—had been raising money and enthusiasm to establish a Working Girl's Club in the city, a resting room for young women and girls in between split shifts or after their day's work. They raised enough money to purchase premises at 25 Irwin Street in the city and stage an official opening in 1927, but the enterprise soon fell over. Cecilia and Katharine's political partnership and friendship, however, endured and they were to work together on new ventures during the Depression.[67]

IF HUGO'S CELEBRITY dimmed over the years, he was still highly regarded as a war hero. In November 1923, he led a guard of honour at a ceremony to unveil a clock placed on the dome of the Midland Town Hall, a memorial for soldiers killed in the war.[68] At an Anzac Day service in 1925, Hugo's businessman friend, Ashton Hunter, presented the people of Northam with an oil painting of Hugo by visiting Scottish artist Duncan Macgregor Whyte.[69] Its acquisition challenges the idea that Northam had disowned Hugo after his Victory Day speech.

Hugo was still showing the effects of the war. When a doctor examined him in June 1923 he noted, 'He has had several turns of palpitations; the slightest thing that irritates him produces an attack'. In November 1923, the doctor granted him an increase to a 40 per cent pension, writing: 'Has increased in weight—and looks well, but he cannot do hard work yet … I have had this officer under treatment and have seen him on good days and bad days … The likelihood of further improvement is somewhat doubtful'.[70]

In December 1925, the government was scaling back the settlement scheme and Hugo's income as soldiers' representative was reduced to a payment for each meeting he attended.[71] Looking for employment, he worked for a short time for a real estate agent named Alfred Leslie Wyly who was later convicted of fraud.[72] As ambassador, Hugo used his good name to induce South Australians to buy up farm land in Western Australia, despite knowing that many Western Australian soldier–settlers were struggling.[73]

Hugo, the putative socialist, had become obsessed with real estate. In August and September 1927, he bought five lots of land in Greenmount and dreamed of making a fortune on a subdivision.[74] As motor car mania swept Perth, 'Mr H. V. H. Throssell, Greenmount' the *Swan Express* declared in February 1928, 'will utilise a Chevrolet car in visiting his extensive estates'.[75] He was borrowing too much and their finances were overstretched. Katharine felt the need to earn more money and took on some freelance journalism, writing feature articles; she was noted attending meetings of the Society of Women Journalists in Perth in 1928.[76]

Like retired sports stars, the glory for returned war heroes was always in the past. Hugo was still respected, but he'd had little success since returning from the war while Katharine was more famous than she'd ever been. In August 1928, a couple of weeks after her win in the *Bulletin* novel competition for *Coonardoo* was announced, Hugo was in Kalgoorlie. Attending a performance by Paddy Hanna's Famous Diggers, a vaudeville theatre troupe made up of returned soldiers, perhaps Hugo had been reminding people it was the thirteenth anniversary of him receiving the Victoria Cross. Paddy Hanna announced it from the stage during the performance and 'the orchestra led the singing of "For He's a Jolly Good Fellow" by all those present'.[77]

ON 28 JANUARY 1929, Katharine and Hugo celebrated their ten-year wedding anniversary. They were now in their mid-forties. Ric turned seven in May and was attending the local primary school in Greenmount. Katharine and Hugo's two de-facto children, Thea and Alan, were now thirteen and nine. After Katharine and Hugo's initial flurry of activism and romance, they had settled into a middle-class life and a marriage which, despite tensions, was tolerable. In the middle of 1929, Katharine sent off a manuscript in time for a novel competition run by Jonathan Cape; it was the third of the remarkable trio of novels from her creative peak, the first about workers in a karri forest, the second about the people living on a cattle station, and the third about a circus.

21

The Karri Forest

Pemberton and Greenmount, 1919–1926

KATHARINE'S FIRST NOVEL written in Western Australia, *Working Bullocks* (1926), was seeded by a motorbike trip with Hugo to Pemberton at Christmas time in 1919. In 1913 the WA government had opened two state-owned mills and a small private town 300 kilometres south of Perth, originally known as Big Brook.[1] In her notebook, Katharine wrote, 'The wall of the forest surrounds the township, dead timber gaunt & blackened etched in silver against the darkness of the trees stretching away for miles across country in every direction'.[2] They stayed for a fortnight in the boarding house, living 'among the karri forests … going out every day to watch the timber men at work, and absorbing the spirit of the place'; Katharine said she even drove a bullock team.[3] She recorded snatches of conversation between timber workers, word sketches of characters she met or heard about, details of logging, handling bullocks, and the sawmill operations, stories about capturing brumbies, descriptions of the plants and animals of the area, as well as the experience of being amongst the trees; she was interested 'above all in the generative power and wild beauty of the land itself'.[4] The bush resembled that around Emerald, a place precious in Katharine's memory. She had many landscapes and industries to choose from in Western Australia—the Wheatbelt which had inspired 'Christmas Tree'; the port workers at Fremantle; the life of the Darling Ranges around where she lived—but it was the karri district which captivated her.

On Boxing Day, she watched a log chop at the town of Greenbushes, and her notes from it inspired a crucial scene in *Working Bullocks*. She was taken with one of the axemen that day, describing his physicality: 'The champion had a grace and poise that was incomparable ... The muscles on his bronzed arms standing out, a pleasant, kindly-face ... Column of his throat that of a thorough-bred bull'. While the unfortunate title of the novel critiques the treatment of timber workers, it also seems to have its origins in Katharine's fascination with this axeman's resemblance to a bull. She was to write of her main character, 'He was a man like one of his bullocks, rooted in deep natural instincts, powerful and intent, with a capacity for dumb and obstinate endurance'.[5]

A timber worker named Norman Smith recalled in 1971 that Katharine

> used to come here and I would give her a lot of information ... and the principal character in that book was an old bloke at Pemberton; had a beard, red headed and that, called Bob Widdeson ... he was a very brawly old fella and generally his job down there—he had a little bullock team of his own—was to clear the log lines, for the state saw-mills when they used to operate down there ... He used to nurse them a lot, I can tell you, they were his life were those few bullocks that he had in the team.[6]

Widdeson was a well-known personality of the district. A local history remembers him as a man of horses rather than bullocks:

> Swamper Robinson drove bullock teams and Jumbo Widdeson horse teams. Horses were generally used for logging in the jarrah bush, and for transporting material by road, but bullocks were preferred for logging in the karri country. They were slower than horses, but stronger and better able to cope with the mud and heavy going in the winter months. Swamper Robinson loved his bullocks and could do almost anything with them in the bush.[7]

The novel reflects the tension between Katharine's admiration of the physical feats of the timber workers, her political concern for their exploitation, and her horror at the great trees being clear-felled. In the eyes of the character Deb, 'The slain giants seemed always on the look out for vengeance—in sullen protest against dismemberment, that tearing of their living flesh by saws in the dark interior of the mill'.[8] Historian Patricia Crawford comments that Katharine, in her notebook, 'observed the mill at work, but most of all she was entranced by the forests, the "wonderful great effect of movement and colour, of light and shadow. And the smell of red gum—the forest through it all"'.[9]

THE NOTES FROM the December 1919 trip lay dormant for several years as Katharine devoted herself to the study circle and then to baby Ric. In 1924 she returned to the notes and began writing the novel; by September she had nearly finished and she wrote to Nettie that she had been to Pemberton 'and addressed a meeting of timber workers on strike. Had a great jaunt & felt a great deal better for the two days. Have just been praying for this strike—and here it is—for me to study as I'm writing the last chapters of my book'.[10] Katharine saw the strike as convenient to her writing; politics was again subservient to writing at this point in her career.

Three hundred fallers and haulers around the towns of Manjimup and Pemberton dropped tools on 5 September 1924. They were piece-workers, paid by the load for their dangerous logging work and had been denied an increase of four pence. By the next week, the mills had stopped as there were no logs coming in.[11] With no reporters on the scene, newspapers were scant on details and Katharine's visit in support of the strike and her speech—a significant celebrity intervention—were not reported. On 22 September, soon after her visit, the strike fizzled out and the workers returned to their jobs at their old rate to await the Arbitration Court.[12]

In the middle of the strike, the *Westralian Worker* published photographs of the makeshift wooden shacks the timber workers and their families lived in. 'In these places women live out a toilsome life and children are born and reared. The timber industry of the Commonwealth is a source of great wealth—but not to the workers in the bush.'[13] It's a contention Katharine fleshes out in *Working Bullocks*.

The hero of *Working Bullocks,* Red, works as a bullock teamster. He is a loner and a man of principle. He faces a series of trials—his brothers thought him dead in the war and sold off his precious team of bullocks; his partner and best friend, Chris, is killed in a timber accident; his glamorous girlfriend Tessa leaves him for a richer man. After noting that Red has just returned from service, the war is barely mentioned again. Yet despite this silence, *Working Bullocks* is a novel about the challenge of returning to civilian life—making money, keeping a job, finding a wife. Like Hugo, another returned soldier, Red has a special way with horses and he finds solace in an elaborate scheme to trap the finest brumby he's ever encountered. Increasingly, he is drawn to Chris's sister, Deb, an 'elemental child of the forest, at one with its trees, flowers, storms and wind-driven surges of emotion'.[14]

Halfway through the novel, a communist named Mark Smith appears—Australian literature's 'first flesh and blood communist'.[15] Mark becomes Red's offsider and the closest he has to a friend. When Deb's other brother, Billy, is killed in a sawmill accident, Mark channels the workers' anger into a strike. Just as Alan's death in the war helped radicalise Katharine, Billy's mother Mary-Ann is radicalised by her son's death and she helps organise the strike. However, the strike soon collapses and Mark Smith leaves the district; the political foray has come to little, reflecting not just the ineffectual strike Katharine observed in September 1924 but also her general feelings about the progress of radicalism in Western Australia. Mark rages at the workers, 'You look like men, but you're not. You're working bullocks. That's all you are … You make me sick, the lot of you!'[16] Mark is particularly frustrated with Red. 'He realized Red Burke had got his creed clearly enough. He had accepted it; it made common sense to him. But he did not want to bestir himself, throw off his lethargy, drugged invulnerability to any further jolt fortune might have in store for him.' The timber workers would 'do anything in the world if you gave them a lead now. Why don't you? There's big things to do'.[17] Perhaps these words channel Katharine's disappointment with Hugo, who had backed away from his speech in 1919, not standing for election as he had been toying with, and not taking his place alongside Katharine in the party.

The novel finishes with the same romantic musical chairs Katharine had played in *Black Opal,* as the estranged Red and Deb find their way back to each other. Red and Deb embody a simplicity and purity of life, two characters in touch with their environment, their work and their appetites.

IT TOOK LONGER than Katharine had hoped to finish *Working Bullocks*; after being inspired by the strike, she was delayed by weeks in hospital with an unknown illness.[18] She finally finished the novel about a year later. She didn't publish it with Heinemann, who had brought out *Black Opal*, complaining that they had 'practically dumped' and remaindered that book.[19] Her fourth novel was published in London by her fourth publisher, Jonathan Cape Ltd, in November 1926.[20] Jonathan Cape Ltd had been founded in 1921 by Jonathan Cape and his partner, George Wren Howard. It was already forging a reputation for a quality list and would publish major authors such as TE Lawrence, James Joyce and HG Wells.[21] Reporting Katharine's contract with Cape, Perth's *Daily News* noted they were 'doing all the more modern and progressive novels'.[22] Katharine's friend Mollie Skinner had published her novel *Black Swan* with Cape in 1925 and may have suggested she try them.

It was to be the major publishing partnership of Katharine's career, with Cape publishing nine of her books between 1926 and 1950. Yet the partnership started badly, with Katharine writing to Vance in June 1927:

> But Lord, Cape, I think are probably the world's worst publishers. My first royalties account was for £23—dears what do you think of that? Despite the notices there has not been a copy of the book in Perth for over three months. My typing bill for *WB* was £25 incidentally. Their arrangements for reviewing & placing the books are so bad & when an edition or rather supplies run out, they have to be replenished from England. No stocks here. So don't publish with Cape, is my advice.

She believed part of the problem was trying to negotiate terms and edits with publishers by post. 'Twixt ourselves *Black Swan* would never have got by but that Mollie Skinner was in London, & revised & revised on the spot. I don't see any possible chance of going myself & just have to take any old terms the publishers offer.'[23]

Jonathan Cape managed to repair his relationship with Katharine, writing to her in 1928 asking 'to let bygones be bygones' and continue as her publisher.[24] She was to maintain a warm correspondence with him over the years and finally met him in person on her trip to London in 1933.

The poor sales of *Working Bullocks* were at odds with its glowing reviews. Before publication, Katharine had left a copy of the manuscript with Hilda and Louis Esson when she visited them in Melbourne in early 1926. Louis read it aloud, slowly, to Hilda. Nearing the end, Hilda wrote effusively:

> The prose is most beautiful—every individual strong and poetical, and the whole thing has an epic reality, a high remote beauty that makes it unquestionably the most important work probably that has ever been done here. One doesn't simply read descriptions of that forest—one lives there, and breathes its air. The people are strong, simple, elemental—and the kinship of the life of nature, bird, beast and tree, and the life of man is most wonderfully expressed.[25]

Reviewing *Working Bullocks* for the *Bulletin,* Louis wrote that it was 'probably the best novel ever written in Australia … a work of genius and a novel of which any country might be proud'.[26] Louis' close relationship with Katharine likely influenced his judgement but his praise was genuine.

The reviewer for the *Mercury* largely agreed with Louis, calling it 'one of the finest novels which Australia has produced' even though her 'sympathies for what one imagines she would call the "down-trodden working classes" has led her into misrepresentation, which one might expect, perhaps, from a hired Labor pamphleteer'.[27] Another reviewer wrote that Katharine 'knows her bush, and the men and women in it and she has the dramatic understanding to make convincing not only the big incidents of the story but also the humdrum lives of the people who live in her pages'.[28] Perhaps the only one who didn't like it was the anonymous reviewer for Sydney's *Catholic Press* who found that its structure was flawed—with several climaxes and anti-climaxes—and that its style 'over reaches' and 'becomes dense and crowded'.[29]

In London, the *Times Literary Supplement* wrote, 'There is something very courageous, surely, in calling a novel *Working Bullocks* ... such a title being likely to put off nine women out of ten—and that is a large proportion of novel readers. In a way, it suits this vigorous uncompromising story of life on the land in Western Australia'.[30] In 1927, Viking published an American edition which would have finally made Katharine some money on the book. The *New York Times Book Review* called it 'a startling and unusual novel'.[31] It had been more than a decade since Katharine had last been published in the United States, and despite the acclaim *The Pioneers* had received at the time, the reviewer assumed *Working Bullocks* was her first book.

Working Bullocks won Katharine a reputation as a major Australian novelist and critics and writers were to look back on it as a landmark in Australian literature. Years later Miles Franklin claimed 'it marked the breaking of the drought in which the novels had merely taken a recess underground for a time like the inland rivers'.[32] On the strength of it, John Sleeman wrote for Britain's *The Bookman* in 1928 that Katharine 'is, to my mind, Australia's greatest living novelist' and *Working Bullocks* 'is the high-water mark of Australian literary achievement in the novel so far'.[33] Hartley Grattan, an American critic, wrote in his 1928 survey of Australian literature, that 'Miss Prichard is the hope of the Australian novel, and literally inexhaustible material lies waiting'.[34]

Katharine was writing far from the centres of literary activity, but that was quintessentially Australian in itself for a nation which saw its identity tied up to 'the bush' and the frontier. In Vance, Nettie and Louis, she was close friends with three of Australia's eminent literary critics. If they inevitably read her work with much sympathy and took opportunities to promote it, they did so out of conviction of its merits. Brenda Niall writes of Nettie, 'Few Australian critics, men or women, have wielded as much influence as she did. In partnership with Vance, but more often in her own right, she helped writers to shake off their colonial deference in the crucial decades that followed Federation'.[35] Nettie wasn't able to buy a copy of *Working Bullocks* in Brisbane—where she and Vance were now living—until April 1927 when she wrote in her diary, 'What strikes me is the confidence Katharine has gained in recent years. She has now set any diffidence aside and writes out of her full self'.[36] In October, Nettie wrote an article called 'The Novel in Australia' for the *Brisbane Courier*. She wrote astutely of the significance and achievements of Katharine's fiction:

> The books of Katharine Susannah Prichard, appearing at pretty wide intervals, are the fruit of an intense devotion to her subject matter. Her gifts are mainly two: first, that of brilliant impressionism, then a rare power of writing group-scenes. One thinks of the opal miners in her second book, *Black Opal*, standing about chaffing one another and discussing the universe, every man of them alive. Or, in her latest book, *Working Bullocks*, there are the groups of timber-getters camped by the road for a smoke-oh, or the unforgettable, hot, timeless Sunday evenings spent by a big bush family and its visitors on a veranda beside some trees of ripe loquats. Such scenes are too difficult for most novelists, who shirk them: yet they enrich a book immensely, and the reader feels that our everyday life is full of unsuspected charm.
>
> So far, Katharine Prichard's novels have been each set in a different spot of Australia—the tall timber of South-east Victoria, the opal fields in Western New South Wales, and the sawmilling country in the south of Western Australia. It is said that her next locale will be the northern inland of Western Australia, a place very wild, very remote, and yet, seen from within, quite a complex commonwealth.[37]

22

The Station

Turee Station, 1926 and Greenmount 1927–1929

Waiting for *Working Bullocks* to appear in 1926, Katharine was ready for her next major project. A trip to Turee Station bore much literary fruit: two of her most acclaimed short stories, an award-winning play, and the best novel she would ever write. The way she remembered it, 'A friend whose husband owned a cattle station in the North-west told me the incident which is the core of "The Cooboo"'.[1] Hearing it 'so inflamed my imagination that I travelled to an isolated cattle station … to be sure of authentic details'.[2] In the story Katharine would write, an Aboriginal woman on a cattle muster is hampered by the infant she's carrying and finally flings him away in frustration and abandons him. The shocking incident has no corroborating historical evidence, and Katharine doesn't say whether, in gathering 'authentic detail', she attempted to verify its truth.

The friend who told the story was Doris Maguire, who had married Joe Maguire of Turee in 1919. Most likely, Katharine knew the Maguires through Hugo, who had worked on a neighbouring station, Ashburton Downs, before the war. Hugo's stories of station life might also have helped pique Katharine's interest as she contemplated the subject of her next novel. It was a part of Australia little had been written about and would build on her experience as a governess at Tarella back in 1905.

She set out on the research trip in September 1926, travelling for a week to reach Turee for a ten-week stay. She took 4-year-old Ric with her rather than leave him with Hugo, but she was only full of praise for Hugo in a letter to Hilda; it was 'wonderful' of him to let her go on the journey, he wasn't even jealous she would be spending most of her time with other men. Ric remembers a model T truck picking them up at Meekathara and 'jolting its way along a track lost in a sea of everlastings'.[3]

Joe Maguire described the location of Turee in a letter to a British newspaper: 'We are just 198 miles from Peak Hill, our nearest post office. Our nearest neighbour is 80 miles away, our nearest railway 267, and nearest port 300 miles. We run a cattle station … and do not meet with a great number of people in these sparsely populated parts'.[4] Katharine got on very well with Joe; he was 'the most likeable type of Irishman' despite the 'little bits of ancient anti-socialist philosophy that he delivers … under the stars when we yarn at night'. He was twenty-two years older than Doris, who, 'being a city girl', was 'nervy and at loggerheads with everything'.[5] They had two young children, Richard and Peggy.

The homestead was made of corrugated iron and daily life was dominated by heat, dust and flies. 'Flies crawl all over your food, and you just take them off—the dust storm powders your meat while you eat. And at present—we're on salt meat, the flour is flavoured with petrol: butter ran out a few weeks ago … and no fruit, almost no vegetables.' At night, the only light came from candles and carbide gas lamps, not strong enough to read or write. 'On the cold nights, when I just came up, we used to sit round the fire in the long kitchen & yarn; but now, after the heat & glare & dust of the day, everybody lies out on the verandah. There's singing & yarning. Sometimes the men play poker or five hundred.'[6]

Each day, Katharine went out riding, 'henna-ed with dust. Sometimes one of the gins rides with me, sometimes mine host, who is really a bit of the country, and sometimes Mick, a stockman who has lived here all his life'.[7] The head stockman, an Aboriginal man named Duck, had been at Ashburton Downs when Hugo was there; Katharine wrote that 'he knows me as "Jim Throssell's woman". Otherwise, along the track I've been known as "Mrs Huge-o" not that I'm any more colossal than ordinary dear. A little less perhaps'.[8]

She was worried about her health, wondering if it would hold out for the long stay. For the first two months she was okay, writing to Hilda Esson, she had 'only had one bad head day. Got a bit scared when I was laid low the other day, as a result of normal conditions returning. But here you say to yourself "I can't be ill. It's no use"—a week nearly from the nearest town & a doctor'. Then, soon after she wrote that on 1 November, she came down with sandy blight. A bacterial infection which causes the eyes to swell and itch with severe conjunctivitis, it can cause blindness. 'I could hardly see for a week, felt miserably ill—in a tin shed by the house, sweltering heat.' It meant she couldn't go on a ten-day cattle muster, 'one of the beastliest tricks fate ever paid me'.[9] In *Coonardoo,* Phyllis comes down with blight too, after being weakened, her father assumes, by the salt meat and lack of vegetables. 'Phyllis lay stretched in her dark room, glad to be still, not to have to open her eyes, or move. Overwhelming weakness and sickness obliterated everything for her. She lay for days in the darkness, the hot stillness.'[10] In Ric's recollection, it was he who had sandy blight while his mother nursed him.[11]

Aboriginal workers lived 80 metres from the homestead in rough timber and iron huts.[12] Katharine didn't question their presence on the station, the dispossession and enslavement it presumed. She wrote, 'I find them poetic and naive. Quite unlike all I've ever been told, or asked to believe about them. I'm doing some character studies'.[13] It was the beginning of a new focus that was to remain with Katharine for the rest of her career. Her 'City Girl in Central Australia' (1906) serial has an Aboriginal minor character and she probably met Aboriginal people while living at Tarella Station back in 1905, but she had not shown interest in them in life or literature until now.

WHILE STAYING AT Turee, Katharine wrote the draft of a three-act play, *Brumby Innes.*[14] The first act is the staging of a corroboree. Joe Maguire's son, Richard, remembers, 'My father asked the official boss, Duck and the high lady, Topsy, to turn on a corrobboree on one evening for Mrs Throssell. The men came up and tramped up and down. Showed her how the kangaroos jumped around. She would have been shown some of the rituals'.[15] As much as Katharine prided herself on the authenticity of the scene, the Aboriginal people were surely conscious of 'putting on a show' for a white visitor. She wrote 'it was the most thrilling and dramatic performance I've ever seen'.[16]

In the play the corroboree is interrupted by Brumby Innes, who drunkenly abducts a 13-year-old Aboriginal girl, Wyalba. In act two, a group of Aboriginal men come to Brumby's homestead seeking revenge; Brumby opens fire, wounding one. As the wounded man lies on a bed, the neighbouring station owner, John, comes to see Brumby with his niece, May, 'a pretty, shallow, city-bred girl', visiting the station for the winter. John wants Brumby to stop stealing his cattle. May flirts with Brumby; when her uncle is out of sight, Brumby rapes her. In act three, four months later, it's revealed John lied in court about Wyalba's age to stop Brumby being sent to prison for under-age sex with her. May is now married to Brumby and a prisoner at the station alongside Wyalba; the play finishes with her unsuccessful attempt to escape.

Katharine based the character of Brumby Innes on Albert 'Brumby' Leake, who owned a neighbouring station, Prairie Downs. It's likely he came over to visit the Maguires while she was at Turee.[17] Joe Maguire's son, Richard, remembers he 'was very good-hearted and if someone fell down, he'd … pull them up without saying anything more about it … Brumby was part of the folklore. He was an old villain'.[18]

Aboriginal people had reason to remember him less fondly. There was an incident at Prairie Downs in late 1925 similar to the events of the play. Leake shot an Aboriginal man named Walgie in the leg and accused Walgie and another man, Spider, of trying to break into his store. Walgie and Spider both testified Leake had been having sex with a 13-year-old girl named Cunie, and had fired shots over their camp when she wouldn't return to him. According to them, it was a confrontation over this that led to Leake shooting Walgie at the homestead. In March 1926, Leake, like his namesake, was charged with carnal knowledge of a girl under sixteen. The girl made a statement saying she was thirteen; Joe Maguire testified that he knew the girl to be at least seventeen.[19] 'Owing to the unreliability of the evidence and the absence of proof of the girl's real age, the bench dismissed the case.'[20]

Leake also inspired Sam Geary, the villain of Katharine's novel, *Coonardoo,* who lives with a harem of Aboriginal 'wives' and lusts after Coonardoo herself. The compiler of a collection of material on

Leake, Peter Bridge, believes Katharine had an intense hatred of Leake, but from her literary portraits of him it seems truer to say that she was fascinated by him at the same time as condemning his behaviour towards Aboriginal women.[21]

Brumby Innes and Katharine's novel *Coonardoo* are both treatments of the theme of interracial sexual relations in the outback. Scholars Wilde and Headon write, 'The White man's sexual use of Aboriginal women had long been tacitly recognised as an acceptable behaviour pattern in the isolated outback, where White women were few, but that acceptance had always insisted that such miscegenation was merely a casual consorting with no deeply underlying emotional attachment'. Katharine, along with Vance Palmer in *The Man Hamilton* (1928) and *Men Are Human* (1930) 'presented a much more complicated view of interracial sexuality'.[22]

Katharine entered *Brumby Innes* in the *New Triad* play competition in 1927 and won. One of the judges, Gregan McMahon, wrote:

> I consider *Brumby Innes* to be in a class by itself. In originality of subject, atmosphere, characterization, virility and technique, it is a very remarkable work, comparable to some of the best of Eugene O'Neill's, and it is, moreover, essentially Australian. It has been objected that the subject matter is sordid, and on that account the possibility of production should be discouraged. I am assuming that the subject matter of the plays presented is no concern of the judges ...[23]

In announcing *Brumby Innes* as the winner, the *New Triad* reported that, 'Messrs J. & N. Tait will produce the winning play, which carries, in addition to the Fifty Pounds Prize, an interest in the takings'; subscribers were even promised a discount on admission. Katharine wrote to Vance just after submitting the play that she supposed it would be 'considered unproduceable' while also insisting that 'it could be produced'. It worried her that Hugo 'doesn't like the play at all. It's too brutal he thinks'.[24] Louis Esson thought highly of it but was sure an audience would get 'the shock of their lives'. He felt Katharine had been 'too sympathetic to Brumby. Nothing can excuse his brutality, not even his "virility", which is his long suit'.[25] The production did not go ahead; the explanation the producer gave Katharine was that the planned season's opening play was given such unfair reviews that he swore to never stage another Australian play.[26]

Brumby Innes was published in 1940 by Paterson's Printing, a Perth company, possibly at Katharine's expense; it was the only play of hers to be published in her lifetime. She was probably hoping that publication would lead to a production, but she died without ever seeing it on stage. In 1972, three years after her death, the Pram Factory in Melbourne finally staged it, with the production filmed and broadcast on television in June 1973.[27]

THE NEXT PIECES Katharine wrote out of her experiences and notes from Turee were the short stories 'The Cooboo' and 'Happiness', both published in the *Bulletin* in 1927 and frequently anthologised as two of her most acclaimed stories. Both are notable for their narration from the perspective of an Aboriginal woman. Today, it is a choice of viewpoint which would be criticised for cultural appropriation; in its context, it was an act of literary empathy. After these stories, Katharine seems to have decided it would not be feasible to write a full-length novel from an Aboriginal viewpoint, and *Coonardoo* reverts to her familiar multi-viewpoint narration.

'Happiness' is an alternative *Coonardoo* in miniature. Nardadu, the viewpoint character, is a grandmother who has lived at a station for many years and the story relates her understanding of the troubles at the homestead. For years, John and his sister Megga have run the station together, but after incurring Megga's wrath for having sex with an Aboriginal woman, John brings home a much younger white bride, Margie. Years of conflict between Megga and Margie culminate in Margie leaving with the children.

A young Aboriginal woman named Coonardoo is mentioned in passing in the story; she would become the title character of Katharine's most famous novel. Katharine said, 'One of the native girls who I used to ride with particularly interested me, and it was her stories about her own people that went into the making of *Coonardoo*'.[28] The woman Katharine referred to was Topsy, whose Indigenous name was Kundri.[29] Elsewhere, Katharine claimed the novel was true to Topsy's life 'in all but the end wh happened to another woman'.[30] Topsy and her husband, Duck, had a daughter named Cooboo, who would, coincidentally, grow up to marry an Aboriginal man named Billy Leake, his name taken from Brumby Leake.[31] The Turee Station manager, John Brown, and his wife, Joe Maguire's sister, Mary, took Topsy, Duck and Cooboo to Queensland with them on a holiday in 1922. According to a police report supporting the granting of permit to take Topsy and Duck, they had grown up at Turee and spoke English very well.[32]

Coonardoo is a tragedy of the repressed love between Hugh, the owner of Wytaliba Station, and Coonardoo, an Aboriginal woman who lives on the station. Katharine claimed to have based Hugh on a particular person she met, and, at some point, he read the novel and came to talk to her, 'appalled that man's inner conflict shd have been so revealed'.[33] The novel spans decades, beginning with the childhood of Hugh and Coonardoo and carrying on into their middle age. Like Katharine's earlier novels, *Coonardoo* presents an idyllic community under threat. Wytaliba's harmonious relationships between the whites and blacks have been set up by Hugh's mother, Bessie. The characters who 'understand' the idyll love the harsh isolation of the station life and treat the Aboriginal people with respect; after Hugh marries, his wife, Mollie, does neither. Before she dies, Bessie sets up an impossible dynamic in entrusting Coonardoo with the duty to look after Hugh while also requiring that they not be sexually involved with each other. Bessie and then Hugh's cardinal rule for the idyll is that—unlike Sam Geary on the neighbouring station—white men must not have sexual relations with Aboriginal women. It is a rule partly borne out of avoiding exploitation but also out of anti-miscegenation. The community is threatened and ultimately destroyed by both the forces of nature—drought—and Hugh's inability to cope with his repressed desire. As in *The Pioneers*, it ends with hope in the next generation—in this case, Hugh's daughter Phyllis is successfully managing the neighbouring station with her husband.

From a literary perspective, *Coonardoo* is the most accomplished of Katharine's novels. She developed the plot with greater skill than any of her other works, not filling it with overly complicated developments nor veering into weaker subplots. The drama is gripping as Hugh's fatal flaws become more apparent over the years and lead to tragedy.

The prose is beautiful, less self-consciously evocative than *Working Bullocks* and less workman-like than the goldfields trilogy which would follow. There are no intrusive communist themes or characters, reflecting not just the isolated setting but Katharine's own retreat from political activism when she wrote it.

Katharine's depiction of the mother–son relationship between Bessie and Hugh is biographically interesting. Later known as a 'doting' mother herself, Katharine portrays Bessie as a mother tied up in her son's life, even from afar while he is at boarding school. In the character of Bessie, Katharine imagined life as a widow with an only son five years before it became her own reality.

Soon before she began writing *Coonardoo,* Katharine met up with Colonel WT Reay's wife Lucinda and daughter Nan in Melbourne; he was still in London and Lucinda was living apart from him.[34] Consciously or not, Katharine may have weaved some of Reay into the character of Hugh. The obvious similarity between the two is their five daughters, 'the joke of the countryside, "his poker hand"'.[35] Hugh's tortured, repressed love for Coonardoo reflects some of Reay's behaviour towards Katharine. The arrival of Hugh's daughter, Phyllis, to work the station with him is another echo. He is delighted when she works alongside him—as Katharine worked in journalism alongside Reay—and devastated when Phyllis starts thinking of marriage. Like Reay, Hugh forbids Phyllis to marry, forcing her to run away to do so.

FOR AN ACCOMPLISHED work, *Coonardoo* was written with extraordinary speed in three months from April to June 1928. 'I was three-quarters through with another story [*Haxby's Circus*], when she presented herself & took charge. Of course there were sketches for her in my Nor-West [note]books; but I worked fearfully hard, & went through the manuscript at least six times before it left me.'[36] The deadline spurring Katharine on was the closing date for the *Bulletin*'s Australian novel competition, which offered a first prize of £500 and retention of royalties for any book publication after serialisation. Entry was open to writers born or living in Australia, New Zealand and the Pacific islands. The entries had to be submitted under pseudonyms; referencing Hugo's time on a station, Katharine called herself 'Ashburton Jim'.

In the foreword to *Coonardo*'s publication as a book, dated 17 March 1929, Katharine defended the authenticity of the novel and gave some insight into the writing process. She claimed 'the story was written in the country through which it moves' and 'facts, characters, incidents have been collected, related and interwoven'. The interweaving of observed material was Katharine's signature process but in this case some of her material has been taken from other books. Scholar Marion Austin-Crowe writes 'a great deal of textual material relating to Aboriginal life and culture which appears in *Coonardoo* can be shown to have been taken almost intact from [Herbert] Basedow's text, *The Australian Aboriginal* (1925)'.[37] In the foreword, Katharine quotes approvingly a particularly offensive claim from Basedow, an anthropologist, about the 'low' place occupied by Aboriginal people on the evolutionary 'ladder'.

Katharine also revealed that she asked Ernest Mitchell, Inspector of Aborigines, to read the manuscript for accuracy. Katharine may have known him through Hugo as, until 1925, Mitchell had been farming in Benjaberring, near Hugo's farm at Cowcowing. 'He has had thirty years' experience of the [A]borigines', wrote Katharine 'and no one in this country has wider knowledge and more sympathetic understanding of the Western and Nor'West tribes'. There wouldn't have been time to send him the manuscript and receive back his advice before the closing date of the competition; perhaps his feedback came after submission but before publication. 'Mr Mitchell suggested an omission and several changes of spelling, but said that he could not fault the drawing of [A]borigines and conditions, in *Coonardoo*, as he knew them.'[38]

The response to the *Bulletin* competition was overwhelming; a special van had to be hired to deliver all the manuscripts on the last two days. In all, there were 542 entries.[39] The panel of five Sydney-based male judges announced their decision in the 22 August 1928 edition of the *Bulletin*. Both Katharine's *Coonardoo* and Flora Eldershaw and Marjorie Barnard's *A House is Built* were awarded first prizes, with Vance Palmer's *Men are Human* third. The two winning novels were not quite judged equal: 'Our first choice is *A House is Built*, an Australian prose epic of marked literary quality. We find, however, such great merit in *Coonardoo*, with its outstanding value for serial publication, that we recommend it also as worthy of a first prize'. Despite the judges' claim of unanimity, their decision suggests a compromise. One of the judges later wrote of the difficult time they had separating the top three entries; the judges thought *Men Are Human* 'splendid' and 'sincere' and 'hailed it as the winner. Then *A House Is Built* came along. There was no more sincerity in it, but its "canvas" was considered greater. Then *Coonardoo* came. There was no more sincerity in it either; but it was, perhaps, "stronger"'.[40]

The *Bulletin* serialised *Coonardoo* weekly from 5 September to 12 December 1928. Katharine thought the illustrations by Cecil H Percival were 'awful', not resembling the country at all, and protested about the *Bulletin's* changes to her sentences.[41] The serial divisions were a problem, too, occurring mid-chapter; 'never was a book so chopped and broken and destroyed', observed Nettie Palmer.[42]

With so much publicity about the competition, expectations were high for the winning entries and *Coonardoo* was read by the large, general readership of the *Bulletin*, a contrast to the small, literary readership *Working Bullocks* reached. With its controversial themes and bleak tone, *Coonardoo* was never going to be a crowd-pleasing serial. The *Bulletin* received many letters of complaint—some of which they forwarded to Katharine—over her depiction of widespread sexual exploitation of Aboriginal women. Instead of publishing criticisms, the *Bulletin* noted, 'Of course, there has been controversy about the authenticity of Katharine Prichard's *Coonardoo.* Do the pictures she draws of life in the far Nor'-West tell the truth or are they fanciful?' From a 'basket full of evidence' they quoted one correspondent from the area who thought it completely true saying, 'The characters fit almost any far-back station'.[43] Responding to this claim, the local conservative member of state parliament wrote to the *Northern Times,* 'I say that the whole yarn is a libel on everyone in the North and North-West, and most of it is exaggerated and untrue'.[44] It was reactions like this that explain the defensive foreword Katharine wrote for the book, insisting on its verisimilitude.

Jonathan Cape wrote to Katharine wanting to patch up their relationship with her after the botched distribution of *Working Bullocks.* She agreed for Cape to have first look at *Coonardoo* in Britain, but handled it through an agent, Curtis Brown, in the hope of a better deal.[45] They reached an agreement in January 1929 and *Coonardoo* was published as a book in June.[46] The standard terms for her novels—perhaps starting with *Coonardoo*—came to be an advance of £150, with 15% royalty on the first 7000 sales and 20% for any sales over that.[47]

Receiving its first true reviews after being the subject of debate in the letters pages of newspapers as a serial, *Coonardoo* was criticised on both ideological and literary grounds. Samuel Rosa, the reviewer for Sydney's *Labor Daily*—a Labor Party paper hostile to communists—disliked it. Granting that it was 'probably the most sympathetic study of a black woman ever written', he found the characters unconvincing and the plot 'not impressive' before ending with the question, 'Is it really necessary, too, that there should be a persistent atmosphere of gloom in a novel dealing with Australian life in the interior? Is there no humor in such a life?'[48] There were some positive reviews, including the *West Australian,* which said 'the ample promise revealed by the author in her previous novels … has become solid achievement in her story of the black gin'.[49] However, even the positive reviews generally failed to predict the long-term significance of the novel. Nettie recognised it in an article in September 1929, and argued that when a writer interprets a theme for the first time as Katharine had done, 'readers are apt to be amazed by the extent of her knowledge and to ignore the aesthetic quality of the work'.[50]

Coonardoo received good reviews across Britain, praising Katharine for its emotional power and its depiction of Aboriginal people. An American edition came out in February 1930. The publisher was William Norton; he had written to Nettie in 1929 saying he wanted to start an Australian list, and she seems to have played a part in him acquiring the American rights to *Coonardoo.* Norton was unhappy with the quality of the British edition of *Coonardoo* and 'corrected the punctuation and typographical errors, expanded the glossary … and gave the novel an attractive new cover featuring cockatoos', delighting Katharine with his 'energy and courtesy'.[51] The *New York Times* wrote:

> *Coonardoo* stands as a forceful piece of social documentation and bids fair to do for Australia what *Uncle Tom's Cabin* did for America … to make the white race face the facts of its treatment and study of the black descendants of the [A]borigines, through an authentic piece of national literature which raises a parochial problem to the level of the universal.[52]

WRITERS DON'T CHOOSE which books come to define them. '*Coonardoo* seems to be the most popular of my books', Katharine said in a 1960 interview, but 'others of my books I consider of more importance, particularly the goldfields trilogy'.[53] *Coonardoo* broke new ground, stirred debate in its time and ours, and has a harsh beauty appropriate to the landscape it depicts. With good reason, it is the novel Katharine is best remembered for—and yet, it is as controversial today as when it was published, albeit for different reasons.

By the 1980s *Coonardoo* was taught in Australian high school and university curriculums, damagingly, as a novel which enabled readers to understand the Aboriginal 'mind' and the plight of Aboriginal people without awareness of its limitations as a 1920s white depiction of Aboriginal people. Wiradjuri academic Jeanine Leane was upset by *Coonardoo* in her high school English class because 'thousands of years of Aboriginal culture and spirituality were being reduced to base instinct'. Her teacher told her not to take it personally, the novel was not about her. 'But it was ... In fact, she was talking about all Aboriginal women. This is because literary representations are never just benign descriptions; they enter into and shape our national discourse.'[54]

Euahleyai/Kamillaroi academic Larissa Behrendt calls the novel a story 'about white sorrow, not black empowerment'.[55] Behrendt and Leane both discuss Katharine's failure to understand the political conditions of Aboriginal people living under settler–colonial oppression or advocate for their empowerment—an ironic failure, given Katharine's politics.[56] Katharine critiques the abuse of Aboriginal people by station owners but assumes the station owners' duty is to show benevolence, rather than liberate the Aboriginal people from slave-like conditions on land which had been stolen from them.[57]

Katharine wrote and published *Coonardoo* at a time of publicity about Aboriginal massacres. In June 1926, police massacred Aboriginal people in retaliation for the spearing of a station owner at Forrest River, now known as Oombulgurri, 1600 kilometres north-east of Turee in the Kimberly. Katharine's acquaintance, Ernest Mitchell, investigated the incident and the Wood Royal Commission followed in 1927. The massacre 'became the catalyst for a wave of concern about the treatment of Aboriginal people in northern Australia'.[58] In 1928, there was another massacre at Coniston in the Northern Territory and Behrendt writes, 'This recent history of violent frontier encounters, along with the backdrop it provides to black–white relations, is missing from the pages of Prichard's novel'.[59] However, there is a significant passage in *Coonardoo* in which the character Saul demonstrates an awareness of these encounters:

> 'You can't help seein' the blacks' point of view. White men came, jumped their hunting grounds, went kangaroo shooting for fun. The blacks speared cattle. White men got shootin' blacks to learn 'em. Blacks speared a white man or two—police rode out on a punishing expedition. They still ride out on punishin' expeditions …'

Saul details a number of atrocities he's seen, trying to educate Hugh's wife, Mollie.[60] The passage suggests Katharine had at least begun to understand the background of injustice and violence. However, this insight doesn't permeate the rest of the novel, and there isn't a sense of the 'fearful reality' for Aboriginal people of punitive killing sprees by white people. Behrendt asserts that many Aboriginal people worked on pastoral properties 'in order to be protected from violence on the frontier'—a very different picture to the contented Aboriginal people in the novel who are glad to be living in servitude at Wytaliba.[61] Katharine was so focused on the sexual exploitation of Aboriginal women that she missed the extent and significance of the wider violence which preceded and undergirded it. There's no indication she heard any local accounts of punitive killings and she would have felt, understandably, that it would be inauthentic to transplant details from the far-away Kimberley to the Turee area. Of course, the lack of accounts told to a white woman on a 10-week stay didn't mean a lack of violence.[62]

The best response to the problems with *Coonardoo* is to reframe the novel. Referring to Kate Grenville's *The Secret River* (2005) alongside *Coonardoo*, Leane writes:

> I am not suggesting that this work and others like it be scrapped—they are important texts that reveal synchronic slices of settler consciousness of and about Aboriginal people at any given time. But I am challenging the notion that these are Aboriginal stories. They are not.

> Any reading of such texts in Australian curricula needs to acknowledge this point. Critical interpretations, both within and outside of school contexts, must also be informed by the growing body of Aboriginal scholarship exploring the politics of representation.[63]

Coonardoo's representation of Aboriginal people was ahead of its time in certain ways but was also very much *of* its time. Katharine would have been disturbed by the knowledge that the canonical status of *Coonardoo* has perpetuated stereotypes about Aboriginal people. In an interview in 1956, she said 'there was a movement for recognition of their rights among the Aborigines' and if she was writing a novel like *Coonardoo* now 'it would reflect these developments'.[64] It is to Katharine's credit that she at least partially identified this shortcoming in her own novel long before critics raised it. Her writings show an evolving understanding of Aboriginal issues over the decades, with *Coonardoo* coming at the beginning of her engagement.

23

The Circus

1917–1930

At age nine, Katharine was captivated when Fillis's Circus visited Launceston and she decided she wanted to be an acrobat. Another encounter when she was twenty-three and housekeeping for her brother Nigel in Pyramid Hill sparked a literary interest in the circus. On the night of 10 November 1917, a trapeze artist named Lizzie Perry was performing with Perry's Circus in nearby Leitchville. 'The young lady was executing one of her most skilful and difficult movements when she fell headlong to the ground.'[1] It was feared her back was broken and she was driven 30 kilometres to Nigel's place. When she arrived, only Katharine was home. Katharine wrote:

> I had to sit with her until Nigel returned from visiting a patient. The girl's agony and the spirit with which she endured it made a deep impression on my mind. Although, when he came, Nigel relieved her pain by injections of morphia and arranged to drive her to the hospital in Bendigo for an X-ray, I was too distressed even to go out and say goodbye to her. After talking to her father, though, I resolved, some day, to write a story about her. She became the Gina of *Haxby's Circus*.[2]

Katharine fictionalised that night in the novel, a car carrying the wounded acrobat, Gina, over a road agonisingly 'full of ruts and old roots' to the 'cottage hospital', only for the unnamed sister of the doctor to tell them he is out on another call. In her delirium, the acrobat thinks the doctor's sister is her own sister.[3]

It was another decade before she began work on *Haxby's Circus* after seeing a performance by Wirth's Circus at Midland on 5 September 1927. She and Hugo were there with 5-year-old Ric. The advertisement declared:

> COMING BY THREE SPECIAL TRAINS
> In all its Glorious Splendour and Opulent Vastness
> WIRTH BROS. LIMITED
> THE GREATEST SHOW ON EARTH
> All New Circus, all New White Waterproof Tents, Menagerie, and Huge Elephant Herd …
> Great Grizzlies that ride bicycles and scooters; that walk on stilts; that skim on skates; bears that amaze and amuse.
> And in conjunction with Wirth's stock company of Acrobats, Animal Trainers, Clowns, Jockeys, Equestriennes, Horses, Ponies and Trained Wild Animals.
> 101 Wondrous Sights and Novelties. The Best and Biggest Show ever seen in Australia![4]

During the performance she told Hugo that she wished she could travel with the circus to research it and after the show Hugo approached the owner, Philip Wirth, who agreed to the request. She packed quickly that night and took the train the next morning to meet Wirth's at Moora, north of Perth, where they performed that night.[5]

Katharine travelled with the circus for two weeks as they put on shows at ten towns across the Wheatbelt and Mid West. Travelling on their own train, the route Wirth's Circus took was guided by the extensive railway networks then in place across Western Australia:

> From Moora, Carnamah, Mingenew, the circus train goes to Geraldton, returning by Mullewa, Dalwallinu, Wongan Hills, Goomalling, Northam, and Merredin, showing in each town for a night, and travelling during the night. Arriving at dawn in a town, the tents, by a miracle of organisation, are up in a few hours, and

> in the same way, when the show is over, within an hour they have collapsed and disappear again.[6]

The train 'was nearly a quarter of a mile long' with 'a retinue of about a hundred and twenty people'.[7] The shows were well attended, Katharine reporting that there would be 'a thousand people appearing from nowhere in towns which appear to be made up of only a post office, hotel, and half a dozen shops'.[8]

Katharine was fascinated by Philip Wirth, writing that 'thrones and chancelleries of Europe may be tottering, but no one doubts the absolute monarchy of Mr Philip Wirth in the cosmos of the circus'. He was soon to retire and she described him training an equestrian performer for the last time—his own daughter.[9]

Katharine recalled of her time with Wirth's:

> They called me the Assistant Lion Tamer. The chief one permitted me to stay in the menagerie while he trained them. It was a special privilege. Nobody else had it. I slept in the circus train but he slept beside his lions. It was a hard time for me. I wasn't allowed to smoke a cigarette all the time. The circus proprietor put me on my honor not to corrupt his little girls by teaching them to smoke.[10]

One of those 'girls', Doris Wirth, remembered that Katharine 'was sorry to leave it, because she had quite a good time with us. We travel by special train, you know, and she had a compartment to herself. She took all her characters from the circus—the dwarf and everybody. No, they didn't mind, they liked her so much'.[11]

The circus Katharine depicts in her novel begins more like Perry's Circus in 1917—much smaller and more worn out than Wirth's, consisting of one family with a few extra hands and certainly no train of its own.[12] At the mid-point of the novel, Dan Haxby, the circus owner, reflects:

> These days, what with picture shows and motor cars, the visit of a troupe of acrobats and riders, such as Haxby's, did not attract the crowds in up-country towns it used to. Besides there was nothing new or original about the show. It was very much what it had been

> ten years ago, second or third rate as compared with great circuses like Wirth's which travelled on its own train, using ten elephants, an imposing menagerie and company of performers, tent hands, keepers and grooms.[13]

Already by the end of the 1920s, Katharine was aware that the golden age of circuses had come to an end. One reviewer, Katharine's old journalist friend Freda Barrymore (nee Sternberg), wrote, 'it looks as if the "Talkies" are having a reactionary effect … Many novelists are collecting material from old time entertainments, such as the circus, and the public is collecting the books built up on them in the same spirit as it seeks out antique furniture'.[14] Only bigger circuses like Wirth's were flourishing, and, echoing this in the novel, Haxby's nearly folds, only surviving because Gina, the protagonist, inherits a fortune and brings it up to the level of Wirth's. The transformation of Haxby's links the two experiences of circuses Katharine was writing about, the revamped circus towards the end of the novel giving her a chance to describe a circus like the grander one she travelled with.

Wirth's traditionally returned to Melbourne every October in time for the Melbourne Cup, opening for a season at their permanent venue, Olympia, on St Kilda Road—a large complex which included the Green Mill Dance Hall.[15] A month after travelling with Wirth's, Katharine was also in Melbourne with Hugo; Louis Esson wrote that she 'gave an extraordinary party' at the Green Mill to thank Wirth's performers and crew. 'They were interesting people of different nationalities, American, German, Danish, Norsemen, trapeze artists, bear-tamers, head balancers, mixed in with … highbrows. The ladies were delightful; and there was dancing, and an elegant supper'.[16] Starting after their performance finished at half past ten, it would have been a late night.

The Throssells became friends with the Wirths, especially Philip's daughters, Gladys and Madeline. 'There was always the best ring-side tickets at the gate for the family when the circus came into town, and the most expensive and luxurious gifts for Katharine and Jim's son: a carved performing bear, a whole box of forbidden chewing gum, a mantel radio, and … a black Timor pony.'[17] Katharine's friend, Annette Cameron, remembers that in the 1960s 'when the circus came to Perth,

Katharine and I went to it, she was still an honoured guest there and we went back and talked with the performers afterwards'.[18]

BY APRIL 1928, Katharine had written three quarters of the circus novel—then titled *Fay's Circus*—when *Coonardoo* seized her imagination and she put the unfinished manuscript aside.[19] In December 1928, Katharine's publisher, Jonathan Cape, announced a novel competition with a prize of £1000 and the possibility of an additional US$4000 advance on royalties from Harper.[20] Entries were closing 31 August 1929. Spurred on again by a competition, Katharine returned to work on *Haxby's Circus.* She had the novel plotted out, but as the deadline loomed Ric and her nephew Bill 'were having mumps and measles all round me and I couldn't give time' so she dropped some of the planned chapters.[21]

Despite travelling through Western Australia with Wirth's Circus, Katharine set the novel largely in Victoria. There are only a few glimpses of Melbourne; it is the regional areas that Haxby's Circus travels through. Katharine drew on her memories and notes of the Dandenongs, the Victorian Goldfields, and especially Gippsland, from South Gippsland near Yarram and up to Mallacoota in East Gippsland where she had stayed on her journey to Lightning Ridge in 1916. Towards the end, she describes journeys much further afield through New South Wales and as far north as Townsville in Queensland, and over to Western Australia. It is a novel which engages her love of travel and the backblocks of Australia.

There aren't obvious autobiographical elements in *Haxby's Circus,* but it is a story of women's lives. Katharine was forty-four and forty-five as she wrote the novel, two ages she specifically gives to characters in the novel. First, it is Gina's pregnant mother: 'Mrs. Haxby was no more than forty-four; but she looked twice that age. Her small square face was weathered and tanned; her grey eyes so flat and unemotional usually, had a light from within now, the luminousness of another soul looking through her'.[22] Gina, in reaction to her mother's enslavement to fertility and self-conscious of her deformed back, decides to live her life free of men, avoiding romance in her twenties and thirties. Then, entering her forties, she embarks on a series of casual sexual encounters, 'suffering some deep dissatisfaction, unrest and discouragement with life'.[23] 'I hate age. People are like fruit, they rot as they grow older or wither up. The world would be a more beautiful place if young and vigorous people ruled it—with their generosity and impulses. Not the old by their weakness, and fear—'. She has a long conversation with her brother-in-law, Jack, about the meaning of life, saying how her friend, Billy Rocca the dwarf, once told her life was a three-volume novel:

> 'Billy was right after all. He said … "The first's the book of ideals and illusions; the second's the book of realities and noble resolutions; the third's the book of the senses and breakdown of the will." I think he was right, Jack. It's the third book I'm up to now.'

Jack helps her break out of her ennui, telling her, 'we've got to keep fighting—even if there's nothing worth fighting for'. She agrees and decides to resist the cruelty and meaninglessness of the world by running the circus well and turning herself into a spectacle as a clown, 'making herself grotesque and hideous to get the brittle crashing merriment of the crowd'. At forty-five she had reached a kind of peace with the world, 'more placid, good-humoured and jolly'.[24]

Gina's transformation from a young and beautiful acrobat to an ageing, humpbacked clown was written as Katharine came to terms with her own ageing. Her hair was greying and she had let slide the ideals of her twenties and thirties for the realities of middle-class married life. She was writing at a time when her return to active political involvement wasn't in sight. Living a comfortable middle-class life at odds with her beliefs, in her mid-forties Katharine likely shared some of Gina's crisis of meaning.

IN DECEMBER 1929 *The Seventh Gate* by British writer Muriel Harris was announced as the winner of the Jonathan Cape Novel Competition. Cape wrote to Katharine offering a contract for publication and advising that her entry 'was within an ace of getting the prize. We had over 600 manuscripts submitted and *Fay's Circus* got into the last six'. Cape insisted on retitling the novel, worried that 'Fay would be thought of as a girl's name' and 'an old-fashioned English surname' was required.[25]

Katharine asked for a delay of a few months to add the unwritten chapters—'four or five' in her estimate—that she had skipped when Ric and Bill were sick. Cape rejected the request and the British edition of the novel was published in July 1930.

About the time the British edition was published, Katharine was waiting to hear back from William Norton about whether he wanted to publish a US edition. Norton wrote, 'I sat up till 3 a.m. reading *Fay's Circus* and then hardly slept the rest of the night for the heavy smell of the animals and for fear I would do a flying header from a trapeze'. He finished his letter 'pledging his word to back it to the limit'.[26] He was also willing to restore Katharine's original title.

Norton had asked for a reader's report on *Fay's Circus* from the critic Hartley Grattan, who wrote, 'Miss Prichard continues to amaze me with her ability to live into diverse situations and I am more sure than ever that I was right in calling her the hope of the Australian novel'. However, he went on to say, 'she has a bad habit of writing too rapidly and too carelessly. If she could be persuaded, in some delicate fashion, that her work would be more enduring if she spent a few weeks on it with a blue pencil, I am sure it would be extremely profitable'.[27] It was a criticism of Katharine's writing made by others, too. Australian novelist Henry Handel Richardson had read *Working Bullocks* and *Coonardoo* by February 1930 when she wrote to a friend, with typical harshness:

> KP ought to sit down for three years & give her mind to improving her style & *learning* to punctuate. Anything so horrible as her punctuation I've never met with. (Norton remarked on it, too.) She throws commas about as old fashioned letter-writers used to make free with dashes. And has absolutely no feeling about separating her subject from her verb. All this makes a truly *il*literate impression.
>
> But the woman has much talent, & insight, & might under certain circumstances, become Australia's chief novelist.[28]

Katharine reacted defensively when such criticisms reached her but despite her insistence that she carefully edited, many of her novels were written in a hurry for competition deadlines while juggling other responsibilities. Driven by deadlines like the journalist she had once been, she wrote quickly in bursts of inspiration, many drafts produced in just months and not substantially rewritten.

Grattan also mentioned a structural problem: the abrupt change in the circus's fortunes from the depths of despair to sudden flourishing when Gina receives a bequest from Billy Rocca. He had put his finger on the gap in the novel, the section Katharine had run out of time to write. Norton gave her the time she needed to complete the missing section—in the end, one and a half chapters of 9700 words. Putting too much stock in Hugo's literary judgement, she read the chapters to him for his opinion. He didn't like them and she told Norton she came close to dropping them. 'The trouble is that having my mind set to the mould of the book, it is difficult to disintegrate and live those phases again. I do not know whether you will like them.'[29] The critic Carol Hetherington writes that the added material not only 'significantly improves the structure of the novel but also enriches and extends the broader canvas of the story'.[30] Katharine expressed her own preference for the American edition but the many reprints of the novel have followed the earlier British edition. When Angus and Robertson sent a copy of the first paperback reprint in 1945, she replied that she wished she had 'thought of giving you a copy of the American edition to print from', only for the oversight to be perpetuated in all the subsequent reprints.[31]

Despite Norton's pledge to back it, *Fay's Circus* was only moderately successful. Norton reported in May 1931 that it 'is getting good press and a fair sale; not quite as good press as *Coonardoo* and perhaps not quite such a good sale either. But after all, these are bad book times and nothing is selling in anything more than a limited way. Sorry not to write you more cheerful news but to a realist realism goes without saying'.[32] The *New York Times* review called it a 'tedious' book; Katharine wrote, 'It's the only thoroughly mean review of my work I've ever seen'.[33] *Fay's Circus* proved to be her final novel published in the United States in her lifetime.

The champion of *Haxby's Circus* was Perth writer Henrietta Drake-Brockman. Her long, glowing review in the *Daily News* judged it 'the best and most moving story she has yet written'. Henrietta praised 'the masterly fashion in which she makes one aware of the essential gallantry that lies somewhere in most human souls'. The characterisation was 'living' and the painting of Australian scenery 'brilliant'. 'One lays down *Haxby's Circus* feeling the richer for reading it, perhaps even a little less bitter over the frequent injustices of life, and certainly more ready to try to extend a friendlier sympathy to all those who bravely face the world in misshapen bodies.' Her one criticism of the novel was the lack of 'even a passing mention of the war'.[34] Later, she would write, '*Haxby's Circus* becomes the most universally compassionate of Katharine Susannah Prichard's novels. The circus represents life itself: the show that goes on, no matter what struggles, joys, disasters, overtake the individual'.[35]

Katharine with her grandmother Susan, brother Alan, and Aunt Chris, outside Clareville, ca. 1887. *KSPP, MS6201/1/13*

The Prichard family—Alan, Tom, Katharine, Beatrice, Edith and Nigel, 1895. *KSP Family Album, NLA*

Left: WT Reay. *Weekly Times, 10 April 1897, p. 11*
Right: Guido Barrachi, 1917. *Papers of Marjorie Pizer, SLNSW, MSS 7428/1/6*

Left: Sumner Locke. *Punch, 20 August 1908, p. 27*
Right: Hugo Throssell, ca. 1918. *Webb and Webb, SLWA, 4387B/38*

Katharine, London, ca. 1915. *KWC*

Hugo and Katharine (right) in the grounds of the hospital, 1915. *KWC*

Hugo and Katharine, Melbourne, 1916 or 1918. *KWC*

Katharine with Thea Bridge and friend, the cottage in the background, unknown visitors in the summerhouse, ca. 1921. *KSPP, MS6201/1/14*

Katharine in front of her workroom, ca. 1930. *KSP Family Album, NLA.*

Turee Station, 1926—left, Katharine and Joe Maguire; right, Topsy/Kundri, picture labelled by Katharine 'a girl like Coonardoo'. *KWC*

Katharine with prospectors at Larkinville, 1930. *KWC*

Left: Katharine and Ric, ca. 1927. *KWC*
Right: Hugh McCrae, 1927. *May Moore, NLA*

Katharine with Helios Gómez and Walter Carmon in the Soviet Union. *KWC*

The last known photograph of Hugo—pictured with his sister Eva Bartlett-Day (right) and nieces, 27 October 1933. *KSPP, MS6201/1/14*

Katharine on her return form the Soviet Union with Ric, ca. 26 December 1933. *KSPP, MS6201/1/14*

Egon Kisch and Katharine (centre) 1934. *KWC*

Left: Jean Devanny, 1932. *NLA*
Right: Doon Doyle (later Stone). *Kalgoorlie Miner, 12 July 1938, p. 1*

Katharine in her sitting room, 1949. *D.Glass, NAA*

Katharine and Paul Robeson, 1960. *John Gilchrist, SLWA*

Katharine with visitors, probably on her front verandah at Greenmount. *John Gilchrist, SLWA*

The last known photograph of Katharine—with Zoya Zarubina on the front verandah at Greenmount, 26 September, 1969. *John Gilchrist, SLWA*

Funeral procession at Karrakatta Cemetery, 4 October, 1969. *John Gilchrist, SLWA*

24

'The Mirage is Breaking Up'

Greenmount, 1929–1930

When Katharine finished writing *Haxby's Circus* she was exhausted; her five-year creative peak had come to an end. 'It became a choice of a holiday or a break down … and she, being a wise woman, chose the former.'[1] On 18 July 1929, she set off on a three-month trip alone. She spent a fortnight at Broome and then a month in Malaya (now Singapore and Malaysia) and Indonesia. 'Men are so sex hungry in the tropics that I'm afraid for you darling', she wrote years later to her granddaughter. 'You don't know all the risks … I do—having been there, when I was not so young—and still a mark for predatory males.' Among the 'unpleasant happenings' she endured was 'going for a drive with an admirer and having to do the Gracie Field act—she fought like a tiger for her honour etc'.[2] Katharine's novel *Moon of Desire* (1941), a romance about pearlers, would eventually come out of her notes and memories of Broome and Malaya.

From Malaya, she sailed right around the top of Australia and down to Melbourne. There was a reunion of old friends on 4 October, when Katharine, the Palmers and the Essons met 'over a sumptuous lobster meal, the sort of festival Hilda knows how to produce with miraculous speed and gaiety'. Nettie wrote of Katharine in her diary: 'In spite of her long days of travel she looked radiantly alive, physically even more graceful than in the past, her mind teeming with impressions of odd characters, remembered bits of dialogue … She seems to be moving along very buoyantly on a full tide of assurance'.[3]

Katharine then took the train to Sydney where she spent time with Christian Jollie Smith, who'd moved there in 1924. Like Katharine, Christian had been working relentlessly for the Communist Party in the early 1920s only to fall ill, in her case with pleurisy. After her recovery, she was less involved with the party, concentrating instead on her legal career, specialising in divorce and industrial cases.[4]

Katharine had written to the poet Hugh McCrae from Singapore, requesting he have dinner with her on 7 October while she was in Sydney.[5] McCrae has been described as 'a man of great charm and attractiveness' with a 'Rabelaisian sense of humour'.[6] They had first met in Melbourne in 1910; Katharine had been an 'earnest' admirer of his poetry but he 'had no time for earnest admirers, just then'.[7] In 1927, McCrae became joint editor of *The New Triad* with Ernest Watt. The short-lived magazine published Katharine's story 'The Cow' in January 1928. In July 1928, Watt met Katharine while he was in Perth. They talked about McCrae's poetry, which sparked Katharine's first known letter to McCrae.

After dinner on 7 October, Katharine sent McCrae another note, the day before she was leaving Sydney, asking if he would meet her for dinner again. He did and he gave her a copy of his poetry collection, *Satyrs and Sunlight* (1928). Their intimate conversation was interrupted by someone trying to talk to them. 'Could have murdered that young man to-night. Why wouldn't he go?' Katharine wrote to McCrae late that night. She stayed up reading his poems, writing:

> Dear Beautiful, Wonderful Hugh—I've never loved anything in all my life as I love your book to-night. It's almost too much. I can't sleep till I say so. Have been pacing this small, stuffy room like one of the beasts you see at the zoo. I'll never love anything so much. I'm sure. Nothing I've ever done is in the least worthy of you. I kneel beside your book & am lost in reverence & adoration.[8]

In the morning, McCrae came again to see her off on the train. 'I remember you always as you appeared to me on the railway station', he wrote to her later. 'I mean at the moment before you entered the carriage finally. Once you had got in I seemed to have lost you; and I've wondered since whether I understood the intention of a gesture you made: a single movement … hardly to be described … never to be forgotten.'[9] She signed off a later letter, 'And so—with the spirit of that gesture you read so well, and I didn't imagine you had ever seen—Katharine Susannah'.[10] In another letter she told him, 'Seeing you in Sydney will always be one of my best memories'.[11] McCrae admitted candidly to Nettie, 'last week, I fell pleasantly in love with Katharine Susannah … It is not so pleasant now; and I wonder if I shall get over it? Of course, she is ignorant of what I felt while I was talking to her; yet she is going to stay in my heart for ever'.[12]

Their letters grew more intimate and flirtatious, a four-year affair of the mind. Separated by the Nullarbor, if their relationship ever had a physical element, it could only possibly have been at the beginning during Katharine's 1929 trip. In her last surviving letter to him years later, she refers to 'whatever it was that bloomed between us for a while'.[13] Was she unsure of what to call it, or circumspect?

Her feelings for him were intertwined with her literary admiration. When she was asked to give a lecture to the literary society at the University of Western Australia in 1931 on current Australian literature, she declared, 'Hugh McCrae, in poetry or prose, is the supreme artist of words among us. He puts words under a spell to carry, colour, emotion, thought, flavour as nobody else does'.[14]

KATHARINE'S THREE-MONTH TRIP ended with her arrival by ship at Fremantle late at night on 22 October 1929. 'Despite the hour,' the *Daily News* reported, she 'went straight to her picturesque home at Greenmount … When asked if she intended beginning work on a new book, Mrs. Throssell said, "Not for a long time; my holiday was purely for a rest, and I am not going to settle down to work yet"'.[15]

A week after her return, the Wall Street stock market crashed and the Roaring Twenties began to give way to the Great Depression. Western Australian unemployment rose from 9 per cent in September 1929 to 25 per cent at the end of 1930.[16] During 1930, a thousand unemployed men were settled in the old army camp at Blackboy Hill in Greenmount, near the Throssells' house.[17] The Depression was coming close, and it was to come even closer.

FOR KATHARINE'S NEXT novel she had settled on the title of *Intimate Strangers*—borrowed from Hugo's account of his romance with Henrietta Watson—before she had written any of it, mentioning it by name in a letter to Louis Esson in November 1928, intending 'a study of the married relation, urban, and as close in as possible'.[18] The tensions in her marriage had been a starting point for the novel and her experiences in 1929 shaped it further—a month-long holiday by the beach in Rockingham in January, the three-month trip without Hugo and Ric and her feelings for McCrae.

She began it in January 1929 before the Depression and finished the first draft at the height of it. The shift in the real world is mirrored in the atmosphere of the novel. The first half of the book is set on a four-week holiday at Calatta, a fictional beachside holiday suburb. As a setting, Calatta brought together two significant places in Katharine's married life: the beach—especially Rockingham but also North Beach and Rottnest Island—and Wandu. Greenmount's Wandu is fictionalised in the Hartog family's house on the coast, Eendracht, the social centre of the holidayers at Calatta. Like Wandu, social life revolves around its tennis courts, bridge games, music and dancing; at the end of the novel, Eendracht is even to be turned into a guesthouse like Wandu.[19]

Elodie and Greg's 15-year-old marriage is strained. Elodie lives with the disappointment of giving up a career as a musician when she fell pregnant a few years into their marriage; she now has two children to look after and a hopeless maid. 'The mirage is breaking up', Elodie murmurs on the beach early in the novel and Greg repeats the phrase. 'He knew what Elodie was thinking as she said that, Greg told himself.'[20] Greg is obsessed with Margaret 'Dirk' Hartog, an athletic young woman from an old Western Australian family fallen on hard times. Elodie has endured his flirtations with different women for years. Now she takes revenge, allowing herself to be charmed by Dirk's worldly cousin, the sailor Jerome Hartog. She contemplates sailing away with him.

In the second half of the novel, Elodie and Greg return home to the suburb of South Perth as the Depression hits. First Greg's income is reduced and then he is sacked; Elodie must become the breadwinner of the family, teaching music and playing at restaurants and nightclubs. Greg's trauma as a war veteran is made explicit in a nightmare: '"God! It was awful," he moaned, clinging to her, weak and distraught. "That first night in the trenches again ... I was digging them out, Elodie, faces and arms and legs, smashed and putrid: then your face turned up ..."'[21] Paralleling Hugo's problems during the Depression, unemployed Greg spends money recklessly. When he loses the family home, he writes a suicide note and takes out his service revolver, only to decide against going through with it.

In the lost first draft, completed before Katharine's trip to the Soviet Union in 1933, Greg did kill himself. 'When I returned home my husband had died like hers. It was too painful then to write of what had happened to me. I changed the end. My literary conscience failed the test, I suppose. So the book was a failure.'[22]

In the published version, the novel ends with Elodie and Greg unconvincingly converting simultaneously to communism, 'the fire of a regenerating idea in which it seemed they would attain freedom and unity'.[23] Katharine seeded the conversion by introducing a communist character, an Italian fisherman named Tony, as Dirk's true love interest early in the novel. Later, Elodie and Dirk attend a rally of the unemployed in Fremantle and hear Tony declare that they must 'organise against the Capitalist system which breeds unemployment and war'.[24] Greg reveals in the final scene that, unbeknown to Elodie, he had 'knocked round with the unemployed a good deal' and now, inspired by Tony and Dirk's parting words as they elope, he tells Elodie, 'I'm thrilled with the idea that there's a big job on hand building this new way of life ... It's like being born again'.[25] By the time Katharine finished the novel, she had thrown herself back into the work of communism. She set out in *Intimate Strangers* to depict the ennui of middle-class life; by the end, she needed to announce the solution she had rediscovered.

Katharine wrote about sex more frankly in *Intimate Strangers* than anywhere else. Over and over, *Intimate Strangers* circles around the questions of finding sexual and personal fulfillment in marriage and out of it, with sexual attraction pulling people away from commitment. There is no simple lesson; the appeal and the problems of adultery are both presented. As in the earlier play *Bid Me to Love,* it is the wife who actually has sex with someone else while the flirtatious husband reveals he has stayed physically faithful. Elodie 'had always believed a woman was not entitled to exclusive rights in a man; nor was he entitled to exclusive rights to her. She despised the frenzy for possession which afflicted so many lovers. There was something ignoble, ungenerous about it'.[26] The climax of the novel has Elodie and Greg recommit themselves to each other at the same time as they applaud Dirk's escape from her marriage. In the moral world of the novel, Dirk's escape is permissible because her oppressive marriage mirrored that of the capitalist oppression of workers, her husband Ted controlling her money and beating her up.

In one incident, Greg is no better. Elodie won't have sex with him while he's infatuated with Dirk, telling him 'I won't be made use of'.[27] Frustrated and insisting a man should not have to be a 'eunuch' in his own house, he rapes Elodie:

> His head fell against her neck. He was kissing her arms and breast with the loose devouring mouth of rage and hunger.
>
> 'Greg!' Elodie besought moving away from him. He clung heavily, overpowering and crushing her. 'Don't, don't! For God's sake,' she pleaded, 'I'll never forgive you.'
>
> He laughed ruthlessly, undeterred, overwhelming and destroying her resistance. When she lay weakened and vanquished, he tried to be tender again, smoothed her hair: whispered, 'Elodie… Elodie, darling.'
>
> She lay limp, unresponsive: perspiration beading in tears all over her body. Her immobility, air of suffering, troubled him. She looked extraordinarily helpless, violated in some supreme way. He was really sorry for her.[28]

Rape in marriage was not legally recognised in Australia until decades later. The scene echoed the message of the Freewoman discussion circle when Katharine was in London. She put that message of the circle directly into the mouth of another character, the more enlightened Jerome: 'Marriage is a business contract … A woman sells out all sexual rights in herself for maintenance, and a man insures to himself a vicarious immortality for himself through his progeny'.[29]

Another instance of rape in marriage in a later work—*The Roaring Nineties* (1946)—reinforces its significance for Katharine. In that scene, Sally and Morris are prospecting at a goldrush when, at night, he 'flung himself upon her' in their tent, 'the crude, vicious copulation … an outrage he had committed against their love'.[30]

Disingenuously, Katharine claimed *Intimate Strangers* 'was a simple story of two friends who recognised themselves immediately when they read the book'.[31] Decades later, Ric Throssell, frustrated at autobiographical readings of the novel, named the friends as Les and Rose Atkinson.[32]

Four years younger than Katharine, Rose was a musician like her fictional counterpart. A newspaper article profiled her at the time Katharine was writing the novel:

> Mrs Atkinson has had a varied and interesting life. She was connected with the theatre and dramatic art for some time, and later was associated with the Melba Conservatorium. She was slow to decide upon her actual work in life, because she is intensely interested in her fellow creatures. She is perhaps, above all things, a lover of beauty, and in her various ventures has managed to include some form of music—of singing or instrumental work.[33]

Like Elodie, Rose seems to have given up the chance for a professional career in music with the birth of her two children. In another similarity to Elodie, the Depression provoked a new interest in social issues for Rose and she worked in both advocacy and practical help for young unemployed women.

Les Atkinson was a teacher, not an office worker like Greg, and he doesn't seem to have served in the Great War; both of these aspects of Greg's character are closer to Hugo. Greg is a frustrated artist, something neither Hugo nor Les were, although Les was an amateur writer, contributing 'light verse to the local press … and articles on children under the name of "Diminie Dee"'.[34] Greg is not convincingly artistic; his art reads like a character element Katharine has grafted on awkwardly. Even if Katharine intended Greg to resemble Les, he talks and acts a lot like Hugo. Ric writes, 'I cannot help seeing much of my father in Greg … in his charm, something about the way he is described, his pride in his physique, his flirtatiousness'.[35]

Echoing the beach setting of *Intimate Strangers,* the Atkinsons had a holiday shack in the bush near North Beach where the Throssells stayed with them at least once.[36] The Throssells may have come to know the couple at Wandu; in July 1927, Rose starred with Hugo in a night of 'mirth, dancing, and music' put on by the Wandu Dramatic Society.[37] The Atkinsons' friendship with Katharine survived them reading the novel and recognising themselves as Greg and Elodie; incidental references to the couple in Katharine's letters to Ric continue into the 1950s. Although the troubled marriage portrayed in *Intimate Strangers* seems destined to end in divorce, in real life Les and Rose remained married until Les died in 1963, at least apparently living out the unlikely happy ending Katharine gave Greg and Elodie.

Despite the fictionalisations of *Intimate Strangers,* the echoes of Katharine and Hugo's marriage from 1929 to 1933 are too loud to ignore. After the beach holiday, Elodie spends months contemplating leaving her family behind and running away with Jerome Hartog to Asia, calling to mind Katharine's long trip by herself in 1929 which culminated in meeting Hugh McCrae. McCrae obviously wasn't present at Katharine's January 1929 holiday in Rockingham but a letter she wrote to him in 1932 when she returned to Rockingham strengthens the association between her memories of the beach holiday and McCrae:

> Walked six miles, along the edge of the sea, barefoot & drenched with spray, after crossing from the island. Dried my clo'[thes] behind a sand dune & went to sleep – again—on hot white sand. Sheltered from the sea breeze: stiff aromatically fragrant shrubs all round. Called to see Prospero, an old Genovese fisherman whose shack of driftwood stands in scrub, back from Cape Peron. He used to play to me on his steel guitar, for hours, when we were here, three years ago: and bawl arias from the operas in a great hoarse voice. But when I knocked & called nobody answered. I opened the door & the hut was empty. 'Prospero—he died two years ago,' men at the nearest camp told me. Sat yarning with them awhile in their boatshed. Anita & and an old Irishman who

> have lived there together for thirty years. The Italian is one of the Medici who has taken the simple life builds boats & mends them; goes fishing, has a queer aristocratic anarchist philosophy, and exquisite manners.
>
> A gorgeous day! Would you have liked to be with me? I wonder.[38]

Katharine wrote directly about Prospero the Italian fisherman in *Intimate Strangers*, not even changing his name; she has Elodie and Jerome meet at his hut.

Intimate Strangers languished while Katharine became preoccupied with party work throughout 1931 and 1932. She had finished a draft when she left for London in May 1933, but she didn't feel confident about it, telling Nettie, 'my book still in the rough & feel as if it will never be done now'. Her headaches were making it hard to write. 'I hate not being able to work—like hell. Tons of stuff to do & only a damaged ache to do it with.'[39] *Intimate Strangers* was not to be published until 1937.

ON 11 NOVEMBER 1929, soon after Katharine returned from her long trip, Colonel WT Reay died in a London hospital at age seventy-one. His wife and daughters had been living in Australia for years. Two of his daughters, but not his wife, had set off for London when they heard he was ill; they did not make it in time to see him. Since the end of the war he had put his energy into reorganising the special constabulary 'to deal with Communistic or other emergencies', an ironic contrast with Katharine's political radicalisation in the same period.[40]

In Katharine's 1929 notebook for *Intimate Strangers*, she seems to have transcribed Reay's final letter, perhaps as a way to preserve it while making it harder for Hugo to find:

> The last letter to K.
> (After ten years—in memoriam)
> My exquisite and adored K—
> Some people believe in the second coming of Christ. I have prayed for the second coming of K. But I am old and ill now, and begin to fear I shall never see your dear face again.

Has he made you happy?
I was afraid he would not.[41]

January 1929 marked ten years since Katharine's telegram to Reay announcing her marriage to Hugo. Did she write back? What could she possibly say, when Hugo had ended Reay's lingering hold over her only to bring new kinds of miseries into her life?

25

Red Star

Greenmount, 1930–1933

IN JANUARY 1932, Victoria Cross recipient Albert Jacka died in Melbourne from nephritis at the age of thirty-nine and the *Daily News* wrote that it

> brings home to Western Australians the question of what has happened, or what is happening to this State's eight VC heroes ... Upon their return from the Great War they were lionised and feted, and, to use the words of one of them, 'were promised the world'. Since those far-away days, however, some of them have experienced what the Diggers call 'a rough spin'.[1]

The newspaper profiled Western Australia's eight Great War Victoria Cross recipients, and, ironically, Hugo was written up as one of those enjoying success since the war.

On a visit to Katharine and Hugo in May 1930, Vance Palmer observed to Nettie, 'Jimmy's got "land" on the brain. He puts all the money they have into land, consequently they're always short ... Of course he takes it half humorously but it's the sort of humour that must be a bit wearing'.[2]

It was a bad time to be in real estate. The final advertisement for W Thomas & Co with Hugo as the manager of the land department appeared on 2 April. After that, Hugo kept placing real estate advertisements in the *West Australian* under his own name, houses and blocks in Greenmount with prices decreasing over the months as he grew more desperate; a lot of them were his own and he was deeply in debt.

In July 1930, a prospector named Mick Larkin found gold south of Kalgoorlie. According to Katharine, 'For a long time my husband and I had been promising ourselves to rush to the first rush which looked like being the real thing'.[3] In November 1930, they travelled 600 kilometres into the desert and spent a week at the newly named Larkinville. For Katharine, it was material for future writing; for Hugo it was a chance to make a quick fortune.

'Within the last month or so', Katharine reported, 'two hundred men have swarmed to the rush … The pegs of mining leases and prospecting areas are scattered through thorn bush, snap-and-rattle, sandalwood and camel bush, for a mile or so on either side of the main camp'. She enjoyed her time on the goldfields, working as camp 'slushie' (kitchen hand) and hearing yarns around the campfire at night. When an old prospector 'red with dust, unfolds a sock, or dingy piece of flannel, to show the twisted effigies of pre-historic pancakes and wild pigs in bright gold … you understand why his hand trembles and his eyes are bright'.[4]

The trip was the beginning of Katharine's chronicling of the goldfields, the biggest literary project of her career. 'Old prospectors … used to come up from the alluvial claims and sit round the camp-fire yarning for hours. I gathered many stories from their reminiscences, and, of course, invaluable material for the goldfields trilogy.'[5] One of the first goldfields stories she wrote, 'Mrs Jinny's Shroud', was published in the *Bulletin* in December 1931. A miniature version of her later novel, *The Roaring Nineties*, it is the story of colourful, tough prospectors looking for gold, resisting pressure to sell out to a mining company, and blowing a fortune only to return to the simple, hard prospecting life they find most meaningful.

On 15 January 1931, two months after Katharine and Hugo's trip, a 17-year-old boy at Larkinville unearthed the biggest nugget ever found in Western Australia. Nicknamed the Golden Eagle, it weighted 1135 ounces and was worth in the order of £6000. Hugo caught the renewed gold fever and returned to Larkinville in February.

With the Depression hitting hard, there were now more than one thousand prospectors hoping to make their fortune. This time, Hugo paid £100 to buy Mick Larkin's original claim. Six weeks later, the *Kalgoorlie Miner* reported, 'Only a few men are on gold … There have been no large finds recently although Mr Hugo Throssell secured about £50 worth of gold a few days ago. Most of the men are unearthing a few weights and are battling on hopefully'.[6] Hugo also claimed land on the road to Larkinville at the same time as another applicant, and the dispute ended up in court.[7] Both men withdrew their claims and Hugo returned home to Greenmount.

On the back of Hugo's disappointment at Larkinville, a clash he was having with the RSL over his role on the Soldiers' Settlement Board intensified. Back in 1919, he'd been appointed by the government as the soldiers' representative, albeit with the approval of the nascent RSL. Some members of the RSL had grown dissatisfied with Hugo's performance and in 1930, a conference of soldier settlers unanimously resolved that the RSL should appoint its own representative to the board, a motion that was then supported by the state congress of the RSL. Hugo wrote to the RSL Land Committee, trying to find out why they were unhappy, but they didn't respond. A deputation from the RSL met with premier James Mitchell and 'complained about Captain Throssell's lack of interest in the Soldier Settlement'.[8] Hugo resigned, dating it Anzac Day, and then spent months demanding explanations.

Katharine would later name Hugo's loss of his job on the Soldier Settlement Board as a major factor in the beginning of his depression. According to her, depression had begun to affect him when the role was reduced to a part-time one and was intensified by the RSL executive's 'contemptible action' in manoeuvring him out altogether.[9] While their dealings with Hugo do seem duplicitous, it's also plausible Hugo hadn't been performing well as the RSL representative, caught up as he had been in his own financial schemes and often away on business.

Katharine wrote to Hugh McCrae, 'The summer was so long & dry this year, that I nearly died of it—what with over-drafts, sleepless nights, & not being able to work … But I revived with the rains, and am working again to be the support of my family & pay off a mortgage of £12,000'.[10] It was a massive debt to have accumulated. In the middle of 1930, Katharine wrote 'the crops have been bad & we've lost our car';

in 1931 they had to let go of their maid.[11] Finally, painfully, in October 1932 Katharine sold off her beloved cottage in Emerald.

Years later, Katharine would write to Ric that 'Daddy's weakness, & the cause of so much suffering & sorrow to me, was a tendency to spend more than he had or could afford. And so all our troubles began, & mounted until the end—you know'.[12] His problem with money was, in another letter, 'his desire to give me all that he thought I should have—and, of course, those extras of living didn't matter to me. I could be quite content with old clo[thes] and our home at Greenmount'.[13]

In November 1932 Hugo had a mental breakdown; after his suicide a year later, Katharine called it 'an incident which foreshadowed what has happened'.[14] The doctor who saw him recorded, 'Worried about his health. Unable to sleep lately. Gets headaches … Everything is a worry and he is a nuisance to himself and his friends. Brain will not seem to work properly. Has lost weight and feels flabby—disinclined for exertion'.[15] Hugo had friends looking out for him and, hearing of his breakdown, one named Jonah Jones arranged a temporary appointment as an inspector of fertilisers with the Agricultural Department. Katharine wrote 'immediately his health improved'.[16]

Hugo's struggles took their toll on Katharine and her severe migraines were back. There's a possible echo of her experience in *Intimate Strangers:*

> All day, Elodie had flogged herself against unfathomable weariness, a headache that frayed every nerve. She fought desperately to do what was necessary … following a blind impulse to take Greg away from anything that reminded him of his trouble. She could keep her legs moving only by an effort of will: the blood barked in her ears: she could not see clearly. An insidious faintness ebbed and flowed through her limbs.[17]

JUST BEFORE THE financial troubles hit the Throssells hard, they spent money building a workroom for Katharine. In May 1930, she wrote to Hugh McCrae, 'A work-room is being built for me in the orchard which you will consecrate by your presence'. As it happened, McCrae's trip to Perth didn't eventuate and so the workroom was not consecrated, but for the first time Katharine had a dedicated writing space. A journalist described it a few years later. 'Dingo pelts were mats; a kangaroo skin rug covered the couch, and the pictures on the walls were the work of Australian artists. The stone fireplace occupied most of one wall, and there were book shelves in the corners. A small jarrah table held a portable typewriter and books and papers were scattered about.'[18] The workroom was 'down past the lemon and orange trees on the hill slope', the window 'overlooking a bank of silver wattle'.[19]

In 1931, Katharine was working on a selection of her stories with Jonathan Cape. Cape insisted on taking the title from one of the weaker stories, 'Kiss on the Lips', based on her observations of impoverished newspaper boys as a journalist in 1909.[20] Advance copies had been printed by January 1932 when Henry Handel Richardson complained to her friend:

> People have now dropped into the horrid habit of sending me books & asking for a par[agraph] or an opinion they can quote! Cape for one sent me KS Prichard's Vol of short stories that they are just about to issue, with a request for an article of 7 or 800 words on her work. As I think some of her books very good, I would have stretched a point in her favour; but alas! when I came to read the stories, I found she had collected the most heterogeneous mass of bits & scraps—some fit only to be the bare bones or pencil jottings of what might ultimately have made a story; & the more finished ones monotonous & hastily written. I couldn't do it—wldn't put my name to that kind of thing.
>
> Don't mention this to NP [Nettie] though, whose pet KSP is.[21]

Richardson failed to see the good in many of the stories, but her 'heterogeneous' comment is fair, the collection spanning two decades across genres, landscapes, readerships and quality. 'An Encounter' and 'Treason' were both published in newspapers in 1917 and 1919 and the former isn't really a short story at all, but a journalistic sketch from Katharine's epic journey along the east coast in 1916. A second group of stories are literary fiction, including some of Katharine's finest stories like 'The Grey Horse', 'The Cooboo', 'Happiness' and 'The Cow'. A third group of stories are 'yarns' from the Australian countryside like 'The Dark Horse of Darran', 'Two Men' and 'The Swop', which attempt nothing more than to entertain. 'White Kid Gloves'—first published in *The Bulletin* in 1928—is somewhere between the popular and literary, a sentimental, romantic story, with some depth, notable for its depiction of shell shock and other effects of the war. Some of the reviewers came to similar judgements as Richardson, but many others were positive. The *Times Literary Supplement* was full of praise, writing 'violent, sentimental, kind, brutal, humorous, her men are alive' and that 'she can bring bush scents and colours and lovely daylight from "down under" into London town, and there is scarcely a convict or kangaroo in her pages'.[22] The *Sydney Morning Herald* gave an appreciative review, summing up, 'There is beauty in these stories and a rare understanding of the people of the outback and the conditions under which they work'.[23]

AFTER RIC'S BIRTH, Katharine had put writing, family and her social life ahead of politics. Things changed during the Depression. In June 1931 she wrote to McCrae, 'I'd like to pitch into [the] work of the Communist Movement again. It is the supreme reality for me. But I can't just now …'[24] However, even as she wrote this, she was already recommitting to the work of the party.

Around this time Katharine apparently contacted the party headquarters in Sydney. The way Jean Devanny told it—her memories coloured by her jealousy of Katharine—it had been so long since Katharine had been connected to the party that the incumbent leaders didn't know who she was. Jean was having an affair with the party leader, JB Miles, and he told her that Katharine was claiming to be a foundation member, but they had no record of it. What did Jean know of her? A reader of thrillers, Miles 'refused to accept my statement that Kathie was regarded as the then leading Australian writer—till shortly afterwards he saw it stated in a Sydney daily paper'.[25]

Perhaps related to Katharine making contact, the party sent the experienced organiser Jack Stevens to Perth to regroup the movement. Katharine remembered him as

> a man of the working class, simple and straight-forward, honest and earnest … When he came to the West as an organiser, there was no Communist Party. There was a group of confused militant

> workers. Comrade Stevens set himself the task of creating order and Communist methods of organisation in this group and of rallying the unemployed about it. Shabby and hungry, he struggled against tremendous difficulties in the work he had undertaken. Very little money could be raised for it, in those days; and he spent every available penny on organisational work and propaganda.[26]

Stevens incited crowds of the unemployed on the Esplanade, collected party subscriptions and sold pamphlets. He was having enough success to worry the authorities. In June 1931 plainclothes detectives arrested him on charges of being a person of evil fame and vagrancy; they said he was 'in this State for the sole purpose of stirring up strife and revolution'. Searching his room in a city boarding house, they claimed he had a formula for starting fires.[27]

At his trial on 2 July 1931, Katharine testified that she'd been assisting Stevens for three months and 'she knew him as a man of the highest moral character, and found it impossible to regard him as a man of evil fame. She had never heard him advocate violence. She regarded his character as similar to that of Jesus Christ, and considered that he was being similarly persecuted'.[28] Her comparison of a communist with Jesus had a whiff of blasphemy and made headlines around the country. The magistrate ruled her evidence had been given in good faith but that she did not know Stevens well, seemingly unaware of how thoroughly Katharine shared his objectives. Stevens was fined, put on a bond and sentenced to fourteen days imprisonment; he ended up serving six weeks because he refused to pay the fine. 'I went to see him there and he had to stand in a horrible barred cage, in the prison uniform, to talk to me, with a warder on guard. I remember that he was very distressed that he had not been allowed to shave.'[29]

As the number of communists around Australia grew, the crackdown on the party's activities continued. In February 1932, the postmaster-general declared he was banning six communist periodicals, including the *Workers' Weekly*, from being carried by post.[30] The ban particularly affected Western Australia, cutting off party members and potential recruits from the main source of news and propaganda.

Western Australian communists responded by founding their own newspaper, the *Red Star*, 'official organ of No. 6 District Committee

CP of A'. The first four-page roneoed issue appeared on 18 April 1932, selling for one penny. Bill Mountjoy was the editor; one of their comrades remembers, 'Katharine not only corrected the English but taught Bill how to write'.[31] Mountjoy, the new state organiser, wrote that 'a friendly typiste cut the stencils and Jack [Stevens] was the machinist'.[32] It ran in this format for sixty-nine issues until July 1933 when the party bought a printing press.

On 12 September 1932 Katharine joined a protest in Perth's city centre of unemployed men who had walked off their work camps at Frankland River in the south of the state and come to the city to demand better conditions. Police arrested eighteen of the demonstrators as they tried to address the public from verandahs along Barrack Street. The demonstrators reconvened on the grass at the Esplanade and addressed a gathered crowd of several thousand. Four of these speakers were arrested after criticising the police. Katharine was shrewd enough to avoid arrest. 'In fact, almost the only person who did not attack the police from the platform was Mrs Hugo Throssell who informed the gathering of her sympathy for the strikers in the demands they were making.'[33] Bill Mountjoy's wife, Jane, was the only woman arrested. According to Ric, Katharine sold a brooch her father had given her to raise the bail and free Jane the next day.[34]

Probably in response to this clash, at eight thirty in the morning on 30 September 1932, detectives with search warrants simultaneously raided the houses of Katharine, the Mountjoys and George Whitbread. She wrote to Hugh McCrae:

> Can you see the criminal, sitting up in bed, to interview the female of the species; and later, passing the time of day with the inspector in charge of the job, herself in yellow silk pyjamas & a black silk gown embroidered with golden dragons? It looked like the first act of a play—the verandah hung round with wisteria, & long sprays of dog roses. The only protest I made was that none of your letters, or Hilda's, should be read, as they were entirely personal.[35]

The detectives took communist pamphlets and books, private letters, and anything else which seemed suspicious—including Katharine's copy of Bernard O'Dowd's *The Poet Militant*—and then proceeded to the rooms of the Friends of the Soviet Union, stripping them bare, even taking away a photo of Lenin. They confiscated all the copies of the new issue of the *Red Star*, which hadn't yet been distributed. The *Red Star* team—probably including Katharine—refused to be intimidated, setting up a new two-page issue of the newspaper that same day.[36] She told McCrae she expected to be arrested any day. 'But so long as I fight the good fight, what does that matter?'

With the rise of Hitler in 1933, the Comintern had been helping set up anti-war groups which would also serve as a communist front, hoping to bring people into the party. Katharine was asked to establish a Western Australian anti-war committee. Two hundred attended a meeting she organised on 13 May 1933.[37] One of the motions on the agenda read, in part, 'We declare that a new world war would be a monstrous crime against civilisation, and must be prevented at all costs' and that all elected to the committee pledged to fight against 'imperialist capitalism, that purveyor to the slaughter house'. Moderates at the meeting, including the League of Nations' representative, academic Fred Alexander, objected to the anti-capitalist elements of the motion and called for amendments which would allow a broader coalition to be formed against war. The moderates were outvoted and the motion passed.[38] The meeting came just before Katharine left on a six-month trip, but on her return she was heavily involved with the organisation, which was to become the Movement Against War and Fascism.

Katharine had placed ads in the newspaper calling specifically on returned soldiers to attend the meeting and register their protest against war.[39] Hugo came, and he was one of two Victoria Cross recipients elected to the committee of forty-five.[40] He spoke at the meeting, saying 'he had seen enough of the horrors of war, and that he would do his utmost to prevent his own boy from going to war'.[41] In her autobiography, Katharine highlighted Hugo's support for the organisation as evidence of his ongoing political commitment.[42] It was a consolation to her, a sign of where he was headed if he had lived. It is, perhaps, woven into Greg's conversion at the end of *Intimate Strangers* after he decides against suicide.

MANY LEFT-WING WRITERS and intellectuals from around the world were making a pilgrimage to the Soviet Union to see the 'workers' paradise' for themselves. Two events in 1933 further fanned the flames of Katharine's desire to go herself. The first was seeing Guido Baracchi. Docked at Fremantle for a day while on the way to the Soviet Union, he came to have lunch at Greenmount on 27 February 1933 with his new lover, Betty Roland. Betty wrote that Katharine 'is gentle and her voice is soft and sweet and I seemed to see a hint of sadness in her eyes. No one could call her beautiful but her face is sensitive and strong'.[43] The visit would have been difficult for Hugo, who knew of Katharine's relationship with Guido. Katharine told Guido that Hugo used to 'humorously' call him her 'greasy, handkissing dago'.[44]

The second push towards Katharine seeing the Soviet Union for herself came on 18 April when she gave an address on the development of communism to the University Historical and Economic Society. She praised the achievements of Soviet Russia and 'deprecated the apathy which existed among University students in connection with social problems'. The respected economics lecturer, Edward Shann, responded:

> He did not want to question the many beautiful pictures of Russia which Mrs Throssell had painted, but others had held different views. He had spoken with one American economist whose recurring comment on Russia was 'Never was human spirit so in bondage'. They must keep an open mind on the question.[45]

Katharine felt she would be able to counter comments like Shann's once she had seen the Soviet Union for herself.

Beatrice, probably aware of her sister's financial and health troubles, wrote saying she was headed to Europe and wanted Katharine to show her around Paris, enclosing the cost of the fare to join her. It would be a chance for Katharine to meet her publishers in London—communication by post had long been a frustration—and secretly journey on to the Soviet Union.[46]

'Too much everything: financial burden, domestic fracas, work & weariness!' Katharine wrote to Hugh McCrae, making a rare reference to tensions in her marriage. 'Miraculously, as soon as I decided to throw in my towel … they withdrew. Every difficulty was straightened out, devotion & sweetness reigned again. Fracas is incidental to domesticity, I suppose. We suppress it, & then don't, and then the *status quo ante* blooms again. I must be an aggravating woman to live with!'[47]

Ric was now eleven. 'Katharine and my father were talking in the garden when I first heard that she was going away. She leaned against him with her head resting on his chest, his arm around her. There was a gravity in their voices, and a sense of parting.'[48] Hugo insisted she go, Katharine claimed, and so she did, on the understanding he 'would do nothing while I was away to make me regret leaving him'.[49]

26

The Real Russia

London and Russia, 1933

'THIS IS A dull ship—and dirty', Katharine wrote to Hugh McCrae from the SS *Baradine*, 'but I sit alone [on] millions of miles of sparkling blue sea & think to you'.

> I was so tired when I came on board. Slept for two days & three nights. And there was a storm. I wakened just to look at it & try to take a walk, but had to do it rushing from pillar to post—waves crashing over the deck. Smoking-room corridors smashed & sea slopping in through the works.
>
> So the move of the sea did not afflict me. I just slept & on the third day, awoke feeling so fit that I ran along the deck & did some physical jerks for sheer joy. It being dawn & nobody but me … about.[1]

All through the trip, her head and heart were full of McCrae. 'Always & always, I think of you, Hugh dear! Have a sense of you with me.' As she travelled up the Red Sea, she wrote to him that she was 'was exclaiming to you, at the black mountains, a full moon, all Arabia behind'.[2] She hoped desperately there would be a letter from him waiting for her in London.

She wrote a letter to Hugo about the same time, echoing her words to McCrae and remembering that he travelled the same route during the war. 'A full moon over the black mountains, the three cornered sails of dhows … made me think of my own dear man & how he had seen & known all these things. How I wanted him … No one else worth while!'[3]

On a stopover at the Red Sea port of Aden, she explored the city with a fellow passenger, an unnamed young woman. The woman offered to buy Katharine a shawl and a necklace; Katharine refused but accepted a gift of 'the most delicious cigarettes & Turkish Delight'. Katharine wrote to Hugo that she didn't have enough money to reciprocate 'My sobriquet is "stingey"!'[4]

She reached London on 22 June 1933. 'London is more of a precocious beast than ever. I feel like a small wild cat in its jaws—all of a dither & frantic to escape.'[5] Her publisher, Jonathan Cape, put on a luncheon in her honour. She remembered proudly:

> Edward Garnett, the distinguished English critic, sat beside me.
>
> 'If Cape takes my advice,' he said, 'he will publish everything you write.'
>
> 'I have already come to that conclusion,' Jonathan Cape replied.
>
> It was an unforgettable occasion.[6]

It may have been at the luncheon that she met Henry Handel Richardson, the expatriate Australian novelist, who had been privately scathing of *Kiss on the Lips* the previous year. Richardson—very recently widowed—invited Katharine to visit her. With the acclaim given to Richardson's *Ultima Thule* (1929), she had eclipsed Katharine in the perception of critics as the most important Australian novelist of the moment. They had a friend in common—Nettie Palmer—who had been corresponding with Richardson and become a strong advocate of her work. Katharine had read *Ultima Thule* in early 1930 and told Nettie she was 'all veneration for it. A great & fine piece of work. Utterly beautiful'. But reading it caused Katharine to feel the tension between her literary nationalism and her communist commitment to internationalism:

> I still feel that HHR writes of Australia as a stranger—not one of us really … I hate her attitude to the life of a little up-country town for instance, it's so thoroughly English. No Australian could feel so

> superior to people who, after all, are creatures of their environment. There is some talk of Henry Handel Richardson doing an introduction to *Haxby's Circus.* I would much rather she did not because I feel that we have nothing in common. I so passionately love the country & am of it—& she belongs to other conditions & probably feels a little superior to my soil besottedness. She is right no doubt. Literature should have no country. But I can't help it. I care first for interpretations of this place—& will, with my eyes open, barter international reputation to give Australia as it is, or as I see it, to the world. If HHR loved Australia & lived here, I would be at her feet. As she doesn't, I can't quite believe in her as *Australian.*[7]

Despite Katharine feeling they had 'nothing' in common, they warmed to each other when they met in person. 'I thought her a charming woman, & quite unspoiled', wrote Richardson. 'I saw her books in her'.[8] The two hoped to stay in touch, with Richardson writing to Katharine the next year, 'Though our glimpse of each other was so brief, write to me sometimes & tell me what you are thinking & doing'.[9]

On 7 July, Katharine went to Paris for a couple of weeks with her sister, Beatrice, and niece, Thea. While there, she signed a contract for a French translation of *Coonardoo* but for some reason, the translation did not eventuate and it was not until 1991 that one was published.[10] Nor did Katharine's other literary hopes for the trip come to pass. Like so many film projects, a much-publicised production of *Haxby's Circus* did not proceed. William Norton, her American publisher, was not in London at quite the same time. He suggested she return to Australia via America so they could finally meet and she was contemplating doing so.[11] As it happened, she did not and he decided not to publish *Kiss on the Lips* or, later, *Intimate Strangers.*

According to Katharine's ASIO file, she contacted the Communist Party headquarters in London, probably to arrange a trip to the Soviet Union. 'Following this she left for Leningrad with George HARDY a well known Communist.'[12] After reaching Leningrad by ship, she took a train to Moscow.

'Making my own wilful way', Katharine wrote, insisting on the independence of her tour and thus the objectivity of her reporting, 'I roamed about by myself, during my first days in Moscow. Nobody suggested what I should do; where I should go. I just arrived and proceeded … feeling rather a motherless foal, so dazzled and bewildered by the beauty and strangeness of everything'.[13] *The Real Russia* (1934), Katharine's book about her travels through the Soviet Union, is an impersonal account. Scholar Jeff Sparrow classifies it as a Stalinist travel narrative, in which the invisible narrator brings back to the West the good news about the utopian transformation of everyday life in the communist state. 'The book is a memoir, but it is not about her.'[14] She came to witness the ideals of communism put into practice, but the revolution of 1917 had been followed by years of civil war and now the brutality of Joseph Stalin's regime. Under Stalin in 1933, there was lip service to communist ideals but tight control over people's lives and millions dying of starvation in Soviet Ukraine as forced collectivisation of farming led to famine. The signs of the betrayal of communism were there for visitors to notice if they looked critically. Yet for those like Katharine who wanted to believe, there were things to admire—economic development, advances in education and health, well-funded arts, and a veneer of egalitarianism. If she had misgivings, she suppressed them.

She made a pilgrimage to visit the body of Vladimir Lenin, architect of the Bolshevik Revolution. 'Processions of children are seen, with a teacher, going to visit him where he lies in the small square temple of red granite … Frail and gentle he looks, lying asleep in his everyday clothes … his long, delicate hands lie outstretched beside him.' Disingenuously, she claimed, 'he is an ordinary everyday person to them, not a saint of any sort—just Uncle Lenin who helped the Russian working-class to organise for the revolution which has given the children schools and school dining-rooms, factories, theatres and flats in the new model dwellings where they live with their parents'. In focusing on the children's reactions, she avoided reporting her own, but her reverence is apparent.[15]

In one chapter of *The Real Russia,* Katharine describes, approvingly, the *chistka*—purge trials—she witnessed. Communist Party members were interrogated over their personal histories and held to account for accusations brought by their fellow workers—from having a 'swelled [*sic*] head' to fraudulently claiming sick leave. 'The 1933 chiska [*sic*], which is not yet concluded, has been drastic and searching, clearing out of the Party all members whose light does not shine by their works.'[16] At this stage of the Stalinist purges, members found guilty were expelled from the party or demoted rather than imprisoned or executed; how would Katharine have reported the murderous Great Purge if she'd been in Russia in 1936?

Originally, Katharine checked in to stay at the Hotel Lux. On 3 August, she turned up at Guido and Betty Roland's place; they were subletting a single large room. Betty remembered that Katharine was unhappy about the atmosphere of the hotel and 'in true Moscow fashion', they 'suggested to Katharine that she move in with us'. The bed had two mattresses and they took one off and put it in the corner for Katharine to sleep on. Guido was working at his desk each night until midnight, and so Katharine and Betty both slept with umbrellas shading them from the light. 'I hope she is not aware', Betty wrote, 'that the situation acts like an aphrodisiac on Guido. I beg him to restrain himself but this has no effect … I trust that she is sound asleep by the time he … comes to bed'.[17]

Betty wasn't jealous of Katharine; she was more worried about Guido's estranged second wife, Neura, who he was still in love with.[18] She found Katharine 'a serene person with a soft voice and a gentle smile; even in this short time I have grown to like her very much'. However, she and Guido didn't see much of her over the three weeks she stayed with them; 'Katharine is very much *persona grata* here, being an important member of the CP [Communist Party] in Australia … She is being taken to a lot of interesting places and is meeting important people'.[19] At the end of August, Guido and Betty farewelled her as they left for Leningrad where Guido was to establish an English-language list for a publishing house.[20]

At the same time, Katharine headed south to the city of Armavir, where she joined the kino train. The kino train had begun the previous year as the brainchild of the famous Soviet filmmaker, Alexander Medvedkin, under the oversight of the Central Committee. The kino train encouraged or shamed farmers to meet the targets of the Five Year Plan by a frenzied process of producing 'film-newspapers' for each place they visited, reflecting the community's work and lives back to them.[21] Katharine wrote approvingly about the kino train in *The Real Russia,* ignoring the famine and deportations that were part of the forced collectivisation it was promoting. 'Films are made on the backward collectives … with close-ups, giving the names of lazy or careless workers, and kulaks who have intrigued against successful development of the Kolkhoz.'[22] The experience was an immersion for her in film as propaganda, a demonstration of how an artform could be used for political purposes.

Her experience of Soviet theatre was also formative. Australia struggled to stage local plays and she was impressed by the many productions she saw in Russia, all of them responding in different ways to the revolution and life in the Soviet state. No longer a commercial enterprise, Russian productions 'convey life and reality without mawkish sentiment, sensational trickery, or a beating-up of thwarted sexuality'.[23] She was thrilled by a production of Maxim Gorky's *The Mother*, the small theatre 'filled to suffocation', the barriers between audience and stage broken down. She also praised a play directed by Vsevolod Meyerhold, quoting approvingly his declaration, 'Art cannot be non-political … a proletarian dictatorship must develop its own forms of expression in the theatre, in literature, in painting and drawing'.[24] Meyerhold, however, was already under suspicion in Stalinist Russia for his 'flagrant modernism'; in 1938 his theatre was shut down and he was arrested on charges of Trotskyism and espionage, before being shot on 2 February 1940 and his name written out of official Soviet history.[25]

On 11 September, Katharine departed on a tour to Siberia with three other writers: 'Walt Carmon, a brilliant, cynical American journalist; Sigvard Lund, a Danish writer, blonde and powerful; Helios Gómez, a Spanish artist and poet, as handsome as Valentino, and Scherer, our interpreter, a Russian, but not a Communist'.[26] Speaking a mix of English, French, Spanish and German, along with their 'odds and ends of Russian', Katharine wrote, 'we were a very gay and comradely party, disagreeing violently in all our languages when occasion arose'. They travelled for five days on a train, Katharine in a luxurious cabin with a writing table and her own toilet, before reaching Stalinsk—now called Novokuznetsk—in south-western Siberia.[27] 'Stalinsk, the city of steel', she wrote, 'flaming to the sky with its towering chimneys, mammoth silos welding the sinews of a new civilisation in Siberia'.[28]

As part of the journey, Katharine visited the house where the great Russian writer Fyodor Dostoevsky lived for a time—probably in

Semipalatinsk (now called Semey and part of Kazakhstan) where he was sent after years in a Siberian labour camp. Afterwards, she read his semi-autobiographical novel based on the experiences, *The House of the Dead* (1862). She commented to a Soviet correspondent in 1956, 'So strange that a man who could depict misery and injustices with such power, was yet lacking in recognition of the innate goodness and genius of mankind to forge a way that would rid it of the oppressions which caused so much misery and injustice!'[29] But of course, Dostoevsky's pessimistic vision was far more relevant to Stalinist Russia than Katharine could see.

Snow started falling as they left a factory tour in Siberia and Scherer, their interpreter, said the forecast was for an early winter.

> Carmon swore in his best American and huddled into his big overcoat; Lund strode away taking the snow on his powerful shoulders; Gomez set off at a run, singing one of his ribald Spanish ditties; I trudged along in my rubber boots and red silk raincoat (made in the Soviet Union) delighted to think for all the autumn sunshine and golden birch woods, we were going to see something of Siberian snow and ice after all.[30]

She sent Ric a postcard on 2 October saying, 'These beautiful hills are all covered with snow now & people go about in big fur coats with fur caps over their ears. Love & kisses darling, & I'll be coming home soon now'.[31] She had contradictory feelings about the weather, having written in a letter before she left for Siberia, 'I'm beginning to feel homesick. It rains every day & already is so cold'.[32]

Returning to Moscow on 14 October, Katharine received three letters from Hugo and two from Ric.[33] In Hugo's final surviving letter, he had woken early on 21 August to write to her and gave an upbeat account of things at home. He had started a rodeo show on their property and it was hard work but so many people were coming he had decided to continue running the show every Sunday:

> One thing that I want [to] impress on you is not to hurry home and to take every advantage of getting the information you want.

> Then when you do decide to honour us again, take [American publisher William] Norton's tip and invitation, and return via New York. We are so well and happy that it would be a thousand pities for you to tear back and not see something of Hollywood and the doings which will be so helpful to you and your work, and don't forget that if your reports of the Bolshies is a favourable one, that the wise guys will only be too ready to say that you scampered through the place in 5 minutes and could not possibly be in a position to form any opinion of the working conditions of such a vast country.

He finished his letter with, 'The sweetpeas are out, wattle almost finished, and the first boronia goes with this for good luck. The only complaints I have are that your jam cupboard is getting down pretty low so see to it Madam'.[34]

Katharine spent three more weeks in Moscow. She made two radio broadcasts on a short-wave station and was desperate for Hugo and Ric to hear them. She wrote to Ric on 2 November:

> I wonder did you hear me on the air, last night. It would be about 9 o'clock in the morning in Australia. You should have been listening. I know Daddy would have tried very hard to hear the broadcast. I sent him 2 wires, really, one on the 26th & that was returned from Greenmount, Queensland. Would you believe it—nobody there knew Hugo Throssell VC? I was so angry because I wanted Daddy to have the message from me first thing, on his birthday.[35]

Ric remembers, 'My Dad and I climbed out of bed early in the morning to hear Katharine's broadcast on a neighbour's short-wave set. We managed to catch a few phrases among the crackles of static before her voice faded again into the senseless, jungle whistles and chatter of the sound-waves. We walked down the hill, silent and disappointed'.[36]

KATHARINE LEFT MOSCOW in early November, arriving in St Petersburg on 8 November. She had dinner with Guido and Betty; Betty records her looking 'thin and tired and pinched with cold'.[37] Much hinges on the conversation Katharine had with Guido and Betty that day. Betty's original diaries are lost but in the published version, she claims Katharine 'was sadly disillusioned. None of her former optimism remained. During the weeks spent here she had seen so much and learnt so much that she had never dreamt of, and her heart was sick'.[38] The only other evidence supporting Betty's account is a sentence by Jean Devanny in a 1953 letter concerned with her own problems with the party, claiming that on Katharine's return to Australia, she confided to Jean about the 'many very bad experiences' she had had in Russia.[39]

If Betty actually wrote that in her diary in November 1933, then Katharine's positive account in the book *The Real Russia* and her continued advocacy for the Soviet Union over the rest of her life would seem dishonest. But Betty is not a reliable witness. Her 'diary' of the time, *Caviar for Breakfast*, was not published until 1979, and by her own admission is only 'based' on the original diaries. An earlier version of the manuscript in her papers is a conventional memoir, with significantly differing details and a milder version of Katharine's disillusionment which reads instead, 'most of her former bright illusions had now faded'.[40] The diary form gives the book more historical authority than it deserves and hides the way the memoir is shaped by Betty's own disillusionment with communism.[41]

The letters Katharine wrote while she was in Russia talk of exhaustion, headaches and homesickness, but also her jubilant excitement at all she was seeing. She wrote to Hugh McCrae from Moscow the day before she left for Siberia, 'If only you could have been here. You would be crazy with the beauty & intense life'.[42] Whatever bad experiences Katharine had were not enough to disillusion her. Her vision was blinkered and her memory selective but her love of the Soviet Union and its people was sincere.

WHEN KATHARINE REACHED London, she took a room at a boarding house. On 20 November, she picked up the morning newspaper to find, buried on page seventeen, a brief report on the suicide of her husband. 'A telegram from Perth (Western Australia) announces the death of Mr Hugo Vivian Hope Throssell, VC. It states that he was found shot at his home yesterday with a revolver by his side.'[43]

A telegram had reached the newspaper before one had reached her; the article claimed she was still in Russia. 'How I lived through the shock and grief, I don't know. And it was weeks and weeks before I could hear what happened.'[44]

She had four days to wait before her ship, the *Baradine* again, left for Australia. She sent off a telegram to Ric. 'She would be home soon. I must be a brave boy till then.'[45] She hadn't been in London long enough to make contact with anybody and now she didn't feel able to reach out. When Henry Handel Richardson heard the news she rang Jonathan Cape, but he didn't know where Katharine was or what her plans were.[46]

A newspaper reported Katharine 'was allotted a special cabin to herself … and during the voyage maintained absolute seclusion. Passengers occasionally heard her tapping on her typewriter, working on her new serious book on Soviet Russia'.[47] On 4 December, two weeks after learning of Hugo's death, Katharine turned fifty. The *Baradine* was in the Suez Canal, having just left Port Said. She had three things left, and she would cling to them the rest of her life: her faith in communism, her writing career and Ric.

27

The Rodeo

Greenmount, 1933

IN AMONGST THE 140 acres the Throssells owned on the other side of York Road was another weatherboard cottage, built in the 1850s as a guardhouse. The warder had lived there while supervising the convicts who built the original York to Greenmount road.[1] Hugo had been renting it out and trying to sell it for years. On 10 February 1933, three months before Katharine left on her trip, the cottage burned down in a bushfire that spread up the valley at four o'clock in the afternoon and threatened orchards and several other houses before being brought under control by firefighters that night.[2] All that remained of the cottage were 'charred timbers and two tall brick chimneys'.[3] Somehow, before the cottage burned down Hugo managed to remove the furniture and haul it out of the bush to safety. He had insured the building for £150.

A question asked in an arson inquiry two months later suggests the insurance company had suspicions. Madame La Reine's hairdressing salon, run by Victoria Ross, had burned down in the city; a police officer had caught a nightwatchman coming out of the building smelling of kerosene. The insurance company suspected that Victoria Ross's husband, John, was involved. Their lawyer, Nathaniel Lappin, asked Ross, 'Have you ever discussed a fire that took place at Hugo Throssell's place at Greenmount?'.[4] Ross said he did not remember doing so and no follow-up was recorded. In May, the Rosses and the nightwatchman were charged with arson; Mrs Ross was acquitted but the other two were jailed. Lappin would go on to work as a police prosecutor in years to come, hunting out communists and manifesting a particular dislike of Katharine, perhaps triggered by his suspicion about the fire.

WITH KATHARINE LEAVING for London on 22 May and no longer restraining Hugo's impulses, he embarked on his grandest scheme to make money: he would turn their Greenmount property into a rodeo. The show would be a source of income and the stream of visitors, enchanted by life in the hills, would buy the vacant blocks he was trying to sell. He was in a hurry. His first description of the enterprise, in a letter dated 21 June 1933 to the local council, sounds innocuous—he was 'establishing a depot to supply horses for mounted hiking'. If that was all he actually intended when he began, it soon snowballed. The next month, when he printed a flyer advertising the grand opening to occur on 30 July, he had added the 'main attraction'—a buck jumping competition—as well as clay pigeon shooting, 'the William Tell Act', a motor vehicle climb up the Freak Hill, Aboriginal people throwing kylies, an RSL band performing and afternoon tea. Hugo had renamed the horses for hire after Katharine's books and Ric remembers the names 'professionally painted in meticulous signwriter's capitals on each tethering post. "Windlestraws" was a long-retired steeplechaser, "Kiss on the Lips" a pretty piebald pony. "Working Bullocks" was a gentle mule that seemed unconcerned by the indignity of being a bullock. Even my silver-maned chestnut was to be called "The Wild Oats of Han"'.[5]

At the end of June, a horse crushed Hugo's foot, breaking two of the bones in his instep.[6] On crutches, he took sick leave from his job as a fertiliser inspector and carried on with preparations for the rodeo. After Hugo was absent from work for five weeks, the director wrote that 'owing to the fact that the necessary money has not been provided on our estimates, it will not be possible to give you further employment'.[7] Perhaps it was a funding problem, but it's possible the director had lost patience with his war hero on sick leave whose rodeo had been in all the newspapers.

Hugo wrote of 'considerable opposition' to his enterprise 'from the powers that be'.[8] As much as Hugo felt persecuted, the opposition was largely due to him ignoring regulations. After constructing a corral, a thatched kiosk, and other temporary buildings, he retrospectively sought permission from the Greenmount Road Board; they told him he had seven days to take them down.[9] Just before the opening, AO Neville, the infamous Protector of Aborigines, wrote to warn that it was a breach of the law to employ Aboriginal people without his permission.[10] Hugo's bigger problem was the law against charging admission for entertainment on a Sunday without special permission. It wasn't an obscure regulation but one that was actively enforced; a dance hall operator, for example, was prosecuted in 1936 after a sting by undercover police officers.[11] Just three days before the opening, Hugo wrote to the chief secretary of the state government asking for permission to charge. He still had some influence; the secretary granted Hugo permission. He would be allowed to cover his costs but any profits would have to go to charity.[12] Later, Hugo was granted ongoing permission to take up a collection after 2.30 p.m. on Sundays.[13] Local 'opposition' might have partly come from other residents objecting to the influx of people each weekend. The day before the opening the Greenmount Progress Association reneged on an agreement to loan him crockery.[14] In August, a number of residents signed a petition objecting to the stench from Hugo's horses.[15]

Two thousand people came up the hill for the opening day on 30 July. Hugo reported 'we took over £70 at the gate for the [entry] charge and £10 odd for afternoon tea, whilst chocolates, oranges and ciggaros [cigarettes] sold readily'.[16] The local newspaper, the *Swan Express,* declared it 'Greenmount's greatest day' as 'happy, laughing crowds wended their way from the station', with a plane performing stunts overhead, the thrill of the dangerous bucking horses, and a 'bounteous luncheon … dispensed in a large marquee'.[17] The *West Australian* saw it differently, declaring 'the programme was very disappointing' with a crowd who 'soon tired of the spasmodic attempts by motor cycles and cars to climb the hill' and supposedly bucking horses who were far too placid.[18]

The rodeos continued through August and into September, still attracting a crowd, but not generating enough money to solve Hugo's financial problems. On 14 September, he wrote to a colonel in the RSL about the possibility of a partnership, inviting the leaders of the RSL to visit and see the rodeo that coming Sunday. 'I am prepared to fall in with any reasonable suggestion', he wrote, 'as my main object in attracting the crowd to Greenmount is to enable me to dispose of some of my building blocks in this locality, and this would be more effectively achieved with your organization in support'. If the RSL were to partner with him, he suggested they could add some military-themed attractions, creating a dugout to display war trophies and trenches from which the public could shoot 'with a periscopic rifle disappearing targets across the creek—a la Gallipoli'.[19] Hugo's qualms about war had been momentarily forgotten. Nothing came of the suggested partnership and that week's rodeo might have been the last, the advertisements having already stopped the week before.[20] A few weeks later, the gossipy newspaper the *Mirror* ran a short satirical list of 'Books That Were Never Written'; the first was 'Rodeo—Hugo Throssell VC'.[21]

In Hugo's letter to the RSL, he talked up his financial situation. 'I have now sold my wheat farm for cash and also have every prospect of selling my Fermoy property at Northam. My foot is mended and the show is a going concern.' The truth was that he was in a financial hole, with bills from the rodeo as well as rates arrears adding up to over £1200 and little income. He had twenty-two heavily mortgaged properties, most of them vacant land. Trying to raise money, he mortgaged the family home to a Harriet Roberts for £400.[22] Years later, when the debt was called in, Katharine wrote, 'This mortgage was one of the desperate things my husband did when I was away from home so long ago … and the last straw I think to his anguish of mind'.[23]

AROUND THE TIME of Hugo's rodeo opening, a woman named Rose Ross and her daughter Enid took over the running of the Wandu guesthouse and, further up York Road at the top of the hill, the Log Cabin tearooms and dance hall. Hugo had enlisted Rose to cater for the rodeo and the two of them became close. Hugo couldn't cook for himself; Ric remembers that after the opening day she stayed on and 'dished up a … forbidden meal of bubble-and-squeak and fried scones soaked in Golden Syrup'.[24] Imagining his father's state of mind in his last weeks of life, Ric writes that Hugo and Rose began an affair. Hugo 'couldn't help playing up to women … But it never did go the whole way. Not till now'.[25] Hugo arranged for Ric to stay with friends from school while he went to live with Rose.[26] Ric doesn't reveal how he knew about the affair—was it neighbourhood gossip or his own interpretation of what he remembered? He imagines Hugo's guilt about it as a factor in his suicide. 'A man should have stuck to [Katharine]. Couldn't even wait a few months for her to come back. Sick with self-contempt, Jim went back to the house at Greenmount … [He] sat at the kitchen table with Katharine's letter in his hand, afraid to be faced with his own disloyalty.'[27]

On 9 October, Hugo saw Dr Heriot. Heriot recorded, 'History obtained with greatest of difficulty, does not wish to discuss his complaints … Not sleeping well—heart worse feels too big … Is financially worried … Unemployed—has only worked Agricultural Bank 10 weeks and run a few Rodeos during past year'.[28]

On 26 October, Hugo turned forty-nine. 'He was born at about midnight', Katharine wrote, 'so they cd never decide the exact date'. The last known photograph of him is dated 27 October. He stands with his arm around his older sister, Eva Bartlett-Day. Next to them are Eva's daughters wearing hats and gloves. Hugo's hair is grey but he's smiling and wearing a suit and tie. They are standing in a garden, probably celebrating Hugo's birthday.

On 7 November, he returned to see Dr Heriot. His insomnia was getting him down. 'He used to dread going to bed', said Hugo's brother-in-law, 'as he had most horrible thoughts as soon as he would lie down'.[29]

Ric hadn't seen his father for weeks when they met in the city to watch a film at the Ambassador Theatre. 'It was good to be with him. I looked around to him happily. He seemed miles away, staring. He didn't know I was there.'[30] On Friday 17 November there was a Greenmount school concert in the evening. Ric recited Tennyson's war poem 'The Charge of the Light Brigade'.[31] It's unknown whether Hugo was there to hear it.

Hugo's much older brother-in-law, George Withers, had known him since he was a boy. On Saturday 18 November, he came out to

Greenmount to help Hugo burn off grass around the property with three other men. Hugo confided in George as they worked:

> [He] drew my attention to his madness in starting his Rodeo Stand which he called Throssell's Folly. He said that the expenses were very heavy and ran him further into debt. He said if he had any pluck he would blow his brains out.
>
> He said his wife left everything in perfect order when she left and he seemed very worried as to what she would think when she came back from England where she was at the time.
>
> He said she would find everything in a muddle and he was far better out of it.

They'd stopped burning off by the time it was dark at half-past seven; George decided to stay the night with Hugo. They walked up the road to the Log Cabin and stayed till midnight, eating and talking with Rose Ross and her daughter. 'After tea he seemed brighter and was telling fairy tales to Mrs Ross's child.'[32]

Returning home, George remembered that Hugo 'had a shower and rub down and said how fresh it made him feel. He then told me how good it was for me to come up and stay with him, and said good night and stated that he was going to sleep in his wife's room. Those were the last words I heard him speak'. Did he mean Katharine's workroom? There's no record it had a bed in it, but it was a strange thing to say if he meant the bedroom he and Katharine shared.[33]

When George woke in the morning, he lay in bed for an hour before he got up. He was expecting for Hugo to call out at any moment for them to get started on the burning off. At ten past eight, he went looking for Hugo. His bed had been slept in, but he wasn't there or in the yard. Eventually, George found him on the back verandah, 'lying in a deck chair in his pyjamas with his feet upon the lattice work and a big wound in the side of his right temple. A revolver in his right hand resting on his right shoulder. A large pool of blood was on the verandah and he was still bleeding and breathing heavily'.[34]

Hugo had been lying there, fatally wounded, for at least an hour. Inexplicably, George hadn't heard the shot, although he thought it might have been what had woken him. George called a doctor and waited with Hugo for the half-hour it took him to arrive. It's unrecorded whether Hugo was conscious. 'When the doctor arrived he was still alive and we placed him on a couch. He expired about 15 minutes after the doctor's arrival.'[35]

The doctor found a suicide note on the shelf. Newspapers reported that it read, 'I can't sleep and feel my old war head. It's going phut, and that's no good for anyone concerned'.[36] He had also made a new will dated the day before his death, leaving everything to Katharine. On the back, he had written, 'I have never recovered from my 1914–18 experiences, and, with this in view, I appeal to the State to see that my wife and child get the usual war pension. No man could have a truer mate'.[37]

An autopsy was carried out on his body the next day and then that afternoon, an hour or two before Katharine heard the news of his death in London, he was buried at Karrakatta Cemetery with a military funeral. When his coffin was lifted onto the gun carriage, 'the pathetic souvenirs of the late Captain Throssell's active service—his Victoria Cross and other war service medals, his weather-beaten plumed Light Horse hat and sword were placed on top of it'. Members of his 10th Light Horse followed the pallbearers, the now middle-aged veterans still showing 'the scars of war', a number of them missing limbs. 'Light rain fell as the cortege drew up at the graveside. Someone offered the chaplain the protection of an umbrella, but he brushed it aside, and the rain streamed down his surplice. Water dripped, too, from the shrubs on to the flag-covered coffin.'[38]

PART 4

COMRADE, 1934–1949

28

'All That Is Left'

Greenmount, 1934–1935

AMONGST KATHARINE'S PHOTOS at the National Library of Australia is one of her and Ric labelled 'on return from SU [Soviet Union]'. She is looking straight at the camera with a sad intensity, her hair white, her face aged. She's leaning against Ric, who is dressed in a Russian peasant shirt, looking older than eleven, and smiling slightly as he looks off to the side.

Ric met her ship on its arrival at Fremantle on Boxing Day. 'I hardly knew her. Her eyes were sunken; her face drawn and splotched with grief. She could barely walk without assistance … There was no welcoming smile, no arms to hold me: a murmured, "Nicky darling", between her tears. I knew that it was I who must comfort her.'[1]

She brought Ric back to their Greenmount home, which had been empty since Hugo's death. 'Dead gum-leaves were piled by the gully wind against the door', Ric remembers. 'The stink of rotten apricots drifted from the orchard … Over the verandas grapes hung in withered wreaths. The wild oats … were hip-high in the dying garden. Everything about the house reminded me of him. I wanted to be able to forget. Katharine found some comfort in remembering.'[2]

Even in her grief, Katharine didn't cry much; she had trouble understanding why others found it a relief. 'When I cry it's usually devastating—nearly kills me. Don't dare to lose control like that.'[3]

Hugh McCrae had stopped writing to her when she needed him most. She wrote a note to him in March 1934 that said only, 'Write to me. I seem to be losing all contact with life'.[4] His silence seems cruel; perhaps he was guilty about Hugo's suicide. When Hugo died, she lost Hugh as well.

After weeks of agonising speculation, one of the tasks awaiting Katharine on her return was to piece together what had happened. It still didn't make sense even once she'd heard all George Withers had to say about Hugo's last day. She wrote to Ric years later, 'I've never been able to understand how Daddy could leave me like that'.[5] One particular fear haunted her: she'd left behind the draft manuscript of *Intimate Strangers*; what if Hugo had read it while she was away and the suicide of the character Greg had pushed him over the edge? Perhaps it was hearing that Hugo slept in his 'wife's room' on that last night that bothered Katharine—if he meant the workroom, it was likely where the manuscript was stored. When Katharine revealed her fear to Ric thirty years later, he reassured her the manuscript couldn't have been the reason for Hugo's suicide; his crippling debt and 'old war head' were reason enough.[6]

The inquest held by the coroner at the Midland Junction Courthouse on 11 December 1933 heard from witnesses and concluded that he 'died as the result of a bullet wound, self-inflicted while his mind was deranged as the result of injuries received during the Great War'.[7] Hugo's brothers and sisters had hired a lawyer to represent their interests in the inquest, and the outcome was probably the one they were seeking, as it made it more likely Katharine and Ric would receive a pension while avoiding too much embarrassing detail of Hugo's financial recklessness.

The Repatriation Commission was making its own enquiries in early 1934, determining whether Hugo's death was related to his war service and, thus, whether Katharine would be eligible for a war widow's pension. The commission asked to interview Katharine soon after her return, but she took weeks to reply, eventually writing on what would have been the couple's fifteenth wedding anniversary, 28 January, and saying she was not up to an interview.

> Nervously and physically, my husband's magnificent constitution was impaired as a result of war service. The Medical Board has the record of his wounds and periods in hospital for meningitis and

> malaria: but I resent the idea that his mind was ever in any way deranged. He feared that it might become so.

In insisting Hugo was not deranged, she was risking her eligibility for the pension. She put his suicide down to him not being able to 'withstand the torture of another crisis of sleeplessness and financial embarrassment', telling the commission:

> I consider that his 'grateful country' made it impossible for my husband to live. He thought he had to die to provide for his wife and child. As far as I am concerned, I could not accept anything that cost him his life; but I feel that I have no right to interfere with what he sought to do for his son.
>
> My own health is uncertain and I may not be able to provide for our boy who is eleven years old.[8]

The doctor consulted by the commission, CW Courtney, disagreed with the coroner's verdict, focusing on the fact that Hugo's depression was not noted in his records until 1929 and on Katharine's comment that he wasn't depressed when he was fully employed. His opinion was that 'it is probable that constitutional and post-war factors were mainly responsible for death by suicide'.[9] Despite Courtney's opinion, the department concluded, 'There may be some doubt in this case but the Commission will give the benefit of it & decide death due to war service'.[10] In April 1934 they granted a pension to Katharine, guaranteeing her a small income.

On its own, the pension would have helped Katharine to pursue her political work and writing without worrying as much about money. However, the financial mess Hugo had left behind was to burden her for many years. Even on paper there was a considerable £546 deficit between his assets and liabilities. Worse, all of his assets were properties, impossible to sell at a good price in the Depression. The mortgages and rates on the properties were precariously balanced with the income from rent and Hugo's share of his parents' estate.[11]

KATHARINE FORCED HERSELF back out in public two months after her return from London, making a speech at a meeting of the Council

Against War in Perth on 28 February.[12] 'Only my belief', she wrote later, 'in the need to work for the great ideas of communism and world peace helped me to survive a grief so shattering. Personal sorrow, I felt, is part of the world's great sorrow, caused by war and an economic system which thrives on war and the preparations for war'.[13] She spent her fifties immersed in party activities, dulling the pain of her grief by working intensely for the cause.

Her series of articles on Russia was accepted for publication by her old newspaper, the *Herald*; the articles ran daily for three weeks from 14 April, prefaced with the disclaimer that her opinions 'sometimes conflict with those arrived at by other equally capable observers'.[14] In the middle of publishing the series, the paper wrote an editorial about the flurry of books on Russia, 'an average of two per day', having the effect of cancelling each other out, for and against the communist project. 'The Communist goes there to see an Arcadia that does not exist outside of [Thomas] More's *Utopia* ... The pseudo-intellectual—often a dreamer ... is taken in hand by the Soviet's powerful propaganda bureau and swears to what has been told him.'[15] The *Herald* didn't publish the last five of Katharine's articles, writing to her that 'we felt we had given readers as much of one subject as they could stand'. This incensed Katharine, and the Western Australian communist newspaper *Red Star* ran a front-page headline 'Soviet Information Banned'.[16] All the articles, including the unpublished ones, were collected as a book, *The Real Russia,* released by Modern Publishers later in the year.

Thirty years earlier, under the influence of Rudolf Broda and Colonel Reay, Australia had been the nation bearing her hope for the world—a young, progressive social democracy. Now it was the Soviet Union, the world's first communist nation, that Katharine believed in; her tour had deepened her love of the nation and her faith in it. Her belief sat uneasily with her ongoing Australian patriotism. She still loved Australia, still strove to express the distinctiveness of its people and places in her writing, but since the Great War its politics had been a source of disappointment and sorrow which only intensified over the decades.

She began a speaking tour, giving lectures on Russia. In July, she gave two lectures in the coalmining town of Collie and went on to speak in Kalgoorlie, probably gathering some material for the goldfields project she had been planning since prospecting in Larkinville. After more speeches in Perth through the winter and spring, her lectures were to continue in Victoria and New South Wales. She wrote again to Hugh McCrae, telling him that each day when she hears the postman whistle she heads through the orchard to check the letterbox at the gate, only to find no letter from him.

> 'Never again will I write to him', she says and returns to work. So the days go.
>
> But the *Westralia* sails on October 25 with all that is left of KS and one son—in long 'uns—steerage. We will be, mostly, with my sister in Victoria, Mrs P. S. Bridge 'Kirinaran', Frankston will find us should a letter, or a Hugh, wander that way. I am due for Sydney in January, but only for a few days.
>
> [I]t seems too impossibly good to be true that I may see you ...[17]

Katharine's sister Beatrice and brother-in-law Patten had left Ceylon and settled on a property in Frankston on the outskirts of Melbourne. Over the following decades, Kirinaran was to be a second home for Katharine, 'a rambling old weatherboard house with endless rooms and corridors' with spectacular views over the bay and crammed with Ceylon memorabilia, including a python skin hanging on the wall.[18] On this visit, Katharine and Ric stayed for two months.

Victoria was holding its centenary celebrations and the Duke of Gloucester, the king's younger brother, had arrived on a royal tour along with the British poet laureate, John Masefield. Katharine met Masefield at a reception, a newspaper recording that she was 'charming in a beige lace frock, and with her grey hair waving down into a bob'.[19] She didn't have much regard for Masefield, claiming in a recollection that everyone was actually crowded around Bernard O'Dowd that night, whom she regarded as Australia's unofficial poet laureate.[20]

Katharine wasn't there because of Masefield or the duke but as the Western Australian delegate to the All-Australia Congress Against War in Melbourne on 10 and 12 November 1934. The congress was held as a counterpoint to the centenary celebrations, which one delegate said were being used 'for the purpose of creating war psychology here in Australia'.[21] The congress's keynote speaker was meant to be

Egon Kisch. Kisch was a communist journalist, born to a Jewish family in Prague. Working in Berlin for years, the Nazis imprisoned him after the Reichstag fire in 1933 and then expelled him. On his way to Melbourne, he was prevented from leaving his ship, the *Strathaird*, at Fremantle on 6 November. Kisch was running late for the congress and had been relying on catching the train from Perth—which was faster than the ship—in order to reach Melbourne in time.[22] The federal attorney-general, Robert Menzies, declared that, in order to protect Australia from 'revolutionary activities', Kisch would not be allowed to land.[23] Kisch was sure that the Australian government was reacting to Nazi pressure. Historian Heidi Zogbaum finds no basis for this, arguing instead that the Australian government had been warned about Kisch by the British security agency only to then be denied access to the details of their intelligence.[24]

The situation had created huge public interest and Katharine suddenly found herself in the middle of it. Katharine and the rest of a Kisch reception committee organised a protest meeting on 9 November. Katharine moved a motion that the meeting 'protests most emphatically against the unreasonable and tyrannous action of the Federal authorities' in detaining Kisch, calling it 'a deliberate violation of the rights of free speech and a flagrant breach of democratic liberties'.[25]

On 10 November, the congress went ahead in the Port Melbourne town hall without Kisch or the New Zealand delegate Gerald Griffin, empty chairs on the stages marking their absence. Katharine reported that the peace movement was growing in Western Australia and warned, 'the capitalists want war, because profits are to be made'. To applause, she declared that although the Shrine of Remembrance would be officially opened the next day, 'the best shrine of remembrance we could build was a mass anti-war movement'. With many of the delegates communists, the chairman dealt with the incongruity of the Soviet Union's militarism by claiming, 'The Soviet Union was carrying out a genuine peace policy, whilst at the same time they were obliged to arm themselves for the defence of classless society'.[26]

When the *Strathaird* reached Melbourne on 12 November, Katharine was selected as the writers' representative to visit Kisch on board. There were only four allowed on board—Katharine; Kisch's appointed lawyer, Joan Rosanove; the communist Jane Aarons who falsely claimed she had met Kisch before and could identify him for the court proceedings; and a Justice of the Peace to witness the identification. At dawn they passed the throng of supporters gathered on the wharf and walked along the gangway onto the ship. When the other three left to attend court, Katharine stayed with him, under orders not to let him out of her sight: 'We had been warned that he might be shanghaied on to a German gun-boat which was lying in the harbour, quite near to the *Strathaird*'. Then, hundreds of supporters surged up the gangway onto the ship and in response, Kisch 'held a gay informal reception … which became an anti-fascist meeting … A lusty singing of the International resounded, and drifted over to the sea to where the Nazi gun-boat lay like a grey shark on the quiet waters of the bay'.[27] The next day, after Kisch's court appeal failed, he jumped onto the wharf. He broke his leg and was forced back onto the ship as it left for Sydney.

In the new year, Katharine and Ric travelled to Sydney on the train and stayed in the city centre in 'a one-roomed flat with [a] gas-ring and balcony, closed-off at one end by ill-fitting sheets of mildewed plywood'. Kisch came to see them and they drank coffee in the restaurant below their flat. Kisch showed Ric a conjuring trick he'd learned in a German concentration camp.[28]

Kisch continued his legal battles through January and February, winning much public sympathy. He finally left Australia in March after the government agreed to pay his legal costs. The affair was a boost to communist morale and made mainstream Australians worried that the government was curtailing free speech.

THE FRENZY OF activity was having its toll on Katharine. After her return to Greenmount, she wrote in March 1935 that her 'beastly machinery'—her heart—had 'played up'. 'Angina, the doctor said, and if I wouldn't go slow he'd give me a year. Don't believe it, of course. But there you are.'[29] For the rest of her life, Katharine was to live with the threat of sudden death from heart failure, warned that overexertion could kill her.

It was lonelier at home in 1935—Ric started boarding school. He had graduated from Greenmount Primary but not won a place at Perth Modern, the selective public secondary school. With Katharine unable to afford a private school, Hugo's classmates from Prince Alfred College set up a fund to pay for Ric to attend the equivalent Methodist boarding school in Western Australia, the recently opened Wesley College in South Perth.[30] As the atheist 'son of a militant communist and a broken war hero', Ric felt out of place 'among the sons of the farmers and professional men of conservative Western Australia society'.[31] His enrolment contradicted Katharine's ethos but there's no record of her trying to justify it to herself or anyone else. It shows that even in this militant period other things still influenced her decisions—in this case, the value she placed on education, her positive experience of South Melbourne College, and maintaining a link to Hugo's legacy.

AT THE TIME of Katharine's trip to Russia, the newly created Union of Soviet Writers had taken control of Soviet literature and was developing a doctrine of socialist realism. The union oversaw the nation's literary journals and ran a publishing house; in order to be a professional writer in Russia it was necessary to be a member. The union's main task 'was to reward or punish writers, depending on their level of cooperation with the Party's agenda'.[32] The Comintern envisioned an international literary network and the union's Foreign Commission liaised with sympathetic writers around the world. In November 1934, Walt Carmon, Katharine's American friend from the Siberian tour, was working for it and he began a correspondence between the Foreign Commission and Katharine which was to last the rest of her life.[33] Carmon's Soviet successors cultivated a literary friendship and exchange with Katharine—she would send literary, cultural and political news from Australia and Australian books; they would send her Soviet publications and would commission her to write articles. She had an opportunity to promote her own work and that of other Australians to the union. Her letters to them became warmly personal and the correspondence her main connection to her beloved Soviet Union.

It was from this exchange and her experiences in the Soviet Union that Katharine developed her ideas about what faithful communist writing—socialist realism—should look like. One element was immersion in the work and lives of the people. In *The Real Russia,* she put forward the ideas of Maxim Gorky; under his influence the 'writers of the Soviet Union were realizing the need of being absorbed into the working life of the people … What people thought and felt about their work, intimate affairs and environment, that was the stuff of literature'.[34] It wasn't a new approach for her—it validated her signature research trips to observe the lives of different industries and places. A second element found in a statement by Katharine from this time was a 'sympathetic understanding of the causes behind the social tyranny of our time'—which is to say writing that exposed the ways capitalism oppressed people for profit.[35] A third element was language. She quoted Gorky saying, 'The simpler the language the better. True wisdom always expresses itself plainly'.[36] It was a principle she adopted, moving away from the influences of DH Lawrence *(Working Bullocks)* and modernism *(Intimate Strangers)* and towards a plainer style in her late novels.[37] The critic Drusilla Modjeska writes, 'She never wrote another novel with the passion of *Coonardoo* or *Intimate Strangers*; in the [goldfields] trilogy the tension was dissipated. She had adopted the literary technique of socialist realism at the expense of that intangible quality evident in her earlier novels'.[38] In a 1956 interview, Katharine offered some further comments on socialist realism: 'I've always maintained that socialist realism does not require a writer to falsify reality; that a story must arise from actual conditions of a place and its people at that time. If there is not a socialist solution arising from the conditions of the story, it is a mistake to drag it in'. Within a capitalist society she understood socialist realism as a responsibility that had to be balanced with the need for readers. 'In our countries we can only go a certain distance if we are going to be published and if we are going to draw ever-increasing numbers of men and women to an understanding of fundamental problems in their lives.'[39]

While in Sydney in January 1935, Katharine and Kisch launched the Writers' League, an Australian section of the Comintern's International Union of Revolutionary Writers.[40] It aimed both to encourage Australian writers to take up the challenge of writing socialist realism and to gain better recognition within the Communist Party of the contribution writers could make to the cause. Kisch and Katharine recruited the communist writer Jean Devanny to lead the Sydney branch. The league met in the bohemian Pakie's Club on Sunday nights, beginning with conversations—led by party members—on working-class writing, followed by a chance for aspiring writers to read from their manuscripts for feedback.[41] Stopping in Melbourne on her way home, Katharine enlisted members of the Kisch Defence Committee to launch a Victorian branch. Nettie Palmer's daughter Aileen, who had just finished her degree and had been a communist for several years, was elected the first secretary.[42] Despite the grand hopes, neither branch lasted more than a couple of years.

IN JUNE 1935 the young journalist Norman Bartlett interviewed Katharine for the *West Australian*, giving a snapshot of her early in a long widowhood. She took him to her workroom for the interview and, perhaps to his surprise, 'was not a disturbing person to meet'. 'She had a self-contained look, as though her personality was controlled from a central core of understanding'. She said her writing routine was to work 'steadily from early morning until about midday, planning well before I start by thinking deeply over the situations and characters, and I take care to have a thorough knowledge of the subject about which I am writing'. *Intimate Strangers* was under contract with Jonathan Cape and was meant to have been delivered at the end of 1934; she was hoping to finish it soon and start on a new novel 'which will deal with the cruelty of conditions which are as active in the lives of many men as drought, flood, fire and the forces of nature'. Anticipating the direction of her writing, she told Bartlett, 'I do not mind if the reviewers hold up their hands in horror and say that at last I have succumbed to the temptation of using the novel as a vehicle of propaganda. I write to please myself, to express what I feel to be true, and not to please the people who review books'. Bartlett left her house after the three-hour interview and 'walked down Greenmount Hill towards the setting sun', wondering 'how many people in Western Australia realise what a truly remarkable woman lives in the rambling wooden house'.[43]

29

On All Fronts

Greenmount, 1935–1939

KATHARINE WAS THE first communist Norman Bartlett had met, and the experience of interviewing her changed him. He became her 'faithful follower' for the next few years as Katharine spearheaded a host of organisations which were fronts for the Communist Party. Looking back, he remembers:

> I have no knowledge how far Katharine Susannah's new role stemmed from her own re-animated enthusiasm and how far she acted under direction. Something of both, in all probability. Certainly, she was not a reluctant or unskilful propagandist. She became the Grey Eminence behind the Workers' Art Guild, the Spanish Relief Committee, the Modern Women's Club and left-wing prompting for more active political commitment on the part of the Western Australian Fellowship of Writers. We, her faithful followers, packed union meetings, sponsored slanted resolutions, provided cheer-leaders at crowded Spanish Relief rallies in the Town Hall, gave a proper kick-off to the collection by waving £5 notes (afterwards recoverable) as tangible tokens of our sympathy for the victims of civil war.[1]

At a May Day celebration in 1935, Katharine announced she was proud to have been a member of the Communist Party since its inception in Australia. Although she was known to have radical views, it was her first public declaration of her membership. Ironically, a few days later her name was included in a list of prominent Western Australians who had been sent a medal to be worn on 6 May for the commemoration of King George V's silver jubilee.[2] Twenty-five years earlier, Katharine had been in London on the fringes of the suffragette movement, a participant in the march to mark the coronation of George V; now she was in the thick of activism as Western Australia's leading communist.

The Comintern in Moscow disapproved of her declaration. It wrote to the Communist Party of Australia in July 1935:

> It has been decided that Comrade Prichard is to devote her energies to antiwar and anti-fascist activities, and to the Writers' League. Being one of the foremost writers in Australia, with also a world reputation, a fact even admitted by bourgeois critics, Comrade Prichard should be prominently used to conduct work among the intellectuals, petty-bourgeoisie, etc., and should not be brought to the forefront as a Party member and activist …[3]

On 2 October 1935 a memo in her surveillance file noted, 'She has been quiet since May of this year'.[4] In reality, she was busier than ever, continuing her work with the Movement Against War and Fascism and helping to start the Perth Workers' Art Guild.

The Comintern was directing the communist parties around the world to change their approach. The new policy was the Popular Front. Instead of taking a hard line against potential allies in the middle class and union movements, communists were now to try to work with them for common goals and take a united stand against the fascist governments who had seized power in Europe. Communist Arthur Rudkin wrote of the strategy that it was so successful in recruiting 'progressive middle class people' that 'for a while the Party was in danger of becoming top heavy with imperfectly assimilated petty bourgeois radicals'.[5]

The Perth Workers' Art Guild was 'to serve as a social hub for the unemployed and the political Left. It was to offer practical opportunities to those traditionally excluded from participation in the arts. It publicly declared its somewhat utopian design as "a non-party organisation dedicated to working class culture"'.[6] Its most important activity was the Workers' Theatre. For several years Katharine had been friends with a theatre director named Keith George; she recruited him to lead the theatre. Then in his thirties, Keith was 'flamboyant' with a 'sparkling intellect', and a distinctive appearance, a 'portly, short and balding' gourmand.[7] His politics were left wing but he wasn't a party member. He and Katharine had different approaches to theatre too—Keith 'has an idea', Katharine wrote to Louis Esson, 'that when he's producing, a play belongs to him, and the author is an unpleasant accident'.[8] Despite their differences, she admired his work immensely.

Building on the approach she'd taken in her suffrage 'playlets' in 1914 and her observations of Russian theatre, Katharine wrote several agitprop plays for the guild to perform. The guild presented three short plays for its inaugural performance on 7 December 1935, including Katharine's rather simple *Forward One*, in which three shop assistants in a Perth dress shop rally together to assert their right to sit down between customers. The *Red Star* reviewed it solely from its propaganda potential, writing, 'With improvements in the content and better presentation this play will become a vital force for the organisation of the shop girls for militant unionism'.[9]

THE SPANISH CIVIL WAR broke out in 1936 when soldiers led by the fascist General Franco fought to overthrow the democratically elected left-wing government. The war was a rallying point for the left in English-speaking countries. Katharine was an organiser of the Spanish War Relief Committee and wrote a play called *Women of Spain* to promote the cause. It was produced by the Workers' Art Guild, first on 31 May 1938 at a small venue, the Myola Club in Claremont, and then as part of a rally at the Perth Town Hall on 27 July. It was the first time the young communist journalist Joan Williams had encountered Katharine and she remembers, 'She spoke slowly and simply, avoiding the padding and circumlocutions that wore out reporters, giving an impression of emotional commitment on a carefully reasoned basis.

When the applause died down, she took up her cigarette in its ivory holder and calmly answered questions'.[10] Historian Dylan Hyde writes, 'The Guild toured *Women of Spain* around Perth between June and August 1938 to assist Spanish Relief Committee appeals, perhaps as a fixed-stage performance at some rallies but almost certainly on the back of a truck at others'.[11]

ON SATURDAY 6 November 1937, the Communist Party celebrated the twentieth anniversary of the Bolshevik Revolution at the Rechabite Hall in the city. The advertisement in the *Workers Star* promised 'short, snappy, and inspiring speeches' from Katharine and two others, one of them an Australian who had just returned from fighting in the Spanish Civil War. Katharine wore a Russian shawl and said, 'If all of you could only see the happy peace-loving Russian people as I have seen them; the women and girls wearing shawls like this one I am wearing to-night, I know that every one of you would devote the rest of your lives in the struggle for Peace and Socialism'. At the end of her speech, she called for 'cheers for the Soviet Union, for Stalin and the Communist Party, which were given with gusto and enthusiasm'.[12] Afterwards there was dancing 'to specially engaged music' and a supper in which 'coffee à la Stalin' was served with 'Marx Meringues' and 'Lenin Lamingtons'.[13]

Katharine didn't believe the reports that were now appearing in the newspapers about the show trials and disappearances under Stalin. Ironically, her firsthand experience of the Soviet Union would have made it harder for her to believe the truth—she had spent months on the ground, witnessing the reality of life under Stalin, and she was sure she knew better than journalists working for the capitalist press.

Katharine was back out in public as a party member and her involvement with the day-to-day operations increased too. Perhaps the Comintern had changed its mind about what her role should be. According to Dylan Hyde, the state conference in January 1938 was held at Katharine's house in Greenmount.[14] She was one of seventeen members elected to the district committee. In a change of tactic, the conference was reported in-depth in the *Workers Star.* Bill Mountjoy, who was re-elected district secretary, was quoted as saying, 'mankind was realising the terrible danger of fascist reaction. But the people, led by the workers, were fighting back'.[15]

Mountjoy's drinking was out of control in 1938. One of his drinking partners was Ron Richards, a detective nicknamed the 'Black Snake', who was lulling Mountjoy into a false sense of security while soliciting information. Charming and 'conversant with party theory', Richards was 'highly intelligent, slick and duplicitous'.[16] Some party members approached Katharine and asked her to intervene. In the only surviving letter from Mountjoy to Katharine, he told her he didn't have time to meet with her about the issue, dismissing the unhappy members as 'ethereal individuals' with 'middle-class ballast'. 'It grieves me', he wrote, 'to see such a brilliant representative of the working class taking the side—even if unconsciously—with those who would wreck the Party'. He flattered Katharine at the same time as putting her in her place: 'there are a number of capable Party leaders in Australia but only one Katharine, whose national prestige is extremely important'. The real leaders of the party were proletarians like Mountjoy. 'I stand guard for the proletarian purity of the Party.'[17] Mountjoy was good at making enemies; Joan Williams wrote, 'Inclined to be a petty dictator, he caused many expulsions and bitterness as he axed possible rivals for leadership … He resented Mrs Throssell's wide influence, possibly because she was a woman, but mostly because she frankly expressed disapproval of his drinking'.[18]

Ric remembers that after Katharine confronted Mountjoy in private, he summoned her before the disciplinary committee and accused her of deviating from the party line.[19] On 6 November 1938 she wrote to Guido Baracchi that the 'situation is rotten … A letter to the CC [Central Committee] which you may hear more [about]. Wish I needn't barge in—but somebody's got to be the scape goat, & I can stand it better than most'. The confrontation was highly stressful; she told Guido she had a 'head-ache—& heart flopping about like a flea on hot bricks'.[20]

The conclusion of the dispute is unknown, but at the state conference in early 1939, Katharine requested permission to refuse the nomination to continue on the district committee and it was granted.[21] She couldn't escape Mountjoy altogether; they were the two most prominent communist speakers in Western Australia and often had to share a platform throughout 1939.

RIC TURNED SIXTEEN in 1938 and Katharine's words about him in that letter to Guido about Mountjoy are revealing: 'My lad's been born & bred for the Party; I know it would be a terrible shock to him to find that Communists were capable of sacrificing party interests for beer. Have got to try & clear things up for his sake'. She was vehemently hoping that she'd raised a communist, even as she sent him to board at Wesley College among the wealthy. Ric remembers, 'I learned to live in both worlds. On my weekends at home … I listened while the grave-faced men of the International Brigade, with the memories of death still hidden behind their eyes, told their stories of Spain'.[22]

Ric insists he wasn't pressed to join the party. 'She told me the way that she saw the issues of the day when I asked, satisfied that the logic of her position would be persuasion enough.' In these teenage years he was intellectually convinced by the 'goals of Marxism', a society 'where all co-operated for the common good', but he was content enough with life that he didn't become politically active.[23] Despite her words to Guido, Ric sensed an ambivalence in her attitude, writing, 'Perhaps she hoped to save me from the rigorous life of self-sacrifice that her own adherence to the Communist Party had come to mean. She wanted success for me without compromising her own ideals'.[24]

KATHARINE WROTE TO Timofey Rokotov at the Union of Soviet Writers in September 1938 apologising for not sending him a requested article, blaming it on a 'weary and over worked brain'. 'I belong to twelve organisations and have to take an active part in their doings: am responsible for many, as well as somehow trying to earn a living.'[25] She was terribly over-committed and realised it, but pushed on. It was partly the urgency of the times, partly her reaction to grief. Perpetual organisational busyness was also a way of life she had learned from both her father and Colonel Reay.

One of the new organisations she helped establish was the Modern Women's Club. According to Katharine, it was begun because the Labor Party had banned its women members from joining the Council Against War and Fascism. At the executive meeting of the council, Katharine said, 'we should have a women's club where the members would be free to discuss any subject which concerned them'; others agreed with her.[26] The club rented premises in the city and had a weekly lunch with a lecture by a visiting speaker. At the official opening in April 1938 the president said, 'We stand for progress especially in the betterment of women's conditions in regard to work, recreation and housing'.[27] Dorothy Irwin remembers the 'chief value' of the club was that 'it provided a meeting place for progressives during a period that was difficult for us all. The weekly luncheons brought people together and gave them a feeling of solidarity that was stimulating'. Echoing how Katharine may have felt, she adds, 'I remember chiefly the crushing work'.[28]

Probably the only non-political organisation Katharine belonged to at this time was the WA branch of the Fellowship of Australian Writers. It was formed after a gathering of eleven Western Australian writers in Perth for dinner with visiting American literary critic, Hartley Grattan, in June 1938.[29] When the branch first met in October, Katharine, Walter Murdoch and historian Jesse Hammond were made honorary life members in recognition of their literary achievements.[30]

KATHARINE WAS OUTWARDLY content to be pouring her life into politics but revealed her unhappiness to old literary friends. 'One day a month is all I get [to write] sometimes and working 18 hours a day sometimes on Party affairs', she wrote to Vance Palmer in October 1935. 'It's devastating—quite impossible to get any concentration. And I'll be stoney [*sic*], motherless broke if I don't earn something soon.'[31] In August 1936, she wrote what would be her final letter to Hugh McCrae for many years, saying, 'It's been a woeful year—living alone & working so hard. To-day, it's raining & raining, & the wind yelps round the house. I say I'm too busy to be lonely. But you know what that means. There's nobody I want to come into my mind, any-more'.[32] When Nettie visited her a couple of months later on the way back from Europe, she wrote to Vance that Katharine looked 'pretty ill—haggard and a bad colour—but game and energetic: She does odd literary jobs when she can find time, but does four furious days' work a week for the party, organising, holding meetings, building up movements that will be spearheads, including a very flourishing Workers' Theatre'.[33]

Her money problems continued through the second half of the 1930s; in April 1939, the shire council advertised in the local newspaper that it would auction off two of Hugo's properties unless Katharine paid more than £20 of rates which were in arrears. Perhaps it prompted her to advertise her 'genuine English Rosewood piano' for £20 two months later.[34]

In Katharine's words, 'by a miracle' she finally finished *Intimate Strangers* in mid-1936 and sent it off to Jonathan Cape.[35] 'I've been in the black depths over it', she told Hugh McCrae in that last letter. 'But Hilda and Louis are pleased … So perhaps it's not as bad as I thought.'[36] The novel would have felt like it came from her distant past; she'd begun it before her political re-awakening in the Depression and finished the first draft while Hugo was still alive.

Katharine's ambivalence towards *Intimate Strangers* was echoed in the mixed reviews after its publication in April 1937. The *Bulletin* gave a harsh assessment, calling it 'disappointing' and arguing that 'the characters are working for the author, not living for themselves'; the reviewer had the feeling that Katharine 'herself has not been happy with it'.[37] The strongest praise came from Perth's *Daily News,* where communists Joan Williams and Bill Irwin were both working. Calling it 'perhaps the finest modern novel written by an Australian', the reviewer wrote it was 'rich in character and understanding: intensely moving, gripping and sincere … It adds immeasurably to our understanding of life and of one another'.[38] The communist newspaper the *Workers' Weekly* praised it for depicting 'the road traversed by many middle class people on their way to the revolutionary ranks of the working class'.[39] A longer review in the same newspaper by Katharine's friend, Jean Devanny, went further:

> It has done for me what personal contact with KSP herself always does for me: it has belted me more firmly for the struggle. It will do the same for you. Read it, comrade, and see how Australia's finest writer, foundation member of our Party, has linked us all together; writer, canecutter, miner, unemployed, seaman—in the enchanted castle of our Party, which cannot be separated from the workers of the world.[40]

Intimate Strangers sold poorly. Jonathan Cape wrote to Katharine in October 1938, 'The reason would seem to be that it was an essential drama of human beings in a modern society, but the setting being ever so slightly different was confusing to the average reader of novels, and was not strongly different to attract people who like books with a definite local colour'.[41] If Katharine needed any encouragement to stay out of the suburbs in her writing and return to the 'backblocks' where she had made her reputation she now had it.

Henry Handel Richardson didn't like the novel and she gossiped from London that she had asked William Norton 'if he was going to publish it in America. He said "My hat, no!" It has fallen like a stone here, & Cape has lost heavily on it. Norton saw C. & inquired why he had handled such a book & Cape said he was "sorry for her!"'[42]

With the limited writing time she had, Katharine was focusing on short fiction, which paid more reliably and quickly. Reflecting this focus, in May 1937 she gave a lecture on the craft of the short story to the Workers' Art Guild. She advised her audience not to let themselves be ruined by the formulas of popular fiction magazines but to try to write about incidents which were 'real and vital' to them.[43] She was to broadcast a version of the same lecture three years later on ABC radio. She finished with a stirring vision for the genre: 'the great short stories ... have been written ... to snatch from oblivion fragments of tragedy and heroism, of joy and comedy for others to laugh over, wonder and weep over, or be exalted and stirred by, to some clearer understanding of our common humanity and the purpose of existence'.[44]

There's a generosity of spirit in Katharine's lecture which is also apparent in her published stories of the time. Even though politics had taken over her life and she was promoting socialist realism, when she wrote short fiction she did so with flashes of humour and diversity of theme. Holidays on Rottnest Island inspired 'The Buccaneers', published in *The Bulletin* in 1935. It's a story of three men who return to the island each year; seemingly lighthearted, it captures the disappointments of ageing. 'Life had never been quite what they imagined it would be, so they lived in their exploits of their youth, sucking from adventurous dreams the rapture and thrills that had never quite materialised.'[45] In 1938 she had one of the best stories of her career, 'Flight', published in *Home*. The story is an early critique of the Stolen Generations policy under which Aboriginal children were being forcibly removed from their families. A constable in the north of Western Australia is unhappy about having to take three Aboriginal girls from their mothers, but he's more worried about looking foolish than about the injustice of it. In the last pages, the point of view shifts to the girls themselves and their devastating inability to snatch a chance for freedom.

Katharine's perspective on Aboriginal issues had been developing since she'd written *Coonardoo* a decade earlier. In February 1939 she attended a conference discussing the Native Administration Act and wrote an article complaining, 'In the wrangle between the Department and the missionary organisations, the right of the natives to dispose of their own souls and bodies is lost sight of'. She urged the state government to convene a conference of Aboriginal people and ask them what should be done to further their interests. 'These people, at least, should be given representation on any board assuming control of their lives and children.'[46] Katharine also wrote an essay in 1939 for the *British Annual of Literature*, 'The Aborigine in Australian Literature'. The essay assumes many racist ideas of the time but it at least begins with an acknowledgement of genocide: 'The early history of our country reeks with the massacre of these people and with the crimes committed against them by ruthless men who would even leave poisoned flour in their huts in order to exterminate men, women, and children'.[47] The next year, when *Brumby Innes* was published, she wrote in a letter, 'If I were writing the play now, I would emphasise their [i.e. Aboriginal people's] right to an independent existence. As it is, the play leaves you with a sense only of the degradation of the natives and the brutality of their over-lords'.[48]

IN 1935, KATHARINE wrote a recruitment pamphlet for the Movement Against War and Fascism called *Who Wants War?*. She warned that weapon makers and fascists wanted another war and that 'Fascism is the last resort of Capitalism to force its will on the people'. The Soviet Union, however, stood for peace and was the one force the fascists feared.[49] Four years later, as the threat from Nazi Germany had grown even clearer, she gave a speech titled 'Peace and War', probably for International Women's Day in March. 'Apathy, credulity and stup[e]fying illusions have brought us to the stage in our history when we must be prepared to defend democracy … or surrender to the cruel and barbarous forces of fascism which have demonstrated their rapacious ambition in Europe and in China during the last year.'[50]

After Katharine and other communists in Australia had spent years speaking out against the danger of fascism, Stalin signed a non-aggression pact with Hitler in August 1939. Australian communists suffered 'the shock of such a sudden and cynical change. The Soviet Union, which had insisted that fascism was the overriding danger to world peace, now stood back to allow Nazi Germany to go to war'.[51] Katharine blamed the British and French governments for rejecting the Soviet Union's overtures for an alliance against Germany. 'A non-aggression pact is not a measure of appeasement. It gives nothing away.'[52]

Ric was in his final year of school and remembers listening to the radio at Greenmount on 3 September 1939 when prime minister Robert Menzies declared that Australia was at war. Katharine was doing something in the next room and Ric wasn't sure if she had heard. When he went in to tell her, 'her eyes filled with tears'.[53]

30

Underground

Greenmount and Kalgoorlie 1940–1942

IN FEBRUARY 1940 Guido Baracchi sent Katharine a telegram to say he'd been expelled from the party:

> Stalinism [is a] betrayal of Leninism ... [I am] continuing full Leninist fight against war and for proletarian revolution and Soviet Union somehow will try to make communist of you love ... Guido[1]

His expulsion came after the party's Control Commission demanded he account for not reporting the 'Trotskyist tendencies' of his friend James Rawling. Guido responded, 'I can only admit knowing that Rawling was returning to revolutionary Marxism, to Leninism'.[2] It was a Trotskyist answer in itself. Leon Trotsky, an architect of the Russian Revolution turned dissident, had been criticising Stalin while in exile and was to be assassinated a few months later.

Guido saw his own expulsion as the culmination of a 'long struggle'. One key moment in his disillusionment was learning in 1938 that his friend in the Soviet Union, Arcadi Berdichevsky, had been missing since the secret police took him away two years earlier. Berdichevsky was interrogated—and later executed—for being part of a supposed Trotskyist group operating out of the apartment Guido had also been living in until 1935. For Guido, it gave 'the Terror—a dizzying 1.8 million people arrested between 1935 and 1940—a name and a face'. Guido's biographer Jeff Sparrow thinks it likely he would have been arrested too had he stayed in the Soviet Union much longer.[3]

Katharine expressed no sympathy with these deviations from the party line. She told Rawling she was appalled by his conduct. 'At this critical period', she wrote, 'to permit oneself Trotskyist divagations strikes me as intellectual dilettantism, incapable of adjusting to the needs of the working-class movement'.[4] When Guido next saw Katharine, she wouldn't speak to him.[5] She had forgiven him sexual and romantic betrayals two decades earlier but not this political one.

Loyalty to the party meant that if Katharine had any doubts of her own, any hesitations, she suppressed them, leaving nothing on the historical record but her hardline support for Stalinism.

ANTI-COMMUNIST SENTIMENT was growing stronger. In early 1940, Katharine was preparing to deliver a series of guest lectures at the University of Western Australia on Australian literature under an arrangement with the Fellowship of Australian Writers WA. Four days before the first lecture, she was barred from speaking after university management learned a notorious communist would be temporarily on the payroll. The fellowship's protests were not enough to have her reinstated but they did secure full payment for her.[6] Katharine wrote to the professorial board, 'To prostitute your power to the service of hysterical obfuscation, at a time like this, in my opinion is servile and cowardly'.[7]

On 15 June 1940, after the fall of France to the Nazis, the Menzies government declared the Communist Party of Australia illegal. That same day, warrants were issued giving police the authority to search houses of prominent communists, including Katharine's.[8] The detectives came the next day. Ric remembers the embarrassment of one of them finding a sex toy:

> 'What's this?' he asked, showing me a rubber gadget that he had fished out from the back of one of the drawers.

> 'I don't know,' I told him, honestly enough, though I had been fascinated by the device and suspected what it was.
>
> 'I think it's my mother's,' I said.
>
> 'Filthy young bastard!' he sneered, with every appearance of utter contempt. 'How'd you like me to tell her what you're up to?'[9]

Katharine had hidden her illegal publications and party papers in a trunk under the plumbago hedge near her writing cabin. However, the detectives still confiscated many other papers, including one of her notebooks and a letter Miles Franklin had just sent her. Katharine wrote to the Ministry of Information, protesting 'the foolish attack which has been made on members of the Communist Party in Western Australia. Communists have always been the most active opponents of Fascism and Hitlerism. They still are'.[10]

The repression of communists was greater in Western Australia than any other state, partly due to Ron Richards' crusade. His long game of gathering intelligence from Mountjoy had paid off and he orchestrated the arrest of a dozen party members, many of them convicted and jailed.[11] Katharine wrote about the prosecutions and the prospect of imprisonment to an editor in Moscow:

> No one, of course, is intimidated by these tactics; no one who attached any importance to his convictions and personal courage, at any rate. It would be giving you a wrong impression, however, to imply that the position is not very difficult, both for me and many others whose sympathies are well-known. I am not in the least concerned about going to gaol at any time. The experiences will naturally provide interesting material to write about some day. But if you do [not] hear from me, now and then, you will understand I am sure what has happened.[12]

As it happened, Katharine escaped arrest. Perhaps Richards believed her prominence as a writer would have brought too much public attention and turned her into a martyr. Party member John McKenzie remembers that in response to the prosecutions, a number of his comrades left their jobs and moved to Sydney, where they would be safer.[13]

Mountjoy was not arrested either. He went into hiding 'somewhere in North Beach' until the party arranged for the Seamen's Union to smuggle him aboard a ship heading east. The committee sent a Gallipoli veteran named Jack Simpson to be his replacement. He stayed in Cottesloe, posing as a retired farmer until he was caught by Ron Richards, prosecuted by Nathaniel Lappin, and sentenced to nine months in jail in May 1941.[14]

In response to illegality, Katharine gave the impression that she was withdrawing from political activity. Suspecting with good reason her mail was being read, she wrote to Hilda, 'For the present, I'm not engaged in any political activity'.[15] It wasn't true, of course. In the days of illegality, Katharine's activities became opaque, her letters and public utterances deliberately misleading. Joan Williams writes that Katharine 'continued on the State committee throughout the illegal period … in conditions which of necessity gave the membership little idea of the official functioning of the apparatus and suspended many of their rights. Despite defects and bureaucracy, the underground organization functioned well, [and] the underground paper was produced regularly and widely distributed'.[16] John McKenzie remembers it more negatively, writing of 'rather futile clandestine meetings' and frustration about the leadership's acceptance of the Soviet line on the war.[17]

Katharine was heavily involved in supporting her comrades through their trials into early 1941, leaving her 'thoroughly exhausted'. She wrote to Hilda, 'Remand, appeal, and interviewing counsel for the defence. It was really a very strenuous time'.[18]

IN THE MIDST of these battles, Katharine was also short of money. She decided to write a novel purely for money, a 'potboiler' Hollywood might be interested in turning into a movie.[19] Calling it *Moon of Desire*, she drew on her notes about Broome and Singapore from her trip in 1929 and constructed an adventure plot about the titular pearl. A pearler, Alec, obsessively shadows Matsu, the Japanese diver he believes has stolen the pearl, leading to a confrontation on the beach which leaves two dead. Alec had hoped the pearl would enable him to marry his fiancée, Ann, but instead it causes their separation, another death, and a recovery mission in Singapore before they are finally reunited. After a passable opening it becomes contrived and tedious. Katharine had finished a draft by May 1940, and wrote to Mikhail Apletin at the Union of Soviet Writers, 'Tragic isn't it to have to write rubbish at the end of one's days in order to live. I have to leave my home soon. Foreclosure of the mortgage'.[20] The foreclosure was somehow averted and she was able to stay in her home for the time being, but the threat remained. In December, after sending *Moon of Desire* to Jonathan Cape, she wrote to Louis Esson, 'Have been so utterly weary of this damned book'.[21]

Katharine held *Moon of Desire* in lower regard than her other novels, conscious of writing it to sell. However, it still has some recognisably Prichardian elements. The romance tropes come from her early fiction; the mystical allure of pearls recalls that of opals in *Black Opal*. The account of the pearling industry, the interweaving of the folklore of Broome, and the colour of Singapore reflect her signature method. Ann's lament echoes that of women throughout Katharine's fiction:

> Ann brooded over every phase of the pearling industry and the sinister undertow it generated in the life of the town … She began to hate pearls and mother-of-pearl: to realize their cost to women like herself and Nell McIntyre, in fear and anxiety about their men, and to the men themselves in fierce and bitter rivalry with each other. Many crimes had been committed for a pearl![22]

Sandra Burchill notes that the novel 'turns away from a deeper exploration of racism, social inequality and poverty', but one point of interest is the section of sympathetic narration through the eyes of Matsu the Japanese diver: 'He had risked his life often enough for the white masters who made a handsome profit on his labour'.[23]

The *Bulletin* reviewer read it as Katharine intended:

> The story is straightforward, bristling with revolvers and knives, and warm with tropic coloring. Those who like the excitements of this sort of novel will find it far better, on this particular ground, than nine out of ten of its kind. Those who look to this author for contributions to Australian literature will possibly read it with some astonishment. Every now and then, when the doings are at

> their wildest and everything, from a literary standpoint, seems to be getting out of hand, the author will come in with a splendid splash of writing in her best style.[24]

The *Sydney Morning Herald* reviewer wrote, 'Against an exotic, tropical background, this competent writer presents in her latest novel a group of characters and a set of circumstances which are as convincing as they are absorbing'.[25] If luck had gone Katharine's way, it might have been the bestseller she hoped but the difficulties of wartime distribution and publicity were against her and it did not sell well. She'd hoped for a lucrative movie deal, especially after the American publisher, Greenberg, offered her a publishing contract in November 1941. She spent more than a year waiting for copies of the published book and news from Hollywood only to discover a letter from Greenberg had gone astray; in it, they had informed her that they weren't proceeding with a US edition.[26]

IN SEPTEMBER 1940, the Workers' Art Guild staged Katharine's play, *Penalty Clause,* for three nights as part of the Perth drama festival. In it, a group of gold miners go on strike over unsafe conditions after a fatality; when they return to work, they find their time on strike has been deducted from their holidays. Katharine was proud of the play and claimed she had inside information that the judges believed it was the best entry but 'were afraid to award the prize to a play with so definite a political content under present circumstances'. She insisted she wasn't concerned with prizes or the praise of 'bourgeois critics'; she was just 'happy to have done something which may be of service to the working class ... The response of the people who heard the play was what mattered, and that was—tears, cheers and an overwhelming enthusiasm'.[27] It was a foretaste of what would happen with her goldfields trilogy after the war. From this point onwards, Katharine was quick to ascribe literary setbacks to politics, reacting to criticism with a complacent confidence in her writing.

She sent a copy of the play to Mikhail Apletin in the hope he might arrange for it to be produced in the Soviet Union. While she was certain it was too left wing to find critical favour in Australia, she was also concerned that it might not be politically palatable for the Soviets. 'In many ways, it may fall short of what you consider it should be. But I was working on actual conditions of a strike which occurred on the goldfields, and anxious not to go beyond the framework of these conditions.'[28]

AN EPISTOLARY FRIENDSHIP had been developing in the 1930s between Katharine and Miles Franklin, the Australian writer who was both a nationalist and a feminist. After the precocious success of *My Brilliant Career* (1901), Miles had spent decades abroad in the United States and Britain accumulating unpublished manuscripts and devoting herself to progressive causes. Returning to live in Sydney, her literary career had revived, with *All That Swagger* winning the SH Prior Memorial Prize in 1936. In Miles's devotion to Australian literature as a writer, advocate and mentor she had common cause with Katharine, while Miles's political ambiguity was a source of tension in their friendship.

In October 1940, Katharine wrote to Miles of her struggles, working hard 'at so many different sorts of jobs—keeping house for my beautiful son who is grown-up now, cooking, sweeping, washing, mending etc, organisational work and lectures, and somewhere in between, I've got to find time to write and earn my living'.[29] Miles encouraged Katharine to apply for one of the new Commonwealth Literary Fund grants and Katharine decided to follow her advice. Asking for financial help did not come easily to her; she wrote in her covering letter in December, 'I am reluctant to apply for a Fellowship … but circumstances at present force me to'. She didn't mention, of course, the heavy toll her political commitments were taking, but wrote of how she had been 'living on much less than the basic wage' for years, and that 'hard work and ill health are making it almost impossible for me to write well. This book of the goldfields which I am anxious to do next year, I should like to make something of real value. With relief from pressing financial anxiety, I think that it may be'.[30]

As part of her application, she detailed her income in 1940. *Haxby's Circus* (1930) and *Intimate Strangers* (1937) were her only novels in print and the royalties paid on them didn't amount to £1. Her military pension of £109 formed the bulk of her income; she supplemented it with £24 from short stories and articles, and £62 from radio broadcasts and a radio play, making a total of £195. The fellowship would be worth £250 over twelve months—about the same as the basic wage for men.[31]

Her application form provided details of her goldfields project, showing it was already well advanced:

> It will probably be of three book length—although my publisher may prefer to print in one volume. Part I deals with the discovery of gold & the prospecting period. Part II growth of the mining industry & the rise of towns. Part III with the slump & return to prosperity in present conditions. I have been working on this book for some time, & Part I is almost completed, having been built on the yarns of original prospectors & personal experiences on the fields ... As the subject of this novel has never been thoroughly dealt with, I want to make it both historically accurate & a good picture of the life of the periods through which the story moves.[32]

The goldfields saga would eventually be published as a trilogy exactly as she envisioned in the application—*The Roaring Nineties* in 1946, *Golden Miles* in 1948, and *Winged Seeds* in 1950.

After Katharine spent months waiting in limbo, the fund wrote in April 1941 to say she had been successful. The awarding of the fellowship was not publicly announced and the security service only found out about it a couple of months later when an intelligence officer read it in one of Katharine's letters to Russia. The officer filed a report saying, 'it seems strange that one so intimately associated with the Communist Party should in any way be recognised'. The security service issued a report recommending that the Commonwealth Literary Fund discreetly submit the names of any writers they were considering for a fellowship for 'comment' to prevent further cases like this.[33]

To start her fellowship, Katharine arranged a ten-week research trip to Kalgoorlie, arriving in late May 1941. More than the heat, it was the noise which struck her, the 'drone of the mine batteries' in her ear, day and night.[34] For the first week, she stayed in the middle of town at the Palace Hotel, 'which is supposed to be <u>the</u> historic & swank hotel of Kal. Not so historic & swank as some of the less reputable pubs where I sometimes go for a pot with old girls'.[35]

A woman named Doon Doyle invited Katharine to stay at her house. Although not a party member, Doon was sympathetic to communism; she was a teacher in her thirties who acted in Repertory Club productions and was married without children to an Irish miner. Doon had met Katharine on a previous trip and idolised her. Doon wrote of Katharine, 'Her conversation is even more exhilarating than her writing. She can deliver a piece of frank feeling with utmost delicacy and gentleness that transmutes it to gem purity'.[36]

'They let me do as I like, work & read', Katharine wrote. 'Marvellous to have no dish-washing & cooking for awhile!' Although Katharine was relaxed Doon wasn't. 'I had an unshakable conviction in her creative art, that amounted to fervour, and the routine of my days revolved around her needs.'[37] Doon arranged trips for Katharine to the mines at Broad Arrow, Ora Banda and Siberia and introduced her to locals for her research.[38] The friendship between the two women was to be an enduring one, even though it was troubled by Doon's tendency to stew bitterly for years over hurts Katharine knew nothing about. *Golden Miles* is dedicated to her.

The three goldfields novels are the only ones of Katharine's to have a strong historical background. *The Pioneers* is set in the nineteenth century but its historical basis is loose; her other novels are set in the present or recent past. Katharine took the research task seriously and had read through the first five years of the *Kalgoorlie Miner* newspaper in Perth. Now for two weeks in Kalgoorlie she spent five hours a day reading the *Miner* from 1897 to 1919. To this research, she added readings in 'mining law, geology and the processes of gold extraction'. Once her research was done, she settled into a routine of writing from half-past seven to noon. In the afternoon, she yarned 'with prospectors, miners, mine-managers, and interesting folks of all sorts', which she felt 'added a good deal to the material I've been gathering for years'.[39] This combination of library research and interviews is reflected in the trilogy in its mix of verifiable historical events and goldfields yarns.

Katharine had always woven folklore into her novels and now she extended that to include her other forms of research. Sandra Burchill writes, 'The three novels are loaded with prospectors' yarns, old miners' tales, anecdotes and ruminations, authentic speeches, real incidents from the period, extracts from official reports, royal commissions and enquiries, commentary from newspapers and technical descriptions of mining processes'.[40] Burchill sees this as Katharine's adoption of the techniques of reportage, a style of writing pioneered by Egon Kisch. The inaugural Writers' League conference in 1935 featured a lecture by Julian Smith on reportage, published as a pamphlet with a message from Katharine. Smith defined reportage as 'the art of setting down observation or chronicling events accurately and in an artistically effective manner', relying on firsthand experience, thorough research, and—in the case of historical writing—seeking out survivors to interview.[41] Burchill notes the 'overall result of this transcription of information is the reduction of human interest', and assigns some of the negative reaction to the trilogy to it.[42] Katharine was conveying a contentious political perspective with a contentious technique.

AFTER YEARS OF limited literary activity, Katharine does seem to have been genuinely focused on her research and writing while she was in Kalgoorlie. Yet in this period of illegality, with the political stakes so high, it seems unlikely she would take ten weeks away from all political activity. Kalgoorlie–Boulder had a party branch, with several members living together on Piesse Street in Boulder in a miner's hut 'affectionately known as the "Kremlin"' which 'national CPA leaders often visited'.[43] She may have justified her trip to herself and to the party by secretly working with the goldfields branch while she was there.

Nathaniel Lappin, the public prosecutor, was staying at the Palace Hotel while he visited Kalgoorlie to prosecute a Yugoslavian named Francis Legeny who had been arrested with several copies of the banned publication *Communist Review*. When Katharine collected her mail from the hotel on 29 May, he cornered her in the dining room, wanting to know why she was in Kalgoorlie. She told him it wasn't the same reason he was here. He criticised her for allowing others to pay her son's school fees and told her, 'You've been shown a great deal of toleration', which she took as a veiled threat. Doon remembers finding Katharine 'white and shaken and barely able to keep the tears from her voice'.[44]

Lappin was the same lawyer who had raised suspicions about the fire that burned down the historic cottage on Hugo and Katharine's land in 1933.[45] During Legeny's trial, Lappin read extracts from one of the publications and declared, 'It reeks throughout its pages of propaganda'.[46] The accused man claimed to not be a communist nor to have ever distributed the material, but he was found guilty and sentenced to seven months' imprisonment with hard labour. It's understandable that Lappin found it suspicious that Katharine's visit coincided with Francis Legeny's arrest and trial. Oddly, intelligence officers didn't even realise she was in Kalgoorlie until Inspector Ron Richards himself spotted her on 30 June 1941, five weeks after she arrived.[47] Despite Lappin's hostility and involvement in prosecuting communists, he hadn't filed a report on her.

THE WAR SITUATION changed dramatically on 22 June 1941, halfway through Katharine's stay in Kalgoorlie, when German forces invaded the Soviet Union. Suddenly the Soviets joined the Allies in the fight against the Axis powers. In late July, Katharine was asked by the Union of Soviet Writers to cable a 1000-word article 'on the Australian people's reaction to Fascist aggression'. After two muddled years, Katharine was free again to unambiguously oppose fascism. She declared, 'Fascism outrages humanity's instinct for progress. It destroys every right the people have won in struggle through the ages against despotic power'. She praised the Soviet Union while criticising the oppressive wartime measures on the Australian home front; since the outbreak of war, 'the workers of Australia have been subjected to more oppressive taxation and more repressive legislation than ever before in their history'.[48]

Katharine was in a strident mood and it led to a temporary breach in her friendship with the Perth writer Henrietta Drake-Brockman. Henrietta wrote a conciliatory letter to her in Kalgoorlie wanting to move past their 'misunderstandings' about the Soviet Union's role in the war, but instead of agreeing to disagree, Katharine replied, 'Am coming home soon: but while you're on the other side of the fence there is little for us to say to each other. I belong entirely to the people who are suffering for their convictions & service to the great ideals of Humanity. Socialism is the only real defence against Fascism'.[49] Somehow the breach had been healed by the time of the next surviving letter from Katharine to Henrietta a year later.

IN AUGUST 1941 Katharine was glad to be back home in Greenmount, seeing Ric at the weekends while he studied at teachers' college. His dream was to work in film production; Katharine had hoped *Moon of Desire* would make enough money to pay for him to study it in Russia or the United States. 'He has a marvellous sense of the theatre', she wrote to Timofey Rokotov at the Union of Soviet Writers, 'better than mine—and a quite modern and original approach. It does distress me that there are practically no opportunities for him to obtain a broad culture here'.[50]

In early October, two independents withdrew their support for the minority conservative government and Labor took office with John Curtin as prime minister. The Communist Party was still illegal but the atmosphere changed for Australian communists—a friendlier government coincided with public sympathy for the heavy Soviet casualties on the eastern front. Communists became involved with committees fundraising to send aid to Russia.

Katharine wrote to the Commonwealth Literature Fund on 12 October, saying that despite 'wanting nothing more than to bring the thing to birth' she would have to stop work on the goldfields trilogy and suspend her scholarship as she was embarking on a speaking tour for Medical Aid to Russia. 'In the suffering and sorrow of our times, I feel … that one is not entitled to put personal inclination before any service that can be given to relieve this tragic pressure.' She said she was 'anxious to do anything I can to aid the Soviet peoples in their magnificent resistance to Nazi aggression'.[51] The Perth branch of Medical Aid to Russia met at the Modern Women's Club. One of its members was an informant to the intelligence agency, and they reported that at a meeting on 9 October, Katharine said the tour was 'in response to a long-distance telephone call' and 'her fare [was] being paid by The Central Cttee'.[52] The report suggests how involved the underground Communist Party was in the aid to Russia campaign.

Her speaking tour took her first to Sydney, Newcastle and Brisbane where she spoke in front of audiences of three thousand and more.[53] 'Was not supposed to speak the first night in Brisbane, but the people called for me, and there was a roar when I stood up, which made me realise that after all, perhaps, I do count for something with my own people.'[54] She told audiences that 'the ruthlessness of the German campaign, combined with Stalin's scorched earth policy, would leave the country in ruins. The Russian people would need not only military aid, but also food and clothes'.[55] At the conclusion of a speech, she would implore the audience, 'Let us do the fair and sporting thing', with ushers collecting donations and placing them in her Russian shawl she had laid out on the platform.[56]

Katharine travelled down the east coast from Brisbane to Wollongong and then to Canberra. When she visited the House of Representatives unannounced, prime minister John Curtin noticed her and sent a steward to invite her to sit on the floor of the chamber. Afterwards, the attorney-general, Bert Evatt, asked Katharine to have dinner with him and his wife. Evatt told her the intelligence officers had been giving him 'an almost hourly report' on her speaking tour; he requested they focus on fascists instead. The esteem Curtin and Evatt showed her meant much to her—she called her Canberra visit a 'thrilling occasion' when writing about it at the end of her life.[57] The federal Labor governments of the 1940s were to be the last of her lifetime, sandwiched by the hostile Menzies governments. After Curtin's death in 1945, Katharine wrote to Ric, 'Glad I saw him that last time. He had many fine qualities—& they will be remembered more than the weaknesses. His life as a model for leading character in play wd be very interesting'.[58]

The months of speaking had exacted a toll on Katharine, and she was a 'wreck' when she reached Melbourne in time to spend Christmas with her sister Beatrice and rest for two weeks.[59] Afterwards, stopping in Adelaide on the way home, a journalist reported, 'Despite her fragility this grey-haired, dark-eyed writer has intense vitality'.[60]

AT THE END of 1941, Ric and his classmates sat their final teaching exams before reporting at Claremont Showgrounds for medical checks, the first stage of compulsory military training. He followed the rest of his class into the signals unit.[61] Katharine was still interstate; when she returned she wrote, 'it breaks my heart to see him in uniform, knowing what may happen. He is the loveliest specimen of young manhood, brown and handsome, only nineteen, but mature for his years … What a fate to have brought him to! Do you wonder I curse the system …?'[62]

In February 1942, after the fall of Singapore to Japan and the bombing of Darwin, the conscripts in Ric's camp were pressured to volunteer for the AIF so they could be sent overseas. Ric was still under twenty-one and needed Katharine's permission; although terrified he would die, she gave it.[63] 'She was concerned that I would think I had to live up to my father's name,' writes Ric, 'chase honours by rash heroics'. A few months later, he was sent to New Guinea. '[S]he fought my imagined battles in the nightmare memories of the First World War, while I bludged and sweated.'[64] She wrote to Doon Doyle about Ric's posting, 'the bottom has fallen out of my world!'[65]

IN A RESPONSE to an unhappy letter from Miles Franklin, Katharine wrote back in June 1942, 'Don't rust out, Miles darling! You've got too much fire & guts for that. The big fight for a better world is on. Let's make our dying worthwhile. You can't be just melancholy—when there's so much to do. The individual—our individual selves, I mean—matters so little in the mass misery & slaughter'. Katharine was approaching sixty and Miles was four years ahead of her; neither of them were confident of living much longer, but in the midst of the war and with high hopes for the communist cause, Katharine had a strong sense of purpose.

She suggested Miles come to Perth and stay with her for a holiday. 'It's quiet here, beautiful country … I'm the world's untidiest person too, & haven't much time to even talk. But I'd love you to come.'[66] As it turned out, a few months later Katharine moved instead to Sydney where Miles lived.

31

Long Live the Party

Sydney, 1942–1943

WHY DID KATHARINE suddenly move to Sydney on 28 October 1942? She told Ric she was moving to be nearer to him.[1] She put it a little differently to Boris Sutckoff at the Union of Soviet Writers, 'My only son is on active service in Guinea, and so my home has been broken-up and in these days of terrible anxiety there is no need to live here, when he is so far away'.[2] Ric was surely a factor, but at a politically crucial time when Katharine was so committed to the Communist Party, the move probably had something to do with the party as well. Perhaps the party leadership requested she move in order to be in the centre of things; her speaking tour the previous year had confirmed her usefulness as a national public figure.

She moved in the last months of illegality, with the federal government lifting the ban on the Communist Party in December. She lived at the Gwydir Flats on Forbes Road in the central Sydney suburb of Darlinghurst, less than two kilometres from the party headquarters on Hay Street. Initially she shared a flat with woman named Glen Mills Fox, a journalist with communist connections, before finding her own flat in the complex in mid-1943.[3] Her first months in Sydney were marked by bad migraine headaches, apparently brought on by the stress of Ric's deployment overseas. Doon Stone remembers, 'His letters revealed a mental depression and horror that terrified her and her suffering for his sensitivity exposed to the nakedness of jungle warfare was … a quivering, throbbing agony'.[4] In early 1943, Katharine stayed in Leura in the Blue Mountains for some weeks to rest. She rang the writer Eleanor Dark, who lived nearby in Katoomba, to apologise for not visiting; she wasn't feeling well enough.[5] By June, she still hadn't seen Miles Franklin either and wrote to say she was 'just beginning to feel fit for human consumption. Trying to make up for lost time'.[6]

Katharine asked Miles in the same letter whether she would see her at the ceremony to mark Henry Lawson's birthday later that month; Katharine had agreed to give a speech. The speech was probably the basis for an article she published on Lawson in *Communist Review* in October. Australians must not 'forever live in his shadow. He had laid the basis of an Australian literature that was to be based on realism, hatred of injustices suffered under the capitalist system, and a desire for social progress, but he did not say the last word on these subjects'.[7] After another Lawson ceremony the next year—held at his statue to mark twenty-one years since his death—Katharine described, 'the usual eulogies, and extravagant claims for Lawson's work. Queer isn't it? The poor man never earned more than about £2 a week and lived in poverty all his life and became a boozing derelict in his last days. Why could not people have been more generous when he was alive?'[8]

Echoing this sentiment, soon afterwards Katharine made a broadcast about Miles Franklin on ABC radio: 'Tributes to writers who are dead always sadden me. I know how much better it would have been to appreciate their work when they were alive. But, today, I am happy to be talking about Miles Franklin, whose novels are among the finest written in Australia, and who still lives and works among us—glory be'.[9] Katharine said that Miles 'has achieved by her work, a brilliant career, the success of esteem: never forfeited her fundamental honesty for financial gain or false values, and she has given us books about Australia which are sincere and beautiful'.[10]

Living in Sydney, Katharine and Miles saw each other enough to turn their epistolary friendship into a face to face one. There was genuine affection between them but also tensions; in July 1944 after having Miles to her house for dinner, Katharine reported to Ric, 'Miles is annoying! Has such a way of ticking people off'.[11]

IN JANUARY 1943, the attorney-general, Bert Evatt, announced a diplomatic cadets scheme. Ric heard about it in New Guinea and decided to apply. Without Ric's knowledge, Katharine wrote to the Foreign Affairs department, 'pleading' for Ric to be appointed, invoking Hugo's name 'and every other argument she could muster'; she wanted him out of danger.[12] In June, the department announced Ric was one of the successful candidates and he began a diplomatic career.[13] As the son of a prominent communist, intelligence services were to view his motivations with suspicion in the years which followed.

Released from the army, Ric was sent to enrol in a course at Sydney University for the rest of the year as part of the cadetship. When the troop train arrived in Sydney six hours late, Katharine was waiting on the platform in 'a coat the colour of spring wattle', Ric writes, 'so that I should not miss her'. Troop movements were secret, but Katharine had heard rumours the train was coming and, according to Doon in a letter to Ric, 'She waited on the station platform, from daylight to midnight, for three days. She had the most fanatical fixation that she must be there to meet you. So there she stayed, cold and exhausted and alone, until you arrived'.[14]

Ric stayed at St Andrew's College near the university. When he visited Katharine on weekends, he was frustrated at the number of uninvited visitors who would turn up. 'She always seemed to be available.'[15] In their conversations about the war, Ric remembers commenting that Stalin seemed more of a dictator than ever. Katharine told him the Russian people needed a 'figure-head', like Churchill to the British, 'to unite them in the effort to defeat fascism'; it would be different once the war was over. Her attitudes had hardened—Ric was shocked to hear her justify the torture of Nazi prisoners for information. 'Katharine had boasted sometimes about her "communist steel", but I had never heard her so openly ready to deny her own nature, her innate sensitivity to others' suffering.'[16] At the beginning of 1944, he moved to Canberra to continue his cadetship.

THE CHANGE IN Katharine which Ric noticed reflected her new role in the party, elected to the Central Committee for a two-year term in April 1943 at the 13th National Congress. At the congress she gave a speech as a foundation member of the party. Nearing her sixtieth birthday, she was feeling her age, lamenting, 'I wish I could be young again to work as hard for the Communist Party of Australia in the next twenty years as I have done in the past'. She captured the mood of the party members at a momentous time as they had just passed through 'the dark days of illegality' and must now look to the future, which was in the hands of the 'magnificent young Comrades here today'. She finished her speech with the acclamation:

> Long live the Communist Party of Australia. Long live our beloved leader, Comrade [JB] Miles. Long live every individual member of the Communist Party that he may prove worthy of the work that lies before him in winning unity of the working class for the defeat of international fascism in this war, for the defeat of fascist tendencies which may arise in the period of reconstruction after the war, and for the building of a Socialist Australia.[17]

Her admiration of JB Miles seems to have been genuine; another time after hearing him speak she wrote to Ric, 'the spirit & energy in that frail body! The intellectual rigour and clear brain!'[18]

Ric writes of Katharine's Sydney years, 'Paradoxically, being close to the centre of political activity meant that Katharine was relieved of many of the minor organizing chores which had come her way in Perth'.[19] Party member Jack Beasley remembers that 'Comrade Prichard's jobs were to write *The Roaring Nineties* and to make a limited number of public speaking appearances'. He depicts the Central Committee as 'very largely a consultative body, meeting periodically to hear reports, discuss aspects of politics … and the work of the party'. It only convened two to three times a year. The real power was in the committee's secretariat—the president, secretary and assistant secretary—as well as the similarly named Central Control Commission. Many references to the Central Committee seem to have been shorthand for this arrangement and give the misleading perception that Katharine took a day-to-day leadership role.[20]

Katharine's articles for the communist newspaper, *Tribune,* show her as a wide-ranging ambassador for the party, commenting on the war and relaying cultural news from the Soviet Union which had been cabled directly to her. In one article she promoted workshops to learn the songs of the working class: 'By singing at party meetings, at demonstrations in the open air, singing as we march and celebrate great occasions, we will give a vital impression of our vigor and what membership of the Party really means.'[21]

A MAN NAMED Wally Clayton was elected to the Central Committee at the same congress as Katharine. Decades later, soon before he died, he was to confess to historian Desmond Ball that he had been gathering information, some of it classified, for the Soviet Union under the code-name 'Klod'. He told Ball he took the information to Feodor Nosov, a Sydney-based correspondent for TASS, the Soviet news agency. Ball, along with David Horner, write of what they call the 'Klod spy ring' in their 1998 book *Breaking the Codes* and allege Katharine was central to it. Other historians think 'spy ring' is an exaggerated descriptor for a network of contacts who may have thought their information was being used for domestic party purposes.[22] 'With one or two exceptions', Ball and Horner write, 'we have made little effort to indulge in speculation', but there are many speculative elements to their case against Katharine.[23]

In their account, Katharine's part in the 'spy ring' dates back to September 1942. Now allies, Australia and the Soviet Union established direct diplomatic relations for the first time and the Soviet Union sent the journalist Vladimir Mikheev to Australia as a correspondent.[24] He stopped over in Perth for a few days before catching the train to Sydney to take up his role. Only learning of his visit at short notice, Katharine organised a reception for him by the Australia–Russia Relations committee at the Modern Women's Club.[25] Ball and Horner write that Mikheev was 'undoubtedly charged with scouting out the Australian scene for the Soviet foreign intelligence service and making preparations for NKGB and GRU [Soviet intelligence agencies'] activities in Australia in 1943'.[26] The Soviets were preparing to establish a legation in Canberra that year, upgraded to an embassy in 1945.

When another Soviet journalist, Feodor Nosov, arrived in Sydney in 1943, Katharine met him and introduced him to other Australian communists. With her appreciation of the Soviet Union and connection to the Union of Soviet Writers, it is an unsurprising thing for her to have done. However, Ball and Horner are certain she knew Nosov was sending sensitive information back to Moscow and believe she was the one who introduced Nosov to Wally Clayton, giving her 'an important role in the establishment of the KLOD group'. They go on to allege Katharine herself was a spy:

> in 1943–45 she was a source of material sent from the KGB Residency in Canberra to Moscow Centre. Most of the material was political gossip, which she would write up in longhand on foolscap paper and give to Clayton to pass to [Soviet diplomat Semyen] Makarov in Canberra. Much of it consisted of summarised accounts of what [Ric] Throssell (who had yet to formally join the department) had related to her about the structure, personnel, interests and policies of External Affairs.[27]

Troublingly, Ball and Horner provide no source for this, the most specific of their allegations against Katharine, meaning there is no opportunity to consult the evidence they are relying on. Is Clayton himself the source, a man Ball and Horner say 'has lied about all the key matters'?[28] Mark Aarons writes of another 'confession' Clayton made late in life that it was 'punctuated by evasion. Passages directly contradict other passages and Clayton's lies are exposed by what he says elsewhere on the tape'.[29] In recent years, journalist Pamela Burton has been refuting espionage allegations made by the now deceased Desmond Ball against her father, John Burton. She writes that when she confronted Ball with his lack of evidence he told her he had secret sources of information he would not reveal.[30] Another objection to what they allege is just what 'political gossip' Katharine could have known that would have been classified or useful to the Soviets. As they acknowledge, her alleged source of information, Ric, was still in the training program and yet to formally join the department.

Some of the radio transmissions Nosov sent back to Moscow were intercepted and decoded by American intelligence in the VENONA project. Publicly released in 1995, one of them contained a report by KLOD about Ric Throssell's appointment as a junior diplomat to Moscow in 1945.[31] Two 1948 transmissions refer to someone codenamed

FERRO, one of them asking whether it was advisable to bring him 'into our work in view of the fact that his mother is well-known in the Commonwealth [Australia] as an influential academician'. In their notes, the intelligence analysts identified FERRO as Ric Throssell, and 'ACADEMICIAN' to be a codename for Katharine. Yet in the decrypted sentence, the term seems to be used literally to mean a university academic or similar, not a codename. The 'codename' ACADEMICIAN does not appear again in the transmissions. In the words of the historian Phillip Deery, 'Venona is fragmentary, raw and "one-way" intelligence data. The cable-senders could exaggerate and the cable-breakers could misinterpret'.[32]

Even if Katharine did help Nosov and Clayton, the degree of her awareness is unknown and Ball and Horner don't allow for her idealistic naïvete in assisting a wartime ally in the fight against fascism. In 1940, Clayton had been responsible for preparing the Communist Party to go underground in the case of illegality. Ball and Horner write of him, 'It is not possible to separate his illegal party work from his espionage activities'.[33] For Australian communists, the lines of loyalty and legality had been distorted by the outlawing of the party. Katharine was proudly Australian and wanted her country to prosper. She saw that as compatible with her loyalty to communism, which she sincerely believed would reshape Australia and the world into a better place.

KATHARINE'S HARDLINE LOYALTY to the party seems to have contributed to the souring of her friendship with fellow communist writer Jean Devanny over the 1940s. New Zealand–born Jean came to Australia in 1929 after the banning of her first novel, *The Butcher Shop* (1926). 'Viewed ambivalently by the party leadership, she was recognised and celebrated as an agitator and organiser by the rank and file ...'[34]

Underlining her connection to Katharine, Jean wrote of how they even looked like each other. 'The facial resemblance Kathie and I bore to each other was constantly under remark. Jonathan Cape, Kathie's London publisher ... when introduced to me he exclaimed: "Oh, I took you for Katharine Prichard!"'[35] Jean envied Katharine's literary accomplishments and was proud of being a better public speaker. Katharine's 'voice was suited only to small hall meetings and the microphone … she lacked the physical stamina to stand up to my scuffling outdoor work'.[36]

The two first met in August 1931 when Jean, on her way to the Soviet Union, stayed with Katharine for two days at Greenmount. 'Katharine's personality I found to be in marked contrast with my own. Her manner was quiet and serene, her expression deeply thoughtful, if not grave. I saw at once that there was nothing of the jack-of-all-trades about her, such as was my bane.'[37] Jean had little money and remembered Katharine giving her £12, an astonishing amount, if true, given the dire financial situation Katharine and Hugo were in. Coming from a working-class background and insecure about her own writing, Jean had the wrong idea about Katharine, assuming she led an idyllic middle-class existence, with 'that inward certitude that comes of a secure childhood, knit through with poise and balance derived from family and educational advantages'.[38] After visiting Greenmount, 'I thought a lot about the conditions in which Kathie lived: a quiet home in lovely surroundings among the hills. For a writer, an ideal environment; while she is writing, at least'.[39]

The pair consolidated their friendship in Sydney in January 1935, a few months after Jean's son had died. 'We had some grand talks together, Kathie and I, in her Kings Cross flat. In all things concerned with the conduct of life we were in agreement; our only differences, and they were amiable, were about literature.' The differences in literary taste Jean noted include Katherine Mansfield (Jean liked her work; Katharine didn't) and Henry Lawson (Katharine liked his work; Jean didn't).[40]

In 1941, Jean was living with four men, all party members, at a remote camp in Emuford in far-north Queensland. A dispute broke out between them, with both Jean and the men making complaints to the party. Jean's account of the incident is ambiguous. She wrote that one of the men hit her face and, 'My privacy was brutally invaded and some of my belongings destroyed'.[41] The unreliable Wally Clayton told Jack Beasley in 1987 that Jean was gang raped by the men.[42]

In her autobiography, Jean accused Katharine of not doing enough to help her. Jean saw Katharine in Brisbane in November 1941 and told her what had happened; Jean wrote that she knew 'I could trust her' to help. In Jean's mistaken memory, Katharine was already on the Central Committee. A couple of weeks later when Jean came to Sydney to speak at the same peace conference as Katharine, Jean was told the party was expelling her for 'political degeneracy'. In Jean's mind, Katharine could have saved her and didn't.[43] Jack Beasley writes that even if Katharine *had* already been on the Central Committee in 1941 her involvement with the case would have been limited; matters of party discipline were handled by the Control Commission, not the Central Committee. Although their friendship initially recovered, Jean's bitterness towards Katharine was apparent years later in her autobiography and in a letter to Miles Franklin.[44]

Jean challenged her expulsion from the party and threatened to write of her affair with JB Miles in an autobiography. It was probably this that prompted Katharine to say in a letter on 23 December 1944, 'I can't believe that you would ever write in a way damaging to the most vital interests of the working class … whatever disappointments and sorrows we have had to face, we can still serve, with our pens, the only cause on earth worth fighting for'.[45] As it happened, Jean's gambit worked and her expulsion was reversed, though her relationship with the party continued to be stormy.

In that final surviving letter to Jean, Katharine goes on to write, 'I often wear the little shell necklace you brought me, and think of you with affection—and grief, dear Jean—wishing that life had not been so difficult for you'.[46] Katharine's opinion of Jean may have been similar to Hilda Esson's; Hilda was fond of Jean 'but her vanity is colossal. There's no argument she's simply right … She's illogical, unsound … but with a native wit and intelligence that deserved a better expression than they ever had'.[47]

HILDA CAME TO stay with Katharine in late November 1943. She was on one of her periodic visits to her estranged husband, Louis, who had been living in Sydney since 1939. His health had been bad for some time and now he had pneumonia. She called on their son Hugh to come and they were both with Louis when he died on 27 November at the age of sixty-five.[48] Years later, Hilda gave Katharine a sad account of her marriage, saying 'the last thing I ever expected was that I would have abdicated from my dearly won freedom by marrying anyone as possessive as Louis … his dependence on me, his fascinating mind, and his real talent, so terribly frittered away, made it impossible for me to break away & find myself'.[49]

There's no record of how often Katharine had seen Louis since she moved to Sydney, but a party member named Harry Gould remembers her helping to nurse him at the end.[50] Their interests had diverged; Louis no longer had much sympathy for communism.[51] She wrote a tribute to him for broadcast on ABC radio soon after his death. 'Latterly', she wrote, 'Louis had become discouraged and disinclined to write at all. Of what use when there is no theatre for the production of plays by Australian dramatists?'[52]

Hilda arranged a private cremation. Leslie Rees remembers, 'I was at this funeral service in a wretched King's Cross parlour, with crude music and blatant lighting effects—just a few people, including Katharine Susannah Prichard'.[53] Afterwards, Hilda and Hugh drove to The Gap with a small group of people who had cared about Louis—Katharine, Frank Davison and Miles Franklin—to scatter his ashes into the ocean.[54]

A week later, Katharine turned sixty, suddenly at an age where her generation was passing.

32

Revival

Sydney, 1944–1946

IN JANUARY 1944 Jean Devanny gave a bleak picture of Katharine's health: 'KSP is very ill mostly. She is under a Macquarie Street specialist. Angina pectoris, you know. I don't think she will live long'.[1] According to Katharine, her doctor had forbidden public speaking because of the strain it put on her. Despite the war, despite the urgency of the political situation, she settled down to write, determined to finish *The Roaring Nineties*, or 'Wasting Assets', as she had titled it at this stage.[2] It had been fourteen years since the publication of *Haxby's Circus,* her last (moderate) success, and in that time her novels had fallen out of print and *Kiss on the Lips, Intimate Strangers* and *Moon of Desire* had sold poorly. But 1944 proved to be a year of revival for her literary career.

In her Darlinghurst flat she 'used to write mostly in her bedroom in the early morning and sometimes on the small dining room table'.[3] She made good progress on *The Roaring Nineties* in January, and enjoyed it. 'Quite drunk with it, & going all day, scarcely able to tear myself away at 12 a. m. or even later. It was almost 2 one morning, when I decided that I'd better go to bed. It's marvellous to have had a week with only minor interruptions.' But she was expecting a more significant interruption in the arrival of a young communist from Perth, Annette Moore (later Aarons and then Cameron), who had been left devastated by a broken love affair. 'So in the West they decided to send her, by plane, to me! Of course, I really don't know the poor kid. Only met her once, but they say … I can cope with that sort of thing. Not looking forward to it you can imagine!' She added that she no longer had patience for people's personal woes; the 'sorrow & pain in the world makes it seem almost egotistical to wail about one's hurts'.[4]

Katharine changed her mind about Annette, writing three weeks later, 'Does all the chores for me. And most intelligent & well read. Don't mind her on the premises at all & most people, I can't abide for very long'.[5] Tensions emerged, though; in April Katharine wrote, 'Two different people have told me she is looking for a flat, although she hadn't mentioned it to me. Is a queer little person in many ways, very secretive … Rather keeps me on the jump, & hasn't been a good stable companion of late'.[6] Despite this complaint, Annette was to be a good friend until the end of Katharine's life.

While in Sydney, Katharine became friends with a communist couple originally from Kalgoorlie, John and Dawn Apthorp, who were now living in Katoomba in the Blue Mountains. From 1943 to 1947, they ran a left-wing lending library and bookshop on the main street of Katoomba, rented cheaply from a 'friendly Russian named Slutzkin'. John remembers typing *The Roaring Nineties* for Katharine. 'The manuscript was done on inferior wartime paper in pencil … being an ex-goldfielder was a distinct advantage in coping with place names and locations.' She sent the manuscript 'in batches of loose pages by courier' which 'arrived at all times of the day or night'. Katharine sometimes came to stay with the Apthorps. 'She loved the Mountains and, whenever possible, would escape from Sydney to spend whatever time she could … I can recall long winter evenings around a log fire discussing the manuscript and people she'd met on the fields while researching for *The Roaring Nineties*.'[7] Katharine finally visited the writer Eleanor Dark on one of these trips in 1943 when Dark showed Katharine the Children's Free Library she had established.[8]

Katharine finished the first full, handwritten draft of *The Roaring Nineties* in March 1944 and then spent several months revising. It was her longest novel yet and she wrote to Jonathan Cape with some trepidation, warning of the length and asking if there was any prospect of publication. 'Quite a thrilling cable from Cape!' she wrote to Ric on 23 October, 'his reply was ... to send it immediately'. It was an unexpected vote of confidence from Cape after the commercial failure of her last three books with him. She was surprisingly unfazed when Cape changed the title from 'Wasting Assets', 'The Roaring Nineties' being what the British 'call the prospecting period on the gold fields'.[9] In March 1945, Cape telegrammed to say he was pleased with the manuscript but couldn't publish it until 1946, due to the paper shortage.[10]

In April 1944, Katharine's novel *Haxby's Circus* was announced as one of the twenty-five initial titles in the Commonwealth Pocket Library, selected by the Advisory Board of the Commonwealth Literary Fund. Each title had a print run of 25,000 in a cheap paperback format sold at a low price or given away to men and women in the services, including prisoners of war. At a time of patriotism, the Pocket Library put Australian classics back in print and encouraged Australians to read their own literature.[11] The selection of *Haxby's Circus* turned it into the most read of her books since the sales success of *The Pioneers.* At the same time, perhaps with the last of their paper allowance, Jonathan Cape published a new edition of *Working Bullocks,* meaning two of Katharine's major novels were back in print.

Before Easter, Katharine called on the Angus and Robertson office to ask why her second short story collection, *Potch and Colour,* was not on sale yet. 'Just as well. Because it had been piled up in the warehouse & forgotten.'[12] It was finally released in May. Many of the stories are goldfields 'yarns', sketches for *The Roaring Nineties*. The *Age* reviewer wrote, 'The distinctive mark of Katharine Prichard's work is sureness. She is never vague, never diffuse. Not only is the writing itself firm and well knit, sober and precise, the stories have an equal definiteness. There are no loose ends'.[13] The *Daily Telegraph* review found 'her prospectors, station hands, farmers, country pub-keepers and outback women have provided raw material for nine-tenths of Australian fiction. But Mrs Prichard invests with fresh interest the characters that two generations of our writers have made familiar'.[14]

The account of these stories which Katharine gave Mikhail Apletin of the Union of Soviet Writers reflects her ongoing struggle to reconcile her writing with her politics. She wrote they were 'chiefly stories which I have had to write for the Capitalist press, so without any special socialist significance, although they are realistic of Australian conditions, and not contrary to my Marxist conception of things and people'.[15] If they were stories she 'had' to write for the 'Capitalist press', they also happened to reflect her career-long interest in the folklore of regions. Her struggle was just as much trying to find Australian stories which could realistically show the working class organising itself to overthrow capitalism.

She also wrote to Apletin that while writing *The Roaring Nineties* 'it was very difficult to separate my mind from problems of the moment and the pressure of this war'. With the manuscript complete, 'For the next few months, I will be writing on subjects of immediate importance, and am going to enjoy it'.[16] One of her subjects was the Ern Malley hoax. In June 1944, Max Harris and John Reed had published an issue of their journal *Angry Penguins* featuring obtuse modernist poems by an Ern Malley; the poems were subsequently revealed to be manufactured by two conservative poets, James McAuley and Harold Stewart, who had been observing with 'distaste the gradual decay of meaning and craftmanship in poetry'. Katharine believed the hoaxers 'have rendered a service to Australian literature … by revealing a tendency to lavish extravagant praise on obscure and salacious nonsense masquerading as poetry'. For Katharine, Harris and Reed were apostates who had once been sympathetic to communism but had then adopted 'the philosophy of irresponsible egoism' in the work they had been publishing in *Angry Penguins* and in their editorialising. They had insisted 'on the unique importance of spoilt children at a party … They have failed to understand that genius which does not seek to serve the community, but merely its own aggrandisement, destroys itself'.[17]

THE ROMANTIC AND sexual elements of Katharine's long widowhood are opaque. Jean Devanny's gossipy claims in letters to Miles Franklin are one of the only sources and, affected by bitterness, they need to be read with caution. Jean wrote to Miles that Katharine 'will have the sense to hold her tongue' regarding the sexual frankness of Jean's autobiography, *Point of Departure,* 'in view of the things she told me of her own mode of life'.[18] In another letter to Miles, Jean was writing about 'just how pressing the sexual impulse is with men' and claimed that in about 1935 Katharine had told her the party needed 'sensible women who would relieve important single workers when needed' and, 'I'll say it for Kath she practised what she preached'.[19] Ric writes in response that this is a fabrication and Jean 'ignores the fact that the Party's attitude to sexual morality at the time was rigidly puritanical'; women offering themselves as 'sexual relief' 'would have been totally repugnant to KSP and contrary to the attitudes to women throughout her writing'.[20]

Jean's picture of Katharine's sex life is questionable but Katharine was certainly not celibate. She wrote to Ric in 1946, 'I feel my Jimmy still with me, though others have come & gone, fulfilling some need of the moment, and broadening one's knowledge and understanding of humanity. So it must be. But my Jimmy & I were great lovers. Nobody could ever take his place with me'.[21] Her words were true for the rest of her life; she never had another publicly acknowledged partner. However, one of those who seems to have 'come & gone' was a man named Andrei, whom she was close to from 1944 until she left Sydney in 1946. English wasn't his first language, but Katharine doesn't mention his nationality, his surname, or how they met; perhaps he was a party member. He had a cottage in Katoomba in the Blue Mountains. He first appears in Katharine's letters to Ric in February 1944, taking her out to lunch. Hating the 'intense cold', she decided on 14 May that she wasn't going all the way to Wentworth Falls just to oblige him. Then in June she wrote Andrei was 'v. charming on Saturday, brought me violets & a big bunch of pink carnations'; he took her to dinner at the Silver Grill and afterwards by taxi to a production of Émile Zola's play *Thérèse Raquin*. In January 1945 she reported to Ric that he was to be in hospital for the next two months with a bad heart.[22] Katharine liked the company of men and the account in *Child of the Hurricane* of her youthful 'beguiling' of them carried over in later life to the cultivation of her 'boyfriends', as she would come to refer to them in her letters to Ric.

FOR INTERNATIONAL WOMEN'S Day on 8 March 1945, Katharine took the train to Newcastle, a coalmining city north of Sydney, attending a luncheon and civic reception before speaking in the evening.[23] 'As the glorious promise of peace draws nearer', she declared, 'we must pledge ourselves to work so that when Victory is proclaimed, the basis for a sound and constructive peace will be assured'.[24] She called on women to make time for reading about politics, attending meetings, and take action to improve local conditions, even if it meant forsaking the 'futile polishing, shopping, and refurbishing of garments' which waste 'the priceless thought and energy of women'.[25] Katharine made several trips to Newcastle and the coalmining town of Cessnock while living in Sydney and was contemplating a coalmining novel to follow on from the goldfields trilogy.[26] Reflecting on the less developed workers' movement on the goldfields, she told Mikhail Apletin of the Union of Soviet Writers, 'I wish I had lived on the coalfields of New South Wales and could have shown the more militant spirit and better organisation of the workers there'.[27] The one literary work to come from the trips was 'Hero of the Mines' (1945), a piece of reportage telling of the effect of a worker's death in a coalmine during World War II.

In May, Doon, Katharine's friend from the goldfields, came to stay on one of several visits over Katharine's time in Sydney. She was serving with the Women's Auxiliary Australian Air Force and, having been granted a divorce on the grounds of desertion, had married Lewis Stone in December 1944.[28] As Katharine worked on *Golden Miles,* the second book of the trilogy, Doon gave Katharine information about the goldfields.[29]

On 9 August, the same day the United States dropped a second atomic bomb on Japan, the Communist Party of Australia held its fourteenth congress in Sydney. Katharine was one of ninety-two delegates and she was re-elected to the Central Committee for another term. The party was on the ascendant, proclaiming that its membership had grown from 4000 to 23,000 over the course of the war. It seemed it was on the cusp of becoming a significant force in Australian politics. Yet it was to prove to be the party's high point, followed by postwar decline.[30]

A few days later, Ric happened to be in Sydney for work when Japan surrendered. He remembers prime minister Ben Chifley's 'slow', 'rough' voice coming over loudspeakers along William Street to announce the war was over. He came home 'to my mother's kiss of thanksgiving' and 'stood with my arm about her for awhile watching the celebrations in the street from balcony of the flat'.[31] Katharine felt relieved and grateful that Ric had survived the war but the 'peace celebrations for so many carried sad thoughts, and I couldn't be altogether joyous—though many are saved further sorrow'.[32]

'HOW VERY DISCRETE [discreet] your mother must be, my sweet', Katharine wrote to Ric in February 1945, 'in relationship with his girl friends. They're mine because they're his, of course, but there's a queer woman-to-woman understanding, or sympathy, between us all too'.[33] Ric's girlfriend in Perth, Iris Wells, had been waiting for him for years and was now asking if she should move over to Canberra to be with him. In the meantime, after a romance with a Janet in Sydney, Ric had become involved with a stenographer in Canberra named Bea Gallacher and seemed serious about her.[34] Katharine was disappointed: 'The making, or breaking, of a man is in the true mate he harnesses with … A sweet little thing isn't enough for the long road. You should choose a wife as you would a horse—for wind, stamina, & character & good breeding'.[35] Katharine liked Iris so much she invited her to come to Sydney to live with her. When she arrived in January 1945 Katharine reported, 'I think she will develop quite a lot here & really has taken her disappointment extraordinarily well'.[36] For the next few months, Katharine gave Ric cheery updates about Iris and praised her, perhaps still hoping he would change his mind.

Completing his cadetship, Ric learned in September that he was to be posted in two weeks to Moscow as Third Secretary to the Australian Legation, a three-year posting. Bea was devastated. 'How could I leave her behind?' Ric asked himself; they decided to marry.[37] When he told Katharine, she wrote back that it was a mistake to 'take on the burden of married life' right now rather than 'travelling free & light'. But 'better this than promiscuous affairs!' and 'what you decide I'll try to abide with a good grace'.[38] The wedding went ahead in Sydney on 29 September 1945 in the sitting room of a Reverend FB Mullens, a couple of days before Ric was due to fly out. According to Doon Stone, 'It was K herself who found a parson willing to perform the ceremony since all civil officers were closed for the weekend'.[39] Katharine and Bea waved goodbye to Ric at the Mascot aerodrome as he left for London on a converted cargo plane. Bea was to follow by sea when a berth was available.[40]

Katharine was excited for Ric to see the Soviet Union, probably believing it would convince him of the truth of communism. Wally Clayton passed on news of this appointment to the Soviets. 'Even before he received the appointment, "CLAUDE" [Clayton] in a conversation with PRICHARD clearly hinted to her that from the point of view of the Party it would be better if he went to a post in Europe, for example in HOLLAND. PRICHARD, however, very much wanted her son to go to the Soviet Union and had her way.' The report assumed the appointment came about by Katharine's influence—presumably with the attorney-general, Bert Evatt—but there's no evidence for that and the new Australian legation was an unsurprising place for trained cadets to be sent. The Soviet intelligence, however, believed not only that Evatt had to be involved with the appointment of a junior diplomat but that there must be a 'real ulterior motive' on his part and they tasked Wally Clayton with discovering what it was and giving 'detailed information about his [Ric's] character', showing how little the Soviets knew about Ric.[41]

AT CHRISTMAS TIME, Katharine's new daughter-in-law, Bea, came to stay with her for six weeks before she could join Ric in Moscow. Katharine had spent the last few Christmases with Christian Jollie Smith at her place in Camp Cove, but Christian, wanting Katharine 'all to herself', hadn't invited Bea, so Katharine didn't go. Katharine warmed to Bea over her stay, but she thought her fragile, and told Ric to be careful of her health in Moscow.[42]

For some time, Katharine had been expecting bad news about the mortgage on her Greenmount house and it came in February 1946. Before his death, Hugo had set up a private mortgage on the house with an elderly woman named Harriet Roberts, who died in 1941. Now, finally, the Roberts estate wanted Katharine to repay the remainder of the mortgage.

Katharine asked her accountant to try to re-mortgage the house to buy her some time. 'Maybe I'll stay there for a year or so.' She needed to return to sort out her papers and possessions and do further research on volumes two and three of the goldfields trilogy. However, she thought it wasn't going to be financially viable to live there in the long term. She was resigned to losing the house but hoped to keep a section of land 'as a relic of our old home', she told Ric, 'but we must not be sentimental, lovey. Life takes us along a broad highway, and though our thoughts cling to the place where we have spent so many happy days, we must go on & camp by the way, wherever we happen to be'.[43]

The situation escalated in March. Her accountant couldn't re-mortgage the place. The Roberts estate foreclosed and began arranging a forced sale. Worried that all her possessions would be dumped, she 'rushed down to the railway office to book a seat West—and they swear there's nothing available until June 17 … And there are no boats sailing!'[44] As it happened, a federal politician, Don Mountjoy, brother of the former Western Australian communist leader, helped her secure a place on the train for early April.[45]

While she prepared to head west, the forced sale was averted by the generosity of Andrei. She hadn't mentioned her predicament to him, but Annette had, and he told Katharine he could lend her the money for a new three-year mortgage. It came just in time, with Katharine's accountant sending a telegram on 25 March that the money would have to be cabled that very day. 'Wonky' with his bad heart, Andrei came straight down from the Blue Mountains to Sydney to arrange the transfer. He was the 'very best friend in a serious emergency'.[46]

In May, he sent a letter to Katharine, who was back in Greenmount by then. 'He's never written to me before—& I suspected that he couldn't write in English. Nearly wept over his effort—which he said betrayed his ignorance, but there were things he wanted to say to me … chiefly, that I mustn't send him interest. He wanted me to use the money on repairs etc.'[47] The irony of his generosity to Katharine was that it separated them; Katharine's sojourn in Sydney was over.

33

The Furies Return

Greenmount and Canberra, 1946–1947

'HOME AGAIN!' KATHARINE wrote to Ric on 5 April 1946. 'And you've no idea how heavenly it feels to be in our little kipsey again.'[1] She had reconciled herself to losing the Greenmount cottage but now, having a reprieve for at least three years, she fell back in love with it. Later in the month she described the state of the garden. 'Most of the fruit trees look the worse for wear. But the fig & mulberry tree quite healthy, also the plums & the apricot near my workroom … The vine has grown all over the side verandah & lots of clusters of black grapes have delighted the birds.' Waiting for the weather to cool down so she could rake up leaves and burn them, she concluded, 'I'm a peasant, at heart, I suppose. I do like it here. Feel my roots are being nourished, somehow. And in Sydney, get that transplanted sort of feeling'. She was 'healthier' in Greenmount and it was cheaper to live, though there were less opportunities to earn a living.[2]

There was a postwar tobacco shortage and in late April Katharine was running out of cigarettes. Hearing the supplies were likely to be interrupted for some months, she decided that if she did have to give up for a time she wouldn't begin again. 'It's such a damned nuisance to be held up in your work & to feel nervy & irritable because there's not a blasted cigarette handy.' But two days later, she managed to buy more and her 'cigarette famine was relieved. I really disapprove of myself thoroughly for missing the little brutes so much. One ought not be dependent on anything like that. I'm going to try reducing the number of my smokes—so as never again to have my work interfered with if I haven't any'.[3]

KATHARINE WAS WRITING to her daughter-in-law Bea as well as Ric. In one letter in April she expressed how glad she was that the two had such a perfect reunion when they met in Stockholm for a week's honeymoon. Echoing her words over the decades about the Furies chasing her through life, Katharine wrote, 'The ancients used to say the gods were jealous of human happiness—& were always trying to prevent mere mortals having something that only the immortals were supposed to enjoy. So it's very rare & precious to have what you & Ric have had together—I'm full of joy for you both'.[4]

Two months later, in July, Bea was taken to a Moscow hospital with paralysis. She fell into a coma and died about a week later, with Ric not even knowing the cause of her illness.[5] Katharine wrote a flurry of letters to Ric, trying in turn to find consolations and explanations. 'I was afraid all the time. It's almost too good to be true, I kept feeling. Always when I've been very happy about anything, something disastrous has happened & I've remembered that saying of the Greeks: "The gods punish those who presume to love or suffer like themselves."' 'When she was with me and I took in her cup of early morning tea, she looked so ill and frail, my heart would contract with pain. I knew somehow she was not going to live long; and after she went, for nearly a week, I just cried and cried.'[6] 'At least your love dream was spared the disappointments & disillusionments most married people know.'[7] 'Don't try to put your grief from you. You must hold it as something sacred and precious you are entitled to. Face the reality of it, I mean; but with the understanding that we don't live for ourselves alone.'[8] 'The way ahead will seem dreary, for a long time, perhaps, darling. One can only hold fast to those objective things that matter. And somehow, in the end, new strength and confidence will come to you.'[9]

At the end of her life, Katharine remembered Bea's death affecting her even more than the other tragedies she had endured. 'Nothing has ever quite so devastated me as the news about her', she wrote to Ric, 'on your account, I suppose, lovey. In the shock over Daddy, I had you to think of living for, but this news which struck at you completely prostrated me'.[10]

BEA'S DEATH IN July 1946 coincided with the publication of *The Roaring Nineties*. The Australasian Publishing Company released an Australian edition simultaneously with Jonathan Cape's British edition, making it more easily available in Katharine's home country than any of her previous books. The novel was met with excitement by Katharine's many friends and admirers in both the Australian literary community and the Communist Party. On 8 August, the Modern Women's Club held a party in Perth to celebrate the novel's publication, with old-timers from the goldfields coming dressed in period costume; extracts were read from the novel, followed by musical items and supper. But Katharine wasn't there and seemed to find no consolation in the publication of a book she had been working on for years. In November, she wrote to Miles Franklin, 'I haven't been to town for months, & see few people. Try not to, because talking even tires me out these days'.[11]

Katharine missed another tribute to her held in Sydney in October. It was a ceremony at Marx House held by the Communist Party to mark the twenty-sixth anniversary of its founding and to honour Katharine. Although not a communist, Miles was invited to speak. Praising Katharine's writing, Miles said, 'She is Australia's most distinguished tragedian. She is uncompromising and relentless, and lets us off nothing'.[12] In the statement Katharine sent to be read out, she gave an account of her conversion to communism and declared, 'How marvellous it is to see the power of Marxism demonstrated in one's lifetime!'[13] She had passed the baton and now saw her party work as largely complete; her role from the time she left Sydney was to write articles and have an occasional ceremonial presence.

Katharine dedicated *The Roaring Nineties* to 'BS'—Bob Saunders. Joan Williams describes him as an 'anti-conscription veteran and socialist … a Kalgoorlie businessman who had gone to the Soviet Union under his own steam in 1924'.[14] Katharine probably came to know him in his role as patron of the Australia–Russia Relations Committee;

'he lived in Kalgoorlie and helped with queries on life on the fields … answering her questionnaires'.[15]

The Roaring Nineties tells of the initial Western Australian gold rush in the 1890s and the establishment of Coolgardie and Kalgoorlie–Boulder. The novel uses a frame narrative, presenting itself as the yarns of prospector Dinny Quinn about the early days. The historical background is never far from the story, forming a spine which moves the story through a series of incidents with a large cast of characters. Sally Gough is the protagonist, a woman who earns money running a boarding house to the shame of her ineffectual husband, Morrie, a fallen aristocrat and a gambler. The struggle between them is an ongoing aspect of the plot, as he gradually accepts her egalitarian ethos in class and gender. Sally's insistence that she and Morrie should not elevate themselves above the others contrasts with their friends Alf and Laura's move up the class rankings, as mining becomes commercialised and Alf betrays his prospector roots to become a mine manager.

Reviews of *The Roaring Nineties* tended to praise Katharine's research and her picture of Australian life, while finding that it has suffered as fiction for her attempt to depict so much history. The *Argus* review—by 'ARC', most likely AR Chisholm—was typical, noting that despite some 'excellent' passages 'occasionally the style sags, as if the author had so much to tell that she did not have time to repolish. The author, however, makes up for these lapses by some magnificent close-ups of the bush … She has it in her blood and thinks Australian'.[16]

Miles Franklin reviewed *The Roaring Nineties* enthusiastically, highlighting its depiction of Aboriginal people and women, two aspects of the novel most contemporaneous reviewers glossed over. 'The Aborigines are made to shine like a vein of gold in a quartz reef through the story.' 'The mining industry … is carried along by an interesting, well-differentiated gallery of men, but it is the women who give most character to the story … Sally's genius for friendship transcends differences of colour, race and religion.'[17]

Joan Williams reviewed the novel from a communist perspective for the *Workers Star.* She praised the way the individual struggles of the prospectors give way to an 'intense class struggle around the rights of alluvial diggers, who had pioneered the fields, against the predatory mining companies'; this aspect 'shows KSP at her best, as a Marxist interpreting history with clarity and vision'. However, Joan found the novel inadequate in its depiction of the solution to unemployment among the miners by not showing 'the organised struggle of the working class'. 'Though this book is the first of a trilogy, the novelist should have found some means of bringing forward this perspective. Its lack is the only flaw in a notable book.'[18] It seems to be this review that Joan misremembers as being for its sequel, *Golden Miles,* writing, 'Bitterly hurt, Katharine appealed to CP general secretary J. B. Miles, who for this and other reasons came roaring over to the West'. It seems unlikely that a generally favourable review would be a primary factor in him visiting Perth, but Katharine's reaction sounds plausible. According to Joan, Katharine defended her book at a meeting, saying she couldn't 'falsify reality' and Joan was reprimanded by JB Miles. 'Deeply ashamed, I hoped that one day Katharine would forgive my arrogance. When I mentioned the episode to her many years later she said with true nobility, "I don't remember anything about it".'[19]

The Roaring Nineties was a commercial success—the first Australian printing of 10,000 copies had sold out by September 1946.[20] It was also an international success, particularly in communist countries, eventually translated into nine languages.

RIC CAME TO stay with Katharine in November 1946 before taking up a post in Canberra for two years from January 1947. Katharine decided she would move to Canberra to be with him for the duration of the posting. She wrote to Miles, 'It's a terrible wrench to leave my quiet & lovely place here … but Ric needs me. So I must be on the move again—though feeling so tired; & not equal to the journey, really'.[21] In Ric's memory, he was guilty about leaving her alone in Greenmount, 'frail and ill', and persuaded her to move so *he* could look after *her*.[22]

Katharine's departure was delayed. Her doctor insisted on removing her appendix before she travelled and she was in hospital for weeks afterwards.[23] She had a lot to organise, packing up her belongings and making arrangements for the house. A friend named Kal McIntyre rented it for £2 a week, with the option of buying it for £900 after two years when Andrei's loan would expire.[24] Katharine prepared herself once more to give up her cottage and finally left for Canberra in late April 1947.

She was unsettled in Canberra. She and Ric were initially boarding with a Mrs D'Arcy in Braddon. 'In the midst of unpackings & radio blaring, small boy asking questions, & mine hostess, an old dear really, being amiably polite and making conversation.'[25] Katharine was preparing three meals a day for Ric. 'Cooking meals, and finding food in Canberra seems to occupy all my time.' Without heating in their bedrooms, it was freezing in the evenings 'so we must sit with the family & be polite, in order to keep warm'.[26]

Back in March, Katharine had written to Ric 'you should hold your horses' after he expressed interest in a woman named Barbara; 'just now, when you're lonely … it's a dangerous time, darling. You're likely to attach yourself to almost anything friendly & charming'.[27] Now Ric was spending his weekends with a woman from his office named Dorothy Jordan—known as Dodie—taking her out to the countryside in 'Natalya', the yellow 1930 Austin 7 he'd bought. Mrs D'Arcy the landlady 'pointed out gently that it was less than a year since Bea had died' but Ric felt no 'obligation to … convention'.[28]

By July, Katharine had found the time to finish *Golden Miles* and send the manuscript to Jonathan Cape.[29] In August, she and Ric finally found their own flat to live in. Katharine told Mikhail Apletin at the Union of Soviet Writers, 'Living at Canberra is very strange after having been in close contact always with the workers in various industries, and the intellectual life of our cities. Canberra is like a garden suburb, thoroughly bourgeois, and remote from the *sturm und drang* of the struggle of existence'. She added her disappointment that *The Roaring Nineties*—'the most important book I have written'—had not yet been translated into Russian. 'I have dreamt that someday, perhaps, in a leisure moment, our great Stalin might read it.'[30]

With a baby due in May, Ric and Dodie married on 3 October. They had a traditional wedding at the historic St John's church and a reception at the Gloucester, Canberra's only licensed restaurant. Katharine wrote, 'I am pleased that the lad has found someone with whom he can be happy and have a normal life. She's a shy, quiet girl, very like his first wife, but intelligent … so there's much to be thankful for … They want me to live with them, but I won't do that'.[31] Her account to Doon Stone hinted at unhappiness: 'When Ric decided to marry a girl he's been seeing a good deal of all the year, I thought it better to leave the flat to them'.[32] She moved out while they were on honeymoon.[33] She'd proved to be unnecessary in Canberra and her two-year stint had finished after five frustrating months.

34

The Cold War Begins

Greenmount, 1947–1949

KATHARINE LEFT CANBERRA on the Murray Valley Coach to Adelaide before travelling on to Kalgoorlie by train. She stayed four weeks researching volume three of the trilogy—soon to be titled *Winged Seeds.* In a letter to Doon Stone, Katharine wrote that she spent some days at a station near the ghost town of Bulong, where some Aboriginal people told her they remembered 'Kalgorla' and 'Meerie'—a tantalising revelation that Katharine's Aboriginal characters Kalgoorla and Meeri had real-life counterparts.[1]

She also stayed a night at Coolgardie with the writer Ernestine Hill. Ernestine and her son, Robert, were camped there with their truck and caravan. They'd been in Perth the previous year and Henrietta Drake-Brockman had introduced them to Katharine.[2] Like Katharine, Ernestine was a chronicler of the backblocks of Australia, but mainly in the form of popular non-fiction such as her travel memoir *The Great Australian Loneliness* (1937); she was also cheerily apolitical. At their Coolgardie camp, Katharine was uncomfortable with the 'flies & red-backed spiders galore' but they didn't bother Ernestine. Katharine told Miles Franklin that Ernestine was 'a strange, otherwhereish creature with big beautiful eyes, a hoarse voice & curious incapacity to argue logically about anything'.[3]

Ernestine was inseparable from Robert. She'd brought him up without a father and during World War II they'd moved to a cattle station in outback South Australia to avoid military service. Born in 1924, he was a similar age to Ric and served as his mother's research assistant.[4] Katharine inevitably compared their situation to her own, writing to Ric when she met them:

> I felt it was rather a tragedy for him, that his mother had kept him out of the war: but that he realized life would have been impossible for her had he been on active service. He looks as if he has decided to devote himself to her. I couldn't be satisfied to know that you were not leading your own life: being an independent person. Complete & sufficient in yourself ... I like to believe that you can go on without me, not hampered in any way by our love for each other, my darling.
>
> I daresay Ernestine feels like that too: but somehow the lad is being kept too close to her—without a job, or training of his own ... Looks a little like you when he laughs, so I had a great sympathy for him.[5]

Katharine's concern about the closeness between Ernestine and Robert seems mixed with her desire for a similar proximity to Ric.

KATHARINE ARRIVED BACK in Greenmount in November 1947 to find her house 'looking so dilapidated & dishevelled'.[6] Kal McIntyre and her extended family were living there and had eighteen months left on the lease but Kal let Katharine have her bedroom back and Katharine halved the rent until they moved out in May.[7]

With Ric making his own life on the other side of the country, Katharine felt more alone than ever. She had written from Kalgoorlie that she had a 'sore sick heart ... when no Sunday letter arrives. It's the only thing I do ask of you, & necessary, if I am to be well & keep going. Need be only a scrap! It's a lonely business wandering about by myself & feeling nobody cares'.[8] After her sixty-fifth birthday on 4 December, she wrote, 'Of course I felt rather forlorn, at first—that morning ... You remember what a fete Daddy used to make of my birthday, Ric darling. And now I feel like something [the] tide's left; but I didn't let myself be sad: started work & forgot everything'.[9]

As she struggled with these feelings of loneliness she was aware she was passing into legend. 'I believe—when the tourists cars go to [the neighbouring settlement of] Mundaring now, the house is pointed out to folks as one of the points of interest now.'[10]

GOLDEN MILES WAS published on 31 May 1948. She dedicated it to 'DS'—Doon Stone—whose help on the goldfields trilogy had extended over many years. The novel spans 1914 to 1927—from the eve of the Great War to the eve of the Great Depression. The untidy narrative takes Sally Gough through a series of trials as her four sons come to adulthood, each representing a different way of living in the world against the backdrop of war and turmoil. Tom is a communist miner who reads political tracts in his spare time; Denny becomes a dairy farmer in the South-West; Lal and Dick enlist to fight in the Great War. The conscription debate divides the family as it divides the nation. Lal is killed, echoing the death of Katharine's brother, Alan. Dick survives, but returns a broken, changed man, echoing Hugo's experience; when he dies in a mining accident Sally is haunted by the possibility it might have been suicide. In the final chapter, Aboriginal people are banned from the town centre and Kalgoorla, Sally's friend and helper, is moved along by the police. In Sally's fury, she decides that Tom is right and the best hope for Aboriginal people is organised political resistance. The novel ends with Kalgoorla standing in the sunset, letting out a cry of defiance.

Katharine asked Ric not to lend his copy of *Golden Miles* around; 'it's v bad for trade—& I do want sales to be good. The reviews are bound to be sniffy because of the book's political bias'.[11] Local communist paper the *Workers Star* summed up the 'bias' well:

> Katharine Prichard exposes the ugly fruit of capitalism—one of the richest goldfields in the world, 25 million sterling paid out in dividends, most of it going to overseas speculators and investors, and for the miner and his wife and kids—a bag and tin humpy in the middle of the red dust. This is capitalism, raw and brutal, eating out men's lungs for profit. But Tom Gough has the answer—give the gold to the people, fight for a Socialist Australia.[12]

Katharine wrote to Ric that the reviews were 'the least enthusiastic I've ever had … though I feel this is probably the best book I've ever written. I'll be very anxious to know what you & Dodie really think of it'.[13] Some of the reviews were merely 'sniffy' while others were brutal, including one in the *Bulletin* which came to represent the consensus on Katharine's work:

> Katharine Prichard as a novelist, after the fine achievement of her early books, has been fighting a long and losing battle with Katharine Prichard as a propagandist. She has not remained the artist, giving her first loyalty to her art, but has divided herself, as it were, into two personalities, the novelist and the propagandist; and while these are at war, contradicting each other on every second page of *Golden Miles,* it is the propagandist who speaks the louder and the more often.[14]

Although there was truth to the *Bulletin's* verdict, *Golden Miles* still had much to commend it as an engaging saga of the goldfields and an authentic account of the lives of miners and their families. The *Western Mail* called it 'a colourful and entertaining tale, one of human courage and endurance and of those human qualities which helped to build Australia into a nation'.[15]

RIC AND DODIE's baby was born in May 1948. They named her Karen Han Throssell, the middle name in tribute to Katharine's alter ego in *The Wild Oats of Han.* Katharine wrote to say she had sympathetic pains on the bus at just the time she was born. 'Hilda always says I have an uncanny prescience about things.'[16] Katharine wrote to publishers, trying to have *The Wild Oats of Han* republished in tribute, but despite some interest the prospect fell through.

Andrei wrote to Katharine in July, saying he had lost a lot of money in business and he was living in a caravan, so he had to 'ask' about the loan. His letter came at the right time as Katharine had £400 from the royalties on *The Roaring Nineties* and was able to repay him. The house was still entangled in Hugo's debts, but she'd been advised that if she subdivided the back of her property into three half-acre blocks and sold them, it would bring in enough money for her to own the house outright.[17]

She had wanted to finish *Winged Seeds* before travelling to Canberra to see Karen Han but in October, Ric learned he was to be posted to Brazil and Katharine dropped her work to visit before they left. She stayed from December 1948 to March 1949 and Ric remembers her becoming a 'besotted' grandmother to Karen.[18] In other ways, it seems to have been an unhappy stay. Her strong opinions about child rearing caused tension with Dodie and Ric. 'Truly, I didn't want to interfere—ever: but there are times when one has to do what is necessary.'[19] Another letter after her departure reveals further anguish: 'I come over all miserable when I realise I can't do any more to help you. You've all become strangers to me—so far away & our lives going in such different ways … I seem to have been thinking a lot of the old days & missing Daddy more than ever'.[20]

At least some of the tension was about politics; she wrote the next month, 'Of course, we agreed not to discuss political matters or to get into arguments about them which distress both of us. But so much is happening these days that I wd like to talk to you about'.[21] The first mention of Katharine and Ric's political differences had come a year earlier, after Katharine's first stay with him in Canberra. 'It does grieve me, of course, that you are not a communist, and don't see eye to eye with me in political matters. Time, maybe, will broaden your outlook.'[22] He had never been a member of the Communist Party, but as a teenager had agreed with its principles; after a long, difficult silence about politics—that most important of topics to Katharine—he seems to have finally told her on that first visit to Canberra that he was a Labor Party supporter and that he felt the best hope for Australia was a centre-left government like it currently had, rather than the radical changes Katharine wanted. After further upsetting conversations during this second stay in Canberra, they had agreed to not talk about politics any more.

THE COLD WAR had begun and Katharine was feeling the political tension. In July 1948, the influential *Sydney Morning Herald* carried a report titled 'How Communist Party Plans Revolution'.

'The Communist Party remains a legal organisation, though by doctrine and action it is dedicated to the destruction of democracy. It is well equipped in Australia for revolutionary action, open and secret. It is a sinister political conspiracy organised on a para-military basis.' Katharine was named, erroneously, as still being a part of the 'Politbureau'.[23] The article was alarmist and wrong; the party had long decided that 'the Australian road to socialism ran through parliament' and did not consider revolution possible or desirable.[24]

The Labor government was distancing itself from communism. The communist-influenced Miners' Federation called a national coalmining strike in the winter of 1949 which brought the economy to a halt. To the shock of many workers, Labor prime minister Ben Chifley jailed the union leaders and broke the strike in late July by sending in troops to work the mines. Then, in October, Communist Party leader Lance Sharkey was jailed for sedition for saying that Australian workers would welcome Soviet troops to Australia.

With a federal election looming, opposition leader Robert Menzies was campaigning with a policy of banning the Communist Party. He accused Labor of being communist in orientation, especially in its attempt to nationalise the banks. Showing the political contrasts in the wider Throssell family, Hugo's nephew, George EL Throssell, was elected chairman of the Bank Employees Anti-Socialisation Committee, a lobby group campaigning against Labor in the lead-up to the election.[25] Stoking fears at a meeting in Kalgoorlie, he warned, 'There are 15,000,000 Communists outside of Russia today. Their objective is world revolution—bloody revolution if necessary ... Relying on the apathy of all Australians they have infiltrated into the country and have worked assiduously and quietly for the past 28 years'.[26]

Katharine's friend and doctor, Alec Jolly, was standing as the Communist Party candidate in the seat of Swan. He was a Midland councillor, but the council banned him from hiring the town hall for a rally. Instead, he held the rally on the large grassed area in front on his house on the night of Friday 9 April 1949. Katharine was one of the speakers. Alec claimed 1500 people came; some were anti-communist protestors trying to disrupt the meeting and others were police, protecting the protestors who tried to drown out the speakers by singing 'Waltzing Matilda' and 'Why Was He Born So Beautiful?'.[27]

The *Daily News* reported, 'residents said today that but for the firm action taken by police an ugly riot could have developed'.[28] Katharine wrote, 'It was a hot night, & speaking in the open air not easy for your little mother, darl—particularly as a bunch of drunken youths were trying to disrupt the meeting'.[29] The crowd cheered when she stood to speak. She said, 'In this most critical period, of Australian history, it is up to all of us to use our courage and common sense to fight the gang of millionaires, warmongers, unscrupulous politicians and their henchmen in their attempt to stampede the people into war'.[30]

When the Liberal Party lost the previous election in 1946, Katharine wrote to Miles Franklin, 'Thanking all my stars that Menzies & Co are on the scrap heap! Had they got a second innings, there'd have been some very uncomfortable times for all of us'.[31] She had written-off Menzies too soon; his Liberal–Country Party coalition won the election on 10 December 1949. Katharine wrote to Ric that the 'present prosperity has made many forget past difficulties … but the fact must be faced, I think—that many workers had lost confidence in the Labor Party'.[32]

IN JULY 1949, Katharine was 'tinkering' with the last chapters of *Winged Seeds* and still not happy. 'Goodness knows whether *Winged Seeds* will have any wings, or [be] the worst flop I've ever conceived! Maybe, tis the atmosphere of these days that makes me so apprehensive.'[33] She posted the manuscript to Jonathan Cape in September 1949.[34] After reading the proofs in May 1950, she wrote to Ric, 'Feel I can die in peace now. My work is done. Not that I've any intention of dying, darling. Am quite well, really. But the book does give, I think, something I've been working for all my life'.[35]

It was published in London in September 1950, with the Australian edition coming out in November.[36] Katharine dedicated it to 'Celia'—Cecilia Shelley, her unionist friend of decades who had grown up on the goldfields and shared her stories for Katharine to draw on. Since Katharine's return to Greenmount, Celia had been helping her a lot, especially in times of sickness. Katharine signed her copy, 'Celia dear—Her book—a slight appreciation of her great work over all the years—from her loving and devoted admirer Katharine Susannah'.[37]

Winged Seeds follows the fates of Sally's grandchildren. It begins in 1936, as Katharine brings the Spanish Civil War to the goldfields by having Sally's communist grandson, Bill, make speeches trying to fire up the apathetic locals. Later, he leaves to fight in World War II and the focus returns to Sally, as she struggles with what to make of the war and relives the grief of the last war. Bill returns home from Greece injured, only to recover and be sent to New Guinea, where he goes missing, presumed killed. Katharine gave to Bill the fate she feared for her own son, Ric. The trilogy finishes wearily, with the two survivors, Sally and Dinny, burying Kalgoorla, the Aboriginal woman whom they have known from the beginning, and finding hope in the winged seeds blown out from her namesake, the 'kalgoorluh' (usually karlkurla or garlgulla) plant. Sally's sons are dead, her grandson Bill is dead, but the ideas they lived for are immortal:

> The life force strives towards perfection. What other imperative is there in living? The struggle had gone on through the ages. The vital germ in a seed attained its fine flowering and full fruit. How then could the great ideas and ideals of human progress be denied and annihilated? They could not. That was what Bill had believed, and what he tried to make people understand.[38]

The reviews were even more negative than for *Golden Miles* and sales were poor.[39] The *Bulletin* was again the harshest. 'Dutifully parroting Communist jargon, twisted into situations to justify political theories, Katharine Prichard's characters become half-comic and half-repulsive, with the disquieting unreality of the tortured.'[40] Other reviewers were more nuanced. Gladys Hains wrote in the *Argus* that despite 'the political turn of the conversations' being 'too suggestive of propaganda' the novel still showed her 'sense of the music of words, her lyrical gift for descriptions of natural phenomena, her deft way of etching a character'.[41] In previous decades the somewhat intrusive political elements of *Working Bullocks* (1926) and *Intimate Strangers* (1937) had not been heavily scrutinised but now the Cold War made readers more sensitive to the communist themes in *Winged Seeds*. 'To express Communist sympathies these days, of course, means that one must take the rap', Katharine wrote to Miles Franklin.[42] But Katharine was deluded in thinking the criticisms of *Winged Seeds* were purely political. The *Sydney Morning Herald* reviewer probably wrote in good faith when they declared, 'a novelist can make a Communist a real and living person and treat him with the utmost sympathy if she so chooses. The objection is merely that Miss Prichard makes young Bill Gough a downright bore'.[43]

Katharine's trilogy has its defenders. The scholar Dale Spender writes in 1988, 'With its combination of the family saga … and working conditions on the goldfields, the trilogy is a powerful and perceptive documentary on Australian political history. It provided me with one of the most illuminating experiences I have had in my life'.[44] Jack Lindsay saw the trilogy as central to Katharine's literary achievement, the culmination of a career depicting men and women at work and grappling, after the pioneering era, with the disruption caused by industrial development as labour becomes something bought and sold:

> The work is a social history, a record of the mines, and an epical novel. Inevitably there are points where the first two aspects threaten to swamp the third; but, taken as a whole, the plan comes off. The story of the mines is told in human terms. The endlessly crisscrossing lines of narrative fall into an easily recognisable pattern, so that a clear significance and an impression of swarming complexity are simultaneously conveyed.[45]

THE BIGGEST PROJECT of her career finished, Katharine didn't know what was next. She had turned sixty-six at the end of the 1940s just as Menzies was elected. Her son was in Brazil with a newly acknowledged political distance between them. Her prospects for the 1950s were not good.

PART 5

KATYA, 1950–1969

35

Legacy

Greenmount, Melbourne, Canberra 1950–1954

SINCE RETURNING TO Greenmount from Sydney in 1946, Katharine had been thinking about putting her affairs in order, ready for the end. A crucial task was sorting out her papers; it would take the rest of her life.

> It's a terrible business trying to clear up my literary outpourings of all the years. There are note books from the time I was twelve, & scores of unfinished m.s. [manuscripts]—which must be all burnt when I fade out. Meanwhile, I can't destroy all of them, because maybe I'll write 'memoirs' someday & then they'd be useful. But I don't ever want any strangers to be delving into those old note books & rough scripts.[1]

Katharine had been contemplating writing an autobiography of sorts for decades. Her original conception was an autobiographical novel in the style of *The Wild Oats of Han.* In the 1928 foreword to *Wild Oats,* Katharine mentions a planned sequel called 'Cuckoo Oats'. At about this time she scrawled chapter titles for it on the back of an envelope; they correlate with incidents in the autobiography she would eventually publish, *Child of the Hurricane* (1963), including 'Confirmation & doubts'; 'Going on the stage opera & Henry V'; 'Father's illness';

'Speech Day'; and 'The elderly lover'. The notes lay dormant; Katharine needed an excuse to write a book focused on herself and it came in the form of a research student's thesis about her.

With Katharine's mind already on her legacy and the hurt over the poor reception of *The Golden Miles,* she was flattered when a teacher named Cyril Cook visited in March 1950 to tell her he was writing his Master's thesis at the University of Western Australia on her life and work.[2] She hoped it would begin her return to literary acclaim. He visited a second time in July, bearing a bouquet of pink carnations. Katharine told Ric, 'He's making a v. conscientious study of "the celebrated works" & concerned about all manner of biographical details. I feel responsible somehow for his getting through. Would hate him to lose because he had chosen your KS for a subject'.[3] Cyril left a draft of a long chapter on Katharine's biographical background in which he used Freud to explain aspects of her life and personality. Katharine reported to Ric, 'Another quaint point in the thesis is that I'm supposed to have a maternal complex because I fell in love with your father "when he was ill in hospital"!' This was 'so remote from the truth', Katharine wrote, because it wasn't until Hugo came to Australia on sick leave a couple of years later that she fell in love with him. 'This attempt at giving biographical details, so out of tune with the facts, has made me realize that I ought to write my own biography, in order to prevent such queer versions being concocted.'[4] When Cyril returned the next week, Katharine 'managed to persuade him that there was no basis for his psychological analysis of your KS's complexes'.[5] She later told him in a letter, 'Freudian theory made a valuable contribution to psychological knowledge in its day; but the tendency to apply it wholesale to normal people has passed, or should have'.[6]

Cyril gave Katharine the gift of a copy of Nettie Palmer's book about Henry Handel Richardson, who had died in 1946. Katharine's letters to Nettie had become less frequent and less intimate. In the background was the mental breakdown of Nettie and Vance's daughter, Aileen, who Katharine remained close to; Katharine felt Aileen was bound by Nettie's 'obsessive personality'.[7] The fact of Nettie writing the Richardson book may have been painful for Katharine—Nettie had become more enthusiastic about Richardson's work than Katharine's. Remarking on the fact Cyril's thesis was about her, Katharine wrote,

'Rather painful & embarrassing to be present at one's own vivisection! At least you spared H[enry] H[andel] that, though I feel sure she would have recognised the real value of your tribute to her work'.[8]

In late January 1951, Katharine noted that her 'Boswell' had stopped by—a reference to James Boswell, famously the biographer of Samuel Johnson. She was feeling positive about Cyril's thesis. 'Seems to know the works of your KS now better than she does herself … & it seems, Professor [Allan] Edwards is pleased with his work & suggested publication. I'm apprehensive of the final result of such a vivisection; but have been amiable & lent him notes & photographs.'[9]

She wrote Cyril a warm letter in June, saying, 'I appreciate how conscientious you have been in your study of the subject for your thesis'.[10] Later that month, he left the completed thesis for her to read. After her hopes his work might lead to an academic rejuvenation of her literary reputation, she was disappointed and angry. 'To take all the information I could give him—which is the only valuable part of the thesis—and then set out to debunk the idea that my work is of any particular value, quoting all the adverse criticism, & not one critic who has given me high marks—from materials I gave him! An amazing performance!'[11]

Two particular claims of Cyril's which upset Katharine were that 'KS depicts herself in all her heroines' and that 'the heroes are "defective males"'. 'Do you see me in the Deb of *Working Bullocks* or Gina of *Haxby's*, or Deidre of *The Pioneers* or Sophie of *Black Opal*?' Katharine asked Ric. 'These characters are all different & separate. He imagines that I am Elodie of *Intimate Strangers*—who of course was Rose A and recognised herself. How is Elodie like Deb or Gina? Yet, this bloke says all my women characters are uniform!'[12] If Katharine was right to claim these women characters are quite different to each other, it wasn't far-fetched to find reflections of different aspects of Katharine in them. Sophie's transition into adulthood fictionalised parts of Katharine's own; a decade later, the world-weary Gina Haxby expressed Katharine's confrontation with middle age. To read her work as completely un-autobiographical would be as much a mistake as to read it as simple autobiography.

Katharine countered Cyril's other claim, about 'defective males', with examples of strong men in her novels—Michael in *Black Opal*, Tom in *Golden Miles*. But there are other male characters who bear out

Cyril's claim—notably the trilogy's Morris Gough, Tom's father, the misguided patriarch who can't provide for his family and is only saved from poverty by Sally's strength and hard work, as well as Greg from *Intimate Strangers* and Hugh from *Coonardoo.* The tragic struggles of Tom Prichard and Hugo Throssell in Katharine's own life left their mark in a pattern of male protagonists who have trouble making their way in the world and depend on the support of resilient women.

After making these complaints to Ric, Katharine wrote a frosty letter to Cyril. 'To have "lived with" my work for two years, & to have failed to realise some of its most significant aspects, surprises me.'[13] Katharine didn't notice Cyril's praise for her work; he even wrote, 'there is much in her novels that deserves the word "genius"'.[14]

In the decades which followed, Cyril taught Katharine's novels in his role as a teachers' college lecturer and followed in her footsteps on his holidays. 'I have made a point of visiting Clovelly [inspiration for her first book of poems], Chelsea [where she lived in London], and Russia.'[15] When Ric Throssell was writing his biography of Katharine in 1972, he wrote to Cyril asking permission to quote from his thesis. On request, Ric sent a draft of the harsh things he had to say about Cyril, explaining that although it was 'unpalatable', there was no getting around the 'fact' that the effect of Cyril's thesis 'was to divert Katharine from a novel on the half-castes to the auto-biography over which she laboured miserably for years'.[16] Ric received back a telegram, 'THESIS IS UNPUBLISHED MATERIAL AND LEGALLY RESTRICTED PERMISSION NOT REPEAT NOT GRANTED TO REFER TO THESIS OR MYSELF'.[17] On the advice of his publisher, Ric removed references to Cyril's name and the quotes from Cyril's thesis, lending the incident an aura of mystery in his biography.[18]

IN DECEMBER 1949, the Fellowship of Australian Writers WA president, John Ewers, published an article calling for Australia to put forward a nominee for the Nobel Prize for Literature, believing it would do much to raise the profile of Australian literature. He approached Allan Edwards, professor of English at the University of Western Australia, seeking support to nominate the essayist Walter Murdoch; Edwards was only willing to endorse Katharine, to which Ewers agreed.[19]

At a meeting on 28 February 1950, Ewers formally proposed that the fellowship nominate her for the prize. Katharine was there to witness the motion carry unanimously, with cheers.[20] They had missed the cut-off for the 1950 prize, but gained support from other state writers' groups for a 1951 nomination. Miles wrote that 'no other candidate is mentioned' in Sydney, although in truth her own name and Eleanor Dark's *were* being mentioned.[21]

Katharine was thrilled about the nomination but she didn't hold the prize winners of the period in high regard. 'When I think of T. S. Elliot [*sic*] winning the last though—with his defeatist, anti-progressive line of thought, & realise present political apprehensions in Sweden I haven't much hope of your KS winning approval, though someday there's a feeling in my bones it may happen.'[22] In June 1951 she was reading William Faulkner, the 1949 winner. 'Don't want to write like that—even if it means winning a Nobel Prize. Feel quite certain it won't come my way—since *Winged Seeds*—and the recession in political affairs. However, as you know darl, I've always been more concerned about going my own wilful way, than anything else.'[23] In November 1951 the Swedish writer Pär Lagerkvist was announced as the winner. She had read some of his stories and made the same comment about his work—'I wouldn't want to write like that'.[24]

Katharine didn't live to witness Patrick White become the first Australian to win the prize in 1973, but in 1957 she read White's novel *The Tree of Man* (1955) and found it 'powerful descriptive writing & characterisation—but tedious in parts, and the moronic types dealt with at great length, leaving one without any exhilaration. As a new writer though, of exceptional ability, I was quite excited to find him'.[25] As her opinions narrowed, she turned against him in the years which followed, writing in 1964, 'Lost in the fog of their own delusions, writers like Patrick White believe they are uncommitted to any social purpose, while, as a matter of fact, they serve the causes of obfuscation and the defeat of human dignity in its demand for truth and justice'.[26]

AFTER A BREAK from political activism caused by her relocations, her bad health and her literary work, Katharine was ready to return to the fray but had to find the right focus for her limited energy.

To have returned to the tedium of backroom state branch work after the prestige of her Central Committee role wouldn't have been attractive. Instead, the Australian Peace Council, formed in 1949 in response to the Cold War, became her focus. The council had a range of people involved, including many progressive Christians as well as communists. Historian Barbara Carter notes that the Communist Party supported the council although 'at that stage peace did not take a central place in the party's program'.[27] Peace had been at the heart of Katharine's radicalisation in the Great War and she now chose to work for a communist-approved organisation dedicated to it, picking up from her involvement in the Movement Against War and Fascism in the 1930s.

She wrote to Miles in January 1950 that she was busy with Peace Council work, attending 'two or three meetings a week, & in this sweltering heat, it's been exhausting'.[28] In April, she travelled to Melbourne as a delegate to the Peace Congress. At the congress, Doon Stone remembers Katharine standing to give her speech before the packed Exhibition building looking 'infinitely frail and indomitable' and beginning with 'the appealing halting words, "my beloved people"'. She went on to say, 'The struggle for peace must have heroes and heroines as dauntless as those who fight in wars. The struggle for peace and social progress demands the highest patriotism'.[29] There was a crowd of ten thousand, with the most high-profile speaker the Dean of Canterbury, Hewlett Johnson, nicknamed the 'Red Dean' for his support for the Soviet Union.

After the conference, Doon drove Katharine to Frankston to stay with Beatrice and her husband. 'My first meeting with K's sister', Doon writes:

> two people so utterly dissimilar that they could have emerged from different planets. B so ... domesticated ... utterly incapable of assessing the fire and grandeur of the flame that burned within K's frail frame, yet filled with anxiety and affection for the 'wayward' sister! I saw a new Katharine there ... consciously divesting herself of all thought and speech that might prove controversial or shattering to the family tie, preserved so carefully through the years. All of this I sensed, but confirmed with inward amusement, when Bee made the opportunity to thank me for my 'kindness to her sister', adding

> with her complete absence of insight that 'Kathy had some funny ideas about things, but she was a dear clever little thing!' It seemed quite incredible to me that her family could be so utterly unaware of K's true mental & spiritual calibre, and of her position among the writers of the world.[30]

AFTER COMPLAINING IN 1949 that men were no longer interested in her, Katharine mentioned having an unnamed boyfriend to dinner in the spring of 1950; she called him 'an old flame'. 'My small dinner party, with boyfriend, came off this week. But I can't feel partyed [*sic*] during my working days; so although he was affable—& affectionate—wanted to stay the night, herself didn't feel disposed. So it was the last bus in the rain for my guest!'[31]

By the end of 1950 Katharine had made a start on the autobiography and several other works: 'facing the New Year with half a dozen designs brewing. Have sketched three. The Deakin play. Novel with half cast [*sic*] problem as subject to be called "Boronia". Dramatic saga built on Aboriginal legends, biography of KS and several short stories. I'd like to do also a monograph on my father. How much of that lot will get done, I wonder?'[32] Katharine was writing the Alfred Deakin play for the Jubilee stage play competition, marking fifty years since federation. With its supporting characters based on her own parents, the project complemented her return to the past in her autobiography. The eventual winner of the competition was Kylie Tennant with her own play about Deakin. When Tennant's play was published, Katharine bought a copy and was gracious enough to conclude that it was probably better than hers and she'd have chosen it also if she was the judge.[33] She did little other work through 1951, writing in March 1952, 'I haven't done any creative writing for a long time, but am feeling I must soon. Perhaps I've been tired, & felt that to finish the trilogy was enough; but now the impulse is churning again, and maybe, soon, I'll get to work'.[34]

LIKE OTHER AUSTRALIAN communists in 1951, Katharine lived expecting illegality. In March 1951 the High Court ruled that the 1950 act to ban the Communist Party of Australia was unconstitutional. Menzies called a double dissolution election, promising a referendum to change the constitution and ban the Communist Party. He won a majority in both houses and announced the referendum would be held on 22 September 1951. At the beginning of the campaign, opinion polls showed the referendum would pass easily. But, helping the 'no' case, Bert Evatt had become Labor leader after the sudden death of Ben Chifley and set about speaking out against the proposal. A week before the poll, Katharine wrote, 'Although the pace is not hectic—nothing like the excitement there was in the anti-conscription referendum of 1916–1917—it may quicken this week'.[35] Her assessment of it probably reflected her lack of active involvement; party member John McKenzie remembers the campaign as the 'most intensive' he had seen and that the 'Australian people were never more politicised'.[36] In a surprise result, the referendum was narrowly defeated. Katharine wrote, 'after the first promising results came through, I was hurried off to a party to celebrate'.[37] Menzies abandoned his attempt to outlaw the Communist Party and instead contented himself with strong surveillance by the Australian Security Intelligence Organisation (ASIO)—the new agency formed in 1949—and the controls offered by existing laws.

ON NEW YEAR'S Day 1952, Katharine's brother Nigel died in his sleep. Nigel and her other brother Alan had been the close companions of her childhood—her sister being so much younger—and now they were both dead. She spent a day in tears. 'Despite the political differences … there was a deep affection between us … I feel as if something of myself had died with Nigel.'[38]

Ric had finished his posting in Brazil and he arrived in Greenmount with Dodie and Karen in June. 'Of course', she reassured him, 'there won't be any political arguments when you come home. We both have our points of view, and I wouldn't dream of disturbing your[s] with mine'.[39] After they left six weeks later, she wrote, 'I'm still feeling so bereft. As if the light has gone out of my world'.[40] At Ric's suggestion, she had an indoor toilet installed that winter—'it looks so grand, almost a throne'.[41]

IN SEPTEMBER 1952, government backbencher and Cold War warrior WC Wentworth was attacking the Commonwealth Literary Fund for directing grants to communists. T Inglis Moore wrote a letter to the *Sydney Morning Herald* claiming this was untrue and not one communist had been funded. It was a strange mistake to make and Wentworth replied with a letter to the editor detailing support given to Katharine and insisting, 'Katherine [*sic*] Susannah Prichard (alias Mrs. Thorssell [*sic*]) is not only a member of the Communist Party in the most exact sense. She is also one of its leading operatives'.[42] Besides his spelling errors, and depending on how 'alias' is defined, his claims about Katharine were true. To Katharine's supporters, his use of 'alias' was a calculated insult, implying a false identity. Bert Evatt's secretary, Allan Dalziel, had a letter published in the *Sydney Morning Herald* under a pseudonym claiming, 'she is subjected to a cheap and sneering gibe which definitely suggests that she is using an alias in the honoured name of Throssell'.[43] Christian Jollie Smith wrote to Katharine to tell her about Wentworth's letter, unwisely advising that it was actionable, and offering to represent her. Katharine told her to go ahead with a suit for libel, claiming damages of £10,000. Katharine wrote to Ric, 'proud I am to have been the wife of my Jimmy, & I can't let this imbecile create a doubt in the minds of many people that I was'.[44] In another letter, she wrote her motivations were to 'discredit' Wentworth and 'make him realise that he can't get away with making damaging statements'.[45] An apology would have been enough for Katharine to drop the action but Wentworth refused. Christian proceeded with the case, but there was a backlog at the Supreme Court of New South Wales and Christian warned Katharine it could be several years before there was a hearing.

On 24 September 1952, two weeks after Wentworth's letter, Katharine opened the *West Australian* to read that her best friend, Hilda, and Hilda's second husband, John Dale, had been in a car accident in Italy. John was dead and Hilda was injured in hospital. Katharine wrote to Ric, 'she's so frail, and I can't believe she will survive. You will realise, darl, how broken-up I am. I had such a strong feeling that this going abroad was going to be disastrous for both of them: begged them not to go'.[46] After living in painful uncertainty for a couple of weeks, sending cables she didn't think would reach Hilda, she received word that Hilda was recovering and expecting to leave hospital.[47]

Hilda's friend, Catherine Duncan, looked after her for a month in Paris until she was strong enough for the trip back to Melbourne. The doctor told Catherine that Hilda had terminal liver cancer, but no-one told Hilda.[48]

Katharine travelled to Canberra for Christmas, staying with Ric and family until mid-February 1953. She then took a trip to Sydney to discuss the libel case with Christian. A doctor advised that her health was not up to a second journey from Perth to Sydney that year, so she decided to stay in Melbourne with Beatrice until the case could be heard. Christian applied for an expedited hearing because of Katharine's health but the case dragged on.

Stalin died in March 1953 just as Katharine was settling in for a long stay at Kirinaran with Beatrice and her husband, the Menzies-supporting 'Pack'. Katharine wrote a tribute for the Union of Soviet Writers. 'How wisely, how indefatigably, Stalin inspired the Soviet peoples to carry out their historic task of Socialist construction! … he was incorruptible, fearless and completely devoted to service of the Soviet peoples, and of the great purpose which seeks to free Humanity from a social system which breeds war, poverty, disease, and prostitution.'[49] Her devotion to him is disturbing to read today. Although some of his atrocities had been reported in 1953, his reputation was less settled. A mainstream newspaper like the *Sun* could carry an obituary which began 'Stalin … will pass into history leaving a question mark behind him. Saviour or tyrant? Superman or ruthless despot? Man of war or man of peace?'[50]

In April, Hilda wrote to say she hadn't been worth visiting because she'd been too ill. 'I wish the wretched doctors could give me some idea of what's the matter.'[51] Katharine came anyway, visiting regularly in May and June. 'We both knew that she could not recover, but in our last days together, talked much as usual, trying to evade realisation.'[52] On Friday 23 June she found Hilda 'so wasted & knowing now that there is no hope'. Thinking it was the last time they would see each other, Hilda dropped the evasion and told Katharine how close they'd been for fifty years and that Katharine had always been there for her in a crisis. On Monday night, Katharine rang for an update and Hilda's son Hugh said she was 'very low' and the doctor thought it would not be long. He rang back later to say she had died.[53]

On Wednesday, Katharine attended the funeral at the Springvale Crematorium. 'It was too harrowing really—I think of Hilda in that long polished box & afterwards committed to the fire—We had talked of it, which of us would survive the other.'[54]

The year before Hilda died, a letter to Katharine evoked the 'memories and dreams and the whole atmosphere and fragrance of our long association':

> Your first words to me at Ormond come back to me when you looked over the fence and we began to talk; your little study; Emerald, and the lovely days at Greenmount, full of sunlight and laughter and burning enthusiasms; our last days—both so tired, but you just as wonderful and charming and wise as ever—my darling, I am just overwhelmed with awe and wonder and admiration! Your spirit burns with even greater intensity than in those early days, when you were so beautiful, so gifted, so emotionally rich and sensitive. You have lived and suffered and rejoiced in a dozen lives, compared to the one humdrum existence most of us achieve.[55]

KATHARINE SPENT A cold winter at Kirinaran, tinkering with things she'd already written—the Deakin play, a film treatment for the goldfields trilogy—but not getting much done as she waited, in limbo, for news of the libel case. 'Here I am still!' she wrote to Miles. 'And feeling marooned! … it's been an awful waste of time, sitting by the fire in the evening listening to murder mysteries on the radio.'[56] She returned to Canberra to stay from October until the new year, reporting to Miles, 'Have been feeling better, here, mostly loafing & sleeping & playing with my grand-daughter—who thinks that was what ga-gas were made for'.[57]

On 27 November 1953, Katharine had to visit Sydney on business relating to the libel case and she stayed with Miles for three nights. Katharine arrived on Friday evening, exhausted from carrying her case from the station; they went to bed at ten, but Miles didn't sleep until 3 a.m., and then Katharine woke her by clearing her throat at 4.30 a.m. 'I'm v. nervous & too lively', Miles wrote in her diary. Katharine spent Saturday in the city; they had dinner together and then a quiet evening.

'K says her work is finished & she wants to die. Very dismal—made me really depressed.' Miles may not have been aware that Katharine was days away from turning seventy, the three score and ten then considered a full life span; it would have been playing on Katharine's mind. In Katharine's account, though, it was Miles' fear of death which stood out. 'I tried to make her feel that the end was not to be feared but anticipated with serenity when our work is done and time approaching for an exit. She, poor darling, however did not seem to be able to take the thought of "not being" philosophically.'[58]

On Sunday, Miles recorded, 'We talked, rested & read—a happy day except for K's depressing manner & philosophy'. Intriguingly, Miles recorded that 'K & Dal had some private business so he came at 2.30 & I did odds and ends'. Dal was Bert Evatt's secretary, Allan Dalziel, who visited Miles regularly. Dalziel was interested enough in Katharine's libel case to have written that pseudonymous letter to the editor, and had told Miles that Ric should punch Wentworth on the steps of parliament; it seems he was helping Katharine in order to cause problems for Wentworth, his political enemy.[59]

Miles made a dinner of lamb chops and potatoes with a dessert of caramel custard and pear pudding. After listening to a feature about Mary Gilmore on the radio that night, they both went to bed and in the morning Katharine left early. Katharine wrote to Miles afterwards to say she was safely arrived '& chewing over my lovely time with you! Such a treat just to hear you talk. I do love the wit & play of your so original mind. Nobody makes me laugh so much'. She sent the letter with a bottle of perfume 'to refresh you on hot days—& make you think of me'.[60]

After an aimless year away from home, Katharine returned to Greenmount in January 1954 with the libel case unresolved. In March, Miles wrote the final surviving letter between the two of them, returning to their conversation on the second night of Katharine's stay:

> You made me so melancholy, dear, by talking about your life being finished—your big writing task done and Ric settled happily and securely, independent of you. It compelled me to face the hateful fact that I must face death without having accomplished one worthwhile thing and I'm not reconciled to death itself. I hope life has

> revived for you since your return to Greenmount and a controlled procedure and warmth, and things that you want to do.[61]

There was at least one more letter, now lost. Miles' friend, Delys Cross, kept Katharine informed as Miles' health deteriorated in the months which followed. Visiting Miles in hospital on 13 September 1954, Delys remembers 'Miles would ask me to read the letter from "my darling Katharine" and "Ah read it again"'.[62] After Delys told Katharine that Miles didn't have long, Katharine extravagantly sent a box of wildflowers by air on the 17th. It was too late for Miles to see them; she was unconscious and died two days later. 'I feel saddened at the thought of how little appreciation & recognition she received. She had an unusual quality: such grit & wit, & yet was defeated, I think, by failure to stand up to certain logical conclusions.'[63]

36

'My Faith Has Never Wavered'

Greenmount, 1954–1959

THE SUMMER OF 1954 ended with one hundred and fifty people attending the official opening of a memorial to Hugo on 24 February. 'At last', Katharine wrote to Ric, 'some tribute is paid to your father's memory'.[1] Back in 1939 Katharine had donated to the road board the triangle of land formed between what had become 'Old' York Road and the new Great Eastern Highway so that a memorial could be built. The long-delayed memorial was a stone rotunda which would serve as a bus stop, metres from her house. A tablet inscribed to Hugo was unveiled by Major General Bierworth. Hugo had been dead twenty years and his generation of veterans had now reached old age; his one living sibling was too ill to attend. Katharine gave a speech, calling for the people of the district to remember Hugo 'not only for his courage … but for his kindliness and friendliness' and his hope that 'negotiation would displace war, because he felt so deeply the sorrow & suffering caused by war'.[2]

In April, junior Russian diplomat Vladimir Petrov defected, revealing he was a KGB agent operating out of the Russian embassy in Canberra. As an ally of Stalin's executed security chief, Lavrentiy Beria, he feared being recalled and purged. The old nemesis of Western Australian communists, Ron Richards, was now deputy director-general of ASIO and negotiated the defection. Katharine wrote to Ric about Petrov. 'At any rate I'm very glad I never met the bloke, or had anything to do with him. My associations with the SU [Soviet Union] have been purely literary—I can't imagine what revelations he would have to make, except in self defence.'[3]

Menzies announced a Royal Commission on Espionage which was to run until August 1955. The Soviet Union recalled all of its embassy staff. Katharine wrote to Mikhail Apletin at the Union of Soviet Writers in June 1954: 'I am sure you will understand how distressed I have been because of the break in friendly relations between our countries … Certain it is however that the treachery and self-serving of an individual cannot change the feeling of warm friendship which many Australians have towards the Soviet Union'.[4]

In one of the ASIO interviews, Petrov, with some help from Ron Richards, named Ric as part of a spy ring operated by Wally Clayton, alias KLOD. Petrov had never met Ric, but claimed his codename was FERRO.[5] Ric was summoned to Melbourne for an interview with Ron Richards. When Katharine heard, she warned, 'He has no love at all for your mother, darling'.[6] While Ric was away, agents turned up and questioned his wife Dodie at home; she was under suspicion too. Katharine wrote, 'How stupid these people are! As if, with a mother known to be friendly towards the Soviet Union, you would do anything in your official capacity to bring you under suspicion even. It would be too obvious!'[7] Ric and Dodie awaited their turn to be called before the royal commission, but they still hadn't heard anything at the end of the year. They came to Greenmount for four weeks at Christmas and spent a lot of time going over the affair with Katharine. 'Katharine blamed herself for everything. She was quite sure it was her reputation that had attracted attention to me.'[8]

In February 1955 Ric and Dodie were called to Sydney to testify before the commission. They were questioned over two weeks about claims made by Petrov and others and about their associations with communists. 'You can't imagine what I am feeling for you!' Katharine wrote to them in the midst of it. 'All on the say-so of a treacherous rat like Petrov, concerned only to save himself from the results of his own misdeeds.'[9] She was anxiously checking the newspapers and turning on the radio for each news bulletin. Hearing their legal costs had run to £600, she sent them a cheque. 'I suppose they will call it "Moscow gold".'[10] Money from Russia was unpredictable; after not receiving anything for the translations of her earlier books, in July 1954 she had been cabled the largest sum of her career—£5835—for royalties on 30,000 copies of one of the goldfields novels.[11]

Ric and Dodie had to wait until September 1955 for the commission's report, which cleared them both, finding that the charges Ric had given information to Soviets 'were only hearsay' and the 'reason that the Moscow centre was so interested in Throssell was probably because of his association with persons who were or had been Communists'.[12] To the family's perpetual frustration, the taint of the accusations would not lift in the decades which followed.

MEANWHILE, THERE WAS finally progress in Katharine's libel case in May 1955 when the court ordered Katharine pay £2500 security before the proceedings began. Frustrated and incredulous, she decided to withdraw.[13] She expected to have to pay the newspaper's costs but to her relief, the final ruling in February 1956 did not require her to.[14] The case caused a rift between Katharine and Christian Jollie Smith; she told Ric 'my legal advisors have both been very remiss in [their] handling of the case'.[15] In 1959 Christian was surprised to finally hear from Katharine after 'years of silence and disapproval at something I did here in connection with her case. I thought [taking legal action] would please her but it didn't'.[16]

TWO ECCENTRIC ARTISTS, Betsey Linton and Kitch Currie, brother and sister, were building a house opposite Katharine's on Old York Road. Once in the 1950s they asked if they could rent her house while she was away for some months. Kitch remembers that although there was electricity and a telephone, 'Otherwise it was in a deplorable condition. The white ants were living a life of Riley and there were no such things as drains'. Betsey remembers, 'if you pulled the plug out [of the kitchen sink] it went down a pipe and straight on the dirt underneath'. Kitch fixed the dry rot in the doors while he was there. When Katharine returned, they were invited to a 'graceful' dinner party with bent forks;

another time they remember Katharine setting up armchairs on the front verandah for an event 'and some of the damned armchairs only had three legs'.[17]

Judy Inveen, Blanche Hunter's granddaughter, grew up at Wandu on Old York Road. Her mother, Iris, was a friend of Katharine's and always cut her hair—usually in a 1920s bob. Judy remembers Katharine from the 1950s and 1960s:

> I knew her as a dignified woman who kept to a circle of friends she trusted. If one was there in the late afternoon she always offered sherry and black olives. She spoke softly and had a quiet sense of humour. Life wasn't easy for her in a small hills settlement like Greenmount. Hugo's heroic ghost pervaded the hills and people were very judgemental of her. In retrospect I admire her so much for keeping her dignity.[18]

IN MARCH 1956, the Western world learned of Soviet leader Nikita Khrushchev's so-called 'secret speech' in which he denounced Stalin's cult of personality and the Great Purge which had seen so many killed. Communists in Australia were reacting in different ways. 'For rank-and-file communists, 1956 forced a re-evaluation of their faith in the communist project and their loyalty to the Party. They had to decide whether that faith and loyalty outweighed their sense of disillusionment and betrayal.'[19] The already depleted party faced further resignations. Katharine, however, was not shaken. In April, in the midst of the crisis, the party published a long article by Katharine in *Tribune*, 'Why I am a Communist', 'a gesture of loyalty to the Stalinist regime, at a time when the faith of many loyal Communist Party members was being shaken to the core'.[20] Later in the year, the party published an expanded version of the article as a booklet.

On 6 May, Katharine wrote to Mikhail Apletin at the Union of Soviet Writers, 'Recent criticism of Comrade Stalin has been much exaggerated and distorted in our press … Whatever the causes for it, the achievements of this illustrious comrade, during times of great stress and difficulty, cannot be forgotten. If he made mistakes—well, "to err is human"'.[21]

She began that same letter by writing, 'To-day, I am sad, because I wanted to go to the celebrations of May Day in Fremantle, but friends who were to drive me could not go, and so I have spent the day alone in my wild hills. Writing to you and Oksana is a consolation'.[22] The words of loyalty to Stalin were written by an old woman stuck in the rain in her lonely cabin, not only far from Moscow but separated from the dwindling local faithful gathering 50 kilometres away at Fremantle.

Katharine was more affected by the suicide of Alexander Fadeyev on 16 May. She had corresponded with him when he had worked for the Union of Soviet Writers and regarded him as 'one of the most outstanding of modern writers'.

> How could such a thing happen to a Soviet writer? Has there been too much criticism? Of course a writer should stand up to criticism and fight for his or her personal point of view. But there are some temperaments on which hostile criticism acts like a blight creating distrust, lack of self confidence …
>
> It seems to me there are too many critics anxious to be critical, rather than appreciate with generous enthusiasm what is fine and of value in the creative work of present day writers. Drastic criticism can destroy a sensitive mind …[23]

Katharine was trying to make sense of his death in terms of the hostile reception her own recent work had received. She hadn't seen his suicide note, in which he denounced the Soviet leaders for betraying communism and killing so many writers. 'The art to which I have given my life has been destroyed by the self-confident, ignorant leadership of the Party and can no longer be corrected.'[24]

In February 1957, she wrote to Apletin, 'The stresses of the past year, I suppose have left their mark on those of us who have been in the struggle for a long time. My faith has never wavered, and I am grateful to an understanding of Marxism which has enabled me to see clearly through difficult times'.[25] Karl Marx's vision of the world sustained her like the teachings of Jesus sustain many Christians. The Soviet Union was to Katharine what the church is to devout Roman Catholics—the bearer of the good news with leaders who should be revered; an institution requiring loyalty even and especially when it seems to have gone wrong.

Then, in October 1957, the Soviet Union launched Sputnik, the world's first artificial satellite, and Katharine's joyous response was that of a believer who thought a revival was now at hand:

> Last night the Soviet star came out of the sky and passed over my garden. What a thrill it was to see that small golden orb and know what it meant! A demonstration to the world of the success and power of Socialism. Triumphs beyond the attainment of scientists in capitalist countries fettered by the system of profit and private enterprise ... This Soviet star was a herald of peace ...
>
> The reaction of people here to the Soviet 'moon' or 'satellite', as they call it, has been remarkable. Everywhere they have been out watching for its appearance just after sun set.[26]

ASIO'S SURVEILLANCE OF Katharine continued; she was in her seventies but apparently still dangerous. Sometimes their sources were egregiously wrong, like the memo stating that 'according to reliable information' Katharine was at the international peace congress held in Sweden in July 1958. ASIO cleared that up, with another officer noting that she had not left her home except to go to hospital in the period alleged.[27] ASIO sources reported on Katharine's occasional attendance at Midland branch meetings of the Communist Party, her brief speeches at May Day rallies, her attendance at meetings of the Peace Council, and a lunch with Victorian party leader Ted Hill when she was in Melbourne. She gave a lecture to a meeting of the Australasian Book Society on 18 February 1960 in Canberra with historian Manning Clark; according to the memo, 'The meeting was said to be dull, uninteresting and purely literary'.[28]

There was at least some invisible sabotage. The department of immigration published a monthly magazine for New Australians called *Good Neighbour*. An article in the August 1958 issue, 'Some Books That Tell of Life in Your New Land', was to include a photograph of Katharine and discussion of her work. But after someone in the department asked ASIO's advice, they were told the director-general 'considers it undesirable that any Communist authors should be recommended to New Australians in an official publication'. A memo advised that 'all reference' to Katharine 'would be excluded' and the published article included only 'safe' writers like Henry Lawson, Eleanor Dark and Patrick White.[29]

KATHARINE WAS MEANT to visit the Soviet Union in 1957 and invited Doon Stone to come as her secretary. The plan was to leave in March, arriving in London and then continuing to a meeting for the World Council for Peace in Vienna before the International Writers Congress in Moscow. But in January Katharine decided she could not handle the trip. She wrote to Ric, 'My beastly heart played up again & I feel that I haven't got the strength for all the journeys & excitement. The least exertion makes me utterly weary'.[30]

Katharine expected the worst part would be Doon's disappointment, but she didn't realise just how hard Doon would take it. Doon had just had her travel vaccinations when she received the letter. 'Before I opened it,' Doon wrote in her unpublished memoir, 'I knew it contained death to the "dream". Between the pathetic lines of the little story of further heart trouble, I read the complete ruthlessness that made K the artist that she is—the determination to carry out her will, cost what it may'. Doon felt 'the last remnants of human feeling in my heart died that night of bitter disappointment and broken faith. I was alone, ill and more desolate than at any time in my life—and tempted, indeed, to add to the tragic suicide pattern of her life'.[31]

Katharine's heart troubles were genuine enough, but Doon also blamed the cancellation on the baby Ric and Dodie were expecting, which has an element of truth. Katharine had told Ric, 'I can't feel happy about going when I'd like to be with you & Dodie for the new babe's arrival'.[32] In April 1957, Dodie gave birth to a boy, and they named him Hugo Alan after his grandfather and great-uncle. 'While we rejoice at the coming of this small person', Katharine wrote to Mikhail Apletin, 'my heart quails to think of the world he will inherit. Maybe it will be better than the one his two dear namesakes had to face'.[33] Ignoring her son's differing political convictions, Katharine embroidered a Soviet jacket for the baby, with a wheat sheath and a hammer and sickle.[34]

The British government was preparing to test nuclear weapons on Kiritimati, an isolated atoll in the Pacific Ocean. Peace activists proposed a bold new protest strategy—sailing a peace fleet into the test area. Two hundred and fifty people volunteered, including Katharine and Aileen Palmer, Nettie and Vance's daughter. They risked a slow death from radiation sickness; Katharine expected there was a good chance she wouldn't survive but wrote, 'I thought I may as well make my dying worth while'.[35] Announcing her intention in a public statement in May, she travelled to the east coast, ready to join the protest. It would have been an appropriate way to finish a life she claimed had begun in the middle of a hurricane. However, sailing a fleet to the middle of the Pacific Ocean proved too difficult to organise, and the protest did not eventuate. The thwarted campaign still came to be seen by some activists as a key moment in the development of the anti-nuclear protest movement, the 'bodies on the line' tactic an inspiration for similar actions in the decades which followed.[36]

Instead of sailing into a nuclear test zone, Katharine spent two months with Ric and family. She wrote that baby Hugo 'already has a lovable personality. He will be good-natured and placid, I think; but his sister … and I have a special bond of affinity'.[37]

She had more time with the family over the first half of 1958 when they came to stay with her for Ric's long service leave. She wanted to give him 'undisturbed time to work on his plays' which 'meant devoting all my time to making domestic affairs run smoothly, cooking nice meals for my beloveds, and being available to look after the children. It was rather strenuous, but I kept fairly well—only twice the tiresome heart behaved badly'.[38] Giving up her own writing and activism to make time for Ric to write was one of a number of ways Katharine helped Ric's literary career over the decades.

Baby Hugo wasn't developing well and on their return to the east, Ric and Dodie learned he had Down syndrome. They decided to put him in a children's home. Katharine said she was with them in their grief. 'If only I were younger & cd depend on my health, I wd have liked to take charge of him for you. But, then, too, my days are numbered & there seems no other way.'[39] He died a couple of months later in September 1958 and Katharine tried to find comfort in the difficulties he had been spared. 'So much love & hope greeted him, and there cd only have been tragedy for him & for all of us' if he had lived.[40] There were happier times ahead for Ric and Dodie with two more children born in the years that followed—Querida in 1959 and then James in 1962.

THE UNFINISHED AUTOBIOGRAPHY hung over Katharine through the decade. In January 1956 she was making progress on it in the midst of the summer heat. She liked writing about her father's time in Fiji but 'I'm still not very interested in writing about myself. Dislike the personal pronoun—the "I … I …" constantly creeping in. It all seems quite puerile and useless!'[41] Her solution was to write the draft with some scenes in the third person, explaining:

> I have always found it difficult to write in the first person, so that in this biography it has been easier to refer to Katharine Susannah as a person about whom I have heard & to whom certain things have happened. Thinking back over the years, I feel quite aloof from her—as if she were someone I had met & known slightly but can scarcely realise as myself.[42]

The switching between first and third person had no literary purpose; she just adopted the viewpoint which came more easily to her as she wrote particular scenes. The autobiography stalled again. She wrote later to Ric, 'must get on with the new novel when I come home & dump these wretched memoirs—which aren't sufficiently important to have spent time on'.[43]

She redeemed an unproductive literary decade with the publication of *N'goola and Other Stories* in March 1959. She had sent off the manuscript in November 1957 saying, 'Am making a gift of them to the ABS because some of the stories wdn't appeal to my usual publishers'.[44] ABS—Australasian Book Society—had been founded in 1952 as a left-wing cooperative publishing society, funded by subscriptions and releasing four books annually.

Vance Palmer wrote a brief foreword for the collection. It's a tribute to Katharine's work, set in the past tense, even though she had another decade of living and writing while he did not:

> Young people today may not be fully aware of the flood of new life Katharine Prichard poured into our writing … [Her novels] brought

> indisputable evidence that a new writer had arisen, one of lyric freshness, of original vision, of dramatic power … She wrote easily in the Australian idiom, weaving a lively and poetic language from images of the natural world around her, from [A]boriginal names, from the talk of blacks, bushmen, or men working on their jobs.

The foreword was Vance's last word about Katharine; he died suddenly of a heart attack a few months later in July 1959.

Although Ric lamented that writing her autobiography diverted Katharine from the planned novel 'Boronia', the project wasn't actually lost altogether—it turned into the titular short story, 'N'goola', which means 'wild boronia'. The story is about Mary, a woman taken from her Aboriginal mother as a child and now trying to live like a white person, yet kept on the fringes of society. An old Aboriginal man who has been searching for his daughter for years comes to town. He tells his story to Mary. When N'goola was born to his wife, she was pale-skinned and rejected by the tribe, but he accepted her as his own daughter, only for her to be removed from the family by the government. N'goola is, of course, Mary, and the story ends happily with a reunion between the two. There's potential in the story for expansion, but it works fine at its existing length, and perhaps Katharine simply decided against turning it into a novel.

Many of the eighteen stories are set in familiar Prichardian territory—a coalmine, the goldfields, a quarry, a station. Some feel incomplete, sketches; others are yarns which work well as entertainments for their time; and several—'Yoirimba', 'The Buccaneers' and 'The Elopement'—are accomplished short stories among Katharine's best. There's an appropriateness in the uneven diversity of all three of Katharine's short story collections. They show a writer at her best and also at her most workmanlike. They show the breadth of her concerns and the range of styles influencing her. They show a working writer, who wrote to change the world but also to entertain and make a living.

THE LIFE KATHARINE had settled into in old age was marked by contrasts. She was a revered literary figure in communist countries but lived an austere life as an eccentric in the hills of Perth. The Soviet

Union was her spiritual home, but she wasn't able to visit, which helped maintain her illusions. She had many friends but, with her family all in the eastern states, she was lonely. 'Sometimes I feel a very un-hugged person, & long for the warmth & physical nearness of my beloveds. I've travelled a lonely road for so long, & yet it's the only one for me to travel, I suppose.'[45]

Returning to Melbourne for the Peace Congress in November 1959, Katharine was presented with the Joliot-Curie Medal for service in the cause of peace, an honour that she said meant more to her than any other.[46] Writing of the congress in her novel *Subtle Flame,* Katharine has her character Sharn describe one international speaker, scientist Linus Pauling, as 'standing out … by the fearless integrity of his personality', while the British author JB Priestly was 'an overgrown wombat' and 'rather a boor'. The opening night, with its reading of the Charter of Hope, was, for Sharn, 'the most thrilling experience of my life'.[47]

After the congress and the public adulation, Katharine went for a 'few days' rest' with Beatrice and Pack and found herself forced to watch television with them. She hated it. She wrote on 22 November 1959 to Ric, 'Have come to the conclusion TV & radio are stealing people's lives from them … Surely TV will die out unless greatly improved. It's like the "canned" music that was popular for a while'.[48] It was a fitting end to the decade, public honour and private frustration, alienated by the new world of the 1950s, on the road, and kept once again from her work. It was also to be her last trip out of Western Australia.

37

'A Personal Thing'

Greenmount, 1960–1964

KATHARINE MADE A substantial start on a new novel, *Subtle Flame,* in 1960, sending off five handwritten chapters for typing in late July and then another six chapters three weeks later.[1] She described the work-in-progress in a letter to Mikhail Apletin:

> My new novel will present a man, face to face with the realities of his time and trying to persuade people for peace, not war. It is a tremendous theme, and will take all my strength to deal with it effectively … Perhaps inference is more effective artistically; but I am more concerned 'to put on brass knuckles' … and convince people of the need for united action, to defeat the intrigues of the war-makers and those who profit by war.[2]

The letter was one of her last to Apletin. They'd grown close; she'd been calling him 'Mik' and he'd been calling her 'Katya' at her request, but then he stopped writing back. 'We had such a warm and friendly correspondence', Katharine wrote to his colleague at the Foreign Commission, Oksana Krugerskaya, 'but now I never hear from him. Tell him, please, I feel thoroughly jilted—and am very sad to lose so good a friend, at seventy-five!'[3] He wrote a final letter, explaining he'd had heart trouble and been immersed in writing his memoirs.

Katharine's progress on the novel came to a halt with two significant international visits. First were two Soviet writers in September 1960, the poet Alexey Surkov with Katharine's pen-friend Oksana as translator, invited by the Fellowship of Australian Writers as a cultural exchange. In anticipation of their visit, Katharine painted the bath, in case Oksana took up her invitation to stay at her house.[4] Katharine met them at the airport with wildflowers. 'Both of them very sincere, simple & yet charming people.'[5] Oksana stayed at a hotel, but Katharine had them to dinner the third night of their stay with thirty guests coming afterwards, 'cushions on the floor of the lounge & the room … packed'. ASIO were very interested in the Soviet writers' movements, and an informant—perhaps one of Katharine's neighbours—wrote down the numberplates of all the vehicles parked near her house that night, including Dorothy Hewett's Ford Zephyr.[6]

It was a rare opportunity for Katharine to see Soviet writers and she spent a long time ruminating afterwards:

> I've been regretting, since, that I asked so many people to meet you on that occasion. I would have liked so much just a quiet talk. There was so much I wanted to ask you about. But I felt I had to share you with the others—all friends and young writers—to whom it was most valuable and important that they should have some discussion with you. So forgive me, dear Oksana, if I erred by spoiling our evening. I can scarcely forgive myself, but the sharing seemed a duty.[7]

They left Katharine with the gift of a model Sputnik which played the Soviet anthem and beeped like the original. The visit meant so much to Katharine that she wrote to Oksana a year later, 'Can still feel your warm and generous personality as you came into this room … If I were a theosophist I could believe you left something of yourself with me'.[8]

The second international visit was by the African-American singer and left-wing activist, Paul Robeson, and his anthropologist wife, Eslanda, who arrived on 30 November 1960. Robeson's Cold War had been even harder than Katharine's; the government deprived him of his passport in 1950 because of his communist sympathies. 'Trapped within the United States in a hostile atmosphere, he found his performance opportunities drying up, with concerts cancelled and recordings withdrawn from sale.'[9]

Finally able to travel again, Perth was the last stop on what would be his only tour of Australia. Such was Robeson's status in left-wing circles that the previous year the Peace Council in Perth celebrated his birthday in his absence, playing his records, with Katharine cooking sausage rolls for the party.[10] When the Robesons arrived at the Perth airport, a crowd of two hundred greeted them with banners and bouquets. Katharine was giving a welcome speech on behalf of the Peace Council when a woman 'dashed between' her and Robeson '& hurled herself against Mrs Robeson in a huge embrace' before Robeson removed her so Katharine could continue. 'Amongst the crowd was a group of Aborigines, greeted by the singer with the words: "I hope that soon they will treat you as well as they treat me."'[11] 'No man I've ever met has so impressed me with his personal greatness', Katharine told Ric. 'He's so simple & unaffected in his manner, so dignified, yet straight forward & uncompromising in what he says. The voice—even when he speaks is deeply moving, but it's the man himself, I think, who demonstrates the greatness of the human spirit.' Katharine attended a concert he gave at the Capitol and then a reception at the Palace Hotel, before farewelling him at the airport.[12]

'CELIA [SHELLEY] HAS been so good to me', Katharine wrote to Ric in 1961, '& I want to do something that will give her a little stand-by in her old age. The block of land I bought from her, when she wanted to go abroad, I'm transferring to her now'.[13] But soon after the gift, Celia turned against Katharine. She broke off all contact and 'said she didn't want to see me or discuss the matter'.[14] Katharine was mystified and shocked at the loss of a friendship of forty years. 'I had thought if I died suddenly & someone needed to take charge here, and arrange for disposal of my belongings, Celia wd do gladly … Now, however, I wd not ask her to do anything.'[15]

After Katharine's death, Ric tried to get to the bottom of the rift between Katharine and Celia and asked various people who knew them both. There were several theories, but finally he interviewed Celia herself and heard her account. His notes read:

> Katharine was sick towards the end. Mentally sick. You know. It wasn't K … 'I don't have to dress. I'm the celebrated authoress,'

> with her arms stretched up like this. 'It's not the time for lying down,' in that haughty voice …
>
> The last straw was the weeding … It has to be cleared right around the house. 'Oh no I can't do that I'm the celebrated authoress. I'm not a peasant.' She ordered me to pull up all the grass all round the house. That was enough. I got on the bus and didn't come back.[16]

Even Joan Williams, an admirer of Katharine's, described her as 'difficult' in her last years, but Celia's accusations don't fit with other accounts of Katharine.[17] She was still mentally sharp in her seventies and eighties and no-one else records her acting haughtily. Yet Celia's falling out with Katharine suggests a similar dynamic to the unspoken hurts Doon Stone felt. It was complicated being the friend of a 'celebrated authoress' and if both Celia and Doon thought they were ready to do anything for her and accepted a degree of subservience, it may have come at a price they couldn't really afford.

Celia told Ric:

> She wrote to me and rang up often. 'What have I done Celia. Tell me what I've done.' I told her in the end.
>
> She said, 'I don't accept that as a reason.' She asked me to lunch but I didn't go. She said, 'You know you're always welcome here whenever you want to come.' She was sick. It wasn't Katharine.
>
> When I heard she died I had a dream. All the trees and shrubs … were all cleared … And K had a box of beautiful materials. She was wearing this beautiful soft pink fluffy thing. Something I have seen sometime.[18]

AILEEN PALMER, NETTIE'S elder daughter, wrote autobiographical pieces with changed names. In a fragment dated 28 January 1961, she wrote about a 'Karin' whom historian Adam Carr identifies as Katharine. 'Karin … has been the most continuous real friend of my life … if anyone makes me think and feel more than another, it's Karin, rather than any of the members of my own family.'[19] Aileen's relationships with her sister, Helen, and mother had become strained. Helen had moved to Sydney in 1952 and was expelled from the Communist

Party after starting a journal in 1957 called *Outlook* which had been giving a platform to dissenting ex-party members.[20] Meanwhile, after Vance's death in 1959, a frail Nettie and mentally fragile Aileen were left living together 'trapped in each other's company … in a relationship of mutual dependence and increasing resentment'.[21] Katharine's support for Aileen's poetry meant a lot to her. In 1957, Katharine offered to pay for the publication of a volume of Aileen's poems called *Dear Life*. 'But the darling sent me only a bill for the roneoed version of them—thinking I cd not afford to pay more.'[22] Katharine sent a copy to Oksana Krugerskaya at the Union of Soviet Writers, saying, 'There is not only high poetic quality in her work, but her mind moves to the themes which are of vital importance to us'.[23] Aileen remained a committed Stalinist like Katharine, and as the two exchanged letters Katharine's 'isolation from political reality' in Greenmount reinforced Aileen's.[24]

KATHARINE CONTINUED HER involvement with the Peace Council. In March 1963, as an early celebration of her eightieth birthday and a fundraiser, the council held a 'Jolly Jumbuck' barbeque in the grounds of her house with a lamb on a spit. The guests 'streamed down to the [amphi]theatre which was beside the big bougainvillea, with a stage on the side verandah. There were over 200 visitors, & lots of fun over the barbecue fires. Boys & girls dancing to the accordion played by a typical Australian stockman'.[25] It was also a launch for a 7-inch record of Katharine reading her stories 'Josephina Anna Maria' and 'The Cooboo'.[26] In September 1963, the council celebrated the Nuclear Test Ban treaty with a supper and speeches. Katharine gave a brief speech. Afterwards, one of her friends said her voice had trembled and she decided to give up public speaking.[27]

Katharine's Communist Party involvement had lessened. One party member recalls it was a 'ritual' of the state conference that on the first night an apology from Katharine was read out 'and a suitable message of greetings agreed to. By this time, Katharine … didn't attend Party meetings any more. I suppose she was nominally a member of the Midland branch, closest to her home in Greenmount … She was a revered figure, seldom seen by most Party members by then'.[28]

IN JULY 1961, Katharine had a heart attack. She downplayed it to Ric, telling him she had a 'nasty heart twang' and she was being looked after well by her friends.[29] In a letter to Beatrice Davis at Angus and Robertson her tone was different. 'A nasty heart attack, last month, made me realise that time is running out for me, and that I must try to put my affairs in order.' She was sending a draft manuscript of *Child of the Hurricane.* 'I regret having given so much time to a personal thing', Katharine wrote in her covering letter, 'but was urged to write these reminiscences when a man here wrote a very distorted version of my youth and childhood in a thesis for his degree'. The manuscript only covered up to her first trip to London in 1908–1909; she was trying to finish another section telling of her work on the *Herald* and wanted to know whether there was a prospect of publication.[30]

After an initial reply thanking Katharine for the submission, it took Beatrice eight months to respond fully, offering publication and encouraging her to extend the story to when she won the Hodder & Stoughton competition to 'make a nicely rounded picture of a young writer up to her first major success'. Beatrice also suggested there was too much about Tom Prichard's adventures in Fiji, that she shouldn't refer to herself in the third person, that the title might be reconsidered for such a 'gentle' book, and asked if Katharine would reveal the name of the Preux Chevalier.[31] A red pen note added to one of Katharine's letters reads: 'BD [Beatrice Davis] minute to DS [Douglas Stewart—her fellow publisher] refers to disappointment over "ordinariness" of *C of H.* Reader's report suggests careful editing by author or publisher'.[32]

Katharine wrote back to Beatrice to say how heartening it was that Angus and Robertson wanted to publish the book. During the long wait for Beatrice's verdict, Wren Howard at Jonathan Cape Ltd had told her they wouldn't be interested in her autobiography, although they would consider *Subtle Flame* when it was finished. Cape himself, her old champion, had died in 1960. She had concluded that Angus and Robertson wasn't interested in *Child of the Hurricane* either and had been tempted to burn the section she'd been working on. 'Only my typist says "don't you dare!" She said she found it "fascinating", so I held my hand, for the time being.' Meanwhile, her 'damned' heart was playing up, 'one angina attack after another and the end of the road in sight, though I don't tell anyone this, and particularly don't want Ric to know I feel like it is'.[33] Her letters to Ric seem so candid that it's a jolt to learn of something so important she was suppressing, presumably because she didn't want to worry him. A few years earlier, Beatrice had arranged with Katharine for Angus and Robertson to reprint *Working Bullocks* and *Coonardoo* and, knowing Katharine was often short of money, she had gone the extra mile to try to sell broadcast and serial rights too. 'I like to think of you as one of my friends now', Katharine had written.[34]

Worried Katharine would die and the remaining chapters of *Child of the Hurricane* would be destroyed, Beatrice replied, 'I would not wish you to worry too much about the revision. Just let us have the MS [manuscript] back as soon as you can: and mark it "not to be burnt" just in case'.[35]

Katharine approached the writing of her autobiography without thinking of it as a literary work; she had no apparent strategy or conscious perspective from which to tell her story. She followed the conventions of autobiography as she subconsciously understood them. She recounted anecdotes from her childhood uncritically, preserving a mix of her own memories and the folklore of her family. A notable example is the story of her birth in the middle of a hurricane. Struggling to finish the book, Katharine took a shortcut, inserting the text of a series of radio broadcasts she'd written in 1941 about her encounters with celebrities while in London.[36] She did little editing to make them fit the narrative, adding to the anecdotal tone. According to one scholar, *Child of the Hurricane* is an 'altogether evasive account … with much detail omitted or glossed over, important information dissipated by family trivia and anecdotal pieces with little apparent significance'.[37] It is all of these things, yet it also reveals as much as it hides. It has the charm of a polite rebel looking back over her early life to recite her best dinner-party stories and settle several scores.

Katharine sent off the last chapters in the middle of 1962 and then, over the next year, agreed to a number of editorial suggestions, including an epilogue with a brief account of her marriage to Hugo. When Beatrice said she was happy with the manuscript, Katharine wrote, 'You know, I feel so much better because you like the *Child.*

The psychological effect seems to have been marvellous in relaxation of tension'.[38]

Child of the Hurricane was published in November 1963, a month before Katharine's eightieth birthday. Reviewers were grateful Katharine had recorded something of her life for posterity but most of them were underwhelmed. The *Sydney Morning Herald* reviewer wrote, 'Perhaps she has left it too late. If it only partly succeeds it is because the valuable passages in it are surrounded and diluted by less interesting chatter ... we might expect a livelier and more richly populated saga of soil and people'.[39] It had the misfortune of being published the same year as Hal Porter's highly praised and more artful autobiography, *The Watcher on the Cast-Iron Balcony*. Katharine wrote to Ric, in the third person, 'I suppose she does seem "sadly old fashioned", when you compare the KS biography with Hal Porter'.[40] She misunderstood the difference between her work and Porter's, thinking that she was being penalised by reviewers for a lack of sexual candour. She wrote to Catherine Duncan, 'It seemed to me that the intellectual development was more important than the sex aspects of that development: other recent autobiographies, Hal Porter's & Xavier Herbert's go into all the details of this, and it's a fashionable tendency these days'.[41]

Although the reviews were lukewarm, readers liked it. Angus and Robertson printed 2305 copies—560 of them for British distribution—and a year later they had just 59 copies left.[42] 'Strangely', Katharine wrote to Oksana Krugerskaya, 'I've had more letters from Australian readers who liked it, too, than I've had for any other of my books'.[43] Relatives and old acquaintances wrote to her in appreciation, including her family's maid, Jessie, dismissed in 1904 for having a lover in her bed, still alive at ninety and not disputing that detail but correcting Katharine's claim she was Irish.[44]

THE COMMUNIST WRITER Dorothy Hewett penned a letter to Katharine at 1.30 in the morning after she had just finished a review of *Child of the Hurricane*: 'I had tears in my eyes not really because of sadness but because of the exaltation of the human spirit that comes through the pages'.[45] The review was reverential. 'In this book she has transmitted the measure of her own heart, the rhythm of her own mind, so that Kattie the child, and Katharine the girl, became living presences. We enter the world of this delightful, tender, iron-willed girl, with her enormous ambitions to be a great writer.'[46]

Dorothy had first met Katharine in 1946 as an undergraduate when she came to interview her for the student newspaper the *Black Swan*. Dorothy revered Katharine not just for her politics but her independence and cultured life. 'I must have been the most utopian starry-eyed convert who ever took out a party card … I approached that interview with Katharine with awe and trepidation.'[47]

Returning to Perth after a decade interstate, Dorothy sometimes visited Katharine in the early 1960s with husband Merv Lilley and 'innumerable children', one of them named Katharine Susannah. Katharine looked forward to these visits as a rare chance to speak to a fellow writer whose opinions she valued.[48] By this time, although still a communist, Dorothy was no longer idealistic about the party. She remembers Katharine questioning her about what was happening over in Sydney at the party headquarters, and particularly what she knew about the expulsion of Helen Palmer. Katharine wanted to know Helen had been treated fairly, and Dorothy, to her later regret, reassured her she had.[49] Dorothy was emerging as a major voice in the next generation of Australian writers, a successor to Katharine, but the cracks in Dorothy's reverence for Katharine were beginning to appear.

JOAN WILLIAMS INTERVIEWED Katharine for an eightieth birthday tribute article in the September 1963 issue of the communist magazine, *Our Women*. Katharine was 'very much aware of a deadly enemy—time … a threat to her plans for work and yet more work'. Joan noted the changes the years had brought to Greenmount; once an isolated spot, now 'there is always in the background the dull roar of traffic thundering eastwards on the road to the Goldfields and beyond'.[50]

The article features the first appearance in print of 'red witch' as a moniker for Katharine. Joan wrote of Katharine's early years in Western Australia, 'She had many friends, especially among the workers, who loved and respected her, but there were others who pointed out her home as if a terrible red witch lived there'.[51] Decades later, in her eighties, Joan complained, 'this witch tag … is one of the myths that has been perpetuated' and she remembered:

> I saw the exact way it occurred, which is a bit different to what people think … My grandmother liked to go out for a Sunday drive. Once when we drove past Katharine's my grandmother said, as we passed her place—my grandma was very much into witchcraft and fortune telling & she said, 'A red witch lives there,' and I repeated this in an interview, and it has grown and grown … [52]

The irony is that it was Joan who devised the 'myth' with her ambiguous wording about the term's usage in the 1963 article. Having read the article, Dymphna Cusack spread it further, saying in a speech to the Sydney Realist Writers for Katharine's eightieth birthday in December 1963, 'her flower-embowered house was pointed out as the abode of a Red witch'.[53] Dorothy Hewett then cemented the name with her centenary tribute to Katharine in 1983 titled 'Happy Birthday, Brave Red Witch'.

In late November, Katharine was basking in the publication of *Child of the Hurricane* and preparing for her eightieth birthday, taking the bus into Perth to look for a new dress. It was the week John F Kennedy was shot dead. 'How appalling the assassination of Kennedy is! Naturally, one asks what forces were opposed to his policies of racial equality and friendship, or at least friendly relations, with the SU [Soviet Union].'[54] A week later, Robert Menzies' Coalition government won the federal election convincingly, increasing its majority over Labor.

Katharine turned eighty on Wednesday 4 December 1963 and friends held a cocktail party for her at the Savoy in Perth. A photograph shows her with brow-line glasses, a large flower pinned to her dress, bouquets on the table next to her. A friend named Bert Vickers is standing to give his speech, already on his third page. In Moscow, at a function held at the House of Friendship, Irene Golovnaya 'said that Katharine was a pioneer not only in Australian literature, but also for the Soviet people'; it was proclaimed that she had sold two million copies of her books in the Soviet Union.[55] In Dymphna Cusack's speech at the Sydney celebration she declared, 'Ridiculous to speak of 80 years where Katharine Susannah is concerned. She is timeless and ageless. A great woman and a great writer, who has become a legend in her own time'.[56]

38

Hardliner

Greenmount, 1964–1968

IN KATHARINE'S WEEKLY letter on 20 July 1964, she told Ric she hadn't been well and was in bed with a hot water bottle. But it was 'just the beastly BP [blood pressure] playing up' and she was sure she would be all right by the time he received the letter.[1] However, her friend John Gilchrist was concerned enough to write Ric a letter the same day saying she had collapsed during the week and had taken a 'very bad turn' since.[2] On 26 July, John picked Katharine up and brought her to his house. He made her a cup of tea at 4.30 the next morning and she held his hand, saying, 'Gil, I'm dying'.[3] A doctor visited, but it wasn't until evening that she was in hospital. She suffered a stroke which nearly killed her. 'I am haunted by the memory of a night of horror … I had lost control of my mental processes. They whirled turbulently in utter disorder—the spate of thought disconnected, and flying in all directions, without rhyme or reason.'[4]

Katharine's doctor, Alec Jolly, and John sent telegrams to Ric telling him to fly over as soon as he could. When Ric arrived at Midland Hospital, she was conscious but only able to speak a few words.[5] Joan Williams remembers Katharine's 'right hand lay paralysed on the white quilt, her voice dragged painfully from some far distance. She seemed too overcome with weariness of life to fight any longer'.[6] Joan was in the midst of editing a selection of Katharine's writings, *On Strenuous Wings,* for the East German publisher Seven Seas Books. She told Katharine there were questions from Germany but Katharine 'turned her face away' and said she was too tired to talk. 'Katharine, so dedicated, disciplined, too tired to talk about writing? We were indeed losing her, I thought, as I stroked her high white brow. Little did I guess the battle she would wage, the willpower that would bring her back from the edge of darkness.'[7]

Katharine spent two months in hospital, finally returning home at the end of September 1964. Her friend Amy Barrett was able to stay with her for a time. 'The sweet peace of home enfolding me again and Amy, like a fussy mother bird, looking after me.'[8]

In October, the communist writer Frank Hardy was in Perth and came to visit. Katharine wore a pink robe and her 'right hand was trembling and withered'. Seeing her workroom, he 'had a feeling about the great labour that had gone on there and felt ashamed of my own recent lack of creative output'. Back at the house, she stoked the fire and 'began to speak of the distant past, as old people will, wandering from subject to subject. I noticed that her voice now seemed to take on the mellow-sweetness I remembered from our first meeting in Melbourne twenty-five years before, educated but not mannered or affected'. When he said he had to leave, she offered him sherry, 'as if reluctant to let me go'. As he looked back, the 'dull light of late afternoon played tricks … she looked like a slim young girl instead of a frail old woman'. '"Blessings," she said, and it seemed a strange word for her to use. At the door, I turned again. She was still standing there, tears in her eyes … I stepped towards her … and kissed her … I hurried away. We each knew we would never meet again.' She had become the ailing old writer that George Meredith had been in her youth.[9]

Amy stayed until November when Joan Williams' mother, Marge Allen, took over. Marge didn't like Katharine's piano and brought over her own; they had to move the spare bed onto the verandah to fit it in.[10] At Christmas, Katharine didn't want to go anywhere so Marge missed her family celebration to be with her.[11] Katharine didn't approve of Marge's weekly round of golf—holding it and bridge to be the self-indulgent pastimes of the apolitical middle class—but otherwise loved having Marge. Marge confided in her daughter that the spartan lifestyle was difficult—the rundown cottage was hot in summer, cold in winter and lacking in modern conveniences.[12] Marge remained Katharine's housekeeper until March 1966, when she was killed in a car accident. 'I'll miss her terribly', Katharine wrote.[13] She was never to have a housekeeper as suited to her; none of the others lasted long and finding replacements became an ongoing problem. Joan Williams, despite her admiration for Katharine, said she was 'domineering and … involved in personal lives of house keeper/companions'.[14]

Katharine was practising writing with her right hand, but it was a great effort. Her handwriting had changed, unsteady and the letters larger. She had recovered well, but six months after the stroke, 'I still feel … a shattering blow has been struck at the resilience and creative energy I once had. Despite skilful treatment there is still a consciousness of depression, uncertainty of movement, and some brain disorder … Has it broken a vital fibre of my contact with life? I don't know. Time will show I suppose'.[15]

Oksana Krugerskaya visited Perth for a second time in February 1965, this time as translator for the novelist Daniil Granin. Too sick to travel into the city, Katharine was only able to see her once. It made her miserable, and she wrote to Oksana afterwards, 'Sometimes I think it would have been better to die, when everybody expected me to, a few months ago, than to be only half alive. Certainly I don't want to live if I cannot regain my creative energy and write again'. Oksana presented her with the gift of a ring. Katharine wore it every day and told Oksana, 'I … regard it as a symbol of mystic union with writers of the Soviet Union'.[16]

In April 1965 she began to write again—two hours every morning. The hardest part was writing without cigarettes. After more than fifty years, she'd been forced to give up smoking after her stroke and, becoming convinced of its link to cancer, implored Ric to quit too. 'Can't you convince yourself that every cigarette you take from the packet is suicidal?'[17] She developed a routine, attempting to write a chapter by hand each week. Her old friend Annette Aarons came on Tuesdays, answering her fan mail and business correspondence and typing whatever Katharine had written.[18] Against great odds, Katharine finished the first draft of *Subtle Flame* in the second week of November 1965.[19]

It was a long manuscript—170,000 words—and politically heavy; she'd been worried from the start about its prospects for publication.

She had complete confidence in the quality of the work itself—it was just, to her mind, that the times were against her. 'All my Welsh guile, literary expertise and passionate faith in the grail of world peace, went into this book to make the story interesting, contemporary, and convincing.'[20] After so many successes in literary competitions over the years, she thought she would have one more attempt. The British publishers MacGibbon & Kee and Panther Books were offering a £3000 prize for 'the best original prose work', calling for submissions which had 'outstanding imaginative qualities or make an important contribution to knowledge, or both'.[21] She posted her entry in March 1966.[22] A letter came in May to say she hadn't won, an anticlimactic finish to her incredible run of competition success.[23]

She sent *Subtle Flame* to Jonathan Cape Ltd next. Their response came back in July 1966, her second rejection in a row from her old publisher.[24] It was '"as much on my account as theirs", they say because they can't see the possibility of it being a best-seller evidently and I can't either, and they talk about "the ever-increasing costs of publishing"'.[25] She hadn't expected any differently, telling Beatrice Davis that she feared Cape 'will find it too Australian and too controversial' and added, possibly hoping to be contradicted, 'I'm not suggesting that it's suitable for A & R [Angus and Robertson]'.[26]

The Union of Soviet Writers wanted to arrange a Russian translation, but she felt it should be published in English first and so she submitted it to the left-wing Australasian Book Society, who had brought out *N'goola and Other Stories* in 1959. Les Greenfield from ABS wrote back in October 1966 to say they would publish it if she could cut the manuscript substantially to 120,000 words. The reader's report praised *Subtle Flame*, calling it 'a beautifully constructed novel, with plenty of good meat in it, and an intense survey of our contemporary way of life'. However, it 'could be effectively told in half its present length … for the entire novel is subordinated to her obsession with peace and disarmament, and … the manner in which she labours the subject almost destroys it'.[27] Katharine disagreed with the criticism but accepted the terms. She found it 'heart breaking' to make the cuts; midway she complained 'it has meant dropping some of my best arguments for disarmament—the facts & figures—so I don't know whether the book will now cut any ice'.[28] In December she informed

Ric *Subtle Flame* had 'gone to its fate' though 'I feel now, I'd just as soon have burnt the ms [manuscript]'.[29]

On 3 August 1967, Katharine appeared on television when she was interviewed on the ABC to mark the publication of *Subtle Flame.* The Australian literary community held such affection for octogenarian Katharine—Stalinist though she was—that launches for *Subtle Flame* were held in Sydney and Melbourne in her absence, as well as one in Perth with her present. The Perth launch was on the afternoon of Saturday 5 August at the Palace Hotel. The communist newspaper put attendance at 100; an ASIO report more generously estimated 110 or 120.[30] 'Started with chandeliers ablaze, in brilliant light—& halfway through there was a blackout', making it hard for Bert Vickers to read out the many messages of congratulations.[31] Two figures of the Perth cultural establishment gave speeches praising her work—Allan Edwards, professor of English, and Mollie Lukis, state archivist—offering Katharine a sense of ongoing recognition outside left-wing circles.[32]

She began her own speech by saying, 'Dear friends—I think of all Australians as my friends!' She had started writing *Subtle Flame* in the midst of the Korean War and now Australia was fighting in the Vietnam War. 'My argument remains the same, how to make the masses of kindly, inert people understand what is at stake for their home and children ... The best defence of Australia in my opinion is organisation for peace.' She finished by saying, 'This may be my last word to you in novel form, my dear Australian men and women. I owe so much to your encouragement and sympathy always'.[33]

The reviews were mainly negative. Cherry Grimm in *Australian Book Review* was scathing: 'The flimsy characterisation, the loose, scanning time-schedule, the superficial emotionalism, above all the continual infelicities of style: the vintage clichés and vintage slang, mark out *Subtle Flame* not as an unsuccessful novel or a minor work, but as a book quite monstrously bad: the final debacle in a notable career'.[34] But other reviewers found elements to appreciate—Nancy Keesing praised Katharine's attempt to capture youth culture and slang when older writers were avoiding it while Maurice Vitner wrote, 'Perhaps it does stumble a little at times, but this story ... has surprising energy and freshness'.[35] By the end of 1967, it had sold 3000 copies, with only 500 left.[36]

Katharine had two other books published in 1967. In May, Angus and Robertson brought out *Happiness,* a volume of short stories she selected from her three collections. She wrote a foreword giving a brief account of the origins of the stories and defending herself from her critics by quoting praise from Nettie Palmer, Hugh McCrae and others. 'All the stories were inspired by intimate sympathy with men and women in the comedy and tragedy of their lives.'[37]

In November, the children's story *Moggie and Her Circus Pony* was published by Cheshire with illustrations by the painter Elaine Haxton. It was part of a short-lived series pairing major Australian writers and artists. Decades earlier, Katharine had written the story for Wirth's Circus. 'Gladys [Wirth] suggested to write a story which cd be sold with the ice-creams and peanuts'; Katharine had been paid £50 for it but had never seen it. Copies had been sold at the circus with the title *The Story of Frisky, The Clever Circus Pony* under the pseudonym 'Val West'.[38]

Adding to the late flourishing in Katharine's literary stocks, a booklet on her in the 'Australian Writers and Their Work' series also appeared in 1967. It was written by Henrietta Drake-Brockman, Katharine's old Perth literary friend from across the political divide. When Henrietta first came to talk to Katharine about it, she joked that it might 'break a life-long friendship' but Henrietta's assessment of Katharine's work was generous and appreciative in putting her novels in their literary and biographical context.[39] Henrietta claimed Katharine as 'fundamentally … an artist of pagan sensibility', summing up her achievement—most apparent in her novels of the late 1920s—as 'the sensuous awareness of people and places, of delight and agony, of action and skill'.[40]

NETTIE PALMER HAD a stroke in May 1964—two months before Katharine—and was moved to a nursing home.[41] She died in her sleep on 19 October 1964. It had been years since Katharine had seen Nettie in person. Katharine happened to write to her days before Vance's sudden death in 1959, saying, 'We've come such a long way on our road to-gether, Nettie dear—and how fortunate we've been to win through after all'.[42] In the last surviving letter from Katharine in January 1964, she wrote, 'I think of you so often & wish we cd meet to yarn about books and the writing fraternity. But here I sit on my hill-top, with few people to talk to whose opinions I value'. She sent her love to Nettie and her daughters and finished with, 'All the best, always, dear Nettie, yours, Katharine Susannah'.[43]

Hilda had been gone a decade and the other of the group of four friends from school days, Christian Jollie Smith, had died in January 1963. Katharine wrote to Ric of Christian, 'Though we didn't see each other often, latterly, there was a bond of deep affection between us'.[44] Katharine, the heavy smoker who had been chronically ill for decades, had outlived her three peers.

THE ONLY CLOSE friend from Katharine's Melbourne years to outlive her was Guido Baracchi. He wrote a long letter to her in April 1965 saying that he'd been told a few years earlier that she'd died from a heart attack, and was attending a tribute to Nettie Palmer when he was shocked to hear a message from Katharine read out.[45] Katharine told Ric that in Guido's letter 'he says: "I love you and have always loved you"—which didn't prevent him from having several wives'.[46]

Katharine was a little cool in her reply to Guido:

> It was a surprise to hear from you. I feel grateful to you always for having introduced me to Marxism, & an understanding of Communist principles. My life has been illuminated by them … It seems that you have been more susceptible to changes in the political atmosphere. But I'm glad to know you take part in marches and demonstrations for peace & the cessation of USA aggression in Vietnam.[47]

As their correspondence continued Katharine's tone warmed. They talked of politics, the old days, and their children and grandchildren. She complimented his poetry; he loved *Subtle Flame,* sending her a telegram, 'What a wonderful picture beauty lives by intelligence humour nobility strength of character without it my cup would have been less full from the heart thank you.'[48]

A SIGNIFICANT NEW friendship in Katharine's eighties was an intergenerational one with an eccentric teenager named David Helfgott. He was a talented pianist and a number of funds were set up to pay for him to study overseas; according to the scholar Cath Ellis, one of these was organised by the Communist Party 'with whom Helfgott's father, Peter, was informally connected. The young Helfgott played at a Communist Party gathering and it was then that he met Katharine'.[49] In November 1963, Katharine invited them to visit her:

> The boy, sixteen, already a brilliant pianist—& his father, a spare, hard-working little man—desperately anxious to give his son a chance to be world famous. David, still a shy, rather callow youth, but if he gets the chance for overseas study, will surely become world famous. He is heard sometimes, on the ABC, and is as mature, as far as his music is concerned, as if he were years older. I liked them both so much.[50]

When Katharine's granddaughter Karen was staying in January 1966, Katharine invited David to dinner, hoping to matchmake as she considered him 'a cut above the youths she has been meeting, intellectually'. 'He played the whole evening for Karen—though I think, did not disturb her allegiance to Tom.'[51]

David began visiting Katharine for dinner on Friday nights. In March 1966 she wrote that he 'played to me for hours. It is a curious attraction for 18 & 80. He is a devout admirer of the writings of KSP & likes to discuss ideas & literature with me, and I am in awe of his brilliant quality as a pianist—& his dedication to music & its interpretation'.[52] After Marge's death in March, her superior piano was still at Katharine's and it was the one David would play on; Katharine asked that Marge's family leave it with her until David departed to study music in London in the middle of the year.[53]

In a letter David sent after he moved to London he wrote that '*The Roaring Nineties* is my "bible" if you know what I mean! I only have to read a bit of it—and immediately *Australia* comes to life—all the hard dry heat—and endless bush and hot desert. Katharine you're the *greatest* genius Australia has ever produced—absolutely!'[54]

Thirty years later—after David's mental breakdown, recovery, and fresh renown as a pianist—the unlikely friendship between David and Katharine was movingly depicted in the Academy Award–winning film about his life, *Shine* (1996). As is often the case in biopics, the actor Googie Withers doesn't resemble Katharine; her character is also much softer than the real Katharine. The casting may not have pleased Katharine, who saw Withers perform in July 1956 when she watched a production of Terence Rattigan's play *The Deep Blue Sea* (1952) with Rose and Les Atkinson. In a letter to Ric, Katharine wrote, 'Didn't like Googie Withers. She was so emotionally over-wrought all the time & her performance seemed to me stagey. Others don't think so. Les & Rose delighted with her'.[55]

KATHARINE HAD AN unhappy friendship with the writer Bert Vickers. He was twenty years younger than her, and they had become close through their work together at the Peace Council. According to the *Australian Dictionary of Biography,* 'He was tall and slim, unpretentious, simple and straightforward, and addicted to his pipe'.[56] In some ways he seemed Katharine's disciple, organising her eightieth birthday celebrations and the *Subtle Flame* book launch, and chauffeuring her around. But he frequently argued with her about politics. 'He's so used to dominating poor Mim [his wife], that he thinks he can dominate me in an argument. And then gets annoyed when I say: "But you're so stupid Bert."'[57] One Sunday afternoon in 1967 Katharine wrote to Ric that she was glad Bert wasn't visiting; but then later he did and they argued about 'freedom'. 'I said there is freedom within the socialist system to criticise administration measures & persons—but not freedom to attack the basis of the socialist system'.[58] After he seemed pleased by a negative review of *Subtle Flame,* Katharine wrote that he had a 'complex that delights in anything that takes me down a peg'. His wife died in May 1967, and Katharine had started cooking him dinner on his Sunday visits; he would drink all her Soviet vodka while still 'never miss[ing] an opportunity to criticise the SU'.[59]

Katharine used to talk of her 'boyfriends', of whom Bert was one. In the late 1960s, these relationships seem to have been platonic; she wrote in May 1968 that her housekeeper 'looks on with amazement, because all my boyfriends are married men, & she doesn't understand their affection for me, & the fact that the wives concerned don't object & that I remain on good terms with the wives'.[60] John Gilchrist—'Gil'—was another boyfriend and he worshipped Katharine with none of the ambivalence of Bert. Gil's daughter remembers, 'Dad was always up there, he used to go up there regularly and look after the house and do all the repairs ... There was tremendous affection between them ... She saw him as the symbol of what she thought the working class hero should be'.[61] In his daughter's memory, Katharine was right and his devotion didn't worry his wife, Roma.

In the last year of Katharine's life, Gil took the only surviving video footage of Katharine. The ten-minute colour video captures her doing ordinary things at her home in Greenmount—writing at her desk, standing outside her writing cabin, posing in front of a blooming wattle bush in her garden, drinking tea on her verandah with friends. All through it she is talking, talking, talking, but her words are lost; there is no sound. Near the end is a scene which belongs at the beginning: Katharine at the driveway, opening the gate as if to invite us in. It cuts to a scene of someone holding open a copy of *Subtle Flame,* and then, shockingly, a procession is following a hearse through the gates of Karakatta Cemetery. Just as she seems so alive, she's snatched away again.

ON THE INTERNET, the most frequently appearing quote attributed to Katharine isn't something she wrote but something Dorothy Hewett claims Katharine once told her: 'Don't sacrifice your life to work and ideals. The most important things in life are human relations. I found out too late'.[62] Years after the event, Dorothy probably wouldn't have been able to remember the precise words Katharine had used and her memory may have been shaped by what she *wanted* to hear while in the process of leaving the Communist Party. But at the end of her life, Katharine was reflecting anew on what mattered. Something she wrote in a letter to Ric in 1962 is similar to Dorothy's quote, but with more ambivalence:

> But all the time my chief happiness is that you are happy in your life with Dodie and the children. When I weigh up the values that seems the most important—to have had a taste of personal happiness with people we love. Fame, for what it's worth, doesn't give it. I suppose it means something to have achieved what you have set out to do,

> but, my own, what there is of it, seems flat & stale now. Service of the great ideals remains something wh cannot be ignored. There'd be no self-respect, if it were; but sometimes, wonder whether I've been stupidly idealistic—for such a confirmed materialist. Though the materialism of Marxism does not mean a rejection of the great ideals, rather an intensification of service to them.[63]

Katharine hadn't wavered in her communism, but in small ways she put relationships ahead of her beliefs, including a plea to Dorothy when they disagreed sharply on a political matter that it shouldn't mean the end of their friendship. It did, however; 'I didn't go to see her', Dorothy remembers, 'I was afraid to discuss controversial matters with her … I didn't want to be the cause of her death'.[64]

The issue they fell out over was the trial of two Soviet writers in 1966. Andrei Sinyavsky and Yuli Daniel were accused of publishing anti-Soviet material, their satires of the Soviet Union having been smuggled out and published under pseudonyms in the West. They were convicted and sentenced to years in prison with hard labour. To Katharine's distress, the Communist Party of Australia made its first public criticism of the Soviet Union over the incident, the general secretary Laurie Aarons labelling the arrests and jailings 'unnecessary and wrong'.[65] The CPA was beginning to split from the Soviet Union, and it would break the hearts of Katharine and the other remnant of loyal Stalinists. She had read Sinyavsky's offending novel, *The Makepeace Experiment*, and wrote to Oksana: 'Who could doubt … the whole purpose of Sinyavsky was to outrage … the whole concept of socialism? I was furious when I read it, and get furiouser and furiouser when I think of the fools who consider Soviet writers should be free to foul their own nest'.

Like many on the left, Dorothy supported the dissident writers and launched a petition to send to the Soviet president calling for clemency. 'I think the petition you sent me is short-sighted and ill-advised', Katharine told her, calling it 'sheer effrontery' to presume to judge the Supreme Court of the Soviet Union for their 'safeguarding' of communism from 'slander'.[66]

For Dorothy, Katharine embodied the rigid Communist Party she herself finally left in 1968. When Katharine died in 1969, Dorothy wrote that brutal obituary for *Overland* called 'Excess of Love: The

Irreconcilable in Katharine Susannah Prichard'. It was polar opposite to the tribute in her 1963 review of *Child of the Hurricane.* Dorothy wrote that it was 'as if, after the suicide of her husband … she willed her own creative death … The sensuousness of her imagery dries up and her style becomes arid and blind'.[67] Katharine 'lived in a dream world up there on the range above the sprawling, changing skyline of Perth, her solitariness partly due to her failing health, partly to her perverse, almost nun-like withdrawal. She moved amidst a narrowing circle of communist friends, who would not argue with her but kept her insulated from reality'.[68]

Yet this wasn't the end of Dorothy's wrestling with the legacy of Katharine. When Ric Throssell interviewed Dorothy in 1972 as part of the research for his biography of Katharine, she told him he overestimated the importance of her obituary and it was 'just how I felt at the time'.[69] In 1983, on the centenary of Katharine's birth, Dorothy wrote that tribute to Katharine which cemented the 'red witch' moniker; its emphasis is different to her earlier piece and it is more generous about Katharine's achievements. '"A year after my death I will be forgotten," she once told me. She was wrong. She was one of a band of Australian women writers who wrote against fearful odds and she is part of the fabric of literature in this country now.'[70]

KATHARINE FELT OUT of step with the times—unfashionable and unappreciated. 'I suppose the young think they're going with the tide these days, disregarding all things old. I've come to the conclusion it's almost a crime to be old.'[71] Although she finally saw the back of Robert Menzies when he retired in January 1966, the Liberal–Country coalition remained in power under the new prime minister Harold Holt. They won an increased majority at the election on 26 November 1966. Katharine had many visitors the next day coming to commiserate with her. She wrote to Ric:

> The Australia I know & loved is passing away—if it hasn't already passed … The struggle for adult suffrage, trade union organization democratic rights—all seem to have been forgotten by the present generation of voters who vote for the conscription of youth & seem

> satisfied for a greater number of Australian young men to be the victims of this cruel war in Vietnam. Sorry darl, I can't think of anything but the shame & disappointment I feel at the moment.[72]

She wasn't just alienated from the conservative-voting public; the left was changing too. Another crisis point for the Communist Party of Australia came in August 1968 when Soviet tanks rolled into Czechoslovakia, crushing the Prague Spring which had seen the communist state giving its people greater freedom. In Perth, a number of party members held a meeting to debate the situation. Katharine wrote:

> I haven't been invited, but couldn't go in any case. Am out of favour with the reformist group in Party affairs. Am regarded as a 'hard-liner'. If that means abide by the principles of Marxism-Leninism, of course I do. And have no patience with this 'open door' policy for the sabotage of socialism as established in Czechoslovakia & the USSR. All this talk of freedom leaves me cold. Freedom for what? … the situation in the Party, at present, is so split by divergences of opinion that I cd not recommend any young person to join it. Although the basic principles are as they always have been the basis for a sound reorganisation of society.[73]

Momentously, the Communist Party of Australia issued a statement condemning the Soviet Union's actions. Katharine sent a letter to the party newspaper, *Tribune*, defending the Soviet Union. She wrote that although it 'grieves' her to disagree with the CPA leadership, 'My confidence remains unshaken that the people of the Soviet Union, and their government, will always defend the socialist system, which they have suffered so much to establish and raise to the great power it has become in the world today'.[74] Katharine's loyalty to the Soviet Union was greater than her loyalty to the CPA and she considered herself an honorary Soviet, even encouraging the Russian form of her name: 'I like it that you should call me Katya', she had told Mikhail Apletin, 'Ric sometimes does'.[75]

The situation festered. ASIO reported that Katharine 'regretted that … $10 was all she intended to contribute [to the party appeal] because she did not agree with the present line'; six members had resigned from the state branch and up to thirty members—15 per cent—supported the Soviet actions and were in disagreement with the party.[76]

KATHARINE WAS NOT able to travel much—she was frail, she had no car, and the buses from Greenmount were infrequent. Instead, she had a lot of visitors, invited and uninvited, some communists, some literary. 'Katharine always turned on the sherry, olives and barbeque shape biscuits', one visitor remembers.[77] She loved to have visitors from the Soviet Union; they revered her and she revered their country. Groups of sailors, tourists and performers would come in pilgrimage with gifts and she would serve refreshments. 'As my doctor said, "One day you are at death's door, & the next when the Ruskies come to town, you have a new lease of life."'[78]

'I find pleasure in the simple things these days', she wrote in April 1967. 'A vase I've just arranged as a poem to autumn with yellow leaves [and] rose berries … Music too, though that's not simple. Sometimes wonderful recitals come over my little transistor—& Clem has lent me his record player.'[79] She took delight in her garden, writing in the spring of 1968 of 'a blaze of colours with bougainvillea growing as high as the pine tree & the pink honeysuckle in masses through the wattle tree near the gate, the Xmas lilies along the path in all their glory. The cerise pelargonium tangling with mauve creeping lantana, nasturtium rioting every[where] … '.[80] She made friends with two magpies she called Caruso and Greedy, feeding them each day when they warbled at her door, and stopping to listen to their 'repertoire'.

IN AUGUST 1968, Katharine was working on an essay commissioned by GA Wilkes for *Southerly* journal, the third in the series 'Australian writers in profile'. She wrote to her granddaughter Karen, 'It's been difficult to talk chiefly about me & my work, preoccupations & intentions. And the academic critics have loved sniping at me. However, let them do their darndest, I have no regrets about writing the way I have—& clearing the way for scientific socialism in Australia'.[81] Even as the weakened CPA broke with the Soviet Union, Katharine was not admitting defeat; a socialist Australia was inevitable sometime in the future.

It was appropriate for *Southerly*, at the centre of Australian literature, to offer the distinguished writer an opportunity to give a testimony at the end of a long life. She wrote to Ric, 'Quite pleased to say my piece in *Southerly*—wh has always been rather supercilious about your KS'.[82] 'Say' her 'piece' she did; the essay is Katharine's defiant last stand.

Calling it 'Some Perceptions and Aspirations', she pushed back against the idea that Australian literature had only truly begun with the recent work of Patrick White and Randolph Stow. Long before the advent of these writers, her generation—and she names Vance and Nettie, Louis and Hilda, Hugh McCrae, and Miles Franklin as well as several others—had 'loved Australia and sought to make others care for the glorious potentialities of the country and people'. She argued that the 'aesthetic and humane philosophy which animated a past decade of writers and poets should not be disregarded'.[83]

In her own work, she wrote, 'I have only hoped to communicate … perception of the beauty and harsh realities of this land: to tell about the joys and sorrows, courage and humour, of men and women I've met in my wanderings through the country districts and cities of Australia'.[84] The sentence sums up well both her aspiration and her achievement, even though it leaves out her attempt to not just describe Australia but transform it politically.

In telling something of the genesis of her works, she also defended them against criticisms—her English was not slipshod; her goldfields dialogue was authentic; *Intimate Strangers* had nothing to do with Sigmund Freud or DH Lawrence. Like most writers, she was deeply sensitive about her work. Only at the end of the essay did she identify a weakness: 'Perhaps I have not made readers dream and laugh enough. The wit and gaiety I admire so much in other writers, I have lacked'.[85]

The issue of *Southerly* containing her essay came out in February 1969. It was her last piece of writing published in Australia in her lifetime, seventy years after her first story appeared in the *Sun* newspaper in 1899.

KATHARINE'S GRANDDAUGHTER KAREN, now twenty-one, flew over to stay just after Katharine's eighty-fifth birthday in December 1968. Their relationship was close, but it wasn't easy: 'I realise something of the same ardent, headlong temperament in both of us', Katharine wrote to her once, 'that's why, I suppose, I'm so anxious about you'.[86] Katharine was unexpectedly old-fashioned about Karen. She once objected to Karen coming to visit by sea because she was concerned about men flirting with her; another time she described her 'shock to see you looking like the imbecilic specimens of brainless girls that the fashion magazines for teenagers want you to become … lank hair, blue eyelids & going about barefoot!'[87] This visit was happier, and Katharine wrote to Ric, 'what a darling sweet herself is: brings me early morning tea & has been acting as my assistant secretary, typing innumerable letters'.[88]

Katharine celebrated her last Christmas with Karen and great-nephew Patten, Beatrice's grandson, who was temporarily living in Perth. It was a hot day, '101 in the shade'—38 degrees Celsius. Katharine cooked roast duckling and they ate plum pudding set alight with brandy. Ric had sent her a recording of Beethoven's piano sonatas and she played it on the verandah. 'It was heavenly hearing it all under the vines, on such a hot still night, after the sunset had faded behind the dark trees.'[89]

In a letter to Ric a few days later, Katharine wrote, 'So the year ends! And what [will] the next bring to us all?'[90]

IN THE NEW year, Karen's boyfriend, Tony, arrived. In the letters to Ric which followed, Katharine kept returning to the subject of Tony and what she called 'the honeymoon'; he wasn't responsible, he didn't share Karen's interests in art, literature and music. She didn't tell Karen though, and Karen had no idea Katharine didn't approve of him.

'I ache over her', Katharine wrote to Ric. 'What life will do to her—and there's nothing we can do to ease the pains & tribulations when they come.'[91] With her own time running out, Katharine was aware that she wouldn't get to see how the lives of her loved ones would turn out, but she'd been through enough to anticipate some of the pain they were certain to go through.

A few weeks later Karen and Tony left on the train to return to Canberra. 'The house has been so quiet—I feel lonesome without that chirpy little song in the morning. Only the rats & my Caruso to talk to.'[92]

39

'My Joy Will Be Complete'

Greenmount, 1969

IN FEBRUARY 1969 Katharine learned Ric would be visiting in March and it became a new focal point for her. She was going to make fig jam. It would be a 'heavenly month'.[1] The next week she had a bad fall in the garden, by the gate, as she was trying to move a hose. Her face was bruised yellow and purple. She told Ric she only hoped she would be looking better by the time he arrived. To reassure him, she listed the many friends who were helping her as she lay in bed recovering. 'You're still the object of my affection', John Gilchrist told her.[2]

Her friends were telling her she needed another housekeeper but she was reluctant; it would be expensive and none of them had lasted long since Marge. Eventually, she found a 'Mrs W', whom she regarded a 'wonder'. She let Mrs W and her husband set up their campervan in the paddock on the condition they didn't bring their cat, out of concern for the safety of the magpies, Caruso and Greedy. When the cat appeared, Katharine was angry and worried for the magpies but decided to say nothing.[3]

In March, she wrote to Ric, 'my joyous thought all the time has been that you'll soon be here … And, I suppose, your next letter will tell me wh plane I must watch the sky for … my joy will be complete just to see you, & feel you'.[4] She went into the shops at Midland and bought a new dress to 'gladden' Ric's eyes; it was the first one she'd bought in five years.

There was a break in Katharine's letters to Ric while he was staying and the details of his visit are lost. It was the last time they would see each other, and although Katharine did not know that for sure, she wrote, 'I did feel as if the light had gone out of my world when your plane passed over—though I didn't see it—waited, scanning the sky, for half an hour, then decided there was so much cloud, I'd probably missed seeing it'.[5]

Sometimes Katharine's love for Ric was almost worshipful, the love of a mother who lost her husband to suicide and whose only child has lived on the other side of the country for twenty-five years. 'As my great day approaches—the day on which you arrived—how can I say all that it means to me?', she wrote before his birthday on 10 May.

> My feeling is one of overwhelming gratitude that life has given you to me—and I don't know who to thank except Daddy. And he always said: 'You chose me to be sire for your son' … No wonder you are such a wonderful person—the best of your father & mother went to making you and rearing you—and you, I feel since, were not infected by any of our qualities wh were not as admirable.[6]

She didn't want to be alone on the day and, as had become her custom, she invited friends to dinner to toast Ric in his absence.

Although she was staunchly atheistic her ceremonies and superstitions had a religious quality. She picked flowers each day and placed them by the photographs of her family as an act of communion with them. 'I've just picked some roses to say good morning to you, darl—actually I've been able to have some fresh flowers for you every day through the hot weather—only once had to fall back on lantana, but it was a pretty little mauve one!'[7]

She was still thinking about her writing, even contemplating learning about television screenplays so she could adapt her story, 'Painted Finches' (1939). However, the only pieces she finished in 1969 were articles commissioned to honour the centenary of Lenin's birth the next year—as many as three for Soviet publications and one for a pamphlet, *Lenin Through Australian Eyes*. Faithful to the end, she wrote, 'Marx and Engels revealed the principles for organisation of socialism … Lenin and the Bolshevik Communist Party recognised the validity of these principles … They changed the dream to a reality, and the Union of Soviet Socialist Republics was founded on the basis of scientific socialism'.[8]

She kept up with her own literary business, negotiating paperback editions, royalties and translations. But she put more energy into promoting the work of her son and her father. When Ric's play *The Day Before Tomorrow* was published she ordered multiple copies and sent them to people of influence she knew. After an article celebrating the centenary of the *Fiji Times* didn't adequately recognise her father's role as an early editor, she decided she must try again to have some of his stories about the Pacific republished in book form. In late September, five days before she died, she wrote asking Beatrice Davis at Angus and Robertson whether they would consider a collection of his stories or whether she had 'better try another firm in fulfillment of my filial duty'.[9]

In June she sent a message of support for the World Peace Assembly and particularly its work on disarmament, urging that they pass a motion opposing germ warfare. In July, she wrote to Karen, 'The struggle against war—& the system wh thrives on it—won't be over for many years but it's the most worthwhile one to work for, surely'.[10] But while supporting the protests against the Vietnam War, she thought that Karen shouldn't get involved until her university exams were finished.

KATHARINE WAS SORTING papers, the endless task which had occupied her for decades. She had told an interviewer in 1967, 'I do not want anything of mine to be published after I am dead that I have not approved of … I do not like to be seen in *dishabille* even in manuscript. I never even liked my husband to see me that way, brushing my teeth and so on'.[11] She wasn't sure what to keep and what to burn and she was taking advice from others in the winter of 1969. 'When Annette [Aarons] was here, on Saturday she urged me to burn a box of letters from you. But when I saw a packet labelled "Ric's letters from NG [New Guinea]"

I cdn't agree.'[12] Katharine wrote about it to her pen-friend, Catherine Duncan in late June or July:

> I'm still on deck—and much as usual, not doing much writing, just enough to justify existence, but tidying and sorting mss like mad—Hate to think of leaving letters & unfinished screeds for all & sundry to read! It's a terrible wrench having to commit some to the flames, though ... I've just discovered the most innocuous letters of mine have been sold to the National Library—& students have been seeking permission 'to have access to them'. So I must sort and burn while there's time.[13]

Catherine was alarmed and wrote back:

> I can understand that you should want to put a time limit on giving students access to personal papers, but in fifty years, dearest Kattie, the KSP you are now will have become someone else—she will have escaped you. It's already astonishing to read letters written ten or twenty years ago. I wrote that? I felt that? Another life, another person. Perhaps in the end it's better to surrender the truth to posterity rather than allow one's self to be deformed by supposition. Anyway I do beg you not to be too ruthless. I cannot believe that beauty in writing can ever belong entirely to one person, or where would be our Heloise and Abelard?[14]

Catherine perceived that future generations would be more likely to remember fairly and truthfully with more evidence available. Her plea may have saved some of Katharine's surviving letters from the fire. 'Suppose you're right about letters', Katharine replied nine days before she died, 'but never think mine are worth anything'.[15]

Before Katharine died she had put aside the letters she wanted preserved.[16] The day after her death, Ric burnt all her unpublished manuscripts. 'There were notes, novels, unfinished short stories and plays—I don't know how many.'[17] The bonfire was a great loss to scholarship and to history, but there are good reasons to think there are no lost masterpieces. Her major research trips are accounted for—she published books from all of them. She didn't work in secret—she usually told her friends about her works in progress, and there are no references to full-length works which had progressed past the stage of notes. She also had such confidence in her work that it's likely she would have tried to publish anything which was fully drafted.

KATHARINE LIVED LONG enough to see the wattle bush bloom in 'all her glory' with 'masses of golden down' in July as the Americans landed on the moon; she lived long enough to feel the winter lift and spring arrive. Mrs W departed—circumstances unknown—and Katharine's loyal friend, Amy Barrett, moved in to look after her. Ric would be visiting again in October, a quick business trip. 'Have just heard a chestnut-breasted whistler … he warbles gloriously in [the] gum tree at the end of the verandah—I've been asking [him] to come & sing to you darl! Though you'll hardly have any sunny hours with me. And October [is] usually a glorious month.'[18]

IN SEPTEMBER, BILL and Dorothy Irwin took Katharine down the road to meet the playwright John Joseph Jones at his ambitious Parkerville Amphitheatre, which was nearing completion. Jones remembers 'the bushland surrounding the playing areas was bright with her beloved wildflowers'. The amphitheatre had three stages and a central pool, and 'as we stood there together on the main stage in the bowl of the amphitheatre Katharine turned and said with some emotion, "I want you to put *Brumby* on here. It's never been done and this is where it should be done"'.[19] It was more than forty years since she'd written *Brumby Innes* and she was still thinking of it, imagining it coming to life. Perhaps she hoped to live long enough to see it. Or perhaps she took comfort in the idea of a posthumous life for her work.

KATHARINE'S DISAGREEMENTS WITH the Communist Party of Australia were intensifying. After hearing that Australian representatives at an international communist meeting in Moscow had publicly criticised the Soviet invasion of Czechoslovakia, she wrote to Oksana, 'I feel sure the next National Congress will see some changes in the leadership. The tendency has been to increase membership by placating middle-class "intellectuals"—among writers chiefly—so I'm very unpopular with many who used to be my friends'.[20] On 22 September 1969, she decided to make her outrage public, writing a letter to *Tribune* stating, 'I am no longer proud and happy to say I am a member of the Communist Party of Australia … I have not deserted the principles of Marxism-Leninism. Some leaders of the National Committee appear to have done so'.[21] The editors wrote back requesting that she cut her letter to fit the limit of 300 words but by the time it arrived she was dead. This disagreement with the party at the end of her life caused her great anguish but she lived in hope it would be resolved by changing leaders at the next congress. Instead, only greater pain awaited her as the anti-Soviet leadership consolidated its grip and the party split. Three days before she died, she renewed her party membership, the breach not yet complete and her criticism of the party unpublished.[22]

TWO REPRESENTATIVES OF the Soviet Women's Committee, Zoya Zarubina and Olga Chechetkina, were visiting Perth as guests of the Union of Australian Women. They stayed with Katharine's friends, John and Roma Gilchrist, and Katharine invited them for morning tea on Friday 26 September. John photographed a smiling Katharine with her arm around Zoya, whom she hadn't met before, their heads touching. It's the last known picture of Katharine. They stand on the verandah at the front of the house, the same one where Katharine danced the Charleston with Hugo in 1927. The stone wall in the background is cracked and the bare chicken wire covering the eaves of the verandah hangs down.

Zoya was a language teacher and sports administrator. As a young woman during World War II, she'd been a KGB translator for Joseph Stalin when he met with American president Franklin Roosevelt. Katharine would probably have been thrilled to learn of this connection to Stalin; it might explain her arm around Zoya. Zoya was less likely to have discussed her role translating stolen plans for the atomic bomb or her dismissal from the KGB in 1951 when Stalin sent her stepfather, a high-ranking KGB officer, to prison. Perhaps fittingly, the ostensibly benign final image of Katharine is coloured with Soviet intrigue.[23]

BACK IN 1954 when Miles Franklin died, Katharine wrote to Ric:

> When I die I'll have a sense of the fullness of my life: that I've had so much in love and work. To have had the best that life could give in your father and you, my darling. In my work, too. To be able to write what I wanted to, and to have used my energy and intellect for the things I believed in. That's why, I suppose, Death has no fears for me. To have lived to the fulfilment of the individual self means that the logical end can be looked forward to quite serenely.[24]

On the day of Katharine's own death, Thursday 2 October 1969, she wrote a letter to her old friend, Doon Stone. Doon had been contemplating moving back west to live near Katharine, but she had written to say she'd decided instead to move to Tuross Head on the south coast of New South Wales. Katharine wished her the best but confessed she was 'green-eyed' about it; 'we both know how to overcome disappointments', she wrote, a little tartly. 'Ric's due tonight on the late plane from Canberra—and I'm aching to see him. Such a strange, lonely life it is, these days.'[25]

For years Katharine had been limiting what she did and avoiding excitement to keep her blood pressure down—but Ric's arrival meant so much to her. She and Amy spent the day preparing the house; his plane was not landing until 11.10 p.m. 'They had made his favourite dish, goulash, festooned the house with flowers and had everything in readiness.'[26] Katharine was tired and said she would welcome Ric in her dressing gown and pyjamas, heading to bed at six o'clock. At 10.15, she was awake and restless, so Amy made her a cup of tea. When Amy brought the tea in, she found Katharine 'breathing heavily' with her face to the wall. She said she was hot and threw off her blankets. While Amy was out of the room, Katharine had a stroke. Amy came back in to hear her stutter, 'Jolly', her doctor's name. Alec Jolly came straight over and gave her an injection to calm her. The way Amy remembers it, Katharine died as the noise of Ric's plane roared overhead on its descent.[27] Her last moments were lived in anticipation of a reunion with her beloved son, trying to hold on just a little longer to see him.

HER FUNERAL WAS held two days later, on Saturday, at Karakatta Cemetery. There were 130 mourners, among them communists, writers, friends, and a wharfie in stained overalls. 'The coffin, draped in a red flag, was decorated with one simple bunch of West Australian wildflowers.'[28] A brief service was held in the crematorium. Joan Williams' husband, Vic, recited a poem he'd written in Katharine's honour. A party member sang the ballad, 'Beloved Comrade', the lyrics promising the fight would continue until it was won.

Katharine requested 'a cremation, the ashes to be scattered over the top of Greenmount … overlooking the lovely prospect and in view of the house where the happiest years of my life have been spent'.[29] Ric carried the cannister of her ashes to the spot where Hugo had always talked of building his dream house and eventually 'wrenched off the lid of the tin and scattered the ash on the dry grass'.[30]

Afterword

Greenmount, 2019

On the night of Wednesday 2 October 2019, the fiftieth anniversary of Katharine's death, I drive to Katharine's Place, home of the KSP Writers' Centre since 1985. The Great Eastern Highway is a constant roar, four lanes of cars and trucks chugging up or hurtling down the Greenmount Hill. I park down the side in what was Katharine's orchard. Her workroom still stands, but its view of the distant city could disappear soon when the neighbours finish building.

Katharine's rundown cottage was at risk of demolition when Ric sold it after her death. I recently met Bronwyn Lewis, who lived in it as a teenager in the 1970s and returned to scatter the ashes of her mother, Patricia, in the garden. It was Patricia who decided to save the cottage, repairing and renovating it, naming it 'Megalong', and opening it to the public as an art gallery.

Katharine's Place is full tonight. As I come through the outside kitchen into the sitting room, an ageing, excited David Helfgott—whom I have never met—kisses me on the cheek like we are old friends before moving off to greet someone else.

Tonight, *Potchnagoola,* a play written by David's sister Louise Helfgott, is staged in the extension, the enclosed north verandah. The title, a combination of Katharine's short story collections, is the name David used to give his time with Katharine. The backdrop to the set is a huge Soviet flag. It's eerie watching two actors play the old Katharine and the young David on this anniversary, like a veneration or a seance.

I feel a collapse of time, a haunting. At the end of the play, the real David plays Katharine's original piano, which found its way back to the Centre in the 1980s. At quarter past ten, I imagine Katharine breathing heavily in her bedroom, beginning her final descent into death. Everyone is talking; we don't stop.

ON SATURDAY, THERE'S a day-long commemoration at the centre. I stand in front of the red flag and announce with my fellow judge the winners of a Katharine Susannah Prichard-themed literary competition. The entries are a tapestry of the mythology around Katharine, Hugo and their house. In judging them, I had to let go of the overriding concern with historical accuracy I bring to my own work. In my biography I am stripping back mythology but with this different hat on I am encouraging it to grow.

One story wrestles with the complicated legacy of *Coonardoo* as an Asian-Australian woman working as a food-delivery driver meets with the ghost of Katharine and is threatened by Sam Geary, come to life from the pages of *Coonardoo* in all his sexism and racism.[1] In another, a character named Kath who suffers debilitating migraines is determined to plant a vegetable garden at Katharine's Place as an act of hope in the midst of a near-future crisis caused by climate change.[2] In some of the non-fiction pieces, memoirists look to Katharine as a secular saint, her life an inspiration and a consolation. Twenty-first century Katharines, personal Katharines, comedic Katharines, they're all there in the competition, along with a Hugo more mythic than ever in the glow of Anzac veneration.[3]

Karen Throssell has flown over from Melbourne for the event, and launches an anthology of the best competition entries called *Kaleidoscope: The Colours of Katharine.* Her speech is warm and generous while still touching on her strong conviction that Katharine's literary legacy must never be stripped of its politics. She speaks of having to overcome the feelings of 'exposure and intrusion that comes from having members of your family as public property', and eventually seeing the positive aspects of that exposure, including the reverence with which many hold Katharine and Hugo and the new knowledge about them that researchers have unearthed.[4]

It's another sad anniversary in 2019—twenty years since Karen's parents, Ric and Dodie, died on the same day in their house in Canberra. Faced with Dodie's death from cancer, Ric took his own life at the age of seventy-six. He lived three decades after his mother, and spent many of those years wrestling with her legacy and his father's. In 1989 he published *My Father's Son*, describing his Kafkaesque attempts to escape the secret suspicions which prevented him being promoted in his diplomatic career. I found a video-taped show about the book, the television crew following him to Katharine's Place for the first time since Katharine's death. He remarked on how it had changed—the outside kitchen enclosed, the wall of his old bedroom taken down to extend the sitting room—but he thought that was a good thing, because Katharine never wanted a museum. He was in his sixties then, dressed in a brown suit and tie, and he was melancholy as he relived the past, well-spoken and thoughtful.

After the launch of the anthology, I stand on Katharine's verandah talking to people who have come to commemorate her. A literary pilgrim who has followed in Katharine's footsteps to Moscow, Turee Station, Kalgoorlie, and many other places. A Queen's Counsel passionate about Victoria Cross winners whose interest in Hugo Throssell has spread to Katharine. A man with disabilities whose story in the anthology tells of how, on a trip to Perth in the 1970s, Katharine's books become crucial to him finding confidence and hope. He thought he saw her ghost at the house. And a writer who has spent three decades working on a history of the Workers' Art Guild, with Katharine a central figure; it has finally seen print and he is signing copies. There's a WH Auden poem with a line about writers becoming their admirers at the moment they die.[5] As a biographer, I tend to think of the writer becoming their *archive* at the moment they die, but in a different sense, Auden was right too. If Katharine's world had narrowed by the end of her life, it seems wide again in this gathering of devotees fifty years into her afterlife.

It's been a strange couple of days, my years of solitary research and writing suddenly having a correlation in the real world outside my laptop, my rows of books, and my visits to libraries. The spring afternoon is over too quickly and I drive back down the hill to the city to return to my silent remembering.

Notes

Abbreviations used in the Notes

AMP = Anne Mahon Papers
ARCF = Angus and Robertson correspondence files for KSP
ASIO-KSP = Katharine Susannah Prichard ASIO files
CHC = Campbell Howard Collection
CLF = KSP file, Commonwealth Literary Fund
CotH = KSP, *Child of the Hurricane* DN = *Daily News* (Perth)
DS = Doon Stone
GB = Guido Baracchi
GBP = Guido Baracchi Papers
HDBP = Henrietta Drake-Brockman Papers
HDB = Henrietta Drake-Brockman
HM = Hugh McCrae
HT = Hugo Throssell
HTRC = Hugo Throssell file, Repatriation Commission
HTS = Scrapbook kept by HVH Throssell
JWP = Joan Williams Papers
KSPP = Katharine Susannah Prichard Papers
KWC = Katharine Susannah Prichard Foundation archives
KSP = Katharine Susannah Prichard
MA = Mikhail Apletin
MFP = McCrae Family Papers
MFS = RT, *My Father's Son*
NAA = National Archives of Australia, Canberra
NLA = National Library of Australia, Canberra
NP = Nettie Palmer
OK = Oksana Krugerskaya
PP = Nettie and Vance Palmer Papers
PROV = Public Records Office of Victoria, Melbourne
RT = Ric Throssell
RTP = Ric Throssell Papers
SLNSW = State Library New South Wales, Sydney
SLV = State Library Victoria, Melbourne
SLWA = State Library of Western Australia, Perth
SMH = *Sydney Morning Herald*
ST = *Sunday Times* (Perth)
THPP = Thomas Henry Prichard Papers
USW = Katharine Susannah Prichard, [letters to Union of Soviet Writers Foreign Commission], Papers, 1935–1969

VP = Vance Palmer
WA = *West Australian*
WSP = Winifred [Doon] Stone Papers
WT = *Weekly Times*
WW = RT, *Wild Weeds and Windflowers*

Preface

1 Williams, 'KSP (Interview)'.
2 *Workers Star*, 22 October 1937, p. 5.
3 See, for example, Dixon, 'Australian', pp. 234–41.
4 Louis Esson, review of *Working Bullocks* by KSP, *The Bulletin*, 31 March 1927, sec. The Red Page, p. 2.
5 *Australian Women's Mirror*, 28 April 1931, pp. 11, 59.
6 Her minor novels, *Windlestraws* (1916) and *Subtle Flame* (1967), also have urban settings—London and Melbourne respectively.
7 'Some Perceptions', p. 236.
8 As one measure of its place in the curriculum, Noel Donnan's 'Brodie's Notes' volume on *Coonardoo,* aimed at secondary school students, appeared in 1981.
9 Corbould, 'Rereading'; Shoemaker, *Black*, pp. 39–62; Leane, 'Whiteman's', pp.48–75; Behrendt, *Finding*, pp. 82–99.
10 Smith, 'Different'; Phillips, 'Novelist'; Barrera, 'KSP'; Carter and Osborne, *Australian*; Hughes-d'Aeth, 'Cooper'.
11 'KSP', p. 17.
12 KSP to Beatrice Davis, 21 September 1961, KSPP, MS6201/10/17.
13 Morrison, 'Leaving'.
14 'Excess', pp. 28, 29.
15 RT to Stephen Murray Smith, 19 July 1970, RTP, MS8071/91.
16 *WW*, p. xii.
17 *KSP*, p. 5.
18 Edmond, 'Double', pp. 318–19.

1. Origins

1 'Presentation to Mr T. H. Prichard', newspaper clipping, THPP.
2 Tom's moderate approach to religion is clearest in his novel, which condemns inflexible Puritanism built on 'the narrow ragged creed of Knox and Calvin'. *Retaliation*, p. 5.
3 Prichard, *Australian*, 1902.
4 KSP to HL White, 27 September 1969, KSPP, MS6201/10/23.
5 Victoria, Australia, Assisted and Unassisted Passenger Lists, 1839–1923 [database], www.ancestry.com.au (viewed July 2015).
6 *CotH*, p. 16.
7 ibid., pp. 15–16.
8 *Australian News for Home Readers*, 20 April 1867, p. 16; *Argus*, 23 August 1867, p. 4.
9 *Argus*, 31 January 1903, p. 16. The *Australian Dictionary of Biography* entry for Frederick states he was 'educated at Ararat, where the family settled'. Reviewing Tom's novel in 1893, a newspaper from the town noted Tom was 'remembered as for some years resident at Ararat'. Ferral, 'Prichard'; '*Retaliation* Reviews', newspaper clippings, THPP.
10 *Cyclopedia of Tasmania*, p. 81; *Brighton Southern Cross*, 13 July 1907, p. 6; *Victoria Police Gazette*, 23 November 1865, p. 1.
11 'Prize Poetry', newspaper clipping, THPP.
12 *Ballarat Star*, 10 May 1869, p. 2.
13 Young, *Adventurous*, pp. 21, 163–214.

14 'Homeward Bound: A Christmas Reminiscence', *Red Funnel*, 1 June 1908, p. 553.
15 *SMH*, 16 March 1872, p. 7; *Cyclopedia of Tasmania*, p. 81.
16 *CotH*, p. 19.
17 KSPP, MS6201/1/5.
18 KSPP, MS6201/1/4.
19 *Argus*, 29 January 1883, p. 1.
20 *CotH*, p. 24.
21 ibid., p. 69.
22 ibid., p. 1.
23 *Argus*, 8 March 1884, p. 13.
24 *CotH*, p. 5.
25 Britton, *Lolóma*, p. 54.
26 *Australian Worker*, 31 August 1916, p. 11.
27 *Argus*, 27 March 1872, p. 4.
28 *Wild*, p. 6.
29 *MFS*, p. 309.
30 KSPP, MS6201/1/5.
31 *CotH*, p. 6.
32 ibid.
33 *SMH*, 15 June 1885, p. 6.
34 *CotH*, p. 8.
35 *Leader*, 20 August 1898, p. 32.
36 Burley, 'Levuka', p. 246.
37 *Fiji Times*, 6 March 1886, p. 2 [microfilm].
38 *Argus*, 20 March 1886, p. 20.
39 *Leader*, 20 August 1898, p. 32.
40 *Fiji Times*, 6 January 1887, p. 2 [microfilm].
41 *SMH*, 19 September 1887, p. 7.
42 *Australasian*, 29 October 1887, p. 28.

2. 'The Memory of a Storm'

1 *Wild*, pp. 1, 214–15.
2 *CotH*, p. 21.
3 *Wild*, p. 13.
4 *CotH*, p. 25.
5 ibid., p. 24.
6 ibid., p. 48.
7 *Tasmanian News*, 5 May 1888, p. 2.
8 *Cyclopedia of Tasmania*, p. 81.
9 *Colonist*, 27 April 1889, p. 23.
10 *CotH*, p. 31. KSP's account of the newspaper changing owners and direction may be confused with the time Tom lost his job on the Launceston *Daily Telegraph* in late 1894. The *Sun* does not seem to have actually changed hands until 1897 and nor did it change focus in 1892. The proprietor was Critchley Parker, who rehired Tom in 1896 to edit another newspaper. Holroyd, 'Parker'.
11 *Wild*, p. 212.
12 ibid., p. 9.
13 Bernie Raselala, message to author, 5 June 2015.
14 Ferrall, 'Prichard'.
15 *CotH*, p. 41; *Launceston Examiner*, 2 February 1895, p. 8.
16 *Wild*, p. 14.
17 ibid., p. 22.

18 *Daily Telegraph,* 18 November 1893, p. 5.
19 *Wild*, p. 136.
20 ibid., p. 145.
21 *Daily Telegraph,* 28 August 1893, p. 3.
22 'Tasmanian Memories', KSPP, MS6201/7/5.
23 The book itself is undated. Library catalogues list its date as 1891, but reviews and advertisements occur in May and June 1893.
24 *CotH*, pp. 29–30.
25 *Daily Telegraph,* 23 December 1893, p. 6.
26 *Daily Telegraph,* 13 August 1894, p. 2.
27 *CotH*, p. 106.
28 *Clipper*, 12 January 1895, p. 5.
29 *Launceston Examiner*, 2 February 1895, p. 8.
30 *Why*, pp. 3–4.
31 *Daily Telegraph,* 8 March 1895, p. 2.

3. 'Enthusiasms and Ambitions'

1 *CotH*, p. 40.
2 ibid.
3 ibid., p. 43.
4 ibid.
5 Victorian Municipal Directory, pp. 372–3.
6 *Why*, p. 4.
7 *CotH*, p. 67.
8 ibid., p. 41.
9 ibid., p. 51.
10 Clerehan, Scully, and White, *Armadale*, p. 7.
11 Education Department correspondence files, 16 October 1896, PROV.
12 *CotH*, p. 52.
13 Katharine claimed that this story appeared in the *Sun,* but she may be confused with the 1899 story. 'Tasmanian Memories', typescript, 19 October 1945, KSPP, MS6201/7/5.
14 *Sun* (Melbourne), 7 April 1899, p. 14 [microfilm].
15 *CotH*, p. 42.
16 *CotH*, p. 53. The professor's name was FS Delmer, according to a 1915 interview with KSP. *Book Lover*, 1 December 1915, p. 1.
17 Burchill, 'Early', p. 90.
18 *CotH*, p. 42.
19 Ferrier, *As Good*, p. 26.
20 *Argus,* 1 January 1901, p. 5.
21 *CotH*, pp. 56–8; *Argus,* 8 November 1902, p. 17.
22 *Pioneers*, 1915, p. 320.
23 *CotH*, p. 58.
24 ibid., p. 63.
25 Hilda Esson to KSP, 4 April 1952, KSPP, MS6201/10/7.
26 *CotH*, p. 63.
27 KSPP, MS6201/8/8, pp. 88-9
28 *CotH*, p. 63.
29 ibid., p. 26.
30 ibid., p. 62.
31 ibid., p. 61.
32 ibid., p. 62.

33 ibid.
34 *Working*, p. 275.
35 *CotH*, p. 107.
36 *Why*, p. 5.
37 Pawsey, 'O'Hara'.
38 Pawsey, 'Poet', pp. 100–1.
39 *CotH*, p. 61.
40 *Record*, 23 August 1902, p. 3.
41 KSPP, MS6201/13/1.
42 *CotH*, p. 60.
43 ibid., p. 57.
44 *Record*, 20 December 1902, p. 4.
45 *CotH*, pp. 60–1.
46 ibid., p. 63.
47 *DN*, 25 September 1902, p. 1.
48 *Wild*, p. 61.
49 *CotH*, p. 104.
50 ibid., p. 66.
51 ibid.

4. Governess

1 *CotH*, p. 69.
2 'Bush', p. 497.
3 *CotH*, p. 69.
4 Amies, 'Victorian'.
5 Matthew, 'Life'.
6 *CotH*, p. 69.
7 ibid., p. 70.
8 ibid., pp. 70–1.
9 ibid.
10 Teacher registrations, PROV, registration no. 5711.
11 *CotH*, p. 76.
12 ibid.
13 *Australasian,* 26 November 1904, p. 38.
14 *Prahran Telegraph*, 1 April 1899, p. 3.
15 *CotH*, p. 77.
16 *Age*, 25 November 1904, p. 5.
17 *Gippsland Standard,* 23 November 1904, p. 2 [microfilm].
18 *Argus*, 5 February 1946, p. 10.
19 *Gippsland Standard,* 23 November 1904, p. 2 [microfilm].
20 *Hurricane*, p. 78; Teacher registrations, PROV, registration no. 5711.
21 *Argus*, 5 February 1946, p. 10.
22 'Some Perceptions', p. 236.
23 'Diana', p. 271.
24 ibid., p. 257.
25 KSPP, MS6201/10/1.
26 *Examiner*, March 30, 1915, p. 4.
27 *Gippsland Standard*, 22 June 1904, p. 2 [microfilm].
28 *Pioneers*, 1915, p. 316.
29 'Notes on Southerly', KSPP, MS6201/10/8.
30 Webster, 'McMillan'.
31 Glowrey, 'McMillan'.

32 Adams, *From*, pp. 26–7.
33 *Pioneers*, 1915, pp. 188–9.
34 ibid., p. 274.
35 'Some Perceptions', p. 237.
36 *Pioneers*, 1915, p. 320.

5. Outback

1 KSPP, MS6201/1/5. 'O'Mimosa' may refer to the songs of the character Mimosa San in the popular Hall, Greenbank and Jones musical comedy *The Geisha, Story of a Tea House* (1896).
2 Depasquale and Crabb, *Tarella*, p. 40.
3 KSPP, MS6201/1/6.
4 *CotH*, p. 79.
5 ibid.
6 ibid.
7 *Barrier Miner*, 9 June 1906, p. 5.
8 *CotH*, p. 80.
9 *Barrier Miner*, 18 July 1891, p. 2.
10 *Barrier Miner*, 16 July 1902, p. 2; *Wagga Wagga Advertiser*, 9 August 1902, p. 4.
11 *CotH*, p. 80.
12 Katharine built on her experience of station life at Tarella with a research trip in 1926 to Turee Station in WA's north-west, the direct model for the station in *Coonardoo.*
13 *CotH*, p. 81.
14 Depasquale and Crabb, *Tarella*, p. 9.
15 *CotH*, pp. 82–3.
16 'City Girl III', p. 48.
17 *CotH*, pp. 84–5.
18 ibid., p. 85.
19 *WW*, p. 15.
20 *CotH*, p. 83.
21 ibid., pp. 85–6.

6. Heavy Rocks, Icy Winds

1 *CotH*, pp. 96–7. Katharine identified the school only as 'Christchurch Grammar', but Cyril Cook's earlier thesis named it as 'St Kilda Christ Church Grammar'. It was probably the South Yarra school begun in 1898 and still running today, but there was another short-lived school of the same name in Hawthorn at this time and a girls' school called 'Christ Church College' at St Kilda. In June 1906, Katharine was one of many private tutors to register as a teacher under new regulations. She did not list her experience teaching at Christ Church, so it's possible her position did not start until the second half of 1906 or even 1907. Cook, 'Critical', p. 26.
2 *CotH*, p. 97.
3 ibid., p. 69.
4 Walter Murdoch to KSP, 29 December 1954, KSPP, MS6201/10/5.
5 *Maitland Daily Mercury*, 7 May 1906, p. 4; *Ovens and Murray Advertiser*, 5 May 1906, p. 2.
6 *WW*, p. 16.
7 'Statement by KSP', typescript, 12 October 1946, SLNSW, A2763.
8 *CotH*, pp. 100–1.
9 *Herald* (Adelaide), 28 March 1908, p. 9.
10 *CotH*, p. 101.

11 *Why*, p. 5.
12 Cook, 'Critical', p. 25.
13 *CotH*, p. 31.
14 *CotH* typescript, KSPP, MS6201/8/1, p. 41.
15 *Australian*, 1902, p. 11.
16 ibid., p. 15.
17 *CotH*, pp. 103–4.
18 'Toorak House Asylum Records', PR7485/1, PROV.
19 *CotH*, p. 88.
20 Victoria, Index to Outward Passengers 1852–1923 [database], www.ancestry.com.au (viewed January 2016).
21 *CotH*, p. 90.
22 *Ovens and Murray Advertiser*, 29 December 1906, p. 3.
23 *Brighton Southern Cross*, 27 April 1907, p. 4.
24 *CotH*, p. 102.
25 ibid., p. 107.
26 ibid.
27 ibid., p. 106.
28 'Proceedings of an Inquest Held upon the Body of Tom Henry Prichard, Caulfield', PROV, VPRS 24, unit 818, item 1907/776.
29 ibid.
30 ibid.
31 ibid.
32 ibid.
33 *Brighton Southern Cross*, 13 July 1907, p. 6.

7. The Preux Chevalier

1 *CotH*, p. 107.
2 *Black*, 1921, p. 244.
3 ibid., p. 76.
4 *CotH*, p. 93.
5 ibid.
6 ibid., p. 94.
7 Defined as 'a deceitful rake' by the Oxford English Dictionary, 'gay deceiver' was a common phrase in newspaper stories at the time.
8 *CotH*, pp. 94–5.
9 ibid., p. 99.
10 *CotH* typescript, KSPP, MS6201/8/8, p. 5.
11 McCallum, 'Child', p. 20; Hay, 'Betrayed', p. 100.
12 *St George Call*, 28 October 1905, p. 7.
13 *Evening Journal*, 16 June 1906, p. 2.
14 KSP to Beatrice Davis, 13 May 1962, KSPP, MS6201/10/9.
15 *Free Lance*, 30 April 1896, p. 3.
16 Langmore, 'Reay'.
17 *Ballarat Star*, 5 April 1911, p. 6.
18 One piece of evidence which doesn't completely fit is that Ric Throssell says the Preux Chevalier had *three* daughters, but he may have had the wrong information from Katharine or realised that mentioning five daughters would be distinctive enough to identify him. *WW*, p. 21.
19 *Herald*, 12 November 1929, p. 7.
20 *CotH*, p. 94.
21 Langmore, 'Reay'.

22 John Lack, 'National Anti-Sweating League', *The Encyclopedia of Melbourne Online*, 2008, www.emelbourne.net.au/biogs/EM01042b.htm (viewed June 2021).
23 Langmore, 'Reay'.
24 Elizabeth Willis, 'Australian Natives' Association', *The Encyclopedia of Melbourne Online*, 2008, www.emelbourne.net.au/biogs/EM00126b.htm (viewed June 2021).
25 *MFS*, p. 62.
26 Langmore, 'Reay'.
27 *WW* draft, RTP, MS8071/4/104, p. 10.
28 NSW Unassisted Immigrant Passenger Lists, 1826–1922 [database], www.ancestry.com.au (viewed July 2016).
29 *Williamstown Chronicle*, 31 October 1908, p. 3.
30 UK, Incoming Passenger Lists, 1878–1960 [database], www.ancestry.com.au (viewed July 2016).
31 *Table Talk*, 18 May 1911, p. 5; *Table Talk*, 23 November 1911, p. 6.
32 *Herald*, 12 November 1929, p. 7.
33 *CotH*, p. 21.
34 *Critic*, 30 November 1901, p. 6.
35 *Coburg Leader*, 6 January 1906, p. 4
36 *CotH*, p. 100.
37 Haller, 'Pygmalion'.
38 KSPP, MS6201/1/4.

8. 'Astir with Great Things'

1 *CotH*, p. 125.
2 Brett, *Deakin*, p. 352.
3 Prichard, 'Deakin', p. 103.
4 *CotH*, p. 126.
5 *Deakin*, KSPP, MS6201/6/6, p. 76. 'Pollard' was Tom Prichard's mother's maiden name.
6 Grey, *Military*, p. 77; La Nauze, *Deakin*, p. 533; Brett, *Deakin*, pp. 359–60.
7 *WT*, 23 May 1908, p. 8.
8 *Swiss*, p. 34.
9 *The International*, vol. 1, no. 1, December 1907, p. 3.
10 'Australian', December 1907, p. 87.
11 'Some Perceptions', p. 244.
12 Foreword to *Wild*, n.p.
13 'KS and Hannah Frances', p. 96.
14 ibid., p. 97.
15 'Kid', p. 39.
16 *CotH*, p. 111.
17 *To Try*, p. 4.
18 ibid., p. 6.
19 *CotH*, p. 111.
20 ibid., pp. 111–12.
21 UK, Incoming Passenger Lists, 1878–1960 [database], www.ancestry.com.au (viewed July 2016).

9. Abroad

1 *CotH*, p. 112.
2 ibid.
3 KSPP, MS6201/8/8.
4 *CotH*, p. 238.

5 ibid., p. 112.
6 ibid., p. 113.
7 *WT,* 17 October 1908, p. 40.
8 'The Exhibition … London, July 30', newspaper clipping, KSPP, MS6201/11/1.
9 *CotH*, p. 130.
10 ibid.
11 ibid., pp. 117–19.
12 *Pioneers*, 1915, pp. 310–12.
13 *Black*, 1921, p. 244; *Black*, 1946, p. 157.
14 Hack, 'Meredith'.
15 *CotH*, p. 126.
16 Lindsay, *George*, p. 8.
17 *CotH*, p. 128.
18 ibid., p. 129.
19 ibid.
20 ibid., p. 125.
21 ibid., pp. 145–8.
22 KSP, interview by Ellis Blain, 1968, KSP [Audio] Collection, NLA, MS2660/3.
23 *CotH*, p. 143.
24 *Williamstown Chronicle*, 31 October 1908, p. 3.
25 *CotH*, pp. 143–5.
26 ibid., p. 145.
27 KSPP, MS6201/8/8.
28 KSP to Catherine Duncan, 31 May 1964, KSPP, MS6201/10/24.
29 'Cow', p. 118.
30 *CotH*, pp. 121–2.
31 ibid., p. 150.
32 ibid., p. 142.
33 ibid., p. 152.
34 ibid., p. 150.
35 ibid.
36 ibid., p. 151.

10. Pomona

1 *Mount Alexander Mail*, 17 April 1909, p. 2.
2 Burchill, 'KSP', p. 42.
3 *CotH*, p. 159.
4 KSPP, MS6201/10/1.
5 Although she seems to have copied his final letter into a notebook—see p. 221.
6 *WT,* 29 May 1909, p. 9.
7 *WT,* 4 September 1909, p. 9.
8 *WT,* 7 August 1909, p. 9.
9 *CotH*, p. 98.
10 O'Dowd, *Poetry*, p. 15.
11 'A Stormy Petrel of Australian Poetry', KSPP, MS6201/7/6.
12 'Tributes to the Memory of Bernard O'Dowd', p. 419.
13 Rees, *Making*, p. 115; Fitzpatrick, *Pioneer*, p. 83.
14 Rees, *Making*, pp. 114, 115.
15 KSP, interview by Campbell Howard, 1961, transcript, CHC.
16 *Ballarat Star*, 5 April 1911, p. 6.
17 *The Burglar,* typescript, KSPP, MS6201/6/1.
18 *Age,* 6 October 1910, p. 10.

19 *Worker*, 20 October 1910, p. 21.
20 *WT,* 15 October 1910, p. 42.
21 Fitzpatrick, *Pioneer*, p. 113.
22 ibid., p. 324.
23 Walker, 'Esson'.
24 Fitzpatrick, *Pioneer*, pp. 76–80.
25 ibid., pp. 109–10; Esson, 'Introduction', p. xiv.
26 KSP, interview by Campbell Howard, 1961, transcript, CHC.
27 'Louis Esson', typescript, 1943, KSPP, MS6201/7/6.
28 *CotH*, pp. 159–60.
29 ibid., p. 167.
30 *Bookman*, May 1915, p. 33.
31 *Sun* (Sydney), 11 October 1910, p. 2.
32 *CotH*, p. 168.
33 New York, Passenger Lists, 1820–1957 [database], www.ancestry.com.au (viewed May 2018).
34 US, Border Crossings from Canada to US, 1895–1956 [database], www.ancestry.com.au (viewed May 2018).
35 *CotH*, p. 168.
36 *Black*, 1921, p. 238.
37 *CotH*, p. 175.
38 *Critic*, 22 March 1911, p. 6.
39 UK, Incoming Passenger Lists, 1878–1960 [database], www.ancestry.com.au (viewed May 2018). It was the same ship which would be torpedoed during the Great War by a German submarine in May 1915, killing 1198 civilians, a factor in the USA's eventual entry into the war.
40 *Black*, 1921, p. 146.
41 ibid., p. 145.
42 ibid., p. 244.
43 *CotH*, p. 176.

11. Freewoman

1 *CotH*, p. 178.
2 Williams, 'KSP (Interview)', p. 26.
3 Van Wingerden, *Women's*, p. 127.
4 Smith, *British*, p. 38.
5 Van Wingerden, *Women's*, p. 144.
6 *CotH*, p. 185.
7 ibid., p. 177.
8 ibid., p. 187.
9 Woollacott, *To Try*, pp. 77–82; *SMH*, 4 April 1906, p. 5.
10 *CotH*, p. 182.
11 *Truth*, 8 October 1911, p. 5.
12 *CotH*, p. 176.
13 *Table Talk*, 23 November 1911, p. 6.
14 *Woman Voter,* 6 October 1911, p. 6.
15 *Table Talk,* 4 January 1912, p. 30.
16 *WW* draft, RTP, MS8071/4/104, p. 10.
17 KSP to Ric and Dodie Throssell, 2 June 1950, RTP.
18 *CotH*, p. 183.
19 Prichard, 'Some Perceptions', p. 237.
20 *CotH*, p. 183.

21 ibid.
22 *Why*, p. 6.
23 Holton, 'Daily', p. 351.
24 ibid., pp. 352–3.
25 'The New Chivalry', *Freewoman,* 2 May 1912, pp. 476–7.
26 'Discussion Circle', *Freewoman,* 2 May 1912, p. 464.
27 *CotH*, p. 178.
28 KSP to Karen Throssell, 26 April 1969, KSPP, MS6201/1/16.
29 Bland, 'Heterosexuality', p. 6.
30 KSP to Dora Marsden, 26 September 1912, Dora Marsden Collection, Princeton University.
31 Bland, 'Heterosexuality', p. 118.
32 'In Loving', p. 712.
33 ibid.; Clarke, 'Sumner', p. 42.
34 'In Loving', p. 712.
35 Albinski, 'Helena', p. 47.
36 *CotH*, p. 192.
37 Beasley, *Gallop*, pp. 33–4.
38 KSP to John Ferres, n.d., KSPP, MS6201/10/23.
39 'In the Heather', *Clovelly,* p. 14.
40 *CotH*, pp. 187–8.
41 *Daily Standard*, 20 May 1916, p. 9.
42 Massachusetts, State and Federal Naturalization Records, 1798–1950 [database], www.ancestry.com.au (viewed June 2018).
43 *Chronicle Telegram*, 12 May 1932, p. 2.

12. Breaking Out

1 'News Notes', *Bookman*, March 1913, p. 289. Hodder & Stoughton sometimes also called it the 'All-British Competition', but never the 'All-Empire Competition', contra *WW,* p. 25.
2 *Sun* (Sydney), 12 March 1913, p. 6.
3 *CotH,* p. 192. In *CotH,* Katharine wrote she took *six* months off from journalism, but an interview from the time specifies it was the first three months of 1914. *Daily Herald* (Adelaide), 17 July 1915, p. 10.
4 *CotH*, p. 192.
5 Whitelaw, *Art*, p. 78.
6 *Darling Downs Gazette*, 21 May 1915, p. 3.
7 *CotH*, p. 193.
8 Matter, 'Pursuing', p. 454.
9 *Bulletin*, 29 July 1915, p. 2.
10 *Dominion* (Wellington, NZ), 29 May 1915, p. 14.
11 *CotH*, p. 192.
12 *Daily Herald* (Adelaide), 17 July 1915, p. 10.
13 KSPP, MS6201/6/1.
14 Hirshfield, 'Actresses', pp. 137–8.
15 *Woman Voter*, 25 August 1914, p. 3.
16 *Weekly Times,* 15 August 1914, p. 10.
17 *CotH*, p. 198.
18 ibid., p. 200.
19 *Socialist*, 12 February 1915, p. 4; *Socialist*, 17 December 1915, p. 4 [microfilm].
20 *Table Talk*, 1 October 1914, p. 6.
21 *CotH*, p. 199.

22 Baker, *Australian*, pp. 25–31.
23 Martin, *Ink*, p. 28.
24 Serle, 'Palmer'.
25 *DN*, 26 March 1930, p. 7.
26 Martin, *Ink*, p. 31.
27 NP to Catherine Higgins, 26 June 1915, PP, MS1174/1499.
28 Martin, *Ink*, pp. 235–6.
29 *CotH*, pp. 134–7, 199; see Nan's signature in Katharine's commonplace book, KSPP, MS6201/1/6.
30 *Sunday Times* (Sydney), 28 February 1915, p. 1.
31 ibid.; *Everylady's Journal*, 6 March 1915, p. 138.
32 *Sunday Times* (Sydney), 28 February 1915, p. 1.
33 *CotH*, pp. 194–5.
34 ibid., p. 195.
35 *Examiner*, 26 February 1915, p. 3; *Weekly Times*, 27 February 1915, p. 22.
36 'News and Notes', *Bookman*, April 1915, p. 1.
37 *Everylady's Journal*, 6 June 1915, p. 1.
38 *Punch*, 4 March 1915, p. 22.
39 *CotH*, pp. 196–7.
40 Carter and Osborne, *Australian*, p. 197.
41 *Times Literary Supplement*, 9 September 1915, p. 302.
42 *Argus*, 17 September 1915, p. 5. At least one other reviewer saw the novel's over-seriousness as its chief defect. *Australasian*, 25 September 1915, p. 46.
43 KSPP, MS6201/10/21.

13. Hugo

1 KSP, interview by Jane Fleming, ABC Radio, 1968, replayed on 'World War One Correspondents', 10 May 2010, www.abc.net.au/radionational/programs/archived/verbatim/world-war-one-correspondents/3112906 (viewed June 2021).
2 *Cairns Post*, 12 August 1915, p. 2.
3 *Weekly Times*, 16 November 1929, p. 6.
4 *Western Mail*, 6 April 1917, p. 38.
5 *CotH*, pp. 201–2.
6 ibid., p. 202.
7 ibid.
8 HT, war diary, KSPP, MS6201/1/7.
9 KSP to RT, 11 March 1962, RTP.
10 *MFS*, pp. 17–18.
11 KSP to RT, 25 Oct 1944, RTP.
12 *MFS*, p. 20.
13 ibid., pp. 22–4.
14 Browning and Gill, *Gallipoli*, p. 15.
15 *SMH*, 18 October 1915, p. 10.
16 *Moora Herald and Midland Districts Advocate*, 26 May 1916, p. 4.
17 Browning and Gill, *Gallipoli*, p. 95.
18 *Observer* (London), 29 August 1915, p. 3.
19 Throssell, 'For Valour', p. 9.
20 *WA*, 28 April 1916, p. 7.
21 Throssell, 'For Valour', p. 10.
22 'Intimate Strangers', KSPP, MS6201/4/4.
23 Hamilton, *Price*, location 3520.
24 HTRC, p. 37.

25 Coronial inquest, HTRC, p. 50.
26 HTRC, p. 37.
27 'Intimate Strangers', KSPP, MS6201/4/4.
28 *DN*, 18 June 1915, p. 3.
29 *Western Mail*, 24 March 1921, p. 27.
30 'Intimate Strangers', KSPP, MS6201/4/4.
31 *CotH*, pp. 202–3.
32 KSPP, MS6201/1/13.
33 *CotH*, p. 203.
34 *Pioneers*, 1963, p. i.
35 *CotH*, p. 203.
36 ibid., p. 207.
37 *MFS*, p. 62.
38 *Sunday Times* (Sydney), 9 January 1916, p. 21.
39 *WA*, 25 December 1915, p. 8.
40 *Sunday Times* (Sydney), 9 January 1916, p. 21.

14. Disquiet

1 *CotH*, pp. 208–9.
2 KSPP, MS6201/5.
3 *CotH*, p. 213.
4 Prichard, 'Radical', p. 84.
5 GB to RT, 10 June 1972, RTP, MS8071/4/94.
6 *Register*, 20 December 1915, p. 6; Sparrow, 'Engineering', p. 146.
7 Macintyre, *Reds*, p. 19.
8 Sparrow, 'Engineering', p. 126.
9 *Fleur-de-Lys,* October 1913, pp. 39–40.
10 Sparrow, 'Engineering', p. 146.
11 *SMH,* 1 January 1976, p. 1.
12 GB to RT, 10 June 1972, RTP, MS8071/4/94.
13 *Argus*, 14 January 1916, p. 8.
14 *Argus*, 12 January 1916, p. 8.
15 ibid.
16 Sally Wilde, 'Armadale', *Encyclopedia of Melbourne Online*, 2008, www.emelbourne.net.au/biogs/EM00086b.htm (viewed June 2021).
17 *CotH*, p. 215.
18 *Graphic of Australia*, 11 February 1916, p. 7.
19 *Punch*, February 17, 1916, p. 32.
20 *CotH*, p. 216.
21 *Bendigonian,* 24 February 1916, p. 10.
22 *Table Talk,* 24 February 1916, p. 28.
23 *CotH*, p. 215.
24 *Weekly Times*, 11 March 1916, p. 9.
25 *Argus*, 22 July 1916, p. 18.
26 '*The Pioneers* in Pictures', *Herald*, undated clipping, KSPP, MS6201/11/1.
27 *Punch*, 9 March 1916, p. 34.
28 '*The Pioneers*: Original Release', National Film and Sound Archive, title 1862, www.nfsa.gov.au/collection (viewed June 2021).
29 Edmondson and Pike, *Australia's*, p. 22.
30 'Australia I: Ti-Tree Studies 1916', notebook, KSPP, MS6201/2/2.
31 'Australia II 1916', notebook, KSPP, MS6201/2/2
32 ibid.

33 ibid.
34 ibid.
35 ibid.
36 *CotH*, p. 218.
37 HTRC, p. 38.
38 *CotH*, p. 217.
39 ibid.

15. The Opal Fields

1 *Leader*, 11 November 1916, p. 43.
2 Cook, 'Critical', p. 33.
3 *CotH*, p. 217.
4 It is debatable whether or not the title should have a definite article. It was originally published in 1921 as *The Black Opal* yet Nettie Palmer (probably reflecting Katharine's opinion) wrote in 1926, 'It is important to get the book's name right, *Black Opal*, not "*The* Black Opal", as I have so often seen it printed—as if it were a treasure-hunt-detective story!' The first reprint in 1946 omitted the definite article, suggesting Katharine restored it to her preferred title, which she also used to describe it in *CotH*. *Australian Women's Mirror*, 27 July 1926, p. 11.
5 'On Purpose', p. 121.
6 KSP to RT, 16 February 1957, RTP.
7 *CotH*, p. 218.
8 ibid., p. 222.
9 ibid., pp. 223–4.
10 KSPP, MS6201/2/2.
11 ibid.
12 Prichard, *Black*, 1921, p. 64.
13 *Sun* (Sydney), 14 January 1917, p. 10.
14 *Sunday Times* (Sydney), 16 July 1916, p. 4.
15 *CotH*, pp. 224–5.
16 ibid., p. 225.
17 'A Brief History of Lightning Ridge', Lightning Ridge Opal Company, http://opalguy.com/history.html; Lloyd, *Lightning*, p. 159; 'Empress of Australia—Famous Opals', Mac's Opals, www.macsopals.com/opal-guide/empress-of-australia/ (viewed June 2021).
18 *Black*, 1921, p. 205.
19 *Brisbane Courier*, 18 September 1916, p. 4.
20 *Black*, 1921, pp. 69–70.
21 *Women Today*, September 1936, p. 3.
22 Beasley, *Gallop*, p. 39.

16. The Omen

1 *Goulburn Evening Penny Post*, 2 September 1916, p. 1.
2 *CotH*, p. 226.
3 *Western Mail*, 13 October 1916, p. 38.
4 *CotH*, p. 232.
5 KSPP, MS6201/2/2.
6 Sparrow, 'Engineering', p. 137.
7 *Western Mail*, 17 November 1916, p. 16.
8 *Weekly Times*, 15 December 1917, p. 9.
9 *CotH*, p. 232.
10 *Graphic of Australia*, 24 November 1916, p. 14.

11 *Argus*, 29 November 1916, p. 1.
12 Alan Prichard, military record, NAA, 6.
13 *CotH*, pp. 226–7.
14 'Australia II 1916', notebook, KSPP, MS6201/2/2.
15 Vickery, 'Lesbia', pp. 102–11.
16 ibid., p. 2.
17 Sparrow, 'Engineering', pp. 149–50.
18 ibid.
19 'Rebel Girl', 9 November 1941, GBP, MS5241/5/39, p. 2.
20 Martin, *Ink*, p. 38.
21 KSP to NP, May 1917, PP, MS1174/1/1641.
22 Roland, *Devious*, 25; Sparrow, 'Engineering', p. 159.
23 Sparrow, 'Engineering', p. 151.
24 1917 Syllabus, Victorian Labor College, University of Melbourne Archives, 1976.0032 unit 40, p. 4.
25 VLC Minutes, 6 July 1917, AT Brodney Papers.
26 Smart, 'Divided', p. 55.
27 *CotH*, p. 239.
28 *Why*, p. 8.
29 Macintyre, *Reds*, location 422.
30 *Age*, 26 March 1917, p. 7.
31 *Worker* (Brisbane), 5 April 1917, p. 11.
32 Cain, *Wobblies*, p. 38.
33 ibid., pp. 81–106.
34 ibid., pp. 169–274.
35 See Baracchi's lecture at a Victorian Socialist Party meeting on 'The Syndicalism of Sorel'. *Labor Call*, 20 December 1917, p. 6.
36 *CotH*, p. 178.
37 Prichard, 'Radical', p. 89.
38 1917 Syllabus.
39 Walker, '[Interview with] Guido Baracchi', p. 18.
40 1917 Syllabus, p. 5.
41 VLC Minutes, 20 November 1917, AT Brodney Papers.
42 *Labor Call*, 20 December 1917, p. 6.
43 Prichard, 'Writer's', p. 29.
44 Sparrow, 'Engineering', pp. 167–77.
45 'To the IWW, a Special Message from the Communist International', Marxists Internet Archive, 1920, transcribed 2003, www.marxists.org/history/international/comintern/sections/australia/iww/open-letter.htm (viewed June 2021).
46 Prichard, 'Radical', pp. 88–9.
47 *CotH*, p. 233.
48 ibid., p. 237.
49 ibid., pp. 237–9.
50 KSP to NP, May 1917, PP, MS1174/1/1641.
51 Clarke, 'Sumner', p. 56.
52 ibid., pp. 50–2.
53 ibid., p. 61.
54 'In Loving'. It is not clear whether the 'go slow' quote is from the final letter or an earlier letter from the hospital. Perhaps the reference to running chickens and books reflects a desire by Katharine to escape the city life to somewhere like Emerald and write.
55 ibid.

56 *Weekly Times*, 24 November 1917, p. 9
57 *Herald*, 14 June 1921, p. 5.
58 Albinski, 'Helena', p. 47.
59 ibid.
60 *CotH*, p. 236.
61 Papers of Bertha Walker, SLV, MS10772, box 2.
62 *CotH*, p. 234.
63 *Argus*, 19 January 1918, p. 11.
64 MS6201/2/2.
65 *CotH*, p. 236.
66 KSPP, MS6201/9/2.
67 *CotH*, p. 236.
68 'Rebel Girl', 9 November 1941, GBP, MS5241/5/39, 2a.
69 Alan Prichard, military record, NAA, p. 52; *Argus*, 22 December 1917, p. 8.
70 GB, speech, 10 March 1965, GBP, MS5241/5/46.
71 *CotH*, p. 248.
72 *Argus*, 22 December 1917, p. 8.
73 ibid.
74 Hilda Esson to NP, 1 February 1918, PP, MS1174/1920.
75 Alan Prichard, military record, NAA, p. 11.
76 ibid., p. 37

17. Retreat

1 Heseltine, 'Australian', p. 183. Heseltine actually cites Katharine's *Intimate Strangers* as a key example of a novel indirectly concerned with the war through its depiction of the after-effects.
2 *Golden*, p. 218.
3 ibid., p. 234.
4 *Subtle*, p. 19.
5 ibid.
6 *CotH*, p. 250.
7 Jordan, 'Shaped', pp. 384–85.
8 PP, MS1174/16.
9 GB to VP and NP, 15 January 1918, PP, MS1174/1/1750.
10 Thurs [18 January 1918], PP, MS1174/16.
11 Jeff Sparrow transcribes it as '2pm', but Baracchi clearly wrote 'am' in block capitals and Nettie repeats that in her diary. 'Engineering', p. 159.
12 *Labor Call*, 21 February 1918, p. 9.
13 NP's diary, PP, MS1174.
14 Roland, *Devious*, p. 25.
15 NP's diary, PP, MS1174.
16 *Prahran Chronicle*, 6 April 1918, p. 5; Larkins, *Book*, p. 107.
17 Larkins, *Book*, p. 137.
18 ibid., p. 133.
19 *Subtle*, p. 34.
20 *CotH*, p. 250.
21 ibid.
22 Alan Rochead Hubert Prichard, Probate and Administration Files, PROV, VPRS 28/P0003 unit 795, item 155/783.
23 Historical Search Statement, Land Victoria, volume 03319 folio 767.
24 Palmer and Palmer, *Letters*, p. 9.
25 KSP to Helen Palmer, 26 January 1961, Helen Palmer Papers, NLA, MS6083/Box 25.

26 The story of the sinful woman washing Jesus's feet with her tears and drying them with her hair is found in Luke 7:36–39.
27 *CotH*, p. 251.

18. Armistice

1 Hospital report, 19 December 1918, HTRC, pp. 41–2.
2 *CotH*, p. 251.
3 ibid.
4 ibid.
5 *Age*, 16 September 1918, p. 4; HT, military record, NAA, p. 5.
6 *CotH*, p. 251.
7 ibid., p. 217. Katharine dates this conversation to Hugo's visit in 1916, but it seems unlikely they were seriously contemplating marriage then.
8 ibid., p. 252.
9 Typescript of *CotH,* KSPP, MS6201/8/8, p. 5.
10 *Argus*, 12 November 1918, p. 6.
11 *CotH*, p. 252.
12 ibid.
13 *Punch,* 12 December 1918, p. 36.
14 *Black*, 1921, p. 256.
15 ibid., p. 266.
16 ibid., p. 318.
17 KSP to NP, September 1919, PP, MS1174/1/2240.
18 KSP to NP, August 1919, PP, MS1174/1/2206.
19 *WW*, p. 84.
20 *Brumby / Bid*, p. 7.
21 ibid., p. 10.
22 ibid., p. 11.
23 *Punch,* 12 December 1918, p. 36.
24 *Caviar*, p. 9.
25 KSP to RT, 26 February 1950, RTP.
26 *Register*, 6 December 1918, p. 4.
27 Hospital report, 19 December 1918, HTRC, pp. 41–2.
28 HTRC, p. 47.
29 *WA*, 3 October 1918, p. 9.
30 *Bunbury Herald*, 5 October 1918, p. 5.
31 *WA*, 19 February 1919, p. 7.
32 *Register*, 21 January 1919, p. 6.
33 NP to VP, 25–28 January 1919, PP, MS1174/1/2025.
34 KSP to Repatriation Commission, 28 January 1934, HTRC.
35 Receipt [loose], HTS.
36 *Age*, 28 January 1919, p. 5.
37 *Argus*, 29 January 1919, p. 7.
38 Curson and McCracken, 'Australian'; Curson and McCracken, 'Flu'.
39 *DN*, 24 January 1922, p. 3.
40 KSP to MA, 30 January 1960, USW.
41 *CotH,* p. 252. Lilly Williams had been the closest of Katharine's aunts and the last to see Tom Prichard alive. She died at the end of that year aged fifty-eight. *Argus*, 22 December 1919, p. 1.
42 Historical Search Statement, Land Victoria, Volume 03319 Folio 767.
43 NP to VP, 25–28 January 1919, PP, MS1174/1/2025.
44 *CotH*, p. 252.

45 Receipt [loose], HTS; Advertisement for Beefine, *Age*, 7 April 1919, p. 4.
46 *Caviar*, p. 9.
47 KSPP, MS6201/10/14.
48 *WW*, p. 40.
49 *Argus*, 4 February 1919, p. 6.
50 *Western Mail*, 21 March 1919, p. 34
51 'Bush', p. 498.
52 *CotH*, p. 69.
53 NP to VP, 1 March 1919, PP, MS1174/1/2065.
54 *Age*, 4 March 1919, p. 4.
55 'Some Perceptions', p. 241.
56 *Gallop*, p. 171.
57 *Subtle*, p. 69.
58 KSP to NP, August 1919, PP, MS1174/1/2206.

19. The New Order

1 *DN*, 13 March 1919, p. 3.
2 'A Century of Population Change in Western Australia', Australian Bureau of Statistics, September 2001, www.abs.gov.au (viewed June 2021).
3 *Australia for the Tourist*, p. 130.
4 *Bathurst Times*, 11 March 1916, p. 4.
5 KSP to NP, September 1919, PP, MS1174/1/2240.
6 *WA*, 28 June 1919, p. 4.
7 *CotH*, p. 254.
8 KSP to NP, August 1919, PP, MS1174/1/2206.
9 Tom Roberts to Elizabeth and Caleb Roberts, 6 December 1919, Hayes Collection, University of Queensland Library, 2/2150a.
10 KSP to NP, September 1919, PP, MS1174/1/2240; Post Office Directory 1919; *WA*, 14 April 1902, p. 1; *Swan Express*, 25 June 1915, p. 3; *Swan Express*, 29 October 1953, p. 4.
11 *WW*, p. 232.
12 *Westralian Worke*r, 4 February 1921, p. 2.
13 Oliver, 'Fremantle's'.
14 *Tribune*, 4 December 1963, p. 5.
15 Blackwell, *Western*, p. 26.
16 *Truth*, 26 July 1919, p. 3
17 KSP to NP, August 1919, PP, MS1174/1/2206.
18 *Northam Advertiser*, 23 July 1919, p. 2 [microfilm], *Northam Courier*, 18 July 1919, p. 1.
19 Gerald Throssell, notes, RTP, MS8071/3/73.
20 *Northam Advertiser*, 23 July 1919, p. 2 [microfilm].
21 *Westralian Worker*, 25 July 1919, p. 4; *Northam Courier*, 25 July 1919, p. 1.
22 *Westralian Worker*, 25 July 1919, p. 4.
23 KSP to NP, August 1919, PP, MS1174/1/2206; Gerald Throssell, notes.
24 KSP to NP, August 1919; *Northam Courier*, 25 July 1919, p. 1.
25 *WA*, 22 July 1919, p. 5; *Westralian Worker*, 25 July 1919, p. 4; *Northam Courier*, 25 July 1919, p. 1.
26 Gerald Throssell, notes; Hamilton, *Price*.
27 *Truth*, 27 December 1919, p. 5.
28 *ST*, 31 August 1919, p. 6.
29 *New*, p. 9.
30 ibid., p. 17.

31 *Truth*, 15 November 1919, p. 2; *WA*, 17 November 1919, p. 9.
32 Cain, 'Australian'.
33 ASIO-KSP, vol. 1, p. 127.
34 Ric Throssell, ASIO file, NAA, A6119, vol. 1, pp. 95, 159–60.
35 *South Australia Police Gazette*, 12 May 1920, p. 178.
36 *WW*, p. 41.
37 *Western Mail*, 12 May 1921, p. 6.
38 *Australasian*, 20 December 1919, p. 51. Earlier in the year, the WA government botanist, Desmond Herbert, had given a paper on the parasitism of the tree. *ST*, 13 April 1919, p. 6.
39 Statement by KSP, typescript, 12 October 1946, SLNSW, A2763.
40 Hilda Esson to NP, 23 April 1920, PP, MS1174/1/2288.
41 *WA*, 13 December 1921, p. 6.
42 Newspaper clipping, KSPP, MS6201/11/2.
43 19 October 1921, newspaper clipping, KSPP, MS6201/11/2.
44 Newspaper clipping, KSPP, MS6201/11/2.
45 Palmer and Palmer, *Letters*, pp. 7–8; *Herald*, 28 September 1920, p. 4.
46 HT to NP, 20 August 1920, PP, MS1174/1/2299.
47 *Western Mail*, 2 September 1920, p. 27; Edith Isabel Prichard, Brighton Burial Register, burial 14529.
48 Bill Earsman to WC Whitbread, 24 December 1920, KSPP, MS6201/10/1.
49 Williams, *First*, p. 185.
50 Earsman to Whitbread.
51 *WW*, p. 232.
52 *Westralian Worker*, 31 December 1920, p. 5.
53 Williams, *First*, p. 90.
54 *Westralian Worker*, 11 November 1921, p. 8.
55 Statement by KSP, typescript, 12 October 1946, SLNSW, A2763.
56 *Westralian Worke*r, 4 February 1921, p. 2.
57 KSP to HL Denford, transcription, 16 February [1923], JWP, MS5425A/188.
58 Prichard, 'Deakin', p. 105.
59 KSP to Denford.
60 ibid.
61 Statement by KSP.

20. York Road

1 KSP to Spencer Brodney, 25 May 1930, Spencer Brodney Papers, SLV.
2 KSP to NP, 14 November 1929, KSPP, MS6201/10/2.
3 'Western', p. 35.
4 'Wild Flower Walkabouts', KSPP, MS6201/7/5.
5 *WW*, pp. 39–40.
6 *MFS*, p. 81.
7 KSP to RT, 9 June 1946, RTP.
8 *MFS*, p. 79.
9 *Roaring*, p. 223.
10 *MFS*, p. 200.
11 Headlam, 'My Aunt', p. 45.
12 KSP to RT, 16 June 1968, RTP.
13 KSP to RT, 4 May 1968, RTP.
14 Headlam, 'My Aunt', p. 45.
15 KSP to RT, 8 October 1956, RTP.
16 KSPP, MS6201/6/3.

17 *MFS*, p. 86.
18 *WW*, pp. 42–3.
19 KSP to RT, 10 May 1953, RTP.
20 KSP to RT, 9 May 1954, RTP.
21 KSP to Dorothy Throssell, 8 March 1948, RTP.
22 KSP to RT, 4 May 1961, RTP.
23 *CotH*, p. 256.
24 'Grey', p. 25.
25 *Australasian*, 25 August 1923, p. 31.
26 KSPP, MS6201/6/3, p. 20.
27 Prichard, 'Lawrence', p. 253.
28 Richardson, *Letters*, letter 462.
29 Prichard, 'Lawrence', p. 252.
30 Palmer, *Nettie*, p. 55.
31 Prichard, 'Lawrence', p. 252.
32 *WW*, 167; 'Lawrence', p. 259.
33 'ML Skinner', *Woman's World,* 1 December 1924, p. 41.
34 KSP to NP, 4 July 1925 [sic – 1928], KSPP, MS6201/10/2.
35 *WW*, p. 170.
36 *Home,* September 1933, p. 70.
37 Palmer, *Nettie*, pp. 54–5.
38 *Art in Australia*, March 1924, p. 23. The March issue was not published until April.
39 Heseltine, 'C. Hartley', p. 357.
40 Souter, *Torrent*, section 5.
41 Prichard, *Happiness*, 1967, p. vi.
42 Burchill, 'KSP', pp. 129–30.
43 'Curse', p. 19.
44 Souter, *Torrent*, section 5.
45 ARCF, MLMSS314/vol. 83/1.
46 *Outline*, p. 219.
47 Royalty statement, KSPP, MS6201/10/1.
48 *Table Talk*, 5 March 1925, p. 35.
49 *Swan Express*, 23 January 1925, p. 5.
50 *Coonardoo*, p. 107.
51 ibid., pp. 116–17.
52 *Roaring*, 195ff.
53 *WW*, p. 64.
54 *Brumby / Bid*, p. 27.
55 ibid., p. 29.
56 ibid., pp. xv–xvi.
57 KSP to VP, 23 June 1927, KSPP, MS6201/10/2.
58 *MFS*, p. 137.
59 Katharine Brisbane, 'Introduction', Prichard, *Brumby / Bid*, p. xxvii.
60 KSP to VP, November 1924, PP, 1174/1/2630.
61 *Swan Express*, 3 July 1925, p. 4. The fourth family member was Katharine's niece, Thea.
62 *DN*, 17 April 1924, p. 4.
63 *Swan Express*, 10 September 1926, p. 7; *ST,* 19 September 1926, p. 3.
64 KSP to VP, 23 June 1927, KSPP, MS6201/10/2.
65 *WA,* 21 September 1928, p. 15; *DN*, 10 May 1929, p. 9.
66 Williams, *First*, p. 95.
67 Batterham, 'Shelley;' *Mirror*, 1 October 1927, p. 4.
68 *Swan Express*, 16 November 1923, p. 5.

69 *WA,* 28 April 1925, p. 8; *ST,* 14 December 1919, p. 6.
70 HTRC, p. 44.
71 RTP, MS8071/03/71.
72 *Advertiser*, 9 March 1937, p. 17; *Advertiser*, 30 August 1949, p. 3.
73 *News*, 4 March 1927, 7.
74 *ST,* 14 August 1927, p. 9; *ST,* 11 September 1927, p. 15.
75 *Swan Express*, 10 February 1928, p. 3.
76 *WA,* 31 August 1928, p. 7.
77 *Kalgoorlie Mine*r, 30 August 1928, p. 4.

21. The Karri Forest

1 'Town Names', Landgate, www.landgate.wa.gov.au (viewed June 2021).
2 Untitled notebook, KSPP, MS6201/2/3.
3 KSP, interview by Hazel de Berg, 1960, NLA.
4 Cook, 'Critical', p. 38.
5 *Working*, p. 92.
6 Norman Smith, interview, 1971, SLWA, OH134.
7 Morris and Underwood, *Tall*, p. 50.
8 *Working*, p. 221.
9 *Contested*, p. 70.
10 KSP to NP, 28 September 1924, KSPP, MS6201/10/2.
11 *Mirror*, 13 September 1924, p. 4; *Westralian Worker*, 12 September 1924, p. 4.
12 *Bundaberg Mail*, 23 September 1924, p. 5.
13 *Westralian Worker*, 12 September 1924, p. 4.
14 Beasley, *Gallop*, p. 55.
15 Joan Williams in Prichard, *Strenuous*, p. 16.
16 *Working*, p. 247.
17 ibid., p. 253.
18 KSP to VP, November 1924, PP, 1174/1/2630.
19 Burchill, 'KSP', p. 96.
20 The first advertisement in *Times Literary Supplement* appears 18 November 1926.
21 Hart-Davis, 'Cape'.
22 *DN*, 6 March 1926, p. 9
23 KSP to VP, 23 June 1927, KSPP, MS6201/10/2.
24 KSP to VP, 15 September 1928, KSPP, MS6201/10/2.
25 Hilda Esson to KSP, [1926], KSPP, MS6201/10/3.
26 *Bulletin,* 31 March 1927, p. 2.
27 *Mercury*, 23 April 1927, p. 15.
28 *Telegraph*, 19 February 1927, p. 7.
29 *Catholic Press*, 10 March 1927, p. 3.
30 *Bunbury Herald and Blackwood Express*, 4 February 1927, p. 12.
31 *New York Times*, Book Review, 24 April 1927, 8, p. 14.
32 *Laughter*, p. 146.
33 *Daily News*, 2 December 1927, p. 11.
34 Grattan, 'Australian', p. 24.
35 *Friends*, p. 250.
36 *Nettie*, p. 24.
37 *Brisbane Courier*, 15 October 1927, p. 22.

22. The Station

1 *CotH*, p. 254.
2 Prichard, *Happiness*, 1967, p. vii.
3 *MFS*, p. 93.

4 *Murchison Times*, 30 April 1920, p. 3.
5 KSP to Hilda Esson, 1 November 1926, KSPP, MS6201/10/1.
6 ibid.
7 Prichard, *Brumby / Bid*, p. iv.
8 KSP to NP, 19 October 1926, PP, 1174/1/2856.
9 KSP to Hilda Esson.
10 *Coonardoo*, pp. 270–1.
11 *MFS*, p. 96.
12 Bill Day to KSP Writers' Centre, 15 April 2002, KWC; Austin-Crowe, 'Coonardoo', p. 99.
13 *WW*, p. 49.
14 Prichard, *Brumby / Bid*, p. xiv.
15 Austin-Crowe, 'Coonardoo', p. 190.
16 Prichard, *Brumby / Bid*, p. ix.
17 Peter Bridge records bush legends of them meeting, and Katharine's jealousy at him being the centre of attention as he told his stories. However, the account of Katharine's visit is unreliable—it also includes the claim that Hugo Throssell was with her at Turee and attacked the governess. Bridge, *Brumby*, p. 71.
18 Austin-Crowe, 'Coonardoo', p. 192.
19 Bridge, *Brumby*, p. 27.
20 *Daily Telegraph and North Murchison and Pilbarra Gazette*, 7 April 1926, p. 3.
21 *Brumby*, p. 71.
22 Wilde and Headon, 'Aborigine', p. 7.
23 Quoted in Prichard, *Brumby / Bid*, p. xiv.
24 Quoted in ibid., p. ix.
25 Quoted in ibid., p. xv.
26 KSP to Douglas Stewart, 24 March 1963, ARCF, MLMSS 3269/vol. 592.
27 Williams, 'Natural'.
28 KSP, interview by Hazel de Berg, 1960, NLA.
29 Austin-Crowe, 'Coonardoo', p. 101.
30 KSP to Douglas Stewart, 25 December 1963, KSPP, MS6201/10/17.
31 Austin-Crowe, 'Coonardoo', p. 110; Bill Day to KSP Writers' Centre.
32 Austin-Crowe, 'Coonardoo', p. 101.
33 KSP to Stewart.
34 *DN*, 2 December 1927, p. 11.
35 Coonardoo, p. 185.
36 KSP to VP, 10 September 1928, PP, MS1174/1/2669
37 'Coonardoo', p. 103.
38 Coonardoo, p. 5.
39 *Bulletin*, 15 August 1928, p. 50.
40 *Bulletin*, 15 January 1930, p. 2.
41 KSP to VP, 10 September 1928, PP, MS1174/1/2669.
42 Quoted in Burchill, 'KSP', p. 142.
43 *Bulletin*, 31 October 1928, p. 37.
44 *Northern Times*, 19 January 1929, p. 4.
45 KSP to VP, 10 September 1928, PP, MS1174/1/2669.
46 *Times* (London), 14 June 1929, p. 10.
47 KSP to Beatrice Davis, 15 November 1954, ARCF, MLMSS 3269/vol. 591.
48 *Labor Daily*, 10 August 1929, p. 9.
49 *WA*, 27 July 1929, p. 5.
50 *Nettie*, pp. 373–4.
51 Hetherington, 'Authors', pp. 420–1.
52 *New York Times*, Book Review, 16 March 1930, p. 4.

53 KSP, interview by Hazel de Berg, 1960, NLA.
54 Leane, 'Other', p. 42.
55 *Finding*, p. 94.
56 'Whiteman's', p. 60ff; *Finding*, p. 94ff.
57 Behrendt, *Finding*, p. 87.
58 Lydon, 'Bullets', p. 285.
59 Behrendt, *Finding*, p. 86.
60 *Coonardoo*, pp. 167–71; Lisa Hill, 'Coonardoo', *ANZ LitLovers*, 17 January 2021, https://anzlitlovers.com/2021/01/17/coonardoo-by-katharine-susannah-prichard/ (viewed June 2021).
61 *Finding*, p. 86.
62 The nearest documented event is 500km west of Turee at Minderoo, where 20 to 50 of the Thalangi people were massacred in 1869. 'Colonial Frontier Massacres in Australia, 1788–1930', The Centre for 21st Century Humanities, https://c21ch.newcastle.edu.au/colonialmassacres/detail.php?r=894 (viewed June 2021).
63 'Other', pp. 42–3.
64 Irwin, 'Australia's', p. 31.

23. The Circus

1 *Cohuna Farmer's Weekly*, 23 November 1917, p. 3.
2 *CotH*, p. 234.
3 *Haxby's*, location 527.
4 *Swan Express*, 2 September 1927, p. 5.
5 Cook, 'Critical', p. 40.
6 *Western Mail*, 29 September 1927, p. 9.
7 *Table Talk* 20 October 1927, p. 19.
8 *Western Mail*, 29 September 1927, p. 9.
9 *Table Talk*, 20 October 1927, p. 19.
10 *Sun*, 27 January 1935, p. 17.
11 *Chronicle*, 16 July 1931, p. 57.
12 Cook, 'Critical', p. 40.
13 *Haxby's*, location 2341.
14 *Townsville Daily Bulletin*, 11 August 1930, p. 3.
15 'A Place Across the River', Performing Arts Collection, 13 September 2016, https://performingartscollection.wordpress.com, (viewed June 2021).
16 Palmer, *Louis*, pp. 87–8.
17 *MFS*, pp. 92–3.
18 Annette Cameron, interview, broadcast January 1984, ABC Radio Archives, AMP, box 5.
19 KSP to VP, 10 September 1928, PP, MS1174/1/2669
20 *ST*, 9 December 1928, p. 10.
21 KSP to VP 7 May 1931, PP, MS1174 /1/3764.
22 *Haxby's*, location 1382.
23 ibid., location 4182.
24 ibid., location 4359.
25 *WW*, p. 59.
26 *Herald*, 29 August 1930, p. 6.
27 *WW*, p. 60.
28 Richardson, *Letters*, letter 477.
29 *WW*, p. 59.
30 'Authors', p. 423.
31 KSP to WG Cousins, 17 July 1945, ARCF, MLMSS 3269/vol. 591.

32 Hetherington, 'Authors', p. 427.
33 *New York Times*, Book Review, 12 April 1931, p. 7; *WW*, p. 61.
34 *DN*, 21 July 1930, p. 4.
35 *KSP*, p. 32.

24. 'The Mirage is Breaking Up'

1 *Sun*, 13 October 1929, p. 4.
2 KSP to Karen Throssell, 4 July 1968, KSPP, MS6201/1/16.
3 Palmer, *Nettie*, p. 54.
4 Skinner, 'Christian', pp. 117–48.
5 KSP to HM, 1 September 1929, MFP, 3607/17(l).
6 Rutledge and Cowper, 'McCrae'.
7 *CotH*, p. 165.
8 KSP to HM, Tuesday [October 1929], MFP, 3607/17(n).
9 HM to KSP, November 1930, KSPP, MS6201/10/5.
10 KSP to HM, April and May [1931], MFP, 3607/17(p).
11 KSP to HM, 4 December 1929, MFP, 3607/17(b).
12 McCrae, *Letters*, pp. 76–7.
13 KSP to HM, 10 August 1950, MFP, 3607/16 (y).
14 'Australian Literature, Present and Future', typescript, MFP, 3607/17 (a).
15 *DN*, 23 October 1929, p. 9.
16 Bolton, *Land*, p. 120.
17 ibid., p. 121.
18 *WW*, p. 84.
19 *Intimate*, p. 331.
20 ibid., p. 4.
21 ibid., pp. 183–4.
22 *WW*, p. 90.
23 *Intimate*, p. 335.
24 ibid., p. 237.
25 ibid., p. 333.
26 ibid., p. 304.
27 ibid., p. 97.
28 ibid., p. 96.
29 ibid., p. 144.
30 *Roaring*, p. 99.
31 'Some Perceptions', p. 240.
32 'Stranger', p. 48.
33 *DN*, 26 April 1932, p. 7.
34 *ST*, 12 December 1948, p. 5.
35 Throssell, 'Stranger', p. 47.
36 KSP to RT, 22 April 1956, RTP.
37 Flyer held privately.
38 KSP to HM, 25 January [1932], MFP, 3607/17(q).
39 KSP to NP, June 1933, PP, 1174/1/4250.
40 *Herald*, 12 November 1929, p. 7.
41 KSPP, MS6201/2/4, p. 206.

25. Red Star

1 *DN*, 27 January 1932, p. 2.
2 *WW*, p. 64.
3 *DN*, 3 December 1930, p. 6.

4 ibid.
5 KSP, *Happiness*, 1967, p. vii.
6 *Kalgoorlie Miner*, 21 March 1931, p. 1.
7 *Western Argus*, 31 March 1931, p. 5.
8 James Mitchell to EA McLarty, [undated], KSPP, MS6201/1/12.
9 KSP to Repatriation Commission, 28 January 1934, HTRC, p. 97.
10 KSP to HM, April and May [1931], MFP 3607/17(p).
11 KSP to HM, 13 July 1930, MFP 3607/17(f); *WW,* p. 64.
12 KSP to RT, 9 December 1945, RTP.
13 KSP to RT, 19 June 1960, RTP.
14 KSP to Repatriation Commission.
15 Dr JS Yule, 4 November 1932, HTRC, p. 48.
16 KSP to Repatriation Commission; *MFS,* p. 119.
17 *Intimate*, p. 327.
18 *WA,* 15 June 1935, p. 5.
19 Isla Marsh, letter to Spencer Brodney, 29 September 1962, SLV, MS Box 1286/6; Williams, 'KSP (Interview)', p. 26.
20 Cook, 'Critical', p. 29.
21 Richardson, *Letters*, letter 691.
22 *Times Literary Supplement*, 14 April 1932, p. 272.
23 *SMH,* 8 April 1932, p. 4.
24 KSP to HM, June 1931, MFP, 3607/17(g).
25 Devanny, *Point*, p. 171.
26 *Workers' Weekly*, 28 January 1938, p. 2.
27 *DN*, 2 July 1931, p. 6.
28 ibid.
29 *Workers' Weekly*, 28 January 1938, p. 2.
30 Lovell and Windle, *Unswerving*, p. 42.
31 Lindsay Brown to RT, 17 July 1972, RTP, MS8071/4/94.
32 *Workers Star*, 14 January 1938, p. 1.
33 *WA,* 13 September 1932, p. 9.
34 *MFS*, p. 119.
35 KSP to HM, 1 October 1932, MFP, 3607/16A(h).
36 *Red Star*, 30 September 1932, p. 1.
37 *Workers' Weekly*, 2 June 1933, p. 1.
38 *WA,* 15 May 1933, p. 6.
39 *WA,* 12 May 1933, p. 1.
40 *Workers' Weekly*, 2 June 1933, p. 1.
41 *Age*, 23 November 1933, p. 10.
42 *CotH*, p. 255.
43 *Caviar*, p. 8.
44 GB to RT, 10 June 1972, RTP, MS8071/4/94.
45 *WA,* 19 April 1933, p. 8.
46 *CotH*, p. 261.
47 KSP to HM, May 1933, MFP, 3607/16(m).
48 *WW*, p. 67.
49 *CotH*, p. 261.

26. The Real Russia

1 KSP to HM, May 1933, MFP, 3607/16(m).
2 KSP to HM, June 1933, MFP, 3607/16(n).
3 KSP to HT, June 1933, KSPP, MS6201/1/11.

4 ibid.
5 KSP to HM, 6 July 1933, MFP, 3607/16(o).
6 Prichard, 'Some Perceptions', p. 237.
7 KSP to NP, 20 May 1930, PP, MS1174/1/3550
8 Richardson, *Letters*, letter 827.
9 Henry Handel Richardson to KSP, 8 May 1934, KSPP, MS6201/10/1.
10 *DN*, 17 August 1933, p. 1.
11 *WA*, 13 September 1933, p. 14.
12 ASIO-KSP, vol. 3.2, p. 37.
13 *Real*, p. 7.
14 'Engineering', pp. 27, 30.
15 *Herald*, 9 May 1934, p. 20.
16 *Real*, p. 173.
17 Roland, *Caviar*, p. 75.
18 Sparrow, 'Engineering', p. 233.
19 Roland, *Caviar*, p. 78.
20 ibid., p. 81.
21 Widdis, *Alexander*, pp. 22–35.
22 *Real*, p. 48.
23 *Herald*, 4 May 1934, p. 12.
24 *Herald*, 5 May 1934, p. 20.
25 Worrall, 'Meyerhold'.
26 *Real*, p. 79.
27 ibid., p. 207.
28 ibid., p. 65.
29 KSP to MA, 6 May 1956, USW.
30 *Real*, p. 96.
31 KSP to RT, 2 October 1933, KSPP, MS6201/1/11.
32 KSP to HM, 10 September 1933, MFP, 3607/16.
33 KSP to RT, 16 October 1933, KSPP, MS6201/1/10.
34 'James Adinmus' [ie HT] to KSP, 21 August 1933, KSPP, MS6201/1/11.
35 KSP to RT, 2 November 1933, KSPP, MS6201/1/10.
36 *WW*, p. 69.
37 Roland, *Caviar*, p. 96.
38 ibid.
39 Ferrier, *As Good*, p. 345.
40 *Caviar for Breakfast* draft, 1969?, Papers of Betty Roland, NLA, MS6772 box 5, file 6, p. 69. The finding aid erroneously claims this is a photocopy of the diary.
41 Moore, 'Burdens'.
42 KSP to HM, 10 September 1933, MFP, 3607/16(p).
43 *Times*, 20 November 1933, p. 17.
44 KSP to RT, 18 July 1946.
45 *WW*, p. 71.
46 Henry Handel Richardson to KSP, 8 May 1934, KSPP, MS6201/10/1.
47 *DN*, 26 December 1933, p. 1.

27. The Rodeo

1 *Swan Express*, 23 February 1933, p. 2.
2 *WA*, 11 February 1933, p. 16.
3 *DN*, 11 February 1933, p. 3.
4 *WA*, 7 April 1933, p. 24.
5 *MFS*, p. 129.

6 ibid., p. 128.
7 EL Sutton to HT, 14 August 1933, KSPP, MS6201/1/11.
8 HT to RSL, 14 September 1933, KSPP, MS6201/1/11.
9 Greenmount Road Board to HT, 18 July 1933, KSPP, MS6201/1/11
10 AO Neville to HT, 28 July 1933, KSPP, MS6201/1/11.
11 *WA,* 6 March 1936, p. 12.
12 Under Secretary, Government of WA to HT, 28 July 1933, KSPP, MS6201/1/11.
13 Chief Secretary's Dept to HT, 9 Sept 1933, KSPP, MS6201/1/11.
14 HT to Mrs Ross, 29 July 1933, KSPP, MS6201/1/11.
15 HT to Dr Buttsworth, 15 August 1933, KSPP, MS6201/1/11.
16 HT to RSL, 14 September 1933, KSPP, MS6201/1/11.
17 *Swan Express*, 3 August 1933, p. 5.
18 *WA,* 31 July 1933, p. 6.
19 HT to RSL, 14 September 1933, KSPP, MS6201/1/11.
20 *Mirror*, 9 September 1933, p. 6.
21 *Mirror*, 4 November 1933, p. 9.
22 Liabilities, 1943, KSPP, MS6201/1/11.
23 *WW*, pp. 138–9.
24 *MFS*, p. 133.
25 ibid., p. 137.
26 ibid., pp. 133, 137–8.
27 ibid., p. 138.
28 HTRC, p. 37.
29 *WA*, 12 December 1933, p. 10.
30 *MFS*, p. 139.
31 *Swan Express*, 23 November 1933, p. 2.
32 HTRC, p. 145.
33 ibid.
34 ibid.
35 ibid.
36 *WA,* 20 November 1933, p. 7. The note was lost by either the police or the coroner and its contents couldn't be verified during the investigation into Hugo's death by the Repatriation Commission. HTRC, pp. 53–4.
37 *WA,* 14 March 1934, p. 3.
38 *WA,* 21 November 1933, p. 14.

28. 'All That Is Left'

1 *WW*, p. 71.
2 ibid., p. 73.
3 KSP to RT, 30 September 1951, RTP.
4 KSP to HM, March 1934, MFP, 3607/16(s).
5 KSP to RT, 11 August 1946, RTP.
6 *WW*, p. 71.
7 *WA*, 12 December 1933, p. 10.
8 KSP to Repatriation Commission, 28 January 1934, HTRC, p. 97.
9 HTRC, p. 19.
10 HTRC, p. 129
11 Statement of Assets and Liabilities at 19 November 1933, KSPP, MS6201/1/11.
12 *DN*, 28 February 1934, p. 4.
13 *Why*, p. 9.
14 *Herald*, 14 April 1934, p. 30.
15 *Herald*, 28 April 1934, p. 6.

16 *Red Star*, 1 June 1934, p. 1.
17 KSP to HM, October 1934, MFP, 3607/16(t).
18 Simon Bridge to KSP Writers Centre, email, 21 November 2005, KWC.
19 *Herald*, 10 November 1934, p. 24.
20 'Tributes to the Memory of Bernard O'Dowd', p. 419.
21 *Workers' Weekly*, 16 November 1934, p. 1.
22 Zogbaum, *Kisch*, p. 33.
23 *Herald*, 9 November 1934, p. 1.
24 Zogbaum, *Kisch*.
25 *Argus*, 9 November 1934, p. 10.
26 *Workers' Weekly*, 16 November 1934, p. 1.
27 Prichard, 'Egon', p. 72.
28 *WW*, p. 78.
29 KSP to Walt Carmon, 27 March 1935, USW.
30 *MFS*, p. 146.
31 ibid., p. 145.
32 Kasoff, 'Union', p. 1610.
33 KSP to Carmon.
34 *Real*, p. 247.
35 International League of Writers, *Report of 1st Australian Conference*, 1935, p. 2.
36 Quoted in Prichard, *Real*, p. 254.
37 ibid.
38 *Exiles*, location 2893.
39 Irwin, 'Australia's', p. 31.
40 'Kisch', p. 78; Clark, 'Soviet', p. 406.
41 *Workers' Weekly*, 8 February 1935, p. 2.
42 *Herald*, 31 January 1935, p. 5.
43 *WA*, 15 June 1935, p. 5.

29. On All Fronts

1 Bartlett, 'Perth', p. 64.
2 *WA*, 7 May 1935, p. 23.
3 Lovell and Windle, *Unswerving*, document 76.
4 ASIO-KSP, vol. 1, p. 92.
5 ASIO-KSP, vol. 3.1, pp. 24-7.
6 Hyde, *Art*, location 1140.
7 ibid., location 408.
8 Quoted in ibid., location 1383.
9 *Red Star*, 13 December 1935, p. 4.
10 *Anger*, p. 65.
11 Hyde, *Art*, location 2893.
12 *Workers Star*, 12 November 1937, p. 1.
13 *Workers Star*, 5 November 1937, p. 4.
14 Hyde, *Art*, location 2445.
15 *Workers Star*, 7 January 1938, p. 1.
16 Hyde, *Art*, location 3829.
17 Quoted in ibid., location 2941.
18 Williams, *First*, p. 139.
19 *MFS*, p. 118.
20 KSP to GB, 6 November 1935, GBP, MS5241/2.
21 KSP to Timofey Rokotov, 11 April 1939, USW.
22 *MFS*, pp. 146–7.

23 ibid., p. 199.
24 ibid., p. 200.
25 KSP to Timofey Rokotov, 11 September 1938, USW
26 KSP, 'Notes on Modern Women's Club', RTP, MS8071/4/94.
27 *Workers Star*, 29 April 1938, p. 3.
28 Dorothy Irwin to RT, 25 March 1972, RTP, MS8071/4/93.
29 Kotai-Ewers, 'Fellowship', pp. 75ff.
30 *WA*, 15 November 1938, p. 11.
31 KSP to VP, 10 October [1935?], KSPP, MS6201/10/2.
32 KSP to HM, 1 August 1936, MFP, 3607/16(x).
33 Quoted in Modjeska, *Exiles*, location 2906.
34 *WA*, 3 June 1939, p. 3.
35 KSP to Sergei Dinamov, 30 October 1936, USW.
36 KSP to HM, 1 August 1936, MFP, 3607/16(x).
37 *Bulletin*, 26 May 1937, p. 2.
38 *DN*, 19 May 1937, p. 4.
39 *Workers' Weekly*, 13 July 1937, p. 3.
40 *Workers' Weekly*, 30 November 1937, p. 2.
41 ASIO- KSP, vol. 1, pp. 77-80.
42 Richardson, *Letters*, letter 1070.
43 *WA*, 21 May 1937, p. 27.
44 Prichard, 'Art', p. 130.
45 *Bulletin*, 11 December 1935, p. 27.
46 *Workers Star*, 24 February 1939, p. 3.
47 'Aborigine', p. 49.
48 KSP to MA, 19 September 1940, USW.
49 *Who*, p. 6.
50 'Peace', p. 59.
51 Macintyre, *Reds*, location 7044.
52 KSP to HDB, 28 July 1941, HDBP.
53 *WW*, p. 92.

30. Underground

1 ASIO-KSP, vol. 1, p. 31.
2 *Tribune*, 23 February 1940, p. 2.
3 'Engineering', p. 255.
4 Quoted in ibid., p. 246.
5 *WW*, p. 239.
6 Kotai-Ewers, 'Fellowship', pp. 122–3.
7 Quoted in Hyde, *Art*, location 4107.
8 ASIO-KSP, vol. 1, p. 14.
9 *MFS*, p. 157.
10 ASIO-KSP, vol. 1, p. 11.
11 Macintyre, *Reds*, location 7307.
12 ASIO-KSP, vol. 2, p. 32.
13 McKenzie, *Challenging*, p. 104.
14 ibid., p. 101; *DN*, 6 May 1941, p. 13.
15 KSP to Hilda Esson, 7 June 1941, KSPP, MS6201/10/7.
16 Williams, *First*, p. 170.
17 Challenging, p. 104.
18 KSP to Esson.
19 Quoted in Hyde, *Art*, location 4629.

20 KSP to MA, 20 May 1940, USW.
21 Quoted in Hyde, *Art,* location 4629.
22 *Moon*, p. 78.
23 'KSP', p. 14; *Moon*, p. 89.
24 *Bulletin,* 26 November 1941, p. 2.
25 *SMH,* 8 November 1941, p. 10.
26 *WW*, p. 98; Carter and Osborne, *Australian*, p. 225.
27 KSP to MA, 19 September 1940, USW.
28 ibid.
29 Ferrier, *As Good*, p. 62.
30 KSP to Commonwealth Literary Fund, 15 December 1940, CLF, p. 113.
31 'What it used to cost', SLV, https://guides.slv.vic.gov.au/whatitcost/earnings (viewed June 2021).
32 CLF, p. 120.
33 KSP-ASIO, vol. 2a, p. 12.
34 KSP to Hilda Esson, 7 June 1941, KSPP, MS6201/10/7.
35 ibid.
36 'Some Recollections of KSP', WSP.
37 ibid.
38 ibid.
39 KSP to HS Temby, 4 August 1941, CLF, p. 99.
40 Burchill, 'KSP', p. 314.
41 Smith, *Newspaper*, pp. 5–6.
42 Burchill, 'KSP', p. 314.
43 Hale, 'My Father', p. 15.
44 'Some Recollections of KSP', WSP.
45 *WA,* 7 April 1933, p. 24.
46 *Kalgoorlie Miner*, 30 May 1941, p. 1.
47 ASIO-KSP, vol. 2, p. 33.
48 ASIO-KSP, vol. 2, pp. 63–5.
49 KSP to HDB, 28 July 1941, HDBP.
50 KSP to Timofey Rokotov, 4 August 1941, USW.
51 KSP to HS Temby, 12 October 1941, CLF, p. 96.
52 ASIO-KSP, vol. 2, p. 7.
53 *DN*, 13 January 1942, p. 5.
54 ASIO-KSP, vol. 2, p. 119.
55 *Newcastle Morning Herald*, 28 October 1941, p. 4.
56 *WA,* 19 September 1941, p. 5.
57 'Deakin', pp. 106–7.
58 ibid.
59 ASIO-KSP, vol. 2, p. 119.
60 *Advertiser*, 30 December 1941, p. 4.
61 *MFS*, pp. 163–4.
62 ASIO-KSP, vol. 2, p. 119.
63 *MFS*, p. 169.
64 *WW*, p. 110.
65 KSP to DS, 13 July 1942, WSP.
66 Ferrier, *As Good*, p. 87.

31. Long Live the Party

1 *MFS*, p. 187.
2 ASIO-KSP, vol. 2, p. 143.

3 KSP to HDB, June 1943, HDBP; Roe, *Stella*, p. 421.
4 Doon Stone, 'Some Reminiscences', WSP.
5 Ferrier, *As Good*, p. 98.
6 ibid., p. 104.
7 'Tribute', 133.
8 KSP to RT, 18 September 1943, RTP.
9 'Her Brilliant', p. 228.
10 ibid., p. 233.
11 KSP to RT, 3 July 1944, RTP.
12 *MFS*, pp. 6–7.
13 ibid., p. 189.
14 *WW*, pp. 119–20.
15 *MFS*, p. 198.
16 ibid., p. 200.
17 *Communist Review*, 1 April 1943, p. 4.
18 KSP to RT, 16 December 1945, RTP.
19 *WW*, p. 117.
20 Beasley, *Gallop*, p. 124; also Aarons, *Family*, location 789.
21 *Tribune*, 17 May 1945, p. 4.
22 McKnight, 'Rethinking', p. 191; Cahill, 'Rupert', p. 263.
23 *Breaking*, p. 10.
24 *WA*, 16 September 1942, p. 4.
25 ASIO-KSP, vol. 2, p. 143
26 *Breaking*, p. 126.
27 ibid., p. 237.
28 ibid., p. 220.
29 Aarons, *Family*, location 2598.
30 Pamela Burton, 'John Burton: Undermined by Dishonest History', *Honest History*, 1 September 2014, http://honesthistory.net.au/wp/burton-pamela-john-burton-undermined-by-dishonest-history/ (viewed June 2021).
31 VENONA documents, National Security Agency, www.nsa.gov/Portals/70/documents/news-features/declassified-documents/venona/dated/1945/30sep_throssel.pdf (viewed June 2021).
32 Deery, 'Remembering', p. 52.
33 Ball and Horner, *Breaking*, p. 220.
34 Ferrier, 'Devanny', 2001.
35 Devanny, *Point*, p. 182.
36 ibid., pp. 180–1.
37 ibid., p. 137.
38 ibid., p. 181.
39 ibid., p. 138.
40 ibid., p. 180.
41 Ferrier, *Jean*, 1999, p. 183.
42 *Gallop*, pp. 126ff.
43 Devanny, *Point*, p. 254.
44 ibid.; Ferrier, *As Good*, p. 317.
45 Ferrier, *As Good*, p. 119.
46 ibid., pp. 119–20.
47 Ferrier, *Jean*, 1999, p. 161.
48 Fitzpatrick, *Pioneer*, pp. 338–9.
49 Hilda Esson to KSP, 4 April 1952, KSPP, MS6201/10/7.
50 Harry Gould to RT, 12 August 1972, RTP, MS8071/4/94.

51 Fitzpatrick, *Pioneer*, p. 332.
52 KSPP, MS6201/7/6.
53 *Hold*, p. 152.
54 Fitzpatrick, *Pioneer*, p. 340.

32. Revival

1 Ferrier, *Jean*, 1999, p. 252.
2 KSP to MA, 6 February 1944, USW.
3 Annette Cameron, interview, broadcast January 1984, ABC Radio Archives, AMP, box 5.
4 KSP to RT, 23 January 1944, RTP
5 KSP to RT, 17 February 1944, RTP.
6 KSP to RT, 30 April 1944, RTP.
7 Low, 'Salt'.
8 Brooks and Clark, *Eleanor*, p. 255.
9 KSP to RT, 26 March 1944, 15 October 1944, 29 October 1944, RTP.
10 KSP to RT, 5 March 1945, RTP.
11 *Daily Telegraph*, 21 April 1944, p. 7.
12 KSP to RT, [undated, 1945], RTP.
13 *Age*, 14 July 1945, p. 9.
14 *Daily Telegraph*, 10 March 1945, p. 13.
15 KSP to MA, 6 February 1944, USW.
16 KSP to MA, 24 October 1944, USW.
17 'Hoax', pp. 199, 200, 201.
18 Ferrier, *As Good*, p. 318.
19 ibid., p. 362.
20 ibid., p. 365.
21 KSP to RT, 11 August 1946, RTP.
22 KSP to RT, 20 February 1944, 14 May 1944, 25 June 1944, 14 January 1945, RTP.
23 KSP to RT, 11 March 1945, RTP.
24 Prichard, 'International', p. 234.
25 ibid., pp. 235–6.
26 *WW*, pp. 120–1.
27 KSP to MA, 17 March 1954, USW.
28 *Argus*, 6 December 1944, p. 8.
29 KSP to RT, 8 July 1945, RTP.
30 *Tribune*, 24 July 1945, p. 1.
31 *MFS*, pp. 216–17.
32 KSP to HDB, 25 August 1945, HDBP.
33 KSP to RT, February 1945, RTP.
34 *MFS*, pp. 201, 211.
35 KSP to RT, Wednesday [undated], RTP, folder 181.
36 KSP to RT, 21 January 1945, RTP.
37 *MFS*, pp. 218–19.
38 KSP to RT, [undated], RTP, folder 182.
39 Doon Stone, 'Some Reminiscences', WSP.
40 *MFS*, pp. 219–20.
41 VENONA documents, National Security Agency.
42 KSP to RT, 24 December 1945, RTP.
43 KSP to RT, 24 February 1946, RTP.
44 KSP to RT, 17 March 1946, RTP.
45 KSP to RT, 29 March 1946, RTP.

46 ibid.
47 KSP to RT, 2 June 1946, RTP.

33. The Furies Return

1 KSP to RT, 5 April 1946, RTP.
2 KSP to RT, 15 April 1946, RTP.
3 KSP to RT, 28 and 30 April 1946, RTP.
4 KSP to Bea Throssell, 23 April 1946, RTP.
5 *MFS*, pp. 238–40; *WW*, p. 140.
6 KSP to RT, 11–13 August 1946, RTP.
7 KSP to RT, 18 July 1946, RTP.
8 KSP to RT, 11–13 August 1946, RTP.
9 ibid.
10 KSP to RT, 20 July 1969, RTP.
11 Ferrier, *As Good*, p. 147.
12 *Tribune*, 18 October 1946, p. 5.
13 'Statement by KSP', typescript, 12 October 1946, SLNSW, A2763.
14 Williams, *First*, p. 113.
15 Burchill, 'KSP', p. 312.
16 *Argus*, 3 August 1946, p. 15.
17 Franklin, *Gregarious*, pp. 211–13.
18 *Workers Star*, 23 August 1946, p. 4.
19 Williams, *Anger*, pp. 130–1.
20 KSP to RT, 23 September 1946, RTP.
21 Ferrier, *As Good*, p. 161.
22 *MFS*, p. 247.
23 KSP to RT, 19 February 1947, RTP; Ferrier, *As Good*, p. 166.
24 KSP to RT, 19 February 1947, RTP.
25 Ferrier, *As Good*, p. 172.
26 ibid.
27 KSP to RT, 10 March 1947, RTP.
28 *MFS*, p. 250.
29 Ferrier, *As Good*, p. 176.
30 KSP to MA, 6 August 1947, USW.
31 *WW*, p. 146.
32 KSP to DS, 5 November 1947, WSP.
33 *MFS*, p. 251.

34. The Cold War Begins

1 KSP to DS, 5 November 1947, WSP.
2 KSP to RT, September 1946, RTP.
3 Ferrier, *As Good*, p. 181.
4 Bonnin and Bonnin, 'Hill'.
5 KSP to RT, September 1946, RTP.
6 Ferrier, *As Good*, p. 181.
7 KSP to RT, 19 January 1948, RTP.
8 KSP to RT, 25 October 1947, RTP.
9 KSP to RT, 8 December 1947, RTP.
10 KSP to RT, 30 November 1947, RTP.
11 KSP to RT, 3 July 1948, RTP.
12 *Workers Star*, 17 September 1948, p. 4.
13 KSP to RT, 18 July 1948, RTP.

14 *Bulletin,* 27 October 1948, p. 2.
15 *Western Mail,* 30 September 1948, p. 14.
16 KSP to RT, 2 May 1948, RTP.
17 KSP to RT, 19 July 1948, RTP.
18 *WW,* p. 151.
19 KSP to RT, 18 March 1949, RTP.
20 KSP to RT, 24 March 1949, RTP.
21 KSP to RT, 10 April 1949, RTP.
22 KSP to RT, 15 March 1948, RTP.
23 *SMH,* 17 July 1948, p. 2.
24 Jeff Sparrow, 'Conceptual Slippage: The Spy Catchers and Dirty Secrets', *Sydney Review of Books,* 21 November 2014, https://sydneyreviewofbooks.com/review/spy-catchers-dirty-secrets (viewed June 2021).
25 *WA,* 13 August 1949, p. 6.
26 *Kalgoorlie Miner,* 29 March 1949, p. 2.
27 *Workers Star,* 14 April 1949, p. 5.
28 *DN,* 9 April 1949, p. 1; *ST,* 10 April 1949, p. 6.
29 KSP to RT, 10 April 1949, RTP.
30 *Workers Star,* 14 April 1949, p. 5.
31 Ferrier, *As Good,* p. 145.
32 KSP to RT, Xmas morning [1949], RTP.
33 KSP to RT, 30 July 1949, RTP.
34 KSP to RT, 1 October 1949, RTP.
35 KSP to RT, 28 May 1950, RTP.
36 Ferrier, *As Good,* p. 257.
37 Book description, Antipodean Books, www.antipodean.com/pages/books/10787/katharine-susannah-prichard/winged-seeds (viewed June 2021).
38 *Winged,* p. 379.
39 Ferrier, *As Good,* p. 267.
40 *Bulletin,* 10 January 1951, p. 2.
41 *Argus,* 24 February 1951, p. 10.
42 Ferrier, *As Good,* p. 267.
43 *SMH,* 27 January 1951, p. 8.
44 *Writing,* p. 255.
45 'Novels', p. 381.

35. Legacy

1 KSP to Bea Throssell, 9 June 1946, RTP.
2 KSP to RT, 26 March 1950, RTP.
3 KSP to RT, 24 July 1950, RTP.
4 KSP to RT, 30 July 1950, RTP.
5 KSP to RT, 6 August 1950, RTP.
6 KSP to Cyril Cook, 19 August 1951, KWC.
7 KSP to RT, 17 March 1968, RTP.
8 KSP to NP, 24 December 1950, PP, MS1174/1/7932.
9 KSP to RT, 28 January 1951, RTP.
10 KSP to Cyril Cook, 4 June 1951, KWC.
11 KSP to RT, 1 July 1951, RTP.
12 ibid.
13 KSP to Cyril Cook, 19 August 1951, KWC.
14 'Critical', p. 192.
15 Cyril Cook to RT, 26 December 1972, RTP, MS8071/4/95.

16 RT to Cyril Cook, 7 January 1973, RTP, MS8071/4/95.
17 Cyril Cook to RT, 19 January 19 1973, RTP, MS8071/4/95.
18 Douglas Stewart to RT, 24 January 1973, RTP, MS8071/4/95.
19 Burchill, 'KSP', pp. 372–3.
20 KSP to RT, 5 March 1950, RTP.
21 Ferrier, *As Good*, p. 239; Roe, *Stella*, p. 488.
22 KSP to RT, 5 March 1950, RTP.
23 KSP to RT, 10 June 1951, RTP.
24 KSP to RT, 19 November 1951, RTP.
25 KSP to RT, 11 February 1957, RTP.
26 'Some Thoughts', p. 203.
27 Carter, 'Peace', p. 61.
28 Ferrier, *As Good*, p. 234.
29 *Workers Star*, 26 May 1950, p. 8.
30 Doon Stone, 'Some Reminiscences', WSP.
31 KSP to RT, 8 October 1950, RTP.
32 KSP to RT, 7 January 1951, RTP.
33 KSP to RT, 29 August 1953, RTP.
34 KSP to RT, 23 March 1952, RTP.
35 KSP to RT, 17 September 1951, RTP.
36 *Challenging*, p. 158.
37 KSP to RT, 23 September 1951, RTP.
38 KSP to RT, 6 January 1952, RTP.
39 KSP to RT, 23 March 1952, RTP.
40 KSP to RT, 27 July 1952, RTP.
41 KSP to RT, Sunday 1952, RTP.
42 *SMH,* 10 September 1952, p. 2.
43 *SMH,* 11 September 1952, p. 2.
44 KSP to RT, 19 October 1952, RTP.
45 KSP to RT, 20 September 1952, RTP.
46 KSP to RT, 24 September 1952, RTP.
47 KSP to RT, 5 October 1952, RTP.
48 Fitzpatrick, *Pioneer*, p. 356.
49 KSP to MA, 7 March 1953, USW.
50 *Sun*, 6 March 1953, p. 4.
51 Hilda Esson to KSP, 20 April 1953, KSPP, MS6201/10/3.
52 KSP to HDB, 3 August 1953, HDB.
53 KSP to RT, 29 June 1953, RTP.
54 KSP to RT, 20 July 1953, RTP.
55 Hilda Esson to KSP, 4 April 1952, KSPP, MS6201/10/7.
56 Ferrier, *As Good*, p. 322.
57 ibid., p. 351.
58 North, *Yarn*, p. 368.
59 Roe, *Stella*, pp. 501, 532.
60 Ferrier, *As Good*, pp. 356–7.
61 ibid., pp. 386–7.
62 Delys Cross, notes about KSP, RTP, MS8071/4/91.
63 KSP to RT, 26 September 1954, RTP.

36. 'My Faith Has Never Wavered'

1 KSP to RT, 7 February 1954, RTP.
2 KSP to RT, 25 February 1954, RTP.

3 KSP to RT, 8 April 1954, RTP.
4 KSP to MA, 24 June 1954, USW.
5 *MFS*, p. 299.
6 ibid., pp. 303–4.
7 KSP to RT, 26 July 1954, RTP.
8 *MFS*, pp. 303–4.
9 KSP to RT, 3 February 1955, RTP.
10 *MFS*, p. 323.
11 ibid.
12 *Canberra Times*, 15 September 1955, p. 1.
13 KSP to RT, 6 May 1955, RTP.
14 *SMH,* 11 February 1956, p. 13.
15 KSP to RT, 17 May 1955, RTP.
16 Quoted in Skinner, 'Christian', p. 264.
17 Betsey Linton and Kitch Currie, interview by Anne Mahon, 22 January 2000, AMP.
18 Judy Inveen, email to author, 7 February 2018.
19 Deery and Calkin, 'We All', p. 69.
20 *Tribune*, 11 April 1956, pp. 6–7; Sparrow, 'Engineering', p. 62.
21 KSP to MA, 6 May 1956, USW.
22 ibid.
23 KSP to MA, 29 May 1956, USW.
24 'Fadeev Kills Self!', SovLit, 2012, www.sovlit.net/fadeevsuicide (viewed June 2021).
25 KSP to MA, 27 February 1957, USW.
26 KSP to MA, 12 October 1957, USW.
27 ASIO-KSP, vol. 4.2, pp. 97–8.
28 ASIO-KSP, vol. 4.2, p. 49.
29 ASIO-KSP, vol. 4.2, p. 93; *Good Neighbour,* 1 August 1958, p. 6.
30 KSP to RT, 6 January 1957, RTP.
31 Doon Stone, 'Some Reminiscences', WSP.
32 KSP to RT, 6 January 1957, RTP.
33 KSP to MA, 9 April 1957, USW.
34 KSP to OK, 8 April 1957, USW.
35 KSP to OK, 11 June 1957, USW.
36 Maclellan, *Grappling*, pp. 94, 103.
37 KSP to OK, 5 September 1957, USW.
38 KSP to OK, 23 June 1958, USW.
39 KSP to RT, 5 July 1958, RTP.
40 KSP to Dodie Throssell, 24 September 1958, RTP.
41 *WW*, p. 181.
42 KSPP, MS6201/8/5.
43 KSP to RT, 7 September 1959, RTP.
44 KSP to RT, 18 November 1957, RTP.
45 KSP to RT, 7 September 1959, RTP.
46 KSP to OK, 15 November 1959, USW.
47 *Subtle*, pp. 275–6.
48 KSP to RT, 22 November 1959, RTP.

37. 'A Personal Thing'

1 KSP to RT, 1 August 1960, 21 August 1960, RTP.
2 KSP to MA, 10 August 1960, USW.
3 KSP to OK, 10 September 1959, USW.
4 KSP to RT, 21 August 1960, RTP.

5 KSP to RT, 11 September 1960, RTP.
6 ASIO-KSP, vol. 4.2, p. 28.
7 KSP to OK, 30 September 1960, USW.
8 KSP to OK, 4 June 1961, USW.
9 Curthoys, 'Robeson', p. 166.
10 KSP to RT, 12 April 1959, RTP.
11 *Tribune*, 7 December 1960, p. 10.
12 KSP to RT, 4 December 1960, RTP.
13 KSP to RT, [1961], RTP, folder 195.
14 KSP to RT, 17 December 1961, RTP.
15 KSP to RT, [1961], RTP, folder 195.
16 Cecilia Shelley, interview by RT, 12 September 1972, RTP, MS8071/4/92.
17 Joan Williams, interview by RT, 5 September 1972, RTP, MS8071/4/92.
18 Shelley, interview by RT.
19 Quoted in Carr, 'Age', p. 411.
20 ibid., pp. 393–403.
21 ibid., p. 410.
22 KSP to GB, 28 July 1965, KSPP, MS6201/10/17.
23 KSP to OK, 11 June 1957, USW.
24 Carr, 'Age', p. 412.
25 KSP to Karen Throssell, 30 March 1963, KSPP, MS6201/1/16.
26 KSP to RT, 23 March 1963, RTP.
27 KSP to RT, September 1963, RTP.
28 Davis, *Causes*, p. 299.
29 KSP to RT, 16 July 1961, RTP.
30 KSP to Beatrice Davis, 21 September 1961, KSPP, MS6201/10/17.
31 Beatrice Davis to KSP, 8 May 1962, KSPP, MS6201/10/9.
32 KSP to Beatrice Davis, 18 October 1961, KSPP, MS6201/10/17.
33 KSP to Beatrice Davis, 13 May 1962, KSPP, MS6201/10/9.
34 Quoted in Kent, *Beatrice*, location 2690.
35 Beatrice Davis to KSP, 24 May 1962, KSPP, MS6201/10/9.
36 KSPP, MS6201/7/5.
37 Burchill, 'KSP', p. 1.
38 KSP to Beatrice Davis, 20 July 1963, KSPP, MS6201/10/17.
39 *SMH,* 9 November 1963, p. 13.
40 *WW*, p. 189.
41 KSP to Catherine Duncan, 31 May 1964, KSPP, MS6201/10/24.
42 CLF, p. 38.
43 KSP to OK, 2 May 1964, USW.
44 KSP to RT, [undated letter, page 3 only, 1964?], RTP, folder 198.
45 Dorothy Hewett to KSP, KSPP, 22 November 1963, MS6201/10/17.
46 *Westerly*, vol. 8, no. 4, 1963, p. 63.
47 Dorothy Hewett, interview, ABC radio, recorded 6 January 1982, AMP.
48 KSP to NP, 25 January 1964, PP, MS1174/1/9931. Two of Dorothy's daughters, including Kate Lilley who was named after Katharine, have spoken of sexual abuse they suffered at the family home in the 1970s which they say was encouraged by Dorothy. Broede Carmody, 'Dorothy Hewett's daughters say grown men preyed on them as children', 11 June 2018, *SMH*, www.smh.com.au (viewed June 2021).
49 Hewett, interview.
50 Williams, 'KSP (Interview)', p. 26.
51 ibid.
52 Joan Williams, interview by Anne Mahon, 22 November 1999, AMP.

53 Cusack, 'KSP', p. 16.
54 KSP to RT, 24 November 1963, RTP.
55 *Tribune*, 11 December 1963, p. 7.
56 Cusack, 'KSP', p. 14.

38. Hardliner

1 KSP to RT, 20 July 1964, RTP.
2 John Gilchrist to RT, 20 July 1964, RTP.
3 John Gilchrist, diary, John and Roma Gilchrist Papers, SLWA, ACC3632A.
4 *WW*, p. 212.
5 ibid.
6 Williams, *Anger*, p. 217.
7 ibid.
8 KSP to RT, [undated, 1964], RTP, MS8074/4/198, pp. 153–4.
9 'Pages From a Diary', typescript, RTP, MS8071/4/91.
10 KSP to RT, 8 November 1964, RTP.
11 KSP to RT, 27 December 1964, RTP.
12 Joan Williams, interview by RT, 5 September 1972, RTP, MS8071/4/92.
13 KSP to RT, 20 March 1966, RTP.
14 Williams, interview.
15 KSP to RT, quoted in 'KSP: "Excess of Love"? Some Comments', p. 26.
16 KSP to OK, 6 March 1965, USW.
17 KSP to RT, 2 May 1965, 28 January 1968, RTP.
18 KSP to RT, 27 June 1965, RTP.
19 KSP to RT, 14 November 1965, RTP.
20 Prichard, 'Some Perceptions', p. 241.
21 *New Statesman*, 7 January 1966, p. 19.
22 KSP to RT, 26 March 1966, RTP.
23 KSP to RT, 8 May 1966, RTP.
24 *WW*, p. 215.
25 KSP to RT, 31 July 1966, RTP.
26 *WW*, p. 215.
27 KSP to RT, 30 October 1966, RTP.
28 KSP to RT, 13 November 1966, RTP.
29 KSP to RT, 19 December 1966, RTP.
30 *Tribune*, 9 August 1967, p. 3; ASIO-KSP, vol. 6, p. 76.
31 KSP to RT, 8 August 1967, RTP.
32 ASIO-KSP, vol. 6, p. 78.
33 KSPP, MS6201/10/19.
34 *Australian Book Review*, September 1967, p. 175.
35 *Bulletin*, 19 August 1967, p. 65; *SMH*, 7 October 1967, p. 17.
36 KSP to RT, 7 March 1968, RTP.
37 *Happiness*, 1967, p. viii.
38 KSP to RT, July 1966, RTP, pp. 114–15.
39 KSP to RT, 30 September 1962, RTP.
40 *KSP*, pp. 5–6.
41 Martin, *Ink*, p. 263.
42 KSP to NP, 11 July 1959, KSPP, MS6201/10/17.
43 KSP to NP, 25 January 1964, PP, MS1174/1/9931.
44 KSP to RT, 20 January 1963, RTP.
45 GB to RT, 10 June 1972, RTP, MS8071/4/94.
46 KSP to RT, 13 April 1965, RTP.

47 KSP to GB, 13 April 1965, KSPP, MS6201/10/17.
48 GB to KSP, 12 December 1967, KSPP, MS6201/10/23.
49 "Cheerio", p. 8.
50 KSP to RT, 3 November 1963, RTP.
51 KSP to RT, 23 January 1966, RTP.
52 KSP to RT, 26 March 1966, RTP.
53 KSP to RT, 26 June 1966, RTP.
54 Quoted in Cath Ellis, p. 11.
55 KSP to RT, 10 July 1956, RTP.
56 Kotai-Ewers, 'Vickers'.
57 KSP to RT, 23 April 1967, RTP.
58 KSP to RT, 20 August 1967, RTP.
59 KSP to RT, 10 September 1967, RTP.
60 KSP to RT, 10 May 1968, RTP.
61 Wendy Kendrick, interview by Anne Mahon, 10 December 1999, AMP.
62 Hewett, 'Excess', p. 30.
63 KSP to RT, 28 January 1962, RTP.
64 Dorothy Hewett, interview by RT, 15 September 1972, RTP, MS8071/4/92.
65 *Tribune,* 23 February 1966, p. 4.
66 KSP to Dorothy Hewett, 18 April 1967, USW, ACC5835A/34.
67 Hewett, 'Excess', p. 28.
68 ibid., p. 30.
69 Dorothy Hewett, interview by RT.
70 *National Times,* 25 November 1983, p. 29.
71 KSP to RT, 16 June 1968, RTP.
72 KSP to RT, 27 November 1966, RTP.
73 KSP to RT, 18 August 1968, RTP.
74 *Tribune*, 25 September 1968, p. 11.
75 KSP to MA, 30 January 1960, USW.
76 ASIO-KSP, vol. 7, pp. 9–10.
77 Delys Cross, notes about KSP, RTP, MS8071/4/91.
78 KSP to OK, 27 May 1962, USW.
79 KSP to RT, 23 April 1967, RTP.
80 KSP to RT, 3 November 1968, RTP.
81 KSP to Karen Throssell, 18 August 1968, KSPP, MS6201/1/16.
82 KSP to RT, 20 July 1968, RTP.
83 'Some Perceptions', p. 236.
84 ibid., p. 235.
85 ibid., p. 244.
86 KSP to Karen Throssell, 4 March 1967, KSPP, MS6201/1/16.
87 KSP to RT, 4 July 1965, RTP; KSP to Karen Throssell, 25 February 1966, KSPP, MS6201/1/16.
88 KSP to RT, 18 December 1968, RTP.
89 KSP to RT, 29 December 1968, RTP.
90 ibid.
91 KSP to RT, 12 January 1969, RTP.
92 KSP to RT, 19 January 1969, RTP.

39. 'My Joy Will Be Complete'

1 KSP to RT, 3 February 1969, RTP.
2 KSP to RT, 9 February 1969, RTP.
3 KSP to RT, 25 May 1969, RTP.

4 KSP to RT, 9 March 1969, RTP.
5 KSP to RT, 30 March 1969, RTP.
6 KSP to RT, 4 May 1969, RTP.
7 KSP to RT, 23 February 1969, RTP.
8 Prichard, 'A Writer's', p. 23.
9 KSP to Beatrice Davis, 27 September 1969, ARCF, MLMSS 3269/vol. 592.
10 KSP to Karen Throssell, 14 July 1969, KSPP, MS6201/1/16.
11 Thomas, 'KSP', p. 55.
12 KSP to RT, 22 June 1969, RTP.
13 KSP to Catherine Duncan, [undated], KSPP, MS6201/10/24.
14 Catherine Duncan to KSP, 14 August 1969, KSPP MS6201/10/24.
15 KSP to Catherine Duncan, 23 September 1969, KSPP, MS6201/10/24.
16 *WW*, p. xi.
17 'Son Destroys Author's Work', newspaper clipping, KWC.
18 KSP to RT, 7 September 1969, RTP.
19 John Joseph Jones, 'A Pigeon Pair of Plays', typescript, KWC.
20 KSP to OK, 30 June 1969, USW.
21 KSP to *Tribune*, 22 September 1969, USW.
22 *WW*, p. 248.
23 Jeffery, *Inside*; Pringle, 'Zarubina'.
24 KSP to RT, 26 September 1954, RTP.
25 KSP to DS, 2 October 1969, WSP.
26 Elizabeth Harris to Faye Davis, 7 October 1995, KWC.
27 Amy Wells [sic – Barrett], interview by Joan Williams, JWP, MS5245A/169.
28 Hewett, 'Excess', p. 28.
29 Williams, 'Rage', p. 18.
30 *MFS*, pp. 362–3.

Afterword

1 Sun, 'Points'.
2 Watts, 'Children'.
3 KSP Writers Centre, *Kaleidoscope*.
4 Karen Throssell, 'Launch Speech', KSP Writers' Centre, 15 October 2019, https://www.kspwriterscentre.com/single-post/2019/10/15/congratulation-to-kaleidoscope-winners (viewed March 2021).
5 'In Memory of W. B. Yeats', Poets.org, 1940, https://poets.org/poem/memory-w-b-yeats (viewed March 2021).

Works by Katharine Susannah Prichard

Referenced editions, short stories, and essays in main bibliography.

Novels and short story collections

The Pioneers, Hodder and Stoughton, London, 1915; rev. edn, Rigby, Adelaide, 1963.
Windlestraws, Serialised in the *Age*, 25 March 1916 – 10 June 1916; Holden and Hardingham, London, 1916.
Black Opal, Heinemann, London, 1921; 2nd edn, Caslon House Publishers, Sydney, 1946.
Working Bullocks, Jonathan Cape, London, 1926.
The Wild Oats of Han, serialised in *Home*, July 1926 – May 1927; Angus and Robertson, Sydney, 1928; rev. edn, Lansdowne, Melbourne, 1968.
Coonardoo: The Well in the Shadow, serialised in *The Bulletin*, 5 September – 12 December 1928; Jonathan Cape, London, 1929.
Haxby's Circus: The Lightest, Brightest Little Show on Earth, Jonathan Cape, London, 1930; American edn, *Fay's Circus*, WW Norton, New York, 1931.
Kiss on The Lips and Other Stories, Jonathan Cape, London, 1932.
Intimate Strangers, Jonathan Cape, London, 1937.
Moon of Desire, Jonathan Cape, London, 1941.
Potch and Colour, Angus and Robertson, Sydney, 1944.
The Roaring Nineties, Jonathan Cape, London, 1946.
Golden Miles, Jonathan Cape, London, 1948.
Winged Seeds, Jonathan Cape, London, 1950.
N'goola and Other Stories, Australasian Book Society, Melbourne, 1959.
Subtle Flame, Australasian Book Society, Sydney, 1967.

Other books and selected pamphlets

Clovelly Verses, McAllan, London, 1913. [poetry]
The New Order, People's Printing and Publishing Co, Perth, 1919. [political pamphlet]
The Earth Lover and Other Verses, Sunnybrook Press, Sydney, 1932. [poetry]
The Real Russia, Modern Publishers, Sydney, 1935. [political travelogue]
Why I Am a Communist, Current Books, Sydney, 1956. [autobiographical pamphlet]
Child of the Hurricane: An Autobiography, Angus and Robertson, Sydney, 1963. [autobiography]
Moggie and Her Circus Pony, Cheshire, Melbourne, 1967. [children's book]

Selected drama

The Burglar (1910), KSPP.
Her Place (c. 1913), KSPP.
For Instance (c. 1914), manuscript lost.

The Pioneers (1923), KSPP.
The Great Man (1923), KSPP.
Brumby Innes (1927) and *Bid Me to Love* (1927), Katharine Brisbane (ed.), Currency Press, Sydney, 1983.
Forward One (1935), in Susan Pfisterer (ed.), *Tremendous Worlds: Australian Women's Drama 1890–1960*, Currency, Sydney, 2000.
Women of Spain (1937), KSPP.
Penalty Clause (1940), KSPP.
Deakin (1951), KSPP.

Selections

On Strenuous Wings, Joan Williams (ed.), Seven Seas Books, East Berlin, 1965. [selections and excerpts]
Happiness: Selected Short Stories, Angus and Robertson, Sydney, 1967. [short stories]
Straight Left, Ric Throssell (ed.), Wild & Woolley, Sydney, 1982. [non-fiction]
Tribute: Selected Stories of Katharine Susannah Prichard, Ric Throssell (ed.), UQP, St Lucia, Qld, 1988. [short stories]
Katharine Susannah Prichard: Stories, Journalism and Essays, Delys Bird (ed.), UQP, St Lucia, Qld, 2000. [selections and excerpts]

General Bibliography

Archival Material

Institutions

National Archives of Australia, Canberra.
National Library of Australia, Canberra.
Public Record Office Victoria, Melbourne.
State Library of New South Wales, Sydney.
State Library Victoria, Melbourne.
State Library of Western Australia, Perth.

Collections

Angus and Robertson correspondence files for KSP, SLNSW.
Anne Mahon Papers, Mundaring and Hills Historical Society.
AT Brodney Papers, SLV.
Campbell Howard Collection, University of New England Library, Armidale, NSW.
Dora Marsden Collection, Princeton University Library.
Guido Baracchi Papers, NLA.
Helen Palmer Papers, NLA.
Henrietta Drake-Brockman Papers, NLA, MS1634/3/23.
Hugo Throssell file, Repatriation Commission, NAA, PP645/1, M5273.
Joan Williams Papers, SLWA.
Katharine Susannah Prichard ASIO files, NAA.
Katharine Susannah Prichard Foundation archives, held at the KSP Writers' Centre, Greenmount.
Katharine Susannah Prichard Papers, NLA.
Katharine Susannah Prichard, [letters to Union of Soviet Writers Foreign Commission], Papers, 1935–1969, SLWA, ACC5835A.
KSP file, Commonwealth Literary Fund, NAA, A463, 1968/5004.
McCrae Family Papers, SLV, MS12831.
Nettie and Vance Palmer Papers, NLA.
Ric Throssell Papers, NLA, MS8071.
Scrapbook kept by HVH Throssell, SLWA, PR5678.
Spencer Brodney Papers, SLV, MS7859.
Thomas Henry Prichard Papers, NLA, MS1147.
Victorian Labor College, University of Melbourne Archives.
Winifred [Doon] Stone Papers, NLA, MS7043.

Newspapers

Unless noted as 'microfilm', Australian newspaper articles cited have been digitised and are available online on Trove, trove.nla.gov.au.

Books, theses, journal articles, and creative works

Aarons, Mark, *The Family File*, Kindle edn, Black Inc., Melbourne, 2010.
Adams, John, *From These Beginnings: History of the Shire of Alberton (Victoria)*, Alberton Shire Council, Yarram, Vic., 1990.
Albinski, Nan Bowman, 'Helena Sumner Locke—Careful!: She Might Hear You'. *Antipodes*, vol. 8, no. 1, June 1994, pp. 47–53.
Amies, Marion, 'The Victorian Governess and Colonial Ideals of Womanhood', *Victorian Studies*, vol. 31, no. 4, 1988, pp. 537–65.
Austin-Crowe, Marion, 'Katharine Susannah Prichard's Coonardoo: An Historical Study', MA diss., Edith Cowan University, Perth, 1996.
Australia for the Tourist, Australian Department of External Affairs, Melbourne, 1914.
Baker, Jeanine, *Australian Women War Reporters: Boer War to Vietnam*, NewSouth, Sydney, 2015.
Ball, Desmond, and David M Horner, *Breaking the Codes: Australia's KGB Network, 1944–1950*, Allen & Unwin, St Leonards, NSW, 1998.
Barrera, Camille, 'Katharine Susannah Prichard, Dymphna Cusack and "Women on the Path of Progress"', in Christina Spittel and Nicole Moore (eds), *Australian Literature in the German Democratic Republic: Reading through the Iron Curtain*, Anthem Press, London, 2016, pp. 117–38.
Bartlett, Norman, 'Perth in the Turbulent Thirties', *Westerly*, vol. 22, no. 4, 1977, pp. 61–9.
Batterham, Linley, 'Shelley, Cecelia Moore (1893–1986)', *Australian Dictionary of Biography*, 2012. http://adb.anu.edu.au/biography/shelley-cecelia-moore-15414 (viewed June 2021).
Beasley, Jack, *A Gallop of Fire: Katharine Susannah Prichard: On Guard for Humanity: A Study of Creative Personality*, Wedgetail Press, Earlwood, NSW, 1993.
Behrendt, Larissa, *Finding Eliza: Power and Colonial Storytelling*, UQP, St Lucia, Qld., 2016.
Blackwell, Bev, *Western Isolation: The Perth Experience of the 1918–1919 Influenza Pandemic*, Homeland Security Communications Research, Canberra, 2007.
Bland, Lucy, 'Heterosexuality, Feminism and *The Freewoman* Journal in Early Twentieth-Century England', *Women's History Review*, vol. 4, no. 1, 1 March 1995, pp. 5–23. https://doi.org/10.1080/09612029500200074.
Bolton, Geoffrey, *Land of Vision and Mirage: Western Australia Since 1826*, UWA Press, Crawley, WA, 2008.
Bonnin, Margriet R., and Nancy Bonnin, 'Hill, Mary Ernestine (1899–1972)', *Australian Dictionary of Biography*, 1996. http://adb.anu.edu.au/biography/hill-mary-ernestine-10503 (viewed June 2021).
Brett, Judith, *The Enigmatic Mr Deakin*, Text, Melbourne, 2017.
Bridge, Peter S, *'Brumby' Leake*, Hesperian Press, Carlisle, WA, 2015.
Britton, Henry, *Lolóma; or, Two Years in Cannibal-Land*, Samuel Mullen, Melbourne, 1884.
Brooks, Barbara, and Judith Clark, *Eleanor Dark: A Writer's Life*, Macmillan, Sydney, 1998.
Browning, Neville, and Ian Gill, *Gallipoli to Tripoli: History of the 10th Light Horse Regiment AIF: 1914–1919*, Hesperian Press, Victoria Park, WA, 2012.
Burchill, Sandra, 'The Early Years of Katharine Susannah Prichard: The Growth of Her Political Conscience', *Westerly*, vol. 33, no. 2, 1988, pp. 89–100.
——, 'Katharine Susannah Prichard: Romance, Romanticism and Politics', PhD diss., University of New South Wales (Australian Defence Force Academy), Canberra, 1988.
Burley, David V, 'Toward the Historical Archaeology of Levuka, a South Pacific Port of Call', *International Journal of Historical Archaeology*, vol. 7, no. 4, 2003, pp. 243–65. https://doi.org/10.1023/B:IJHA.0000014312.75099.26.

Cahill, Rowan, 'Rupert Lockwood (1908–1997): Journalist, Communist, Intellectual', PhD diss., University of Wollongong, 2013.
Cain, Frank, 'Australian Intelligence Organisations and the Law: A Brief History', *University of New South Wales Law Journal 296*, vol. 27, no. 2, 2004.
——, *The Wobblies at War: A History of the IWW and the Great War in Australia*, Spectrum, Melbourne, 1993.
Carr, Adam, 'An Age of Certainty: Three Generations of Melbourne Radicals, 1870–1988', PhD diss., University of Melbourne, 2001.
Carter, Barbara, 'The Peace Movement in the 1950s', in Ann Curthoys and John Merritt (eds), *Better Dead than Red*, Allen & Unwin, Sydney, 1986, pp. 58–73.
Carter, David, and Roger Osborne, *Australian Books and Authors in the American Marketplace 1840s–1940s*, Sydney University Press, Sydney, 2018.
Clark, Katerina. 'The Soviet Project of the 1930s to Found a "World Literature" and British Literary Internationalism', *Modern Language Quarterly*, vol. 80, no. 4, 1 December 2019, pp. 403–25. https://doi.org/10.1215/00267929-7777793.
Clarke, Sharon, 'Sumner Locke Elliott: Writing Life', PhD diss., University of Wollongong, 1995.
Clerehan, Rosemary, John Scully, and Ros White, *Armadale Primary School: The First Hundred Years, 1884–1984*, Armadale Centenary Publication Committee, Armadale, Vic., 1984.
Colebatch, Hal, 'Katharine Susannah Prichard, Literary Icon and Stalinist Liar', *News Weekly*, 12 October 1991, pp. 17–19.
Cook, CM, 'A Critical Study of Katharine Susannah Prichard as a Novelist', MA diss., University of Western Australia, Perth, 1952.
Corbould, Clare, 'Rereading Radical Texts: *Coonardoo* and the Politics of Fiction', *Australian Feminist Studies*, vol. 14, no. 30, 1999, pp. 415–24.
Crawford, Patricia, and Ian Crawford, *Contested Country: A History of the Northcliffe Area, Western Australia*, UWA Press, Crawley, WA, 2003.
Curson, Peter, and Kevin McCracken, 'An Australian Perspective of the 1918–1919 Influenza Pandemic', *New South Wales Public Health Bulletin*, vol. 17, no. 8, 1 August 2006, pp. 103–7. https://doi.org/10.1071/nb06025.
——, 'Flu Downunder: A Demographic and Geographic Analysis of the 1919 Epidemic in Sydney, Australia', in Howard Phillips and David Killingray (eds), *The Spanish Influenza Pandemic of 1918–1919*, Routledge, London, 2003, pp. 110–31.
Curthoys, Ann, 'Paul Robeson's Visit to Australia and Aboriginal Activism', in Frances Peters-Little, Ann Curthoys, and John Docker (eds), *Passionate Histories*, ANU Press, Canberra, 2010, pp. 163–84.
Cusack, Dymphna, 'Katharine Susannah Prichard', *The Realist*, no. 14, 1964, pp. 14–16.
Cyclopedia of Tasmania: An Historical and Commercial Review, Maitland and Krone, Hobart, 1900.
Davis, Geoffrey, *Causes*, Geoffrey Davis, Mount Lawley, WA, 2013.
Deery, Phillip, 'Remembering ASIO', *Overland*, no. 203, 2011, pp. 51–8.
Deery, Phillip, and Rachael Calkin, '"We All Make Mistakes": The Communist Party of Australia and Khrushchev's Secret Speech, 1956', *Australian Journal of Politics & History*, vol. 54, no. 1, 2008, pp. 69–84. https://doi.org/10.1111/j.1467-8497.2008.00485.x.
Depasquale, Paul, and Judith Crabb, *The Life and Work of Tarella Quin*, Pioneer Books, Adelaide, 1981.
Devanny, Jean, *Point of Departure: The Autobiography of Jean Devanny*, UQP, St. Lucia, Qld., 1986.
Dixon, Robert, 'Australian Fiction and the World Republic of Letters, 1890–1950', in Peter Pierce (ed.), *The Cambridge History of Australian Literature*, Cambridge University Press, Cambridge, UK, 2009, pp. 223–54.

Donnan, Noel, *Brodie's Notes on Katharine Susannah Prichard's Coonardoo*, Pan, Sydney, 1981.
Drake-Brockman, Henrietta, *Katharine Susannah Prichard*, OUP, Melbourne, 1967.
Edmond, Martin, 'Double Lives: Rex Battarbee and Albert Namatjira', Doctor of Creative Arts diss., University of Western Sydney, 2013.
Edmondson, Ray, and Andrew Pike, *Australia's Lost Films: The Loss and Rescue of Australia's Silent Cinema*, NLA, Canberra, 1982.
Ellis, Cath, '"Cheerio for Now Darling"', *National Library of Australia News*, October 1998.
Esson, Hilda, 'Introduction', in Louis Esson, *The Southern Cross and Other Plays*, Robertson & Mullen, Melbourne, 1946.
Faithfull, Denise, '"Progressive" Publications: *The Realist Writer* and *The Realist*', Unpublished essay, n.d.
Ferrall, RA, 'Prichard, Frederick John (1851–1920)', *Australian Dictionary of Biography*, 1988, http://adb.anu.edu.au/biography/prichard-frederick-john-8111 (viewed June 2021).
Ferrier, Carole (ed.), *As Good as a Yarn with You: Letters between Miles Franklin, Katharine Susannah Prichard, Jean Devanny, Marjorie Barnard, Flora Eldershaw, and Eleanor Dark*, Cambridge University Press, Oakleigh, Vic., 1992.
——, 'Devanny, Jean', in *The Oxford Companion to Australian History*, OUP, Oxford, 2001. www.oxfordreference.com (viewed June 2021).
——, *Jean Devanny: Romantic Revolutionary*, MUP, Carlton South, Vic., 1999.
Fitzpatrick, Peter, *Pioneer Players: The Lives of Louis and Hilda Esson*, Cambridge University Press, Oakleigh, Vic., 1995.
Franklin, Miles, *A Gregarious Culture: Topical Writings of Miles Franklin*, UQP, St Lucia, 2001.
——, *Laughter, Not for a Cage*, Angus and Robertson, Sydney, 1956.
Glowrey, Cheryl, 'McMillan, Angus (1810–1865)', *Australian Dictionary of Biography*, 2017. http://adb.anu.edu.au/biography/mcmillan-angus-2416 (viewed June 2021).
Grattan, C. Hartley, 'C. Hartley Grattan's View of "Australian Literature" in 1928', *Antipodes*, vol. 2, no. 1, 1988, pp. 20–4.
Green, HM, *An Outline of Australian Literature*, Whitcombe & Tombs, Sydney, 1930.
Grey, Jeffrey, *A Military History of Australia*, 3rd edn, Cambridge University Press, Cambridge, UK, 2008.
Hack, Daniel, 'Meredith, George', in *The Oxford Encyclopedia of British Literature*, OUP, Oxford, 2006. www.oxfordreference.com (viewed June 2021).
Hale, John, 'My Father, Len Hale', *Papers in Labour History*, vol. 29, n.d., pp. 14–17.
Haller, Benjamin, 'Pygmalion', in *The Oxford Encyclopedia of Ancient Greece and Rome*, OUP, Oxford, 2010. www.oxfordreference.com (viewed June 2021).
Hamilton, John, *The Price of Valour: The Triumph and Tragedy of a Gallipoli Hero, Hugo Throssell, VC*, Kindle edn, Pan Macmillan, Sydney, 2012.
Hart-Davis, Rupert, 'Cape, (Herbert) Jonathan (1879–1960), Publisher', *Oxford Dictionary of National Biography*, 2004. oxforddnb.com (viewed July 2020).
Hay, John A, 'Betrayed Romantics and Compromised Stoics: K. S. Prichard's Women', in Shirley Walker (ed.), *Who Is She?*, St Martin's Press, New York, 1983, pp. 98–117.
Headlam, KB (Thea), 'My Aunt—Katharine Susannah Prichard', *LiNQ: Literature in North Queensland*, vol. 11, no. 2, April 1983, pp. 45–53.
Heseltine, Harry, 'Australian Fiction since 1920', in Geoffrey Dutton (ed.), *The Literature of Australia*, Penguin, Ringwood, Vic., 1964, pp. 181–226.
——, 'C. Hartley Grattan in Australia: Some Correspondence, 1937-38', *Meanjin*, vol. 29, no. 3, 1970, pp. 356–64.
Hetherington, Carol, 'Authors, Editors, Publishers: Katharine Susannah Prichard and W.W. Norton', *Australian Literary Studies*, vol. 22, no. 4, 2006, pp. 417–31.

Hewett, Dorothy, 'Excess of Love: The Irreconcilable in Katharine Susannah Prichard', *Overland*, no. 43, 1969, pp. 27–31.
——, 'Happy Birthday, Brave Red Witch', *National Times*, 25 November 1983.
Hirshfield, Claire, 'The Actresses' Franchise League and the Campaign for Women's Suffrage 1908–1914', *Theatre Research International*, vol. 10, no. 2, 1985, pp. 129–53. http://dx.doi.org/10.1017/S030788330001066X.
Holroyd, JP, 'Parker, Frank Critchley (1862–1944)', *Australian Dictionary of Biography*, 1988, http://adb.anu.edu.au/biography/parker-frank-critchley-7954 (viewed June 2021).
Holton, RJ, '*Daily Herald* V. *Daily Citizen*, 1912–15: The Struggle for a Labour Daily in Relation to the Labour Unrest', *International Review of Social History*, vol. 19, no. 3, 1974, pp. 347–76. https://doi.org/10.1017/S0020859000004703.
Hughes-d'Aeth, Tony, 'Cooper, Cather, Prichard, "Pioneer": The Chronotope of Settler Colonialism', *Australian Literary Studies*, vol. 31, no. 3, 2016. http://dx.doi.org/10.20314/als.17437df508.
Hyde, Dylan, *Art Was Their Weapon: The History of the Perth Workers' Art Guild*, Kindle edn, Fremantle Press, Fremantle, WA, 2019.
Irwin, EW, 'Australia's Katharine Susannah Prichard', *New Frontiers*, vol. 5, no. 2, 1956, pp. 29–32.
Jeffery, Inez Cope, *Inside Russia: The Life and Times of Zoya Zarubina*, Eakin Press, Austin, Texas, 1999.
Jordan, Deborah, 'Shaped on the Anvil of Mars: Vance and Nettie Palmer and the Great War', *Australian Journal of Politics & History*, vol. 53, no. 3, 2007, pp. 375–91. https://doi.org/10.1111/j.1467-8497.2007.00464.x.
Kasoff, Brian, 'Union of Soviet Writers', in James Millar (ed.), *Encyclopedia of Russian History*, Macmillan, New York, 2004, pp. 1610–11.
'Katharine Susannah Prichard: "Excess of Love"? Some Comments', *Overland*, no. 44, 1970, pp. 25–8.
Kent, Jacqueline, *Beatrice Davis: Backroom Girl of Modern Literature*, Kindle edn, Pan Macmillan, Sydney, 2013.
Kotai-Ewers, Patricia, 'The Fellowship of Australian Writers (WA) from 1938 to 1980 and Its Role in the Cultural Life of Perth', PhD diss., Murdoch University, Perth, 2013.
——, 'Vickers, Frederick Bert (1903–1985)', *Australian Dictionary of Biography*, 2012. http://adb.anu.edu.au/biography/vickers-frederick-bert-15891 (viewed June 2021).
KSP Writers Centre (ed.), *Kaleidoscope: The Colours of Katharine*, Wild Weeds Press, Greenmount, WA, 2019.
La Nauze, John, *Alfred Deakin: A Biography*, MUP, Carlton, Vic., 1965.
Langmore, Diane, 'Reay, William Thomas (1858–1929)', *Australian Dictionary of Biography*, 1988. http://adb.anu.edu.au/biography/reay-william-thomas-8170 (viewed June 2021).
Larkins, John, *The Book of the Dandenongs*, Rigby, Adelaide, 1978.
Leane, Jeanine, 'Other People's Stories', *Overland*, no. 225, 2016, pp. 41–45.
——, 'The Whiteman's Aborigine', PhD diss., University of Technology Sydney, 2010.
Lindsay, Jack, *George Meredith: His Life and Work*, Bodley Head, London, 1956.
——, 'The Novels of Katharine Susannah Prichard', *Meanjin*, vol. 20, no. 4, 1961, pp. 366–87.
Lloyd, Stuart, *The Lightning Ridge Book,* self-published, Mumbil, NSW, 1968.
Lovell, David W., and Kevin Windle, *Our Unswerving Loyalty: A Documentary Survey of Relations between the Communist Party of Australia and Moscow, 1920–1940*, ANU Press, Canberra, 2008. https://doi.org/10.26530/OAPEN_459400.
Low, John, 'The Salt of the Earth: John Apthorp', Australian Society for the Study of Labour History, n.d. https://www.labourhistory.org.au/hummer/no-15/john-apthorp/ (viewed June 2021).

Lydon, Jane, 'Bullets, Teeth and Photographs: Recognising Indigenous Australians between the Wars', *History of Photography*, vol. 36, no. 3, 2012, pp. 275–87. https://doi.org/10.1080/03087298.2012.673315.

Macintyre, Stuart, *The Reds*, Allen & Unwin, St Leonards, NSW, 1998.

Maclellan, Nic, *Grappling with the Bomb: Britain's Pacific H-Bomb Tests*, ANU Press, Canberra, 2017.

Martin, Sylvia, *Ink in Her Veins: The Troubled Life of Aileen Palmer*, UWA Publishing, Crawley, WA, 2016.

Matter, Laura Sewell, 'Pursuing the Great Bad Novelist', *Georgia Review*, vol. LXI, no. 3, 2007, pp. 444–59.

Matthew, Kate, 'The Life of an Aussie Governess', *Traces*, 28 December 2013. https://tracesmagazine.com.au/2013/12/the-life-of-an-aussie-governess/ (viewed June 2021).

McCallum, Mungo, 'Review of *Child of the Hurricane*, by Katharine Susannah Prichard', *Nation*, 14 December 1963, p. 20.

McCrae, Hugh, *The Letters of Hugh McCrae*, Robert David FitzGerald (ed.), Angus and Robertson, Sydney, 1970.

McKenzie, John, *Challenging Faith*, Fremantle Arts Centre Press, South Fremantle, WA, 1993.

McKnight, David, 'Rethinking Cold War History', *Labour History*, vol. 95, 2008, pp. 185–96.

Modjeska, Drusilla, *Exiles at Home: Australian Women Writers 1925–1945*, Sirius, Sydney, 1981.

Moore, Nicole, 'The Burdens Twain or Not Forgetting Yourself: The Writing of Betty Roland's Life', *Hecate*, vol. 18, no. 1, 1992, pp. 6–26.

Morris, John, and Roger Underwood, *Tall Trees and Tall Tales: Stories of Old Pemberton*, Hesperian Press, Victoria Park, WA, 1992.

Morrison, Fiona, 'Leaving the Party: Dorothy Hewett, Literary Politics and the Long 1960s', *Southerly*, vol. 72, no. 1, 2012, pp. 36–50.

Niall, Brenda, *Friends and Rivals: Four Great Australian Writers – Barbara Baynton, Ethel Turner, Nettie Palmer, Henry Handel Richardson*, Text, Melbourne, 2020.

North, Marilla (ed.), *Yarn Spinners: A Story in Letters between Dymphna Cusack, Florence James and Miles Franklin*, UQP, St. Lucia, Qld., 2001.

O'Dowd, Bernard, *Poetry Militant: An Australian Plea for the Poetry of Purpose*, T.C. Lothian, Melbourne, 1909.

Oliver, Bobbie, 'Fremantle's "Bloody Sunday"', in Charlie Fox, Bobbie Oliver, and Lenore Layman (eds), *Radical Perth, Militant Fremantle*, Black Swan Press, Perth, 2017, pp. 35–42.

Palmer, Nettie, *Nettie Palmer: Her Private Journal Fourteen Years, Poems, Reviews and Literary Essays*, Vivian Smith (ed), UQP, St. Lucia, Qld, 1988.

Palmer, Vance, *Louis Esson and the Australian Theatre*, Georgian House, Melbourne, 1948.

Palmer, Vance, and Nettie Palmer, *Letters of Vance and Nettie Palmer, 1915–1963*, Vivian Brian Smith (ed.), NLA, Canberra, 1977.

Pawsey, Margaret, 'John Bernard O'Hara: Poet and School Proprietor, 1862–1927', in Marjorie R Theobald (ed.), *Family, School and State in Australian History*, Allen & Unwin, Sydney, 1990, pp. 91–113.

——, 'O'Hara, John Bernard (1862–1927)', *Australian Dictionary of Biography*, 1988, http://adb.anu.edu.au/biography/ohara-john-bernard-7893 (viewed June 2021).

Phillips, Glen, 'The Novelist as Occasional Poet: Patrick White and Katharine Susannah Prichard', in Cynthia Van Den Driesen and Bill Ashcroft (eds), *Patrick White Centenary: The Legacy of a Prodigal Son*, Cambridge Scholars Press, Newcastle upon Tyne, UK, 2014, pp. 196–209.

Prichard, Katharine Susannah, 'The Aborigine in Australian Literature', *British Annual of Literature*, vol. 2, 1939, pp. 49–53.

——, 'The Art and Craft of the Short Story', in *Straight Left*, 1982, pp. 126–30.
——, 'Australian Literature', *The International*, vol. 1, no. 1, December 1907, p. 87.
——, *Black Opal*, Heinemann, London, 1921.
——, *Black Opal*, 2nd edn, Caslon House, Sydney, 1946.
——, *Brumby Innes and Bid Me to Love*, Katharine Brisbane (ed.), Currency Press, Sydney, 1983.
——, 'Bush Fires', *New Idea*, 5 December 1903, pp. 497–8.
——, *Child of the Hurricane: An Autobiography*, Angus and Robertson, Sydney, 1963.
——, 'Christmas Tree', *Australasian*, 20 December 1919, p. 51.
——, 'A City Girl in Central Australia: III – Horse Breaking and Stock Branding', *New Idea*, 6 July 1906, pp. 45-8.
——, 'The Cooboo', *Bulletin*, 31 March 1927, pp. 57–8.
——, *Coonardoo: The Well in the Shadow*, Jonathan Cape, London, 1929.
——, 'The Cow', in *Stories, Journalism and Essays*, Delys Bird (ed.), 2000, pp. 112–19.
——, 'The Curse', in *Happiness*, Angus and Robertson, Sydney, 1967, pp. 1–20.
——, 'Danny Niel', *Australasian*, 15 December 1917, pp. 41–2.
——, 'Deakin and Evatt', in *Straight Left*, 1982, pp. 101–12.
——, 'Diana of the Inlet', *Equinox*, vol. 1, no. 7, 1912, pp. 251–90.
——, 'Egon Erwin Kisch', in *Straight Left*, 1982, pp. 70–81.
——, 'Flight', *Home*, 1 April 1938, pp. 27–8, 86, 88, 93.
——, *Golden Miles*, Australasian Publishing Co., Sydney, 1948.
——, 'The Grey Horse', *Art in Australia*, no. 10, 1924, pp. 17–26.
——, 'Happiness', *Bulletin*, 10 December 1927, pp. 11–14.
——, *Happiness*, Angus and Robertson, 1967.
——, *Haxby's Circus*, Kindle edn, HarperCollins, Sydney, 2013.
——, 'Her Brilliant Career: Miles Franklin', in *Straight Left*, 1982, pp. 228–33.
——, 'Hero of the Mines', in *N'Goola and Other Stories*, 1959, pp. 51–4.
——, 'Hoax Renders Service to Literature', in Delys Bird (ed.), *Stories, Journalism and Essays*, 2000, pp. 198–204.
——, 'In Loving Memory: Sumner Locke, Novelist and Playwright', *Everylady's Journal*, 6 December 1917, pp. 711–12.
——, 'International Women's Day: 1945', in *Straight Left*, 1982, pp. 234–42.
——, *Intimate Strangers*, Collins, North Ryde, NSW, 1990.
——, 'The Kid', *The Bulletin*, 17 January 1907.
——, 'Lawrence in Australia', *Meanjin*, vol. 9, no. 4, 1950, pp. 252–9.
——, 'Lips of My Love', *The English Review*, April 1914, p. 10.
——, *Moon of Desire*, Jonathan Cape, London, 1941.
——, 'Mrs Jinny's Shroud', *The Bulletin*, 16 December 1931.
——, *The New Order*, People's Print and Pub. Co., Perth, 1919.
——, 'N'goola', in *N'goola and Other Stories*, 1959, pp. 11–24.
——, 'On Purpose and Propaganda', in *Straight Left*, 1982, pp. 117–21.
——, *On Strenuous Wings*, Joan Williams (ed.), Seven Seas, Berlin, 1965.
——, 'Painted Finches', in *Potch and Colour*, 1944, pp. 111–129.
——, 'Peace and War', in *Straight Left*, 1982, pp. 41–61.
——, *The Pioneers*, Hodder & Stoughton, London, 1915.
——, *The Pioneers*, rev. edn, Rigby, Adelaide, 1963.
——, 'Radical Origins in Australia', in *Straight Left*, 1982, pp. 82–9.
——, *The Real Russia*, Modern Publishers, Sydney, 1934.
——, *The Roaring Nineties*, Australasian Publishing Co., Sydney, 1946.
——, 'Some Perceptions and Aspirations', *Southerly*, vol. 28, no. 4, 1968, pp. 235–44.
——, 'Some Thoughts on Australian Literature', in *Straight Left*, 1982, pp. 200–6.
——, *Straight Left*, Ric Throssell (ed.), Wild & Woolley, Sydney, 1982.
——, *Subtle Flame*, Australasian Book Society, Sydney, 1967.

——, 'Tribute to Henry Lawson' in *Straight Left*, 1982, pp. 131–3.
——, 'Western Wild Flowers', *The Home Annual*, 15 October 1940, pp. 35–7, 72–4.
——, *Who Wants War?*, Franklin Press, Perth, 1935.
——, *Why I Am a Communist*, Current Books, Sydney, 1957.
——, *The Wild Oats of Han*, Angus and Robertson, Sydney, 1928.
——, *Winged Seeds*, Australasian Publishing Co., Sydney, 1950.
——, *Working Bullocks*, Jonathan Cape, London, 1926.
——, 'A Writer's View', in *Lenin Through Australian Eyes*, Novosti, Sydney, 1970, pp. 23–32.
Prichard, TH, *Australian Popular Delusions*, Critchley Parker, Sydney, 1902.
——, *Retaliation: A Tale of Early Melbourne*, Sun Printing and Publishing Company, Melbourne, 1893.
Pringle, Robert, 'Zarubina, Zoya Vasilyevna (1922–)', in *Historical Dictionary of Russian and Soviet Intelligence*, Rowman & Littlefield, Lanham, USA, 2015.
Reay, William Thomas, *The Swiss Army: Organisation and Training*, Herald and Weekly Times, Melbourne, 1907.
Rees, Leslie, *Hold Fast to Dreams*, APCOL, Sydney, 1982.
——, *The Making of Australian Drama: From the 1830s to the Late 1960s*, rev. edn, Angus and Robertson, Sydney, 1978.
Richardson, Henry Handel, *Henry Handel Richardson: The Letters*, Clive T Probyn and Bruce Steele (eds), 3 vols., Miegunyah, Carlton, Vic., 2000.
Roe, Jill, *Stella Miles Franklin: A Biography*, Fourth Estate, Pymble, NSW, 2008.
Roland, Betty, *Caviar for Breakfast*, rev. edn, Collins, Sydney, 1989.
——, *Devious Being*, Collins, London, 1990.
Rutledge, Martha, and Norman Cowper, 'McCrae, Hugh Raymond (1876–1958)', *Australian Dictionary of Biography*, 1986. http://adb.anu.edu.au/biography/mccrae-hugh-raymond-7327 (viewed June 2021).
Serle, Geoffrey, 'Palmer, Edward Vivian (Vance) (1885–1959)', *Australian Dictionary of Biography*, 1988. http://adb.anu.edu.au/biography/palmer-edward-vivian-vance-7946 (viewed June 2021).
Shoemaker, Adam, *Black Words, White Page: Aboriginal Literature 1929–1988*, new edition, ANU Press, Canberra, 2004.
Skinner, Carolyn Margaret, 'Christian Jollie Smith: A Life', PhD diss., Macquarie University, Sydney, 2008.
Smart, Judith, 'A Divided National Capital: Melbourne in the Great War', *La Trobe Journal*, no. 96, September 2015, pp. 28–58.
Smith, Ellen, 'Different Workers: Political Commitment and Subaltern Labour in Katharine Susannah Prichard's *Brumby Innes*', *Journal of Postcolonial Writing*, vol. 51, no. 6, 2015, pp. 648–60. https://doi.org/10.1080/17449855.2015.1106418.
Smith, Harold L, *The British Women's Suffrage Campaign, 1866–1928*, Longman, London, 1998.
Smith, Julian, *Newspaper Reporting and Modern Reportage*, Australian Writers' League, Sydney, 1935.
Souter, Gavin, *A Torrent of Words: Leon Gellert: A Writer's Life*, Xoum, Sydney, 2012.
Sparrow, Jeff, 'Engineering Your Own Soul: Theory and Practice in Communist Biography and Autobiography & Communism: A Love Story', PhD diss., Royal Melbourne Institute of Technology, 2007.
Spender, Dale, *Writing a New World: Two Centuries of Australian Women Writers*, Pandora, London, 1988.
Stead, Henry, 'Dear Comrade Apletin', paper presented to the Anglo-Russian Research Network, Pushkin House, London, 5 October 2018.
Sun, EJ, 'Points of View', in KSP (ed.), *Kaleidoscope: The Colours of Katharine*, Writers Centre, Wild Weeds Press, Greenmount, WA, 2019, pp. 78–87.

Thomas, Tony, 'Katharine Susannah Prichard Interviewed', *The Critic*, 22 December 1967.

Throssell, Hugo, 'For Valour', in *Westralia Gift Book*, VK Jones & Co, Perth, 1916, pp. 5–11.

Throssell, Karen, *The Crime of Not Knowing Your Crime: Ric Throssell Against ASIO*, Interventions, Melbourne, 2021.

Throssell, Ric, 'Katharine Susannah and Hannah Frances: Katharine Susannah Prichard's Legacy to Children's Literature', in Eleanor Stodart (ed.), *Writing and Illustrating for Children: Seminars 1975–80*, Children's Book Council, ACT Branch, Dickson, ACT, 1985, pp. 96–100.

——. *My Father's Son,* William Heinemann, Melbourne, 1989.

——, 'Stranger Fiction', *Westerly*, vol. 39, no. 1, 1994, pp. 45–9.

——. *Wild Weeds and Windflowers: The Life and Letters of Katharine Susannah Prichard*, Angus and Robertson, Sydney, 1975.

'Tributes to the Memory of Bernard O'Dowd', *Meanjin*, vol. 12, no. 4, Summer 1953, pp. 405–19.

Van Wingerden, Sophia A, *The Women's Suffrage Movement in Britain, 1866–1928*, Macmillan, Houndmills, UK, 1999.

Vickery, Ann, 'Lesbia Harford's Romantic Legacy', in *The Intimate Archive: Journeys Through Private Papers*, NLA, Canberra, 2009, pp. 81–132.

Victorian Municipal Directory, Arnall & Jackson, Melbourne, 1896.

Walker, David, 'Esson, Thomas Louis Buvelot (1878–1943)', *Australian Dictionary of Biography*, 1981. http://adb.anu.edu.au/biography/esson-thomas-louis-buvelot-6115 (viewed June 2021).

——. '[Interview with] Guido Baracchi', *Overland*, no. 97, 1984, pp. 16–20.

Watts, Rachel, 'Children of the Hurricane', in KSP Writers Centre (ed.), *Kaleidoscope: The Colours of Katharine*, Wild Weeds Press, Greenmount, WA, 2019, pp. 55–61.

Webster, Theo, 'McMillan, Angus (1810–1865)', *Australian Dictionary of Biography*, 1967. http://adb.anu.edu.au/biography/mcmillan-angus-2416/text3203 (viewed June 2021).

Whitelaw, Bridget, *The Art of Frederick McCubbin*, National Gallery of Victoria, Melbourne, 1991.

Widdis, Emma, *Alexander Medvedkin*, IB Tauris, London, 2005.

Wilde, William H and David Headon, 'Aborigine in White Australian Literature', in William H. Wilde, Joy Hooton, and Barry Andrews (eds), *The Oxford Companion to Australian Literature*, OUP, Melbourne, 1994, pp. 2–10.

Williams, Justina [Joan], *Anger & Love*, Fremantle Arts Centre Press, South Fremantle, WA, 1993.

——, *The First Furrow*, Lone Hand Press, Willagee, WA, 1976.

——, 'Katharine Susannah Prichard (Interview)', *Our Women*, December 1963, pp. 26–27.

——, 'Rage That Engenders: The Last Decade of Katharine Susannah Prichard', *Southerly*, vol. 32, no. 1, March 1972, pp. 17–29.

Williams, Margaret, 'Natural Sexuality: Katharine Prichard's *Brumby Innes*', *Meanjin*, vol. 32, no. 1, 1973, pp. 91–3.

Woollacott, Angela, *To Try Her Fortune in London: Australian Women, Colonialism, and Modernity*, OUP, Oxford, 2001.

Worrall, Nick, 'Meyerhold, Vsevolod', in *The Oxford Companion to Theatre and Performance*, OUP, Oxford, 2010.

Young, John MR, *Adventurous Spirits: Australian Migrant Society in Pre-Cession Fiji*, UQP, St Lucia, Qld., 1984.

Zogbaum, Heidi, *Kisch in Australia*, Scribe, Melbourne, 2004.

Acknowledgements

I acknowledge the Whadjuk people of the Noongar nation, traditional custodians of the land on which I wrote this book.

Many thanks to Karen Throssell, Katharine Susannah Prichard's granddaughter and literary executor, for permission to quote from the works of Katharine and Ric and for her gracious interest in my research.

I thank the Edward and Janet Palmer Estates for permission to quote from the Papers of Vance and Nettie Palmer.

The first half of this book was written for my PhD and my supervisors, Tony Hughes-d'Aeth and Van Ikin, were generous with their time, astute in their feedback, and skilful at bringing out my best. It was a pleasure and an honour to work with them. Van not only took me on in his retirement but was my first reader for the second half of the book too. Earlier versions of chapters 2 and 39 were first published in *Westerly* as '"The Memory of a Storm": *The Wild Oats of Han* and the childhood of Katharine Susannah Prichard, 1887 to 1895' (vol. 60, no. 2) and '"As My Great Day Approaches": Katharine Susannah Prichard in 1969' (vol. 64, no. 2).

This research was supported by an Australian Government Research Training Program (RTP) Scholarship. I've been glad of the collegiality of academics and other postgraduates in the School of Humanities at the University of Western Australia and beyond. The Words and Thoughts creative writing group gave feedback on my work and literary stimulation. My colleagues at Morling College have been supportive over many years.

The Document Delivery team at UWA fulfilled countless requests with professionalism and courtesy. Thanks to the staff of National Library of Australia, State Library of Victoria, Melbourne University, Public Record Office of Victoria and the State Library of Western Australia. The National Library of Australia's Trove digitised newspapers and other digitisation projects have made an immense difference to my research. A number of volunteer organisations have helped in my quest, including the Brighton Cemetorians, Emerald Museum, Glen Eira Historical Society, Mundaring and Hills Historical Society and Yarram District Historical Society.

The KSP Writers' Centre's ongoing interest in my research has been a great encouragement, and I particularly thank Glen Phillips, Shannon Coyle, Mardi May, Elizabeth Lewis, Tabetha Rogers Beggs, Lisa Wolstenholme and Valerie Everett. I thank the KSP Foundation, which runs the centre, for permission to use their photographs of Katharine.

I have been nourished by the literary friendship of many, including Laura Sewell Matter, Tracy Ryan, John Kinsella, Laurie Steed, Melinda Tognini, Madelaine Dickie, Jonathan Morling, Miriam Wei Wei Lo, James Quinton, Siobhan Hodge and Cassie Lynch, and fellow bloggers Lisa Hill, Bill Holloway, Michelle Scott Tucker, Sue Terry and Karenlee Thompson. Biographers John Burbidge and Sylvia Martin encouraged a novice. Nicholas Jose, Judith Brett, Nicole Moore, Janet Blagg, Terri-ann White, Kate Noske and Josephine Taylor kindly gave expert opinion on sections of the manuscript. Many Facebook friends have helped decipher Katharine's difficult handwriting. For help with translation, thanks to Bernie Raselala, Aldo Magagnino, Tony Quicke, Diana James and Michael Hobby. Thanks to John and Irene Mills for their hospitality in Canberra.

Thanks to the other writers and researchers interested in Katharine and her world who have enriched me on the way, including Graham Barwell, Riley Buchanan, Sandra Burchill, Leigh Dale, Denise Faithfull, Emily Gallagher, Louise Helfgott, Dylan Hyde, Deborah Jordan, Brigid Magner, Henry Stead, and Trevor Todd. Special thanks to Anne Mahon for preserving her superb research on Katharine for future scholars. Many people have generously shared their knowledge, including Ross Burgess, Jocelyn and Dick Cook, Bill Day, Timothy Dauth, Nicholas Hasluck, Judy Inveen, Dale Kessell, Dianne Lane, Cate Remfry, Rosalie and Adrian Roberts and Karen Zammits.

It's an honour to publish with Nathan Hollier, Catherine McInnis and the rest of the team at Melbourne University Publishing, and I thank them for bringing this book to print. I was fortunate to have an excellent copyeditor in Katie Connolly and a great cover from Klarissa Pfisterer. Thanks to Patrick Cannon for page design and typesetting, and Karen Gillen for indexing.

Thanks to my family for their ongoing support—David and Suzanne Hobby, Joshua Hobby, Catherine and Keith Gorman, Rob and Diana James, Russell and Nadia James, and my nephews and nieces. My beloved grandmother, Beryl Winning (1932–2021) asked each week how 'Katharine' was going. My love and gratitude to my wife, Nicole Hobby, whose belief in the project has been crucial; she's put up patiently with Katharine and shown much wisdom and insight. Without Thomas and Sarah—both born during the project—I'd have finished sooner but with far less love and joy.

Index

THE MIEGUNYAH PRESS

This book was designed and
typeset by Cannon Typesetting
The text was set in 11¾ point Adobe Garamond Pro
with 14½ points of leading
The text is printed on 80gsm uncoated woodfree
This book was edited by Katie Connolly

THE
MIEGUNYAH
PRESS